THE PEOPLE OF THE PARISH

.

THE MIDDLE AGES SERIES

Ruth Mazo Karras, Series Editor
Edward Peters, Founding Editor

A complete list of books in the series
is available from the publisher.

The People of the Parish

COMMUNITY LIFE IN A LATE MEDIEVAL

ENGLISH DIOCESE

Katherine L. French

PENN

UNIVERSITY OF PENNSYLVANIA PRESS *Philadelphia*

10 9 8 7 6 5 4 3 2 1

Published by
University of Pennsylvania Press
Philadelphia, Pennsylvania 19104-4011

Library of Congress Cataloging-in-Publication Data

French, Katherine L.
The people of the parish : community life in a late medieval English diocese /
Katherine L. French.
p.   cm. — (The Middle Ages Series)
Includes bibliographical references and index.
ISBN 0-8122-3581-9 (alk. paper)
 1. Parishes—England—History—Middle Ages, 600–1500.   2. England—Religious
life and customs.   3. England—Church history.   I. Title.
BR744   .F74   2000
274'.23/905—dc21   00-055181

CONTENTS

ACKNOWLEDGMENTS

Over the course of writing this book I have built up many debts and garnered much encouragement. It is now my great pleasure to acknowledge those debts and thank those who have helped and encouraged me. I have worked on this project in many places. The History Department at the University of Minnesota was its first home. There I found a collegial group of scholars who supported me both formally and informally. In particular I want to thank Barbara Hanawalt, who helped nurture this book from its earliest incarnations to its final form as a book. Throughout it all, she has remained enthusiastic and supportive about the project. In England, I am grateful to all the staff of all the archives I worked in, but especially those at the Somerset Record Office where I did most of my research. At SUNY-New Paltz, the History Department, and in particular Carole Levin, now of the University of Nebraska, provided further encouragement for the often difficult process of revising a manuscript while also learning how to be a professor. At the Harvard Divinity School, where I was a Research Associate and Visiting Lecturer in the Women's Studies in Religion Program, Clarissa Atkinson, Deborah Valenze, Susan Shapiro, Amina Wadud, Carol Karlsen, and Rebecca Krawiec all listened patiently and asked thought-provoking questions as I talked about my ideas about what it meant to belong to a medieval parish.

The long process of writing a book is also not possible without a great deal of financial support. The History Department at the University of Minnesota and an Eileen Power Fellowship from the London School of Economics provided support for both travel and research, and a Charlotte W. Newcombe Fellowship allowed me the luxury of writing full time. At SUNY-New Paltz, the Dean of Liberal Arts, the Academic Vice President, and several Research and Creative Projects Awards provided further research funds for trips to England and the Newberry Library in Chicago. Although I was officially working on another project, my year at the Harvard Divinity School made completing this book possible.

In dealing with the particulars of assembling this book, James Stokes and Robert Alexander shared with me their in-depth knowledge of Somerset sources, and Robert Palmer shared his as yet unpublished work with me to help my discussion of legal jurisdictions. I also want to thank Jai Kasturi who created much of my appendix, Stephen Hana who drew the maps, and the Courtauld Institute of Art in London, Fred H. Crossley, Maurice H. Ridgway F. S. A., Dr. Christopher Wilson, and the National Monuments Record Centre for permission to use their photographs. I also want to thank Manchester University Press for permission to reprint my article "Parochial Fund-Raising in Late Medieval Somerset." The anonymous reader at the University of Pennsylvania Press and Robert Swanson saved me from many mistakes. Both took great pains with my manuscript, and it is a much better book for their efforts. Remaining errors are of course my own.

One of the joys of academic work is the intertwining of friendship and intellectual exchange. In addition to those named above, I would also like to thank the following people for their help on this book. Help comes in many forms: Some read drafts, often at the last minute. They did so cheerfully and willingly. Others talked to me endlessly about my ideas, helping me to explain them better, and most at one time or another pulled me away from my computer and reminded me that all work and no play is boring. My deep felt thanks and appreciation to Sandy Bardsley, David Benson, Clive Burgess, Eric Carlson, Jay Carter, Sue and Russell Clarke, Gary Gibbs, Edmund Kern, Rebecca Krugg, Beat Kümin, Caroline Litzenberger, Shannon McSheffrey, Maureen Morrow, Stella Neiman, Oliver and Caroline Nicholson, Allyson Poska, Gary Shaw, Tim Spurgin, and Dan Swartz.

Lastly, I owe my biggest debts, emotional, financial, and grammatical, to my family, my parents David and Louise, and my brothers Andrew, Stephen, J. D. and Jim Ciulik, and their wives, Lisa, Peg, Jane, and Kirsten. Although usually mystified by why I am so interested in this time-period, they nevertheless share my interest in wanting to know how things fit together. This book is for them.

A man who was once asked why he did not weep at a sermon when everyone else was shedding tears replied: "I don't belong to the parish."

—Henri Bergson, *Laughter: An Essay on the Meaning of the Comic*, 1928

INTRODUCTION

In 1379, the king's court called upon nine parishioners of the Lancashire parish of Walton to remember the baptism of John, the son and heir of
Robert de Walton. Their memories served to verify John's age and whether he
was old enough to receive his inheritance.

John de Sotheworth, forty and more, was at the church for a loveday between William
Robynson and [tear] of Kirkdale when John was baptized.

John del Twys, forty and more, was at the church to hear mass before going to buy fish
at Bootle, and was present at the baptism.

Robert de Eld, forty and more, was at the church to hear news from Ireland of the Earl
Edmund of March.

Henry de Penketh, forty and more, was at the church to buy corn from Robert
Wilkynson.

Henry de Twys, forty and more, was at the church to hear mass before going to
Kirkdale to buy two oxen from Robert Wilkynson of Kirkdale.

William Laghok, forty and more, was at the church to hear mass before going to
Litherland to see a corpse and wreck on the seashore.

John de Hey, forty and more, was at the church to see John del Hethe.

John de Andern, forty and more, was at the church for a cockfight between John de
Silkes and Robert del Heth.

John de Bugard, forty and more, was at the church to see a man from Liverpool.[1]

In this picturesque proof-of-age, jurors offer a variety of reasons why they
were at the local parish church and, therefore, able to witness John's baptism.[2]
Only three claimed they had come to the church to hear mass; the rest had
other—nonreligious—reasons for being there. Their recollections, however,

testify to the centrality of the parish church in their lives. Business, legal settlements, sociability, and entertainment, in addition to worship, brought them to the church. This book examines the role of the laity in parish life and organization in one medieval diocese, Bath and Wells. Focusing on the parishes in one diocese emphasizes the range and diversity of late medieval English parish life. In the post-plague period, the laity had broad responsibility for administering their local parishes, and this task, as it was mediated through local needs, priorities, and lay organizations, shaped their perception and practice of orthodox Christianity. The interplay of local parish administration and ecclesiastical expectations made the parish a dynamic and vibrant association around which the laity could create a community identity. Understanding how the parish operated refines our understanding of lay piety and Christian orthodoxy in the two centuries before the Reformation. Parish dynamics also provide valuable insights into everyday lives, local social and gender hierarchies, and the communal decision-making process. The world of the late medieval parish united secular and sacred concerns.

The parish was one of the basic units of public worship and was the shared responsibility of the laity and the clergy. By design and definition, it was a geographic unit of regulation and coercion. It provided much of the focus for spiritual and moral instruction and ecclesiastical authority. As a benefice, it provided a living for the incumbent through tithes; as the primary forum for public worship, it offered its members religious instruction and the sacraments; as a jurisdiction, it administered moral correction and extracted goods and money from parishioners to support the clergy. Membership was mandatory and determined by where one lived.[3] Generally, the parish church held both baptismal and burial rights. Even when the laity lived far from the parish church and attended weekly services at a dependent chapel, they typically went to their parish church for major holy days, for burials, and for baptisms. Some chapels had partial parochial rights, such as a cemetery but no baptismal font or vice versa. Although one could hear mass in a cathedral, chapel, or monastic church, most received baptism, went to confession, and were buried in their own parish church or churchyard.

From the Norman Conquest to the thirteenth century, the number of parishes grew throughout England. Norman landlords, in an effort to provide their peasants with access to worship and themselves with lucrative tithes, set up churches on their lands or created parishes out of local chapels. By the thirteenth century, England had about 9500 parishes, although no one ever made a complete survey.[4] After the plague in the fourteenth century, this trend reversed; ecclesiastical officials still occasionally granted parochial status to existing chapels within a parish, but an overall drop in the number of parishes occurred, as bishops tended to consolidate them rather than create new ones.[5]

Poverty and declining revenue could make a parish untenable for the incumbent. In 1535, when the government carried out the survey of all church lands in England called the *Valor Ecclesiasticus*, the surveyors counted 8800 parishes for all of England, showing an estimated 7 percent decline in the number of parishes during the middle ages.[6] This decline reflected the slow recovery of the population after the plague, not administrative or spiritual dissatisfaction with the organization of local religious life. The parish continued to be the basic forum of public worship, but it was, I believe, socially and culturally much more than that. Comparing the parishes of one diocese shows how location and resources combined with shared liturgical and spiritual needs to create a unique religious culture that became a forum for community identity.

Bath and Wells

Because of the diocese's size and the surviving medieval records, the parishes of Bath and Wells are particularly conducive to a comparative analysis. Bath and Wells was not huge and sprawling; it did not encompass parts of many counties. It stretches only seventy miles from east to west and fifty miles north to south at its widest point. Located in England's West Country, the diocese is contiguous with the medieval county of Somerset; throughout the book, I will use the two names interchangeably (see Map 1).

Christianity came to the West Country in the seventh century. Soon after the Anglo-Saxons had converted, they began settling in Somerset, Devon, and Dorset.[7] The earliest churches were the monasteries in Bath (676), Glastonbury (688), and Muchelney (c. 693).[8] Little documentation about the foundation of these minster churches survives. Minsters were a class of monastic church that provided the laity with the sacraments; their foundation in the Anglo-Saxon period was an important part of Christianizing the population. By the eighth century, minsters existed on royal lands, but we know little about how quickly other landholders founded them on their own estates.[9] The minster at Wells, founded in 909, became the seat of a new diocese.[10] As part of the monastic reforms of the mid-eleventh century, the bishop of Wells, John of Tours, moved his seat to the reformed monastic house at Bath.[11] Other bishops acted in a similar manner; placing their seats in old Roman cities provided the continent-educated bishops with the prestige and status they had come to expect from their office.[12]

By the thirteenth century, however, episcopal business had grown, and the bishop of Bath felt the need for a church closer to the center of the diocese. Politically, this not only benefited diocesan administration, but also helped him curtail the strong influence of Glastonbury Abbey. The construction of a new cathedral in Wells by Bishop Jocelin in 1239 further enhanced episcopal

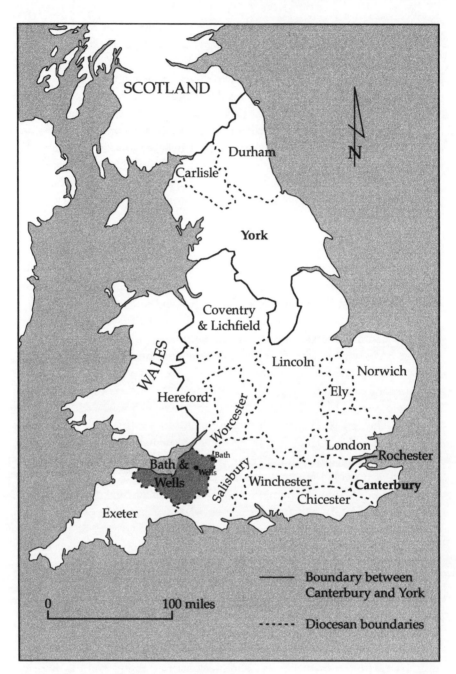

Map 1. Pre-Reformation dioceses of England.

dignity and autonomy. The episcopacy's prestige reached a new level when Jocelin's successor, Bishop Roger, became the first bishop designated the bishop of both Bath and Wells.[13]

The continued spread of Christianity in the Anglo-Saxon period necessitated the foundation of more churches for the laity.[14] Like the rest of England, the origins of Somerset's parochial organization lie in the Anglo-Saxon past.[15] Landlords founded minsters, and these churches provided fonts for lay baptism and churchyards for lay burial. Although the Domesday Survey conducted in 1086 mentions only seventeen churches in Somerset, place-name studies, archaeology, and archival research suggest that this is an inaccurate figure. There were possibly more than twenty minster churches in Somerset, all associated with large estates.[16]

Those communities living far from the minster attended dependent chapels, but the minster received their tithes. This system, however, could not accommodate the growth in population or the change in the political landscape that developed after the Norman invasion. Gradually, dependent chapels would become independent parishes. As the fallout from the Norman invasion divided estates, landholders set up new churches on their lands for the dependent population or appropriated the tithes for existing chapels, thus increasing the number of parishes. Landholders increasingly put secular priests, rather than monks, in charge of these new foundations; without monastic ties, these priests were more amenable to secular landlords' and episcopal concerns.[17]

The move to create new parishes continued into the fourteenth century but did not happen in a uniform or consistent manner. Some minsters, such as Wells, were powerful enough to resist the division of their territory. Of its twelve dependent settlements, only Wookey and Westbury became parishes.[18] Other minsters, such as Crewkerne, were divided into several parishes. The chapels of Misterton, Wayford, Seaborough, and Eastham all became independent in the thirteenth century.[19] In other instances, the chapel received some new rights but never achieved full independence. In 1326, Bishop Drokensford granted members of Congresbury's chapel of Wyke the right to bury their dead and have their own services. Their chaplain was, however, still to be appointed by the vicar of the parish church of Congresbury.[20] Chapel status did not automatically relegate the community to obscurity or poverty. St. Mary Redcliffe, in the suburbs of Bristol, is one case in point. It remained a chapel of Bedminster, although it was far wealthier and had a more prominent congregation than the parish.[21]

After the demographic crisis of the fourteenth century, the number of parishes throughout England and in Somerset declined. Throughout the period of this study, bishops combined parishes, since low population provided inadequate funds to support the living. Despite its general unwillingness to change parish boundaries, the episcopal organization was not insensitive to the shifts in population.[22] For example, the parish of Curry Rivel absorbed the chapel or parish of Earnshill in 1352 after the plague had killed off latter's inhabitants.[23] By 1444, both the parishes of Freshford and Woodwik were so poorly endowed that, when the rector of Woodwik resigned, the bishop demanded an inquiry into the feasibility of joining the two.[24] Four years later, having completed his investigation, he combined the two churches into one parish.[25] In 1502, Bishop Oliver King joined the two parishes in the town of Ilchester at the rector's request.[26] It is unclear how many parishes existed in Somerset before the plague, but by the end of Henry VIII's reign there were about five hundred.

Parishes and chapels were the bottom rung of diocesan organization. Most dioceses, Bath and Wells included, were divided into successive jurisdictions for ease of administration. Parishes with their chapels were grouped into rural deaneries, which in turn were grouped into archdeaconries.[27] By the thirteenth century, Bath and Wells had three archdeaconries: Taunton, Wells, and Bath. While the position of rural dean rotated among the rectors of the deanery, the archdeaconry was a real clerical benefice; appointment to this office gave the candidate a living.[28] Each deanery had its own court that addressed a variety of spiritual, moral, and administrative issues such as adultery and failure to attend church, but it also oversaw the appointment of diocesan administrators and the probate of wills. Although bishops were theoretically at the top of this administrative pyramid, they did not have complete power within their dioceses. Dotted throughout were jurisdictions called peculiars where the bishops had only limited authority.[29] Each peculiar had its own complement of courts, although their competence varied greatly. Most of the peculiars in Bath and Wells were attached to the cathedral and its officials. Glastonbury was also a peculiar, but with more curtailed authority than the others.[30] Throughout the middle ages, the bishops of Bath and Wells tried with little success to limit Glastonbury's power. Of the twenty parishes that are the primary focus of this book, six were in peculiars.[31] Unlike the vast diocese of York, the peculiars of Bath and Wells were not especially contiguous and thus did not compromise the bishop's authority over large sections of the diocese.[32]

The medieval bishops of Bath and Wells were all capable men with long experience in public affairs.[33] Their prominence in national politics kept them away from the diocese for long periods. Nicholas Bubwith (1408–25), a close councilor to Henry V, served as one of England's representatives to the Council of Constance in 1414.[34] His successor, John Stafford (1425–43), was a doctor of civil law and lord chancellor of England. In the sixteenth century,

Thomas Wolsey occupied the see (1518–23) while he was Cardinal of St. Cecilia and Archbishop of York (1514–30). Because Bath and Wells was merely a way of augmenting Wolsey's income, he took little notice of the diocese, granting wide powers to his vicar-general.[35] In 1523, Wolsey went to Durham and resigned his seat at Bath and Wells. Sometimes prominence led to notoriety. Robert Stillington (1466–91) spent little time in the diocese. He was a staunch Yorkist during the Wars of the Roses and spent the years after the accession of Henry Tudor in prison dying there in 1491.[36] After Stillington's death, the diocese was vacant until an Italian, Hadrian de Castello, became an absentee bishop. During his entire tenure (1503–17), he never once visited the diocese. His disinterest was a scandal that the king tolerated because de Castello had surrendered to him all episcopal patronage within the diocese. But when de Castello became implicated in a plot to poison the pope in 1517, Henry VIII finally banished him.[37]

The bishops of Bath and Wells were also university-educated men who generally came to the see after other experience in royal service. Thomas Bekynton's prior employment brought him into contact with Italian humanism.[38] Bekynton (1443–65) received his education at Winchester and New College, Oxford. While a fellow at New College, he attracted the attention of Humphrey, Duke of Gloucester, a patron of other humanists.[39] The duke appointed Bekynton his chancellor sometime in 1420, and he held that position until 1438 when he became secretary to Henry VI. Bekynton's humanistic interests are most obvious in his diplomatic correspondence. His ability to write to the Roman Curia in Renaissance-style Latin impressed many and gained him the diocese of Bath and Wells upon Stafford's transfer to Canterbury.[40] Despite his prominent connections, Bekynton, a local man, appears to have spent more time in the diocese than either his predecessors or successors.[41] One of the Reformation bishops, John Clerk (1523–41), who succeeded Wolsey at Bath and Wells, was previously a theology professor at Cambridge and a monk of Bury St. Edmund's. Unlike most of his predecessors, he had received his education on the continent, at Bologna. He was primarily a diplomat and spent much of his episcopate in the service of Wolsey and the king. He died while on a mission to the Court of Cleves explaining to the duke why King Henry VIII was divorcing his sister Anne.[42]

The diocese of Bath and Wells had prestige, and the king often used it as a reward for good service; it was also a stepping stone more than once to the archiepiscopate of either Canterbury or York. Henry Bowet (1401–7) left Bath and Wells to go to York as the compromise candidate in a clash between the king and the pope over who should replace the executed Archbishop Scrope.[43] The king recognized John Stafford's hard work in the government with promotion to Canterbury in 1443. Because of the prominence of many of the men who served Bath and Wells, episcopal administrators largely ran the diocese. Most bishops turned over diocesan administration to their vicars-general and suffragan bishops, but administration of the diocese could still reflect the bishops' national concerns.

Episcopal administration had a number of concerns and responsibilities. Collection of tithes, the income that financed any clerical administration, was paramount, but also of concern was pastoral care, including moral behavior, and Christian education. By the fifteenth century, because of the threat of Lollardy, assuring the orthodoxy of both the clergy and the laity took up an increasing portion of episcopal and crown business.[44] Sir John Oldcastle's revolt in 1414 compelled the church and the crown to work together to fight off this challenge to both religious and royal hegemony.[45] The Leicester parliament of 1414 gave both secular and ecclesiastical authorities the authority to investigate and enforce orthodoxy and the quality of religious practice. The full force of statutory law punished those found in violation of defined standards of orthodoxy, but the differences between orthodox and heterodox beliefs and practices were not always clear. Both professed Lollards and their orthodox rivals shared concerns for greater purification of religious practice and the promotion of individual religious conscience.[46] It was thus up to the bishops, as they governed their dioceses, to explain the distinctions between heterodoxy and orthodoxy. Bristol was a hotbed of Lollardy; because of its proximity to Somerset, heresy concerned the bishops of Bath and Wells. The prominence of Bristol in local trade made it easy for heretical ideas to spread across the county, something the episcopal hierarchy wanted very much to avoid.[47] Numerous trials took place against people living in Bristol and in the surrounding parishes of northern Somerset.[48] Bishop John Stafford (1425–43), also a doctor of civil law and lord chancellor of England, held the diocese's first recorded heresy trials. The dioceses also worked together to promote orthodoxy by initiating uniform practices. It was during the fifteenth century that English bishops within the province of Canterbury accepted the guidance of Lyndwood's *Provinciale*, which set out guidelines for their responsibilities and diocesan organization.[49] They also championed a common liturgical use for the province, the Sarum Rite.[50]

The wealth of the diocese made it an attractive see and helps explain its use as a "reward" in royal policy. Over the course of the late middle ages, the bishops of Bath and Wells drew income from an increasingly wealthy diocese. Somerset's wealth came from a diverse and rich countryside. The geographic diversity of its 1,630 square miles helped its inhabitants develop a prosperous economy.[51] Geographers divide the county into five different regions[52] (see Map 2). In the west, bounded by the Tone and Parrett Rivers, is the moorland

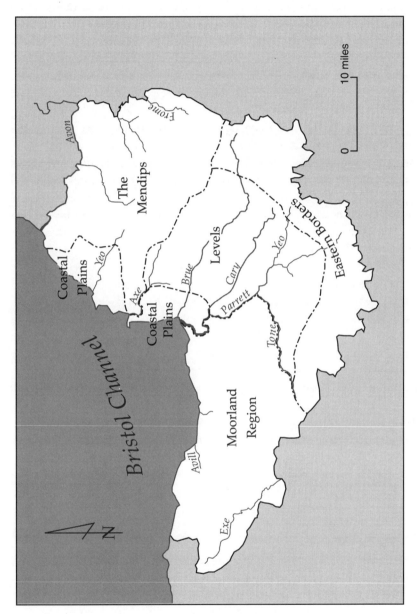

Map 2. Geographic regions of Bath and Wells.

region of Exmoor and the Quantock Hills. Poor drainage and soils from the underlying limestone made this area better suited to sheep farming and tin mining than to agriculture. The central part of the country is called the Levels. Although it is very low-lying and marshy, drainage programs made it the agricultural heart of the county in the middle ages. With four rivers, the Axe, Brue, Cary, and Parrett, the area was also to become a center of trade. Along the eastern and southern edges of Somerset, a border area makes up the third geographic region. It is more hilly than the Levels, but still offers fertile soil for agriculture. In the Anglo-Saxon and Norman periods, it was mostly forest. The fourth region, the Mendip Hills, lies to the north and is the highest area in the county. Finally, there is a coastal plain in the northwestern part of the county, where the Yeo River feeds into the Bristol Channel.[53]

This diverse geography fostered a varied and prosperous economy. Whereas in 1334 Somerset ranked twenty-third out of thirty-eight counties in lay and clerical wealth, by 1514 it was second only to London.[54] This prosperity came from the diversification of crops and livestock and the attendant increase in trade. Somerset farmers grew not only wheat, but also barley, oats, woad, and hemp. Livestock consisted predominantly of sheep, but cattle were also important. In the late fifteenth century, enclosure became common, especially in the western parts around Exmoor and the Quantocks, and sheep farming rose in prominence.[55] The coastal location and navigable rivers encouraged trade. There was regional trade with Bristol to the north and Devon and Cornwall to the southwest; trade also extended to other European countries. Much of the trade, however, depended not on water routes, but on an ancient and extensive network of roads. By the end of the middle ages, about forty markets of varying sizes and specialties had replaced the seasonal fairs as centers of commerce.[56] The 1504 will of Dennis Dwin illustrates the wide area covered by Somerset merchants which made the region so prosperous. He described himself as a "merchant of Ireland [and a] citizen and burgess of the [Somerset] town of Bridgwater."[57] He wrote his will while on a trading mission in Bordeaux. The sixteenth-century depression checked Somerset's growth, and mid-sized towns such as Bridgwater and Stogursey suffered.[58] Despite these difficulties, the region still retained a dense population and a diverse economy. According to Joan Thirsk, it was the third most densely populated county in England by the end of the sixteenth century.[59]

The diversity of Somerset's landscape is important for understanding local religious life. As I will show, the resources available to the parishioners combined with local politics and administrations to influence the shape of parish involvement. The laity practiced orthodoxy within a specific environment that determined much of their behavior and thus much of their level and method of involvement in the parish community.

Regional Sources

There are many different kinds of sources for studying local religion. Some of the earliest and most abundant are wills. The large number that survive throughout England show differences in regional practices and changes over time. They illuminate many issues such as religious concerns at the point of death, local devotions, and the uses of charity. Many of the first studies of local religion drew from these sources.[60] Their drawback is that they only address the interests and concerns of a relatively elite group of people at a particular moment of their lives, as they were preparing for death. They do not inform on a lifetime of religious involvement, and may, in fact, reflect more the desires of the cleric writing the will than those of the testator.[61] Another source for the study of local religion is the deeds of land and property given or sold to the clergy or the church. These are a haphazard source, surviving more frequently in towns than in the countryside. Visitation reports are another source for the study of local religion. These reports catalogue the moral infractions of the laity, clergy, and monastics.[62] Very few survive for England from before the Reformation. Because so few survive, they show only a snapshot of community behavior. They cannot be used to address issues of continuity or change in parish life or the decision-making processes behind them. Similarly, church court records identify individual transgressions, but little about the collective nature of local religious life.[63] Churchwardens' accounts are the best sources for these latter issues. These records are the yearly accounts of the laity's fundraising and expenditures to maintain the parish. They are unique in that they address lay priorities and community concerns. When there are several decades of accounts, they can reveal much about community decision-making and long-term local involvement in parish life. Although mediated through layers of ecclesiastical and local administrations, they constitute, nonetheless, one of the few sources available for studying the parish from the laity's perspective.

Not all of these sources survive for the diocese of Bath and Wells. There are virtually no ecclesiastical court records and no visitation reports. What do survive in relative abundance are churchwardens' accounts. The parishes in this diocese that have left churchwardens' accounts are the primary focus of this study. One diocese means that only one episcopal administration influenced parochial behavior and organization. Thus, we can attribute many of the differences among parishes to local factors rather than episcopal ones. Bath and Wells has churchwardens' accounts still extant from twenty different parishes (see Map 3). Although the records represent only about 4 to 6 percent of the total parishes of the diocese, the surviving churchwardens' accounts span the period between the Black Death in 1348 and the end of Henry VIII's reign

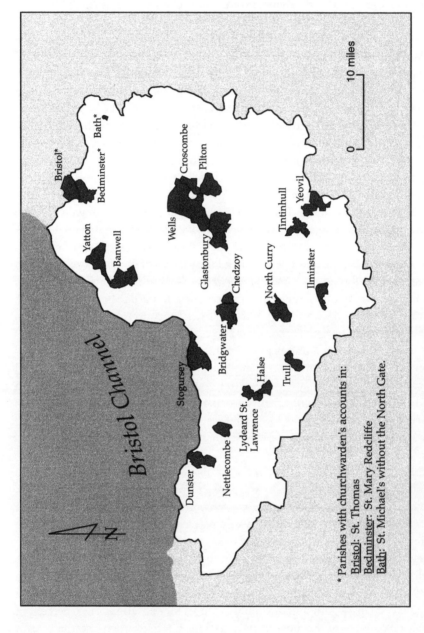

Bristol Channel

Bristol*

Bedminster*

Bath*

Yatton

Banwell

Wells

Croscombe

Pilton

Glastonbury

Chedzoy

Tintinhull

Yeovil

North Curry

Ilminster

Stogursey

Bridgwater

Dunster

Nettlecombe

Lydeard St. Lawrence

Halse

Trull

N

0   10 miles

* Parishes with churchwarden's accounts in:
<u>Bristol</u>: St. Thomas
<u>Bedminster</u>: St. Mary Redcliffe
<u>Bath</u>: St. Michael's without the North Gate.

Map 3. Parishes in Bath and Wells with churchwardens' accounts.

in 1547. They comprise an unusually rich and early collection of church-wardens' accounts. Four sets start in the fourteenth century—one half of the total number of surviving fourteenth-century accounts in all of England.[64] Seven sets begin in the fifteenth century, and the remaining nine accounts appear at varying points in the early sixteenth century. These accounts come from parishes all over the diocese, representing different kinds of settlements. The range and length of accounts allow for not only a discussion of differences among parishes, but also a discussion of change over time—change that was often initiated by the parishioners themselves.

Just as most of the diocese was rural and dependent on agriculture, so too were most of the parishes with surviving churchwardens' accounts. There are accounts from twelve rural parishes. They varied in location, proximity to ecclesiastical patron, wealth, size, and population. Both Banwell and Yatton, in northern Somerset, encompassed large geographic areas and had sizable congregations of four hundred and five hundred communicants respectively.[65] Yatton had two dependent chapels to help serve this spread-out congregation. Both parishes were also reasonably well-off. Their probable status as former minsters explains their large size.[66] Croscombe, located in the central part of the diocese, was small, having only 220 communicants.[67] The nearby parishes of Pilton and Tintinhull were also small, probably representing equally small populations, although we have no population figures.[68] Size and location would help determine not only the wealth of a given community, but also the quality and character of its religious life.

The town parishes in this study reflect the history of urban development in Somerset. There is a lengthy and early set of churchwardens' accounts from one of the five parishes in the old Roman city of Bath: St. Michael's without the North Gate. By the late fourteenth century, Bath had become a center of cloth manufacturing, and by 1525 it had a population of roughly twelve hundred.[69] Despite the bishop's overlordship, the city developed its own civic government with a mayor and aldermen. With the bishop more occupied with the cathedral in Wells, the city acted reasonably independently throughout the middle ages. There are also early accounts from the parish of Bridgwater, which included the port town of the same name on the Parrett River and seven hamlets.[70] The town started as a settlement around a Norman castle, and in 1200 it received a borough charter from King John.[71] By the fourteenth century, however, it was the focus of local trade in wine, dyestuffs, and food, as well as cloth-finishing. The merchant guild oversaw town government so as to further facilitate commerce. Prosperity followed, and by 1400 the population had reached sixteen hundred.[72] By the mid-sixteenth century, however, there was noticeable decay. The parish served only six hundred communicants, probably half of what it had served in the fifteenth century.[73]

We also have records from the parish of Wells, which had two thousand parishioners (including twelve dependent settlements outside the town), and the parish of Glastonbury, which had seven hundred parishioners.[74] The large, ancient, and powerful ecclesiastical establishments of Wells and Glastonbury dominated these parishes. Their presence, however, contributed wealth and prestige to the area and benefited the local population. Wells, in addition to being the seat of the bishop, was an important center of the leather trade. Resistance to both the bishop's and the cathedral's influence marked the city's civic culture.[75] Glastonbury never achieved this level of independence from its ecclesiastical overlord. The abbey had founded the town in the twelfth or thirteenth century, and it tightly controlled the town and its business up to the abbey's dissolution in the sixteenth century. The local economy depended on a marketplace, the wool trade, and the industries that supported the constant influx of pilgrims to the abbey's shrine.[76] Accounts also survive from smaller market towns in the county. Sporadic ones remain for Yeovil, and a set starts in the early sixteenth century for Stogursey. By the mid-sixteenth century, Stogursey had 646 communicants and Yeovil 822.[77] Despite their size, neither parish was as wealthy as Bridgwater and they like Bridgwater, suffered economic difficulties in the early sixteenth century. The diocese of Bath and Wells also included three parishes from the suburbs of Bristol: Bedminster (and its larger, wealthier, and much more famous chapel, St. Mary Redcliffe), Templemead, and St. Thomas. After the Reformation, Henry VIII incorporated them into the new diocese of Bristol. Miscellaneous churchwardens' accounts survive from St. Mary Redcliffe and St. Thomas, and although they are late (1530s and 1540s) and of short duration (one to two years), they show a kind of parish life distinct from that of smaller towns or rural parishes in the rest of the diocese.

Although I have based most of this book on the analysis of churchwardens' accounts, I have supplemented them with other ecclesiastical sources. Bishops' registers exist for the period covered by this study—the second half of the fourteenth century, all of the fifteenth century, and the first half of the sixteenth century. Thus, it is possible to study the laity's organization of their parishes in conjunction with episcopal supervision of parish organization and administration. I have also made use of the wills and some court records. Both of these sources are very problematic because of their limited survival for this diocese; the wills survive only in an early twentieth-century printed edition, as the originals were destroyed in World War II.[78] Nevertheless, using what remains does provide additional information on lay activities within the parish. The abundance of churchwardens' accounts which focus more on collective behavior than court records or wills do more than makes up for this lacuna.

For over a century, scholars have been interested in the laity's ability to organize themselves and to appoint lay leaders—the churchwardens. Early scholars equated this lay organization with the origins of English democracy.[79] Although these works idealized and homogenized parish life and activities, they also showed how much the parish depended on lay involvement. Not until Charles Drew's study of the origins of the office of churchwarden did anyone look at how the laity acquired so much influence in parish life and administration.[80] His pamphlet occupies an important place in understanding the parish and its evolving position within ecclesiastical law. Drew traced through synodical legislation the development of lay responsibilities for the nave and churchyard. In the process, he helped explain the purpose of church-wardens' accounts, documents that are central to studies of the late medieval and early modern English parish.[81]

The late medieval English parish is currently a popular focus of attention for scholars of the Reformation. They have set about characterizing the parish and its activities during this period as a way of tracing the reception and processes of religious reforms in the 1530s and 1540s. By examining the state of pre-Reformation religion at the parish level, scholars—particularly historians—feel that they can better gauge the spread of Protestantism. In a sense, current understanding of the late medieval parish is the creation of Reformation scholars, who have suggested that its religion is somehow lacking. A. G. Dickens started this trend by proposing in his book, *The English Reformation*, that the religious reforms of the 1500s had their origins in a long-standing tradition of anticlericalism espoused most obviously by the heretical group, the Lollards, but felt by the majority of the English population.[82] Such claims have not gone unchallenged. Scholars have lined up on both sides of the debate, and the activities and concerns of the laity at the parish level have become, if not an explicit focus, then an implicit one in recent work on the Reformation.[83] One of Dickens's detractors, J. J. Scarisbrick, started his book, *The Reformation and the English People*, with a discussion of the late medieval parish and its religious practices.[84] He argued that "there was little sign of lay disenchantment with the ecclesiastical ancien régime, no angry alienation, no seething discontent, little expectation that the old order would not, could not and should not endure until the end of time."[85] Looking at wills and parish guilds, he argued that the conservative and ritualistic nature of English parish life continued well into the reign of Elizabeth. According to Scarisbrick, the English Reformation came from above, imposed on an unwilling population by a king eager for a divorce because he was desperate for a male heir.

Once historians started examining churchwardens' accounts, they tended to arrive at similar, albeit less dogmatic, conclusions. Ronald Hutton's article, "The Local Impact of the Tudor Reformations," was the first study to use churchwardens' accounts to address the question of the laity's rate of compliance with religious reform.[86] Hutton concurred with Scarisbrick about the conservative nature of the laity, adding that the rapidity with which the reforms were instituted was a testament more to strong governmental pressure and coercion than to the presence of latent Protestant beliefs among parishioners.[87] Soon after Hutton's article appeared, Robert Whiting published his book, *The Blind Devotion of the People: Popular Religion and the English Reformation*, a study of the diocese of Exeter during the sixteenth century that also used churchwardens' accounts.[88] He argued that lay interest in parish life had declined by the early sixteenth century.[89] Lay ambivalence toward the parish explained why royal and episcopal authorities had met with little trouble in setting up a Protestant church in place of the Catholic one. Whereas Scarisbrick held that deep commitment to Catholicism, tinged with pagan superstition, had prevailed well into the reign of Elizabeth, Whiting argued that his economic analysis of churchwardens' accounts showed otherwise.

In light of these treatments of the topic, Eamon Duffy has attempted to rehabilitate the late medieval parish. Motivated by the frequent characterization of parochial religion as "popular religion" and the indictment this label makes against the quality or sincerity of religious practice, his book, *The Stripping of the Altars: Traditional Religion in England, 1400–1580*, rejects a model of religion dependent upon a dichotomy between popular and elite.[90] Instead, he has filled his mostly East Anglian parishes with knowledgeable and committed Christians, united in their devotion to what he calls "traditional religion," a fully Christian religion neither lacking legitimacy nor in need of reform. Duffy portrays the parish as a place where the universal Church was physically embodied in shared venerations, symbols, and liturgies.[91] Within a normative or universal discussion of a parochial system, he asserts that parishioners developed a sense of community identity as a consequence of their commitment to the liturgy. Both Whiting and Duffy have limited their studies to particular regions in England, projecting general observations about the status of medieval religion from these regional studies. The pictures that emerge are quite different, which speaks as much to the importance of regional variations as it does to the historians' concerns and methods.[92]

Beat Kümin's recent book, *The Shaping of a Community: The Rise and Reformation of the English Parish, c.1400–1560*, takes a broader view by looking at ten different parishes scattered throughout England, which represent a range of sizes and wealth as well as regions.[93] Although not denying the importance of local variation, this work uncovers trends and experiences shared by all parishes between 1400 and 1560, while simultaneously looking at the effects of size and wealth. Kümin's approach also shows how readily continental approaches to the Reformation can be applied to England.[94] In order to realize their religious program, Henry VIII and his successors sought to expand on the duties and responsibilities of the parish and its officials. In the end, this process not only facilitated major changes at the local level, but also strengthened the crown's position with respect to its subjects. The parish became as much a governmental unit as a religious one.

The studies that precede mine have not generally focused on the late medieval parish for its own sake, and they have not emphasized the interaction of local concerns with institutional expectations. Rather, they have focused on changes to the parish over the course of the Reformation. My perspective does not offer a general picture of English parish life or the particulars of one community alone. Instead, I present the coherence of one diocesan administration to reveal differences among parishes within that diocese and how these differences reflect the creation of a community identity. Furthermore, I am interested in how community identity affects the reception and practice of orthodoxy. The differences among parishes suggest a range of practices and expressions within the bounds of orthodox Christianity. Although I am most concerned with the diocese of Bath and Wells, the ways in which parishes differed from each other are by no means unique to this area. My findings thus have broader implications for how we view religious practice throughout late medieval England. Because of these interests, I am almost solely concerned with the laity's perspectives and actions. Although the frequent close association of clergy and laity makes it impossible to ignore the clergy, they will not be a major focus of this study.

I consider religious practice to include a broad range of activities that promote and enhance worship. Religious practice goes well beyond attendance at the mass and veneration of the saints. The flexibility and scope of parish involvement meant that, in order to help their souls, men and women could participate in a variety of ways commensurate with their social status, economic resources, and gender. They came together in groups and also worked as individuals. This variety casts parish participation in more complex terms than those offered by simplistic models of coercion and exploitation or of Christian fraternity vaguely equated with egalitarianism. Obligations and collective and individual religious concerns combined to form unique local religious cultures based at the institution of the parish. This approach also recognizes that for most of the laity, religion was not so much a set of ideological concepts as it was certain sets of activities and prescribed behavior.

The six chapters in this book draw on the information in and organization of the churchwardens' accounts to explore different aspects of parish life and lay organization. The format and purpose of these documents create a vision of the parish as a shared project or common concern. Churchwardens' accounts are records of accomplishment—leaders chosen, funds raised, buildings repaired. Failures and shortcomings are not always explained. Emphasizing the collective nature of parish life is no naive or romantic excursion. These accounts must be read within the context of the hierarchical ecclesiastical organization that sought to govern religious life.

Chapter 1, "Defining the Parish," examines how the interaction between the parish and the episcopal hierarchy created opportunities for the formation of a community identity. By setting standards of sacramental performance, moral behavior, and financial support, the bishop's administration sought to impose a uniform vision of communal life in the parish. Yet the laity cannot be viewed as simply passive recipients of diocesan directives. Episcopal regulation compelled the laity to act as a corporate body, ultimately capable of articulating parish needs and concerns back to the ecclesiastical hierarchy. The rest of the book turns then to the internal dynamics of parish organization and lay piety as revealed largely through the churchwardens' accounts. Chapter 2, " 'The Book and Writings of the Parish Church': Churchwardens' Accounts and Parish Record Keeping," provides a critical look at churchwardens' accounts. Their varying quality and format delineate further differences among local administrations and show how groups of largely nonliterate people used records to protect and define their parish communities. I argue that creating churchwardens' accounts was a community-defining exercise that acknowledged the importance and uniqueness of a parish's own church space, history, and ritual. Chapter 3, " 'A Servant of the Parish': The Office of the Churchwarden and Parochial Leadership," focuses on the organization of lay parochial leadership. The strength or weakness of a warden helped shape the relationships and involvement that characterized life in a particular parish community. The evolution of parish leadership shows the parish as more than a coercive unit responding only to outside administrative demands. The laity constituted a body with the ability to express a will. Chapter 4, " 'Received of the Good Devotion of the Town and Country': Parish Fundraising," examines how the laity raised money to support the parish. Here the differences between urban and rural parishes become quite pronounced, as different types of parishes followed different strategies for meeting their annual expenses. Chapter 5, " 'Curious Windows and Great Bells': The Architecture of Community," looks at the church building and its interior organization. The building itself was one way that the parish community identified itself to the outside world. Analysis of the interior furnishings such as rood screens, seating arrangements, and chapels and side altars shows how the community identity of a parish incorporated both status and gender concerns into its community identity. Chapter 6, " 'The Worthiest Thing': Liturgical Celebration and the Cult of the Saints in Place," assesses how the laity wove their community identity into officially sanctioned religious practices. When read against didactic literature, churchwardens' accounts reveal a great deal about the local nature of piety and orthodoxy. Although parishioners shared the same spiritual concerns and practiced many of the same devotions, worship can be understood within the context of locally-specific parochial organizations. Thus, within the practice of orthodoxy, we see a convergence of local and institutional concerns.

I DEFINING THE PARISH

Community Identity

Because the parish served as a religious focal point for both urban and rural Christians, it was the center for a variety of associations and obligations that encompassed all aspects of life. The laity's involvement in their parishes went well beyond attending the liturgy and paying tithes. Episcopal mandate also required them to maintain the nave and churchyard and to supply various liturgical items such as mass books, candlesticks, and chalices, while the clergy took care of the chancel. Meeting these requirements necessitated that the laity organize themselves into an administrative structure that could, among other things, raise and spend money. This exercise in collective planning and action catalyzed the formation of community identity. But each parish's unique resources, location, status, wealth, and needs distinguished it from all others. Such local characteristics and priorities evolved into local religious cultures that became forums for community identity.

Institutional authority, in the form of episcopal expectations and requirements, was a part of parish life and community identity. Power, authority, and coercion were, therefore, part of the parishioners' experience and part of the formation of a community's identity. They cannot be stripped away to reveal the "true" or "real" medieval parish, because the parish did not exist separately from the institution of the Church.[1] At the same time, clerical and episcopal expectations for the parish were carried out within unique local contexts and depended on specific resources and needs. Part of the process of forging the community of the parish was the impressing of an administrative ideal onto a specific place.

Applying the concept of community identity to the parish offers a way of understanding the visible and meaningful differences between parishes and how they affected Christian worship and lay piety. Once members of a given parish developed certain patterns of liturgical practice, fundraising, social interaction, and decision making, they would go to great lengths to protect them. The desire for salvation that could be advanced through involvement in the church was infused with the desire to honor the traditions of the particular parish. Granted, parishioners generally wished to follow the practices of the larger Church, but a strong sense of identification with the parish could come into conflict with the ecclesiastical hierarchy. Understanding these differences between parishes offers a new perspective on the religious practices of the late middle ages.

As an analytical concept, the notion of community, and hence community identity, is not without its critics or its problems. Both the definition of *community* and the term's use in medieval studies show a spectrum of viewpoints. Often scholars understand it in overly simplistic ways. Historians in particular have long portrayed the parish as the quintessential medieval community, which disappeared in the drive toward industrialization.[2] Both John Bossy and Gervase Rosser have argued that the central element in community is a voluntary and a socially homogeneous membership, and that, because this did not constitute the parish's membership, it could not meet all religious and social needs. This failure to meet all such needs was thus a failure of community formation.[3] Critics of this rather rigid understanding of community contend that it reflects an unrealistic and naive understanding of the medieval past.[4] In particular, Miri Rubin argues that, as used by historians, the concept of community is "a static notion, [that] obscures difference and conflict: as it seemingly highlights the peculiar medievalness of the Middle Ages, it whitewashes shades of tension, distance, difference."[5] Gary Shaw reminds us that a community is not the same thing as an interest group; while common characteristics might make up a class, a race, or a gender, they are not the same thing as a community.[6] Both Rubin and Shaw reinvigorate this concept by incorporating into it the very elements that Bossy and Rosser argue destroy community. Rubin wants a definition that takes differences into consideration, such as those of occupation, gender, and wealth. Rather than existing as entities comprised of homogeneous people, communities instead reflect a process of social interaction directed at common goals. Furthermore, Shaw argues, communities must be self-identified as such, and members must participate willingly, for the good of the group, in the process, creating traditions, a group mentality, and institutions.[7] Community encompasses much more than collective action or pure volunteerism.

This richer multivalent concept of community informs this book. I contend that the parish is, in fact, such a community, defined by a broader range of characteristics than administrative necessities, geographic borders, or social similarity. Lay interaction in the parish resulted not only from mandatory attendance at mass, visitations, court appearances, or tithe gatherings, all seemingly coercive aspects of parish life. Parishioners also assembled for local saints' days, family and neighborhood baptisms, marriages, funerals, parish fundraising activities, theater productions, and building maintenance, events which involved individual choice and personal interest. The laity participated in many different activities and groups within these borders, and such activities fostered important relationships. The ability to form guilds, which, in Bath and Wells, often helped support the parish, and the role of gender and status in internal organization show the flexibility, rather than the putative rigidity of the late medieval parish.[8] Groups within the parish, such as parish guilds, or groups that spanned many parishes, such as merchant guilds or town confraternities, may alter the identity of a parish, but in and of themselves, they do not compromise its integrity. Although the parish was a coercive unit in some senses, it was also a place where lay activity in a variety of forms—which were needed and encouraged—allowed individual choices. The result was a sense of belonging, a sense of community.

Although scholars have rightly criticized views of medieval communities that over-emphasize harmony and fraternity, both were very much medieval values applied by medieval people to assemblies of parishioners and guild members.[9] Medieval theology called specifically for the creation of what we often think of as community. The second great commandment of Jesus, "you shall love your neighbor as yourself" (Mark 12:31), created the basic moral doctrine of *caritas*—charity, in the broadest sense of the word.[10] Charity required social integration and the creation of continual fraternity. Indeed, medieval preachers and the parish clergy directed their efforts to promoting the notion of Christianity as fraternity and community.[11] John Mirk's fourteenth-century sermon for a parish's patronal saint's day states that "the church is an ordained place where Christian people should come together in charity, to worship our God in peace, each one with the other."[12] The anonymous author of the fifteenth-century didactic work *Dives and Pauper* wrote that "Singular prayer of one person is good in chamber and in oratory and better in church, but common prayer of a community in church is better than singular prayer, for Christ said in the gospel that if two or three are gathered together in his name that is charity, there is he in the midst of them."[13]

Although practice fell far short of the ideal, the parish's membership shared goals and values for community life that they continually articulated in word and deed. Furthermore, permanent lay organizations, and lay leaders worked hard to foster the shared mentality of fraternity.[14] When social status, gender, and occupation, which often coalesced into guilds or other sub-parochial groups, endured as distinguishing characteristics among parish members, these differences in some ways supported efforts to attain harmony and charity. They could siphon off tension and competition in affirming ways. Parish leaders could draw upon the variety of skills and interests represented by different groups to enhance the life of the parish.[15] In writing about guild feasts, Rosser argues that, "The motifs of hierarchy and community were not in competition with one another. . . . The reality of social inequality notwithstanding, the language of fraternity was open to appropriation at every social level, thus helping to shape the lived reality of each."[16] Despite his earlier contention that the medieval parish was not an effective community, Rosser's observations about guild interaction are apt. Medieval parishioners integrated their status consciousness with their religious concerns for social integration. The formation of community identity put into practice the theological demands for charity.

The laity expressed and acted upon their understanding of community through their involvement in parish activities, whether they were participating in the liturgy or in the repair of the church building. They worked collectively to build and keep a worthy home for the host. The laity used their local resources and, at times, the legal system to build and maintain their parish. The church itself became the physical reminder of a shared past, present, and future. The community's priorities and history literally became inscribed in the building's shape, furnishings, and decoration.[17] Parishioners' participation in parish affairs took place in accordance with their status, gender, age, wealth, interest, and local expectation. Although the clergy required minimal participation, no one ever delineated maximum participation. There was a great deal of room for personal choice. Such choices not only furthered the ideal of charity and social integration, but also enhanced parishioners' status, wealth, and interests. Some identified with their parish so strongly that when they moved away they still maintained contact. Stephen Forster, a London fishmonger, was born and baptized in the Somerset parish of Staunton Drew.[18] In his will, proved in 1458, he left this parish £20 for new vestments and ornaments. He also bequeathed an additional £20, "to be distributed by my executors in the marriage of poor girls, the relief of poor widows, and other poor and needy persons dwelling in the said parish of the Blessed Mary of Staunton Drew and three other parishes next adjacent."[19] Forster's bequests are not particularly meaningful if we understand the parish only as a clerical benefice and involvement only in coercive terms.

Although the parish was a focus of community identity, not all members shared in it in the same ways or to the same level. Alienation because of poverty, politics, or personality could shear off groups and individuals from the whole. The community of the parish could be inclusive, but it was not necessarily so. By possessing the qualities that placed them outside the group, these individuals, who are all but invisible in the records, helped, in a sense, to define further the community. It is important to remember Miri Rubin's concerns about a false sense of harmony and unity permeating the use of concepts of community. The community of the parish drew support from Christian theology and ecclesiastical mandate and administration, but those alone did not compel all parishioners to share in the community's identity in the same way.

As a working definition in this book, *community* denotes the repeated interactions over time of a group of people with shared goals, interests, concerns, and ideals. This continual interaction creates a group history that can enhance the group's identity. Although for the late medieval parish this interaction usually focused on a particular geographic area, location alone did not create community. Members had to be willing to work for the group and its preservation and not just for individual self-interest. At times coercion from both within and without the group arose to maintain community. The exercise of coercion itself does not negate the presence of community, but by definition other factors must also draw the group together.[20] Mandatory membership alone could not inspire the sense of belonging and investment in the group that characterize community. Some individuals, whether by choice or by behavior, remained perpetually outside the community.

We can see something more of this process of identification when that community failed, as it sometimes did. In such instances, both the internal and the external forces that worked to create community came into play in an attempt to reassert the parish community. As many parishes were large and included more than one settlement, parishioners could live far away from their parish church. Sometimes these distant settlements had a chapel for weekly services, and the parishioners attended the parish church only on major holy days, such as Easter, or for baptisms, confession, and burials.[21] Those attending the chapel often resented the parish church. Resentment could be initiated by the local gentry, who had a financial or political interest in the chapel's independence, or by the rest of the parishioners, who felt that it was unfair to have to support both the parish and their own chapel. Sometimes animosity could stem from neglect by the clergy in charge. One possible solution to this problem was to petition either the bishop or the pope for independent parochial status for the chapel or for extended rights for the chapel. I would suggest that this resentment points to an understanding of community and parish life that had been, in part, fostered by interaction with the episcopal administration. Although those who worshiped at a chapel did not feel particularly loyal to the parish, they *believed* that the parish church *should* be the focus of their loyalty. The petitioners hoped to change the status of their chapel in order to meet these expectations.

In 1405, the parishioners from the town of Leigh-on-Mendip, in the parish of Mells, petitioned the pope to expand the rights of their chapel. They claimed that from time immemorial they had received all sacraments except for burials in their chapel. Their rector, however, had recently been neglecting his duties to them. As they explained in their petition, "the said town and chapel being distant two English miles from the said church, it is very difficult for them, on account of the dangers of the roads, floods, and divers other impediments, to convey their dead to the said church—as often as it shall be expedient."[22] The townspeople wanted burial rights for their chapel but agreed to maintain its status as a chapel with respect to the rector of Mells.[23] The pope apparently granted their petition. Some fifty years later, however, the parishioners in Leigh-on-Mendip again challenged this relationship, and this time the bishop tried to smooth the relationship between the two groups. The parishioners who lived in Leigh were supposed to take turns supplying holy bread to Mells, and they now had refused. The laity only received the Eucharist once a year. On every other occasion, at the end of mass, the priest distributed pieces of a blessed bread, called "pax bread," to the assembled worshippers.[24] That they chose the holy bread as a point of rebellion was probably not a coincidence. It embodied ideas of Christian community and was, thus, a potent symbol for the members of the chapel. Their refusal to participate in this tradition signaled their alienation from the larger community of the parish. The laity can be presumed to have understood something of the Christian ideology of community that sharing holy or pax bread symbolized. The churchwardens from Mells brought the rebels before the bishop, who upheld the "ancient custom" and required those at Leigh to continue supplying bread in their turn.[25]

This case, which is by no means unique, is a good place to begin exploring a variety of issues related to community identity. For the parishioners at Leigh, their place within the community of the parish of Mells had broken down, and they were currently more identified with the chapel, where they went to weekly services and received most of the sacraments. Thus, they wanted their family members buried close by, where the living could easily pray for them and not forget them. Once their rector started ignoring them, their physical distance from the mother church at Mells exacerbated their alienation. There were likely other local issues, such as Leigh's economic prosperity, that were also driving the two groups apart. It was surely not just the cost of a loaf of bread that those attending the chapel resented, but their exclusion from the community identity of the larger parish. In response, they had formed one around the chapel.

This case also illuminates something of the ecclesiastical hierarchy's relationship to the parish. The formation of a community identity, as we will see in this chapter, was not only in the hands of the laity. The proper role of the bishop was to have a clear idea of what the relationship between the two groups should be and to achieve an accommodation between the two. Part of the identity of a parish, as this case suggests, was its place in the ecclesiastical hierarchy. Leigh, a chapel of Mells, was a benefice that the bishop sought to protect through both his authority and the symbols of community present in the liturgy. Granting a chapel its independence would diminish the rector's income, because he would no longer receive the tithes from Leigh; a new rector would. The obligation to provide holy bread did not impinge heavily upon the corporate life of the parishioners and could, in fact, from the bishop's perspective, be a way of trying to incorporate the two groups into one community of the parish. Community definition was not a simple one-way process. As the petition shows, the parishioners' own interests were often tied to location and autonomous sacramental rights. In contrast, the ecclesiastical hierarchy's concerns were tied to understanding the parish, not just as a geographical location, but also, and more importantly, as a benefice. Preserving it was a sign of the bishop's own authority and position within the diocese.

Petitions to either the bishop or the pope requesting greater rights for their chapels were quite common and reveal how widely shared were the ideas of parish identity.[26] Those attending chapels generally requested a consecrated churchyard for burials and a font in the nave for baptisms. Usually the petitions claimed that the parish church was too far away and that the roads were in poor condition, prone to flooding, or plagued by outlaws, so that bringing a baby for baptism, having a woman churched, or carrying a body for burial was a hazardous and difficult business. Those attending the chapel of Trull, dependent on the parish church of St. Mary Magdalene in Taunton, wanted similar independent rights and applied for them in 1476. Their petition stated that, "The chapel is distant one mile and that some of the houses of the said persons are distant two miles of those parts or there abouts . . . that in winter the roads are very muddy, and that the said persons cannot sometimes conveniently carry the said bodies to the said churches."[27] Through descriptions of the geography that prevented the laity from easily going to the parish, the petitions define the chapel-goers in terms of their physical and emotional separation from the parish and the sacraments. It is no coincidence that the sacraments that the chapel clergy could not perform—baptism, the Easter Eucharist, confession, and burial—were tied to the human life cycle and helped connect the laity to their parish in bonds of community.[28] The petitions express not just a desire for the sacraments, and, thus, participation in the universal Church, but a desire for the sacraments to be performed in the most meaningful place for them—near their homes and surrounded by family and neighbors. The petitions thus declare the importance of place in the practice of Christianity. They powerfully express community identity through the blending of specific locale and access to the sacraments. Although the petitions are often overstated and a bit dramatic in tone, they illustrate the interconnection of place and corporate religious activity. Those attending a chapel were acting on their understanding of proper or "normal" parish life, and they felt that their particular circumstances did not fit that model.

Formulation of Episcopal Oversight

Models for "normal" parish life came, in part, from interaction with episcopal regulation. In the rest of this chapter, I will show how the parishes of Bath and Wells fit into the administrative hierarchy of the diocese and how episcopal administration sought to regulate parish life. The goal is not just an institutional overview, but a discussion of how the laity interacted with this regulation and its consequences for the formation of collective action and corporate identity. The laity's compliance with pastoral reforms did not consist of blind, passive submission. Late medieval Christians interacted with episcopal administration in ways that expressed their own care and concern for their parishes. As we will see in subsequent chapters, local organization of the parish became more than just an avenue of compliance with episcopal mandates; it was also a meaningful way of practicing orthodoxy.

Over the course of the late middle ages, English parishes grew in self-confidence and influence. They became capable of defining their own needs and interests and, in turn, articulating them to the ecclesiastical organization that oversaw them. Episcopal and papal regulation of the parish inadvertently fostered this self-awareness. Whereas, in the twelfth century, parishioners mostly fulfilled duties and had only a few rights with respect to their parish,[29] by the fifteenth century, the laity had turned these duties into meaningful spiritual and political actions that they strove to preserve and expand. This change in the laity's relationship to the parish grew out of ecclesiastical reforms of pastoral care in the twelfth and thirteenth centuries. Bishops wanted greater clarity of organization, ease of revenue collection, and consistency of clerical oversight and religious practice. In achieving this level of diocesan organization, the bishop, through his administration, both coerced the laity into following these reforms and convinced them of their value. The laity's interaction with the bishop's administration compelled them to act collectively, and by the fourteenth century the laity had organized themselves on a permanent basis so as to meet episcopal demands.[30] This experience of collective action became a form of religious activity and a way of protecting their community. Yet the parish's strengthened position in the religious, economic, and legal realms of late medieval England appears to be an unintended consequence of these reforms. By the fifteenth century, this corporate action had moved beyond simply responding to episcopal needs, and it now addressed the laity's own needs and concerns.

Late medieval bishops of Bath and Wells were usually too busy with political concerns to take a very personal role in diocesan pastoral care. Most of the interaction between the parishes and the bishop was carried out by his administration under the auspices of either his vicar-general or the suffragan bishop. Through this administration, the bishop sought to impose a uniform vision of communal life on the parish by setting standards of moral behavior, financial support, and sacramental performance. To be sure, the bishop was often more concerned about the financial underpinnings of his administration, but these concerns were not completely separate from the sincere practice of religion. Both bishops, and their administrations, justified their expectations for parish life and behavior with calls for the proper and regular performance of the mass.

Although pastoral care was not a new issue for church councils, at the Fourth Lateran Council in 1215, Pope Innocent III articulated a new level of concern for organizing and regularizing lay interaction with the Church.[31] The council's decrees sought to define the church's authority in both spiritual and temporal affairs in order to further the organization and centralization of the church.[32] The Fourth Lateran Council and King John's death a year later provided a kind of watershed for the English Church. Exhaustive episcopal reorganization was not needed, but the council provided the impetus for reform and greater supervision of parishes.[33] The decrees were wide-ranging and touched on doctrinal, administrative, and behavioral issues.[34] Innocent III wanted to provide for clergy instruction in doctrine; the definition and regular administration of the sacraments, especially confession and communion which all Christians were now to receive at least once a year; and the uniform and correct implementation of canon law. He also addressed jurisdictional issues in an attempt to sort out the often haphazard and erratic relations between monasteries and cathedrals, between bishops and their cathedrals, between bishops and the lower clergy, and between secular and ecclesiastical courts. In many places, parish and diocesan boundaries needed adjusting, and the concept of the cure of souls needed definition and regulation of practice.[35]

If the Fourth Lateran Council established the possibility of a reformed pastoral mission, the numerous diocesan synods following the council made it a reality. Prior to the council, English bishops dealt with parish behavior in a piecemeal fashion, if they dealt with it at all. Parishes had fallen largely under the purview of landlords or minsters, and bishops had exercised little direct influence over the laity's religious practices.[36] After 1215, however, bishops grew more willing to regulate parish life by addressing the quality of pastoral care. This would be a feature of parochial life and organization in the later middle ages. Between 1219 and 1268, nearly all English dioceses held synods to create statutes that reiterated and expanded upon the Fourth Lateran decrees.[37] Bishops shared their statutes with one another, and some statutes, like those of Oxford (1222), Salisbury (c. 1238–44), and Worcester (1240), were especially influential, as other bishops copied and adapted them for use in their own dioceses.[38] Taken together, they illustrate the kinds of concerns the English episcopacy had for the administration of their dioceses and the parishes within them. The result was a body of legislation that outlined some shared goals for the English Church and its organization. By 1456, canonist William Lyndwood tried to standardize these goals in his compendium of statutes, the *Provinciale*.[39] A guiding principle for much of the pastoral reform of the thirteenth century was a desire to break down the local traditions, loyalties, and customs of parishes. The parish clergy were the focus of this project, because they were to be representatives of a universal Church.[40] Yet synodical requirements for greater adherence to an idealized norm of parochial support and involvement could not and did not erase the tension between local parish concerns and interests and institutional demands and desires. Although parish regulation was now a greater concern for bishops than for secular landlords, the statutes did not reinvent the parish, nor did they erase local traditions or differences.[41]

Sometime between 1252 and 1258, the bishop of Bath and Wells, William Bitton I, contributed his own statutes to this growing episcopal legislation.[42] His eighty statutes outline episcopal expectations for the parishes in his diocese and fall into essentially four broad categories: (1) the sacraments and their administration, (2) the condition and contents of the parish churches, (3) clerical duties, responsibilities, and behavior, and (4) the organization and administration of the diocese.[43] Intended to control collection of revenue, they also provided an important institutional framework for lay involvement in the parish. Bishop Bitton sought to establish regular performance of the sacraments. This meant not only establishing the proper schedule for their celebration, but also the form of their celebration. The statutes stipulated that the church fabric must be solid and clean. The ornaments had to shine. There had to be one chalice of silver, if possible, but gilt would be allowed, and there had to be a dish for the priest to wash his hands in before the mass. Mass had to be celebrated with two candles on the altar, and a bell had to be rung after the consecration so that the laity would know what had happened.[44] Churches needed to have mass books for the parish liturgy.[45] There had to be a stone font of sufficient size with a cover.[46] Furthermore, the churchyard needed a fence or wall to prevent animals from digging in the graves, and the laity were not to build booths or stalls in it or to hold markets, "dishonest games," or fights within its confines.[47] These last concerns suggest that there was already some sort of collective life revolving around the parish.

The statutes did more than list rules: they made the laity actors and agents in their own parish by giving them responsibilities. The sixteenth statute required the laity to lock up the host, chrism, and holy oil, and to cover the font.[48] The bishop wanted them secure and properly housed, and this meant that the church also had to be in good repair. To this end, the bishop divided responsibility for the church between the laity and the clergy. He specifically stated that, whereas the rectors or vicars would maintain the chancel, "the body of the church is to belong [*pertinere*] to the parishioners."[49] The twenty-second statute required a secure and honest custodian, preferably not a layperson unless no other individual was available, for the liturgical items.[50] These two statutes had strong implications for the future of lay organization. To meet these responsibilities, the laity were going to have to organize themselves. In these two statues, we can see the beginnings of the office of the churchwarden in this diocese and the potential for corporate activity.

Bath and Wells was not the first diocese to divide responsibility for the church building between the laity and clergy in this manner, and this division was to be repeated with greater specificity in other statutes.[51] As Charles Drew has pointed out, the implications of these statutes were not immediately obvious. Despite allowing for the possibility for lay control of the church and its contents, bishops did not envision that lay leadership or initiative would result from their decrees. However, lay involvement in the maintenance of the parish developed relatively quickly in Bath and Wells upon the publication of the statutes. [52] Ultimately, because of either episcopal neglect or growing concern for salvation after the plague, the laity did develop permanent organizations that helped them furnish and maintain their parish churches. [53] The earliest surviving churchwardens' accounts for Bath and Wells are from the early and mid-fourteenth century, some seventy to one hundred years after the publication of the statutes. They show parishioners already in the process of supplying books, vestments, and other liturgical items beyond the level required by the statutes.[54] The appearance of churchwardens' accounts is not then the first instance of lay organization on behalf of the parish.

Although these requirements created further financial burdens for parishioners, the people more than met such challenges. In fact, it is possible that laity did not feel their obligations to their parish to be especially onerous. The statutes allowed a great deal of opportunity for collective and individual choice, and providing for the parish church became a source of local pride and a forum for personal and corporate piety. These obligations, therefore, facilitated the development of parish cohesion, lay organization, and ultimately community identity. The laity recast mandates from the bishop into ways of developing and expressing their own concerns for the parish.

The bishop's statutes show that the bishop was already aware of the laity's activities in the parish, and he was worried about propriety. He admonished his clergy against the laity's celebrations of ales in the church, lest the clergy ruin their reputation with drunkenness and other immoral behavior. The bishop also feared that the laity were using their churchyards for nonreligious occasions, a circumstance that was not unlikely, given the central location of many churches. Yet the clear distinction between religious activities and secular activities that existed in the mind of the bishop was less obvious to the parishioners. As we will see in a later chapter, fairs and ales, held in the churchyard, were to become popular ways for some parishes to raise money to maintain the church. Thus, many activities deemed improper by the bishop comprised right and proper religious behavior in the minds of the parishioners. Although not akin to worship perhaps, these activities nevertheless expressed their Christianity and allowed them to adhere to the bishop's requirements.

Episcopal Oversight

As a means of instilling liturgical uniformity, clerical competence, and clerical and lay morality, the statutes established visitations and courts as mechanisms of oversight.[55] Yet visitations also allowed local concerns and individual needs to be articulated and in a sense required such communication.[56] To participate in a visitation, the laity had to organize and act in a corporate fashion to be able to address the bishop's concerns and state their own. Here, concerns for universal religious practice confronted particular locations characterized by unique economic conditions and social relations. Parishioners responded to direction from the bishop according to local resources and preferences.

Although no visitation reports survive for Bath and Wells, we have the questions the visitors asked the wardens.[57] The questions are undated, and may, in fact, have only served as a guideline. Surviving visitation reports from other dioceses show that different visitors emphasized different issues at different times.[58] These questions, however, were designed to find out what was going on in the parishes and to reaffirm the goals and aspirations laid out by the statutes. The bishop or his visitors wanted to ensure that the churches were proper houses for the host and that the clergy were performing the liturgy correctly and with proper piety. In particular, the visitors inquired about performance of the mass and the condition of liturgical items, books, vestments, the churchyard, and both halves of the church building itself—the nave and the chancel. The visitors asked: "If the church's chancel, nave, or bell tower were well covered? If other parts of the chancel, nave, or bell tower were in ruin? If the churchyard might be well enclosed or if cattle grazed there?"[59] The visitor was also to ask after the moral character of the laity and clergy: "Did the parish chaplains, and other clerks honorably celebrate in the church? Were they frequenters of taverns or were they scholars? Were the parishioners criminals, adulterers, or fornicators? Were either the clergy or the parishioners heretics, usurers, or soothsayers, or other kinds of criminals?"[60] Finally, the visitors inquired about the state of the church's finances, whether the parishioners paid their tithes, if the vicar was in residence, or if he or the rector was involved with usury.

Ideally, the bishop was to hold a visitation every third year.[61] Despite the best of intentions, however, they did not hold them this often. When they did hold them, concern with the condition of the church's property often took priority over sacramental or moral issues.[62] Surviving visitation records are rare for England in the period prior to the Reformation,[63] and, although none survive for Bath and Wells, the bishops' registers show that they did, indeed, take place. Despite the bishops' best intentions, however, he often did not conduct them in person. In 1333, Bishop Ralph of Shrewsbury declared his intention to visit ten parishes and five chapels in the northeastern part of the diocese.[64] In April 1477, Bishop Robert Stillington had intended to finish his visitation of the diocese, but "important business affecting the welfare of the realm and the English church" kept him away.[65] In 1506, Bishop Hadrian de Castello, who never even visited the diocese, delegated his visitation duties to his official along with most of his other duties.[66] In general, the fourteenth-century bishops, John Drokensford and Ralph of Shrewsbury, appear more personally involved in their visitation duties than their fifteenth-century successors were. By the fifteenth century, episcopal visitations were generally in the hands of professional administrators like the vicar-general, and only in serious cases did the bishop need to become involved. Far more regular were smaller visitations conducted by the archdeacons and their rural deans.[67] Rather than physically visit each parish, the archdeacons or the rural deans set up court in a central location in their district and had the churchwardens come to them. Churchwardens' accounts show wardens attending such visitations every year. The accounts for Stogursey record annual parish expenses at a visitation usually held in Bridgwater, while the wardens from Tintinhull went either to Montacute or Ilchester for their visitation.[68] In 1443, the Tintinhull wardens attended the bishop at his visitation in Ilchester.[69]

Attendance at a visitation took place according to an elaborate process that required planning and organization on the part of both the clergy and the laity. The statutes required the rector to provide food and lodging for the visitor and his entourage.[70] Churchwardens' accounts show that the wardens sometimes traveled far enough to necessitate spending a night away from home. Accompanying them was the parish clerk who carried the parish's banner. The wardens, the clerk, and their horses all needed food and lodging. The accounts for Tintinhull show that, in 1457, the parish paid for the wardens' expenses at the visitation and "for carrying the [parish] banner up to two times, being for the year past not allocated, and this year."[71] If problems had to be sorted out, that too would cost the parish money, as the wardens found out the next year when they had to pay 3s. 8d. for a concord between the parish and the rector.[72] We can imagine that visitations were noisy and protracted affairs. They gave the churchwardens a chance to meet their counterparts and compare their parishes with those in the area. With comparisons came competition for position and visibility. Robert Grosseteste, Bishop of Lincoln, wrote in his diocesan statutes that "rectors of churches and priests should not permit their parishioners to compete with each other over whose banners should go first in the annual visitation of the mother church, because brawls and even deaths result form this."[73] Sometimes the wardens declared that everything was as it should be, and no problems plagued the parish.[74] Some issues, such as lack of proper liturgical items or a ruinous church fabric, could be addressed at the visitation with instructions to remedy the situation. In 1512, the visitor cited the parishioners of Nettlecombe for broken windows, which they repaired.[75] Other issues, such as moral infractions or lengthy and complicated disputes, were outside the jurisdiction of the visitation and had to be turned over to the proper diocesan court. Most parish issues went first to the lower courts of the archdeacon. As there are no surviving records in Bath and Wells for these courts, we know little about them.

Although attending the visitation did not constitute a major parish expense, the appearance of such expenditures shows that the bishop's expectations had compelled the laity to respond. The parish needed leaders and an organization sufficient to finance and arrange the trip to the visitation. Episcopal administration also needed the wardens and lay organization to implement it. Visitations sought to bring parish religious practices and lay and clerical morality into line with episcopal expectations. This reassertion of Christian orthodoxy also maintained the parish's place vis-à-vis the ecclesiastical hierarchy. Yet although the visitation process served to enhance conformity, it also allowed the laity to voice some of their own religious concerns. Religious and administrative instruction had to proceed far enough so that there was a shared appreciation for what could be wrong in the parish. The laity had to be able both to recognize and to report on defects. In fact, parishioners may have reported on matters of little interest to the authorities in hopes of finding a remedy for their own concerns. In some instances, however, the laity and the clergy shared the same concerns, including a desire to deal with anything that interfered with masses for the good of their souls.

Because the visitors forwarded some of their findings to the bishops, bishops' registers documented some of the more serious concerns.[76] They covered issues ranging from lay resentment of episcopal interference to decayed chancels and clerical wrongdoing. These episodes reveal some of the dynamics existing between parishes and the episcopal hierarchy. Parishioners appear to be quite concerned with liturgical improprieties and moral laxity. Typical of findings during visitations were concerns expressed over the state of the vicarages and their attendant lands and buildings or clerical failure to perform sacramental duties.[77] In a visitation conducted in 1335, the visitor discovered that the rector of Yeovilton was not maintaining the chancel or the ornaments in an appropriate fashion.[78] Sometimes it was laxness or incompetence that led to decay; sometimes the clergy pleaded poverty.[79] Although this monetary concern appears to manifest only the bishop's financial interests in the parish, this decay ultimately hindered the performance of the mass. In January 1445, Bishop Bekynton demanded that his vicar-general and commissary-general conduct a full inquiry into the value of all the vicarages in the diocese, because he had found in his last visitation that many were so poorly endowed that the vicars, priests appointed by rectors to attend to the cure of souls in parishes, could not suitably maintain themselves.[80] From the parishioners' perspective, these situations all interfered with the sacraments.

The cases that appear in the bishops' registers are the more serious ones and should not be construed as typical. They do show, however, that the parishioners' concerns were not general, random, or uninformed. They were often quite specific about their spiritual needs and concerns. During the visitation Bekynton conducted in 1444, he heard complaints from the parishioners of St. Mary Magdalene in Taunton.[81] The parishioners were upset that their clergy, consisting of the vicar and numerous chaplains for the side altars, were not celebrating as regularly and as seriously as they should. The parishioners accused the clergy not only of laxness, but also of not wearing their vestments. "[They] ought to be content with their surplices and caps, and more over, they ought not during the said mass, or any service, to wander and pay attention to the walls or windows of the church, but should with devotion and attention read, chant and sing the psalms."[82] In a 1504 visitation, the parishioners of Bicknoller complained to the bishop that one John Pounceford refused to continue to endow "a taper before the image of our lady in the time of the saying of the mass at Bicknoller & a torch to give light at the sacring time there with 3d. to be given to the priest yearly to pray for the souls of certain persons called the Wayfildes whose names [have] been largely. . . specified in the mass book at Bicknoller."[83] Pounceford's unwillingness to honor his family's obligations threatened the community of the parish, both those living and dead. In both cases, the bishops found in favor of the parishioners, thereby recognizing and sharing their spiritual concerns. All such breaches hindered prayers for the dead. The laity's concerns were understood in terms of ritual performance, but bishops had encouraged them to think about religion in these terms. The ecclesiastical and royal hierarchy repeatedly used ritual to reinforce its position.[84]

Lay involvement in the visitation was not limited to informing on clerical laxity. The visitor expected the parishioners to be knowledgeable about the parish's history, patronage, and worth. Parishes might have many clergy. Usually the rector did not perform the weekly services but turned them over to a vicar. His living was carved out of the much larger living the rector earned from the parish. When the rector or vicar died or moved, it was standard procedure in Bath and Wells to inquire among the "honest and faithful men of the parish" about who had the right to present the benefice. In 1467, when the parish priest of Tintinhull died and the bishop needed to find out who should be presenting the new one, he called upon John Stacy, Robert Afte, John Browne, and Peter Bretyil to tell him how long the church had been vacant and who held the advowson—the right to appoint the new incumbent.[85] As this procedure shows, the bishop expected and relied upon parishioner involvement.

These cases notwithstanding, we should not assume that visitations were harmonious affairs, where churchwardens and diocesan officials always saw eye to eye. In some case, parishioners saw the visitors as unwanted intruders. One of the most violent responses to episcopal authority came in 1349, when Bishop Ralph of Shrewsbury conducted a visitation at Yeovil. The parishioners rioted over unspecified causes. A crowd attacked the bishop and his attendants, locking them up in the church overnight. The next day the bishop made his way to the rectory, where the parishioners again besieged him.[86] Once the riot and bloodshed were over, the bishop threw the full weight of his authority behind apprehending and punishing the offenders, by placing the parish under interdict and demanding penance. The bloodshed necessitated a second episcopal visit to reconsecrate the churchyard for burials, thus ensuring the bishop a future chance to observe local behavior. In the end, he was content to punish only the perpetrators, hoping this would set an example for the rest of the community. The bishop still allowed the parishioners to bury their dead in the churchyard, even though it had not been reconciled after the violence, and he suspended the interdict during the Christmas season.[87]

Regarding those who participated in the riot, he was not as merciful. As the proceedings against the perpetrators progressed, the bishop identified fifty-seven individuals as participants. They included a tailor, a parish clerk, a tanner, a baker, and probably a glover, a skinner, and a carpenter. At least one woman, Margota Weston, along with her husband, Richard, was also involved. That the account listed members of so many occupations and a woman as participants in the violence suggests that the riot cut across a wide section of the parish.[88] Once the bishop had tried and convicted the perpetrators, they were to turn over their weapons to the vicar and perform public penance designed to identify and separate them from the rest of the parish both emotionally and physically. They were to process around the church of Yeovil on three Sundays and feast days with bare head and feet and carrying tapers weighing one pound. After the mass, they were to offer the tapers to the high altar. The vicar was then to read out what crimes they had committed. Finally, the offenders had to process through the marketplace on three separate occasions and visit the churches of Wells, Bath, Glastonbury, Bristol, and Somerton, and finally make a pilgrimage to Canterbury. Their ringleader, identified as Richard Bardolf, was also to pay a fine of £20.[89] The combination of a fine and pilgrimages made this a very expensive punishment. Although Bath, Wells, Glastonbury, Bristol, and Somerton were all within the diocese and relatively close, Canterbury was clear across the kingdom; traveling there would entail a much longer and more expensive undertaking and remove the troublemakers from the parish for a longer period of time.

The bishop designed the punishment to reinforce his authority in a number of ways. He sought not only to publicly humiliate the rioters, but also to reinforce the link between his position as bishop and the sanctity of the church and its saints. It was part of his office to protect the church. His punishment also served to identify the parish as a community and cut out those who did not meet his notions of a community. The rioters' bad behavior was held up as a potential threat to the whole parish. If the bishop had not lifted the interdict, no one would have been able to receive the sacraments. The punishment showed that offending the bishop or disobeying his directives could result in formidable obstacles to the laity's ability to work for salvation by receiving the sacraments and having a proper Christian burial.

Interaction with the episcopal hierarchy thus compelled parishioners to act in specific ways. They had to act as a corporate body with leaders who could speak to the physical and moral condition of the parish. They were also compelled to know their parish's history and rituals. Failure to participate in the visitation could have serious legal repercussions, but it could also lead to spiritual consequences, when there was a failure in sacramental performance. Lay organization and local knowledge, however, made it easier for the laity to promote and act on their own spiritual concerns. In this fashion the laity created meaning out of their compliance with diocesan regulations. It was also in this manner that episcopal administration could foster one aspect of community identity.

Issues reported out of the visitation were only one part of the business of episcopal courts. There were four diocesan courts. The two busiest and most systematic were the commissary court and the consistory court. By the fifteenth century, the bishops had turned these courts over to professionals, the commissary-general and the vicar-general respectively. Much of the business of both courts was administrative and bureaucratic. When a testator held property in more than one archdeaconry, the commissary court, rather than the archdeacon's court, probated the will.[90] The consistory court oversaw the formal appointment of a number of diocesan court officers, including the rural deans.[91] In this capacity it also dealt with litigation over appointments and benefices and cases involving small amounts of money.[92] Additionally, the consistory court had license to hear morality issues such as defamation and marital disputes. Although the commissary and consistory courts did not generally deal with issues of collective parishioner behavior, churchwardens, as lay leaders of the parish, dealt these courts when necessary. They could be important venues for protecting the interests of the parishioners. In 1460, the churchwardens of South Petherton were apparently unable to collect a bequest from the executor of their late vicar's will.[93] As proctors of the parish's goods, it was their responsibility to go to the consistory court to secure the parish's bequest. Cases that made their way to either the commissary or consistory court usually concerned individual rather than communal behavior.[94] Most parochial issues of a communal nature, such as failure to maintain the chancel or nave, appear initially to have been dealt with through fines administered at the visitation or by archdeacons at their courts. Failing these lower courts, such cases went to either the bishop's personal court or the vicar-general's court, where punishment could be as serious as excommunication or interdict.

These latter two courts were more flexible venues. They consisted of the bishop's own court, called the *audience*, and the vicar-general's personal court which was held in the bishop's absence. These two courts generally dealt with the routine appointment of clergy to benefices or with serious issues, such as heresy, which fell outside the jurisdictions of the other two courts. Although the bishop and the vicar-general could hear any case they desired, they generally did not hear *instance* cases—those brought to court by a plaintiff and not by the Church's own actions or oversight.[95] One case that came before the vicar-general's court was between the monks of the priory of Dunster and the parishioners of Dunster. Rather than providing the parishioners, over whom they had cure of souls, with their own church, the monks shared their church with the parishioners. Parishes throughout England found themselves in similar situations.[96] The most common practice was to turn over one section of the church, such as an aisle or a chapel, to the parishioners. Although this situation was common enough in the Anglo-Saxon and early Norman churches, in the wake of the reforms introduced by the Fourth Lateran Council, these shared situations became less and less satisfactory.[97] The monks and the laity often resented each other, and confusion frequently developed over ill-defined rights and obligations. The rivalry could become so intense that the relationship sometimes degenerated into violence and litigation.[98]

The situation in Dunster was uneasy, and in April of 1498 the monks and parishioners assembled before the vicar-general's court. At issue were the scheduling of services, controlling the offerings and tithes, and maintaining the building. The monks felt that the parochial processions in and around the choir interfered with their services, the vicar William Bonde felt that his rights and privileges with regard to the monastery and its control over the parish were arbitrary and unclear, and the parishioners wanted clarity over what part of the church fabric was their responsibility. Much of the settlement tried to clarify the vicar's relationship with the priory; however, a portion of the resolution went to the heart of the laity's concerns over their community identity. The vicar-general physically divided the church. The monks received the chancel and choir and the parishioners the nave. In the nave, at the altar of St. James, the vicar and his successors were to celebrate divine services without the prior's interference. This meant that the vicar could now perform high mass for the parishioners, whereas before the prior had been the main celebrant. The vicar and his parishioners could also conduct processions in the nave or churchyard without disturbing the monks. In effect, this arrangement created two separate churches in one building and clarified each group's financial responsibilities toward their respective parts of it. By using this particular legal venue, the parishioners and their vicar were able to address particular issues relating to the parish's identity vis-à-vis the priory. Now the two religious communities were further distinguished not only by their lifestyles but by their separate sections of the church. Episcopal oversight, even when handled by professional administrators, compelled the laity to act as a group on behalf of their parish. Although the parish remained of concern to the bishop primarily as a benefice, his oversight provided the laity, such as those in Dunster, with the opportunity to articulate what they thought was important.

Equity Courts

Because of the laity's continued organization to ensure church maintenance, the parish over the course of the fifteenth century became an increasingly significant economic, and, ultimately, legal, force. While the bishop may still have thought of the parish as a benefice, it was becoming much more than that to the parishioners. Within the context of their parochial administrations, set up to meet the bishops' demands, the laity found that they could articulate and expand their own religious interests by endowing side altars, lights, and masses for the dead. To meet the financial and religious obligations of both the bishops and the laity, parishes (not individuals) began to acquire land, create contracts with artisans, and inherit goods and other valuables. Because of their collective action, they were now able to define their parish and its needs in other ways.

These goods and activities needed legal protection. Parish leaders did not want to assume personal liability for parish financial obligations, and the laity as a group did not want one or two individuals controlling the goods and property they had amassed for their parishes for the benefit of souls. Thus the laity's involvement in their parishes assumed a large economic dimension. The bishop's jurisdiction was increasingly unable to deal with the issues and disputes that arose out of these increased responsibilities. Episcopal jurisdiction did not include the means of adjudicating contractual law. Common law was also not ideally equipped to handle the legal complications that arose from the parish's growth in status and the increase in lay activism. With parishioners acting as de facto corporations, they needed a legal venue that could better address their contractual disputes.[99] As early as the reign of Edward I (r. 1272– 1307), English lawyers had a clear concept of the legal corporation, but it did not include the parish. A corporation was "an organized group of men . . . treated as a unit which has rights and duties other than the rights and duties of all or any of its members."[100] The law considered a mayor and commonality, abbot and convent, or dean and chapter to be corporations, but parishes were not.[101] This situation put many of the laity's parochial concerns outside the immediate purview of the common law. According to common law, the parish was to be treated as a perpetually underage person who required guardians, a role the law expected the patron to assume.[102] The patron was the person (or institution) who presented a candidate to the bishop to be appointed incumbent. The patron, even when he (or she) was a member of the laity, had different interests in the parish than those of the rest of the parishioners. To many parishioners, giving the patron charge over the valuables they themselves had given, inherited, or purchased was a lot like putting the proverbial fox in charge of the hen house. Only gradually did the law come to acknowledge that the lay component of the parish, separate from patrons and clergy, owned property and had separate interests that needed protection.[103]

The parish's lack of legal status in the eyes of common law developed from its strictly ecclesiastical origins. "The parish is originally a purely ecclesiastical district and during the Middle Ages it is not a unit in the geography of . . . temporal law."[104] As lay parochial organizations became more permanent, legal jurisdiction over parishes became increasingly unclear. Instead of simply dealing with parish patrons as church guardians, courts now faced the money-raising capacities of parishioners who owned property and made contracts in the name of their community.[105] Although not legally defined as such, parishes were in fact acting like corporations. A strong ecclesiastical court system might have been able to address the laity's corporate behavior, but the ecclesiastical courts' powers were diminishing in the fifteenth century, at the same time that parish organizations were expanding.[106] Church courts appear to have been effective within their jurisdictions, but their jurisdictions were shrinking. The economic and contractual orientation of most fifteenth- and early sixteenth-century parish organizations lay outside the competence of the episcopal courts. Bishops and their courts were not equipped to deal with lay parochial concerns arising out of broken contracts and contested land.[107]

Scholars disagree somewhat on the effectiveness of the ecclesiastical courts. Richard Wunderli found that the men and women of London were suspicious about the quality of justice handed out in the consistory and commissary courts.[108] Studies of Chichester, Canterbury, and Lincoln, however, show that the Church courts were effective and busy.[109] The very few surviving ecclesiastical court records for Bath and Wells also suggest that the ecclesiastical courts still served an important function for this diocese. During the fifty-year period covered by the one surviving consistory court book, *instance* cases increased.[110] These cases, in which a plaintiff charges a defendant rather than the defendant ending up in court by the Church's own regulatory process, provide a good measure of a court's effectiveness. They suggest that litigants outside the ecclesiastical hierarchy found the consistory court to be an acceptable place to try cases. If people had in general found that justice was not obtainable there, it seems reasonable to assume that they would have gone to another court. Yet, even if these courts were able to address some grievances, their jurisdictions did not easily include the collective action of the laity working on behalf of their parishes.

As well-defined as jurisdictions might be in theory, in practice litigants would try their cases in whatever court they thought might work to their advantage. Typically justices in the courts of common law did not throw out a case over matters of jurisdiction. Thus we know that the laity did in fact try their cases in common-law courts, and would continue to do so throughout the middle ages. They would, however, have to craft their argument in terms that common law could address.[111] This often meant that churchwardens had to take more personal responsibility for church property than either they or the rest of the community might wish. Eventually, the jurisdictional murkiness of the lay component of the parish gave the laity a new venue for their disputes. Increasingly laity, who were acting on behalf of their parishes, turned to the equity courts. The equity courts were relatively new. They had been set up to deal with weaknesses and gaps in the common law, such as those pertaining to lay administration of the parish. Parishioners understood the legal limbo their organizations occupied and often explained it in their petitions to the Court of Chancery. As two Essex churchwardens, who could not convince a fellow parishioner to return some money they had entrusted to him for safe-keeping, explained sometime around 1465: "for as much that your said suppli-cant be not capable in the law to take action as parson & wardens of the parish church of Abbeswearley they can have no remedy by the course of the com-mon law & so in this case they be without remedy without [that which] your gracious lordship be showed to them in this behalf."[112]

Three equity courts—the Court of Chancery, the Court of the Star Cham-ber, and the Court of Requests—developed out of the chancellor's duties and responsibilities in the royal chancery. The oldest court was the Court of Chan-cery.[113] By the reign of Edward III (r. 1327–77), the Chancery and the chancel-lor had ceased to travel with the king and remained at Westminster, ultimately becoming the third largest court there. Few Chancery petitions relating to any common-law issues appeared before 1420. Between 1420 and 1450, however, as the inadequacies of common law became more obvious, the number of petitions quadrupled, while at the same time their concerns became more specialized.[114] Under the Lancastrian kings, Chancery developed four specific areas of legal concern: (1) cases outside the common law, such as ecclesiastical or maritime law; (2) quasi-ministerial matters of interest to the king; (3) cases in which the common-law courts could not enforce a settlement; and (4) cases in which the law was at fault.[115] The laity generally had their parish cases heard under the auspices of the first, third, and fourth areas of legal concern. During the fifteenth century, the Court of Chancery became increasingly popular.[116] To help with Chancery's growing caseload, two other equity courts developed in the late fifteenth century, with slightly different jurisdictions. The Court of the Star Chamber was established in 1487 by the Star Chamber Act. It was designed to be a tribunal for special matters of law and order.[117] During its early years, it also dealt with disputes surrounding land tenure that included riot or forcible entry.[118] In practice, the differences in the jurisdiction of the Court of Chancery and that of the Star Chamber were minimal, and their proceedings were quite similar. The third equity court, the Court of Requests, also developed out of Chancery's equitable jurisdiction and owed its popu-larity to Wolsey, then chancellor of England, who further advanced it as a court for the poor.[119] Initially, he intended it to be similar to the Court of the Star Chamber, but dealing with civil rather than criminal matters.[120] As an alternative to the common-law courts, the equity courts, particularly the Court of Chancery, became quite popular. Chancery's appeal grew out of its prestige, supposed incorruptibility, and the existing system's perceived slowness and inadequacies.[121] The populace perceived the king and chancellor as having more recourse for dealing with violence and the means to enforce decisions.[122] Petitioners felt that the Chancery was immune to local pressure, quicker, and more flexible.

This development in the royal court system allowed the laity's parish organization to evolve into more than a creature of diocesan regulation. Equity's ability to address parochial issues and lay concerns gave the king or his courts a way of regulating and defining parochial behavior. The growth of the equity courts and the expansion of lay obligations to the parish prompted the laity to view their parish participation in ways that extended beyond the bishops' original intentions. By the fifteenth century, parish support, which the bishops had mandated to ensure the maintenance of the parish church, came to include notions of property and legality outside the control of the bishop or his court. Although the bishops' administrations had sought to define internal parish relationships in terms of Christian morality and correct celebration of the sacraments, secular law now also defined and regulated these in terms of contracts and legal obligations to the organizations set up by the laity themselves. By the fifteenth century, an individual's promise to give money for a new roof or aisle was seen as both a religious obligation and a legal contract.

A Chancery petition dating from between 1538 and 1544 shows how the parochial leadership in one Somerset community could define their religious practice in both business and legal terms.[123] The parish of Kilmersdon decided to add a new aisle that would enlarge the church. The plaintiff, the churchwarden during the start of construction, claimed that "one Thomas Rychmonde otherwise shepherd husbandman said in convocation with your said supplicant to know his mind that he would give toward the building and making of a new isle for the enlarging of the said parish church . . . £6 13s. 4d."[124] Later, Thomas Rychmonde refused to pay the money he had promised, although he did not deny his financial commitment to the new aisle project.[125] The churchwardens saw his refusal not only as a legal violation, but also as a threat to the community spiritually.[126]

The issue of proper performance of the mass had assumed a larger legal dimension than that anticipated by the episcopal statutes. Although performance of the mass was not directly at issue in most court cases, petitioners in Chancery petitions knew it was a sound tactic to cast their arguments in terms that showed how the mass would be threatened. Indeed, they were following the same logic that the bishops used in their visitation questions—all parochial failings ultimately led back to the central issue of proper performance of the sacraments. Contractual disputes among the laity over parish maintenance had altered the terms in which the laity debated parish issues. With the increased use of equity courts, the laity developed alternative terminology and definitions to describe their parochial involvement, a vocabulary that had been unavailable to them in the guidelines of the episcopal statutes and the procedures of the episcopal courts.

Conclusion

The churchwardens' ability to act for their parish become more pronounced over the course of the fourteenth and fifteenth centuries. This consolidation of the parish community would seem to compensate for what some scholars have referred to as the decline of the village community.[127] Collective regulation and action was still an important part of local life, but, after the plague, local life revolved more around the parish. Whether the laity attended mass in a chapel or parish church, both the laity and the bishop considered the parish a physical place, wherein the laity should practice acceptable and "normal" parish life. As we will see, differences existed from parish to parish, and they were often celebrated. Such variations, however, were not allowed to stray too far beyond clear standards for economic and spiritual practices. Too much variation or laxity could cause anxiety and distress to either the laity or the bishop. In general, the laity wished to fit into the perceived model of parochial Christian practice, and the bishop was committed to ensuring orthodox practices and beliefs within the diocese.[128] Yet as the laity took collective action to follow the bishop's directives, they began to forge distinct communities with a capacity to act for themselves.

2 "THE BOOK AND WRITINGS OF THE PARISH CHURCH"

Churchwardens' Accounts and Record Keeping

The Parish as a Textual Community

By the thirteenth century, English law, government, and religion all depended on writing and record keeping.[1] Consequently, the number of people able to acquire and to use the skills of reading, writing, and numeracy on a daily basis (mostly urban men) seems to have increased throughout the late middle ages.[2] Literacy rates in late medieval England varied according to class, level of urbanization, occupation, and sex; even the most optimistic estimates, however, show that the majority of the population still had to hire scribes and have documents read to them.[3] Studies such as those by Michael Clanchy and Brian Stock on the increasing use of writing and the growth of literacy also show how literacy and orality cannot be simply opposed.[4] Thus, medieval people often functioned within a context framed by writing, without actually possessing the skills of reading and writing. Simultaneously, political, ecclesiastical, or legal expectations of literacy existed in a context created by persistent local oral practices.[5]

There are gradations of literacy. One may read, but not write, and one may do either in many or few languages with varying degrees of competency. In the middle ages, literacy originally referred to Latinity—the ability to read and write Latin—but as the vernacular languages gained in prominence, the term *literacy* took on other connotations.[6] The commercialization of the late medieval economy and the reality of a cash economy made it necessary for merchants to keep accounts. Writing, reading, and numeracy became tools for success at business, a practice that we may fairly label practical literacy.[7] Schools and private tutors taught the skills of reading and writing separately, so that a person might know how to read English or Latin but be unable to write. Similarly, listening to a text being read out loud provided access to written information, yet those participating might not possess the skills of reading and writing.[8] The differing levels of familiarity with writing and reading led to various strategies for using written records. These strategies are visible in the recordkeeping practices of the late medieval parish and have implications for the creation and perpetuation of a community's identity. The amount of surviving parish material makes it possible to look at the relationships among recordkeeping practices, the character of local religion, and ideas of community formation. Using these records is difficult, however, because they are often vague, incomplete, and unclear. Yet their variety and vagueness can actually tell us something about how communities of people with greatly divergent literacies created and used these records. Examining how parishes kept and used their records reveals some of the internal processes of community formation and identification.

Our best insights into parish life are churchwardens' accounts. These documents record the laity's parochial income and expenditures on behalf of their portion of the parish church—the nave and its contents. Creating these records was one aspect of how the laity, or at least a portion of them, forged a community identity around their parish involvement. This process worked in tandem with episcopal oversight. Although churchwardens' accounts were the result of diocesan regulation and thus were imposed from the outside, the processes of creating and using churchwardens' accounts were internalized and reflective of local concerns.

As we have just seen in the last chapter, diocesan regulations compelled the laity to organize themselves. Although we can read the diocesan statutes as anticipating the development of lay parochial organizations, led by lay officials called churchwardens, the statutes for Bath and Wells are not themselves clear on exactly how the laity were to organize. At most they suggest that a member of the laity might serve as a custodian of the liturgical items, in the absence of a clergyman.[9] There is no discussion of keeping accounts and no discussion of accountability. The earliest statement of these responsibilities comes from the diocesan statutes of Exeter, Bath and Wells' neighbor to the south. Bishop Peter Quinel issued these statues in 1287, some thirty years after Bishop Bitton wrote his for Bath and Wells. In his diocesan statutes, Peter Quinel urged parishioners to elect responsible custodians, or churchwardens, to manage parish resources, explaining that these wardens were to render to the parish and its clergy an annual written account of their activities and the church's contents.[10] He directed that the custodians should come before the rectors or vicars of the churches (or at least before parochial chaplains and five or six trustworthy parishioners, whom the rectors or vicars have selected for this) and they should render every year a faithful account of the stock of the churches. And it should be recorded in writing, which writing we order to be presented to the archdeacon of the place when he should visit.[11]

The close geographic proximity of the two dioceses made it possible for practices in Exeter to influence Bath and Wells and vice versa. Only thirty-seven years after Quinel's statutes went into effect, the first churchwardens' account appeared in Bath and Wells.[12] We can speculate that Quinel realized that lay custodians would need greater supervision and thus mandated the keeping of written records. The parishioners could also have realized, because of the way some conducted their business, what sorts of advantages the accounts provided them. Whatever the explanation, Quinel did not invent churchwardens' accounts or parish organization. It is likely that his statutes reflect practices already in existence somewhere in his diocese. While financial accounts might have been new to the parish, they were not new to the cash economy of the thirteenth and fourteenth centuries.[13]

Some two hundred years later, rendering churchwardens' accounts had become routine enough that they were the subject of litigation and discussion. A Chancery case from 1536 reveals something of how some Somerset parishioners had come to understand this process and what it meant to parish organization. In 1536, Richard Partridge and Thomas Newght, churchwardens for the parish of Axbridge, brought suit against their predecessors in the Court of Chancery. [14] The two men alleged that the former wardens had refused to render an account of the money they had received and spent during their tenure as the parish's churchwardens. Furthermore, the former wardens refused to surrender the goods and income entrusted to them while in office. Clearly frustrated, the current wardens explained that

with the assent and by the commandment of the whole parish thereafter [in the] said year determined [they] have diverse and sundry times required them to make account or receiving thereof unto them according to their old accustomed usage and that to do they have refused and yet do refuse contrary to right and good conscience to the great destruction and decay of the said church.[15]

What made this such a serious matter, Partridge and Newght emphasized, was that the churchwardens were the ones

unto whose hand and possession and under whose charge and keeping was much money, plate, vestry implements, and ornaments of the said church and they at that time took upon them the care and charge thereof and of diverse other advantages and moreover that they should . . . make a true account thereof at the year end and of such advantage and moreover as they should get and obtain thereby for that year and the use of the said church as other procurators of the same church their predecessors did before time.[16]

Complete responsibility for the church money and precious objects gave the wardens control of a potentially substantial amount of money—money raised by the parishioners. Thus the former churchwardens' behavior not only threatened the parish financially but also hampered its liturgical performances, thereby threatening the community spiritually as well.

As a narrative of parish administration gone wrong, this case describes record keeping, its relationship to parochial leadership, and the parish's understanding of its importance. The corporate nature of parish finances meant that the accounts represented and recorded the shared contributions of parishioners that became manifest in the church and its liturgy. Without the accounts, not only could the wardens not perform their jobs, but also the very nature and quality of parochial life were called into question. The requirement to keep records became meaningful to parish communities throughout England in ways that differed from the motivations that had initially inspired the bishops' reforms. For the bishops, accounts were to ensure that the church was properly stocked and maintained so that the sacraments could be administered; for the churchwardens, the parish's ongoing spiritual and communal activities depended upon regular rendering of accounts.

Determining that a document is in fact a churchwardens' account is not as obvious as one might think.[17] There is tremendous variety in the form and content of documents listed in archive catalogues as churchwardens' accounts. Some have only brief entries, listing simply the total amount of money earned and including little information on how the parish raised or spent its income.[18] Others are much more detailed and illustrate much more than just the parish's financial state at the end of the year. Ronald Hutton's book *The Rise and Fall of Merry England* follows a very strict definition, and he lists 194 accounts dating before 1547.[19] Beat Kümin in his book, *The Shaping of a Community*, used a much broader definition of churchwardens' accounts that included the audit accounts, and his list has 234 sets of extant accounts dating before 1547.[20] These variations make it difficult to come up with exact numbers of churchwardens' accounts for all of England or for any given diocese or county.[21] The majority of these records now labeled as churchwardens' accounts come from London and southwestern England. The diocese of Bath and Wells alone has twenty accounts (see Table 2.1) and the diocese of Exeter, just south of Bath and Wells, has another twenty-five sets.[22] These two dioceses account for 19 percent of the pre-1547 accounts. London has another twenty-six accounts, which constitute 11 percent of the total pre-Reformation accounts. In con-

Table 2.1. Churchwardens' Accounts for the Diocese of Bath and Wells (b=borough)

Parish	Date	Type	Language	Comments
1. Bridgwater (b)	1318, 1366–1471, 1548	rolls	Latin and English	28 accounts + guild accounts
2. Bath (b)	1349–1577	rolls	Latin	77 accounts
3. Glastonbury (b)	1366–1564	rolls	Latin	21 accounts (torn)
4. Wells (b)	1377–1547+	city corp. books	Latin	totals only
5. Tintinhull	1433–1678	books	Latin and English	mostly complete
6. North Curry	1443, 1460	rolls	Latin	
7. Yatton	1445–1604	books	Latin and English	
8. Yeovil (b)	1457–1549+	rolls	Latin and English	13 accounts; transcripts of lost accounts
9. St. Mary Redcliffe (Bristol) (b)	1470, c1530, 1548	book	English	misc. pages
10. Croscombe	1474–1560	book	English	original lost
11. Pilton	1498–1538	book	English	incomplete
12. Stogursey (b)	1502–1546	book	Latin and English	
13. Nettlecombe	1507–1548	book	English	
14. Chedzoy	c.1508	rolls	English	written on back of 14th-century manorial account
15. Banwell	1515–1602	book	Latin and English	
16. Lydeard St. Lawrence	1524–59	book	English	totals only
17. Trull	1524–49	book	English	with guild accounts
18. Halse	1541–58	book	English	totals only
19. Ilminster	1542–1608	book	English	totals only
20. St. Thomas (Bristol) (b)	1544	book	English	with guild accounts

trast, few records survive from the northern part of England and those that survive are from the sixteenth century.

Episcopal demands to keep churchwardens' accounts suggest, therefore, a paradoxical situation: most late medieval parishioners could neither read nor write, but at the same time they had to keep records.[23] Perhaps we distinguish too sharply between oral and literate modes of thinking. Understanding literacy and orality as completely separate and mutually exclusive, rather than as interactive practices, obscures the degree of literacy medieval people might have actually possessed. By making certain accommodations, nonliterate or quasi-literate communities could create, employ, and exploit documentation.[24] Both the pace of increasing literacy and the ways oral and written practices influence and interact with each other shaped the process of accommodation.[25] How did people access and use writing without actually being able to read and write?

Writing influences social organization and group dynamics by creating what Brian Stock calls textual communities. Looking at heretical groups, he explored how texts both organized a group's internal behavior and provided a basis for solidarity against the outside world.[26] Neither the presence of a written version of a text nor literacy in the strictest sense of the term was necessary for a group's cohesion, Stock argued, as long as one member had mastered the use of texts and could use that knowledge to influence the community's actions and thoughts. These insights are helpful for understanding churchwardens' accounts and their role in the parish community. We can view the late medieval English parish as such a textual community in many different ways: through clerical instruction in doctrine, through the liturgy recited by a priest from a mass book to the congregation, and through the laity's provision of financial records concerning their maintenance of the church. This chapter will focus on how the need to keep churchwardens' accounts transformed the laity into textual communities and how these dynamics furthered the development of community identity at the parish level.

The issue of how texts influence a community's organization, as Stock has pointed out, is important, because it raises questions of how nonliterate or quasi-literate people accessed and incorporated the process of writing into their social organization.[27] This is a crucial issue, for throughout the middle ages such individuals had to account for themselves, protect themselves, and express themselves through the medium of writing. Parishes, unlike the heretical communities discussed by Stock, created some of the very records that defined them as a textual community. Furthermore, again unlike the groups studied by Stock, literacy was not a prerequisite for parish leadership. These issues relate to how communities used records, the significance records had for the community, and the role of the community's oral practices in creating and using their records.

As I will argue, a parish's oral practices are an important consideration in understanding how parishes created and used these records. Paul Zumthor has addressed the role of orality in medieval writing in his work on oral poetic performances. Zumthor is concerned with the social role of the voice or vocalization.[28] He contends that since all medieval literary texts were intended to be read out loud, the human voice must have a prominent role in our understanding of medieval literature.[29] In the absence of a written text during a performance, the voice created a bond between the audience and the performer, establishing a position of prestige for the performer and his or her voice and making the audience aware of itself as a corporate body.[30] When the performer relied on a prepared script, it, rather than the poet, became a source of authority. A written text, interposed between the performer and the audience, mediated the role of the voice and shifted the character of the group's self-awareness.[31] In quasi-literate groups, such as the late medieval English parish, written records have an ambiguous, not an absolute, position. The relevance of written records to their audiences lies not in the audiences' ability to read them personally but in the ability of one or a few individuals to read them out loud to an audience which then comments on and interacts with the records through this "public reading." Both Stock and Zumthor are willing to understand literacy as something less than absolute; their models of literate and oral interaction make it possible to discuss the social role of writing and record keeping in groups which, though only marginally literate, nonetheless produced and used written records. The involvement of writing in group dynamics comes into play quite clearly in churchwardens' accounts which grew from the communal nature of lay parochial administration.

Greater evidence for how quasi-literate groups used writing and orality appears in the fifteenth and sixteenth centuries. With the developments in English law, the increased bureaucratization of the church and government, and the growing commercialization of the late medieval economy, written records were now an integral part of local and national organization and regulation. Thus, in the late medieval English parish, both assumptions held by the literate about how to administer and organize property, and the still largely oral conventions of local communication and organization, continuously informed lay recordkeeping practices. We can often pinpoint these differences in the parish records themselves. For example, a Chancery petition from a parishioner of the Middlesex parish of Harmondsworth claimed that in 1540 he had leased the parish's church house. The wardens had "made a bill of remembrance which was read before all the whole parishioners then being present, where unto they all agreed that the same your orator should have a pair of indentures of the same for certain of his life time to be made by the said wardens and by their whole assent and agreement."[32] Subsequent wardens had challenged the validity of the lease, saying that they needed the house for storage and that their predecessors had no business leasing out the church house.[33] What is important for our purposes, however, is that someone had written up the agreement which they then read out loud to the parishioners. Despite both written and oral proof of the lease, the succeeding churchwardens challenged it.

The different uses of written records, especially those employed by both parishioners and the clergy, reflected not only different relationships to writing but also different priorities for the parish. For the laity, writing became more than just a means of recording information on paper or parchment to meet the demands of the ecclesiastical hierarchy; it was part of the process by which the laity transformed the practice of episcopal-mandated record keeping into a manifestation of community organization and local identity. This writing often reflects the oral or quasi-literate status of most medieval parishioners.

Throughout the fourteenth, fifteenth, and sixteenth centuries in many parishes in Bath and Wells and all over England, the churchwardens, in collaboration with the clerk, wrote up a set of accounts detailing the year's income and expenses. Internal evidence, as we will see, suggests that this process of composition relied on both notes kept on scraps of paper and the wardens' often imperfect memories. Upon completion of the accounts, they had to be audited. This could be done by a meeting of the parishioners as a whole or by a select group of them. At this meeting, someone, often the parish clerk, read them out loud to inform the assembled group of their contents. The parishioners would first hear what money and goods had been received and from what sources. Income might come from the rents of parish-owned property, but it also might come from a church play, a parish ale or revel, or bequests from members who had died during the year. The clerk would then read how the parish spent money, reporting both regular annual expenses, such as the purchase of church decorations for Christmas, Easter, or saints' days, and special projects, such as constructing a new tower or aisle or fixing the rood screen. By the meeting's end, the accounts had been corrected and approved via oral communication. Then, in some parishes, the clerk drafted a final copy of the accounts. In other parishes, there was no such final copy; corrected accounts still survive. The surviving accounts are, then, the product of a process that combined both literacy and orality.

Community identity grew from the combination of specific location, particular financial needs, idiosyncratic economic realities, and local traditions that made each parish unique. Even the dates for the parish audit varied from community to community. When the members assembled to hear and amend the accounts, they would be reminded of just what made their parish unique and which individuals had contributed during the year to the community's goals. Annual meetings helped define the parish year and its administration and thereby helped to affirm who was part of the community and what membership in it meant. This process might, in fact, only define the parish community in a narrow and exclusive sense. Some parish customs dictated that only householders could participate in parish decisions.[34] This would prevent some, such as married women, from participating in this aspect of the community. With respect to this level of parish involvement, married women, young adults, and servants would have to rely on their personal relationship with the householder in order to influence parish politics.[35] Yet the annual meeting was but one opportunity for a parishioner to define him- or herself as a part of the community. The parish community did not have a single form, and a meeting of the parishioners—or a portion of them—to audit the accounts would still enable them to hear about the contributions of the lowly laundress and the wealthiest patron.

By reading the accounts, the clerk gave a performance that articulated the year's events and familiarized the community with the records and their contents. Through the recitation, or performance, of the records, each member present was privy to written information. At the same time, those assembled could influence how the clerk kept the records by correcting and commenting on them. The presence of written records helped orchestrate this local interaction and helped organize the parish. We must read these records with an eye toward how the parish composed them and accessed their contents, so that we can see these documents not only as sources of information sent to episcopal administrators about parish maintenance, but also as symbols of locally-constructed community identity.

For late medieval parishes, record keeping included not only writing but also performance, or, to use Zumthor's term, vocalization. Literacy was necessary insofar as someone had to write out the accounts and read them out loud. But although the creation of these records acknowledged a parish's need to comment on their contents, it did not lead to widespread literacy, nor did it lead to the elevation and supremacy within the parish of those who could read and write. Parochial record keeping in late medieval England invoked implicitly oral ways of behaving, and, conversely, oral contracts and local organizations incorporated the expectations laid down by writing-based governmental administrations and legal systems. As a result, we should invest writing and the power it offered with a significance and meaning that draws upon community expectations for local religion and interaction.

Literate and Oral Practices in the Parish

Our own reliance on written sources reinforces the impression that writing was at the heart of parochial administration, even if most parishioners neither read nor wrote. This is not necessarily the case. While visiting England in the thirteenth century, an Italian notary observed that the English were more willing to forgo an official written contract than the Italians.[36] Michael Clanchy believes the notary was overstating his case, but the Chancery Court's increasing caseload was in part related to its ability to address oral transactions. This implies that spoken business practices were still entrenched.[37] Parishes created their written records within a context of both literate and oral practices. Common law courts accepted only written contracts as evidence in contract disputes.[38] If no written contract existed, petitioners had to turn to the equity courts, run by the chancellor and subject to his discretion, rather than the letter of the law and precedent. Plaintiffs and defendants alike knew that, in principle, the chancellor could accept oral contracts, and so they often referred to their verbal agreements and the problems they caused.[39] Chancery's standards of proof meant that court petitions are one of the few textual sources in which people from all parts of society commented directly on what writing meant to them. Because the act of litigation required orally conducted business to be committed to parchment, such acts explicitly moved the petitioners from the realm of the spoken word to that of the written word. Looking at how the laity conducted the business of their parish in both literate and oral ways opens up new possibilities for understanding churchwardens' accounts as instruments for forging textual communities.

The issues that came before the Chancery Court demonstrate that not all writing or all opportunities for written records were of equal value. The presence of churchwardens' accounts does not mean that the community took every opportunity to document their financial business. Parishioners might put their trust in corporate writing projects such as churchwardens' accounts, but this behavior did not automatically transfer to the realm of personal interaction in which personal trust was bond. It also did not mean that, having committed business to paper or parchment, the community would necessarily refer to these records during later disagreements. What follows is a discussion of oral practices in parish interaction and business as explained by parishioners in their Chancery petitions. In order to show how parish record keeping reflected both oral and literate ways of acting, we need to understand that churchwardens' accounts developed out of more than the Latin literate world of the church and, therefore, reflect much more than the Church hierarchy's concerns and priorities. Their method of composition and the presence of oral practices imbedded in churchwardens' accounts means they also reflect lay concerns. Evidence for this sort of behavior is scarce, and I have not confined myself only to cases from Bath and Wells. The evidence from Bath and Wells does suggest, however, that reliance on oral contracts was not an especially regional phenomenon, although it was probably more prevalent in the countryside than the city. The following cases show quite clearly that the laity used many kinds of business practices.

According to the following Chancery cases, communities relied on memory and oral practices well into the sixteenth century. They were an appropriate and expected part of local life that drew the community together and also reinforced certain collective religious goals. Even if plaintiffs fabricated the claims that they operated orally, they were willing to craft petitions based upon the presumption that parishes could and did transact business without writing. Nonetheless, their ability to describe business arrangements in terms of absent documentation points to the extent to which writing did organize community activities even when it was absent.[40] A Norfolk parish, St. Martin's in Fincham, kept no record of the £3 loan it made to its parish clerk, William Grene. After his death, around 1500, the churchwardens could not collect the money and sought legal intervention. In their petition to Chancery, the wardens stated that because they "have no writing" that recorded the delivery of the loan, they could not collect from Grene's executors.[41] Sometime around 1500, the Wiltshire parish of Steeple Ashton operated in a similar fashion when it contracted with Thomas Lovell, a freemason, to build a new church steeple. The Chancery petition explains that "the said covenants & bargains & payments to be made at the days as is aforesaid were made & done between the said Robert & Thomas Lovell by simple contract & not by written obligation or other wise."[42] During the 1530s, in Radbourne, Gloucestershire, John Payne served as churchwarden for nine years.[43] During his tenure, he incurred debts totaling twenty marks. Since Payne kept neither records of his debts nor any accounts whatsoever, the new churchwardens had no way of recovering the parish's lost revenue. In all cases, the plaintiffs show clear knowledge of what part of their business could have been recorded in writing. Within Somerset, we find that in the parish of Croscombe wardens kept churchwardens' accounts, but this did not prevent Richard Maudeley, a parishioner there, from using an oral contract to hire a carpenter to build the church a rood loft.[44] When the carpenter failed to do the work or return the advance on his salary, there was no written record of the transaction to protect Maudeley's investment. Here we see a corporate willingness to keep records but an individual's reluctance to do so, even when working on behalf of his parish.[45] What is more, we know that in 1497 he and his wife Alison had given a service book to the parish.[46] Whatever the reason Maudeley did not write out a contract, it was not because he was unaware of the uses of writing. Other parishes in Bath and Wells also relied on oral agreements. In Yeovil, the community became embroiled in a pew dispute in the early seventeenth century. In trying to resolve the situation, witnesses testified not only to how the churchwardens distributed seats but also to how the parish elected the wardens.[47] None of the witnesses giving depositions referred to any written sources in accounting for parish tradition; instead, they relied on the memories and recollections of "diverse old and ancient men of the parish of Yeovil." Yet this parish kept churchwardens' accounts, which, had they been checked, would have dated both the election and the seating arrangements back to the mid-fifteenth century.[48] Thus, even at this late date, the practice of deposing witnesses validated dependence on memories and oral testimony even within the highly bureaucratized and literate world of the courts. Legal procedures accommodated oral exchanges and reaffirmed their legitimacy.

The involvement of local oral practices with the legal system's literate expectations becomes more explicit in another Chancery case from sometime between 1538 and 1544. This property dispute juxtaposes a skill dependent on writing—forging deeds—with reliance on memories as a source of local knowledge. The petition also suggests the parishioners' awareness that the administration of their parish could depend simultaneously on both oral and literate practices. In this case, the plaintiff, Edmund Colleton, cousin and heir to the late William Colleton, challenged the Devon parish of Halwell over ownership of a parcel of land.[49] Edmund claimed that immediately upon William's death, six parishioners conspired and forged deeds which gave them control of a certain acre of land and prevented him from inheriting this land. The defendants' counter petition survives and shows what strategy the six men employed to deny the accusations; not only do they declare their innocence, but also they counter the accusation of forgery by claiming that the parish was an oral community, dependent on the memories of old men. Their petition states that

the said John Ryder in the bill named and . . . other[s] the wardens and feoffees of the said church of Halwell, have been seized & possessed of the said acre of ground to the use of the said parish by the space of this 80 years and more as it shall be duly expressed by old men being yet alive within the said parish.[50]

Although the defendants invoke written contracts and the writing-based assumptions of common law, they establish the antiquity of their association to the "said acre of ground" through oral testimony. This defense circumnavigates the whole issue of the charter's legitimacy by presenting an entirely different means of operating and organizing their parish. The competing descriptions of how this parish conducted its business arrangements expose the tension and interdependence between oral and literate ways of functioning. The wardens' response to the forgery charge suggests a basic understanding of the different ways to organize a bureaucracy. The defendants did not simply check old churchwardens' accounts, which would have shown whether the parish had collected revenue from this acre of land or not. Instead, they turned to the elder members' oral testimonies. In this case, the defendants refused to engage the plaintiff's expectations that written records were the basis for all parish administration. Instead they crafted a defense based upon the possibility that a parish still could function orally, and they expected the chancellor to understand this as well. Should that defense fail, they could try another strategy based on literacy; they could then address the contents and legitimacy of the contested charters. Their "forged" charters, in Clanchy's terms, "recreated the past in acceptable literate form" which could be presented at another court case.[51]

A parish's unwillingness to commit everyday activities and exchanges to paper, especially on behalf of the church, may reflect the lack of trust that was implied once a business agreement was put in writing.[52] Sometime in 1507, the churchwardens and parishioners of Shepton Mallet in Bath and Wells lent £52 to three parishioners.[53] Trusting the men, the parish kept no record of the transaction. Two years later, the men refused to repay their loan, and without any records, the parish had little legal recourse. In their petition to Chancery, the wardens made much of the parish's trust and confidence in their fellow members, claiming that the three men had promised them and the parishioners

that they would truly content & repay the same £52 unto the said late wardens or their successors immediately after the said 2 years ended without any condition or delay. & said late wardens & parishioners having great credence & confidence in their fair words & promises of the said Edmund, Thomas, & Nicholas and also trusted that they would not break their said promises. [T]he same late wardens according to their request then and there at the said parish church by the assent of the said parishioners delivered and lent unto the said Edmund, Thomas, & Nicholas the said sum of £52 sterling.[54]

The situation in Shepton Mallet suggests that the community placed its trust in oral practices. It may be, then, that the increasing dominance of writing and documentation shifted the character of exchanges from an atmosphere of trust and intimacy to a legal, authoritarian, and distrustful one which some parishes or individuals might have wanted to avoid.[55] The reluctance to swear oaths, even orally, had a strong religious basis because of the danger of swearing false oaths. Susan Brigden, in her study of sixteenth-century piety in London, points out that many felt that "it was a profanity that men would swear 'for every light trifle,' and that 'it was high time for the world to be at an end when no man trusteth not another.'"[56] She goes on to show that prohibitions against perjury as well as a strict code of honor informed this community behavior. It was not that writing was unavailable, but that it perhaps seemed inappropriate when two individuals conducted business.

The cases just discussed raise questions about the role of writing, particularly churchwardens' accounts, in establishing local precedents. Brian Stock implies, however, that textual communities would have used written records in such a fashion. We have to be careful of how broadly representative of parish behavior we assume these cases were. They do not necessarily show that parishes systematically ignored the information contained in their accounts. Successful appeals to previous records were not likely to result in litigation. They do show, instead, how deeply entrenched oral practices still were in the parish.

The potential protection that writing offered did not mean that parishes taught their members to read and write or that they demanded that the church-wardens be literate. Churchwardens participated in written ecclesiastical culture in a variety of ways: by keeping accounts, acting on the written instructions after a visitation, appearing in a variety of local secular and religious courts, and as executors or beneficiaries of wills. Writing helped safeguard the relationship that parishioners had to the abstraction of the parish. Yet parishioner-to-parishioner relations did not yet need the authority of written contracts, because people believed in the efficacy of a personal oath. The ability to hear and comment on the accounts during the annual meeting further mediated the authority of writing.

Oral and Written Practices in Churchwardens' Accounts

Although parishioners did not immediately resort to the protection of writing when required by either the legal system or the episcopal hierarchy to keep accounts, they had a variety of strategies available for gathering and preserving information when they did need written support. In acquiescing to episcopal demands, parishioners took one source and symbol of the bishop's control—written accounts—and made them a locus of communal responsibility and activity. The records gave authority and legitimacy to the lay component of the parish community.[57] As such, the records reflected the ways in which parishes operated, and they helped define each community by becoming part of the local religious culture. The challenges of language and the lack of the skills of reading and writing separated the parishioners from their records. Unable to comprehend Latin easily or to read and write English, parishioners had to develop ways to relate to their records without those skills. Their strategies are inscribed in the accounts, which we must read not only as a record of lay activities in the parish but also as ways of negotiating with legal and religious institutions that demanded written records.[58]

A central figure in the negotiating process between the literate episcopal bureaucracy and the quasi-literate parishioners was the parish clerk. As few churchwardens seem to have written their own accounts or any of the other documents that the parish might have required, both wardens and parishioners depended on the skills and knowledge of clerks to create the physical records.[59] Although John Symones and John Hayne very carefully signed their account in 1531 when they were churchwardens for Banwell, their signatures did not match the handwriting of the accounts.[60] Similarly John Broun, church-warden for Tintinhull from 1448 to 1452, also signed the account of 1447 to signify that he had taken office, but he did not write his account either.[61] Accounts regularly record money spent on paper, parchment, and the salary of someone other than the warden to write them.

The responsibility for writing out churchwardens' accounts did not fall to a single group of people specifically trained for the purpose. Who wrote the accounts and their positions within the parish varied. Sometimes the scribes' names appear, but not frequently enough to reconstruct the writing habits of most parishes. For example, in 1446, the vicar of Yatton received 14d. for providing the book and writing the account.[62] John Thurbane served the same parish in the late 1460s and, in 1502 a parish clerk named Richard took over the record keeping.[63] John Paris did some record keeping for Bridgwater in the 1450s but not apparently during the years he served as warden (1429, 1431, 1445, 1453).[64] In the neighboring diocese of Exeter, the vicar of Morebath, Christopher Trychay, wrote out the accounts during his incumbency.[65] In Ashburton, another Exeter parish, we know the names of most of the men who kept the parish's accounts. Ten different men wrote them over a period of sixty-eight years; all but one were laymen.[66] Yet although their skills made them important to parochial administration, there is little evidence that writing out the accounts gave parish clerks any special status within the bureaucracy. They were paid for their work in the same manner as any other artisan working for the parish.

The scribe did more than simply write out the accounts. Some parishes accommodated different levels of literacy by having the scribes inform the participants of a document's contents by reading it out loud.[67] There are numerous examples of clerks reading accounts or other documents to the assembled parish. For example, the accounts for Banwell often included the expense of reading the accounts to the assembled parish: "for reading of the book of accounts—8d." and again, "for saying of the evidence of the church—8d."[68] The language in the 1516 account from Yeovil parish also suggests that the warden or scribe read his account to the parish. The account's heading states: "First in the same day James Dyrdo made his account read of the whole parish."[69]

A switch from Latin to English further facilitated reciting the accounts for the community. The Latin-literate episcopal hierarchy that imposed record keeping on the parishes also set up Latin as the language of parochial records, even though it was not the parishioners' language of daily communication.[70] Initially, churchwardens' accounts were kept in Latin, and, in a sense, a language barrier separated the parishioners from the documents they themselves were helping to create.[71] As the availability of clerks familiar with Latin declined, the writing of accounts gave the community greater access to the records' contents. In some parishes, the wardens and clerks dealt with the laity's lack of Latinity by keeping two sets of records, one in English and another in Latin. Bridgwater accounts from between 1428 and 1431 are in English, while those from both previous and subsequent years survive in

Latin.[72] The English ones seem to have served to inform the parishioners of the contents of the Latin ones (which no longer survive). At least as early as 1473, the parish of St. Edmund's in Salisbury had two such sets; in 1500, the parish paid John Hampton, Jr., 3s. 3d. "for his labor in writing and making this present account in Latin with a reckoning in English in the big book called the 'Journal.' "[73] The parishes of Wimborne Minster in Dorset and St. Michael's in Oxford also have some surviving English accounts that duplicate the Latin ones.[74] Other parishes gradually abandoned the use of Latin altogether and began keeping their accounts exclusively in English. Given the literary and bureaucratic traditions of the capital, not surprisingly, some of the earliest churchwardens' accounts in English come from London parishes.[75]

Although this transition was not uniform or immediate, most communities, including those in Bath and Wells, had switched to English by the early sixteenth century[76] (see Table 2.1, #12–20). Exceptions to this practice include the parish of St. John's in Glastonbury, which has sporadic accounts from 1366 to 1574, all of which are in Latin, and St. Michael's in Bath, which did not keep accounts fully in English until 1541/2.[77] The haphazard switch from Latin to English proves the local nature of record keeping and argues for the strong role played by individual scribes. When the vicar drew up the Tintinhull accounts in 1507, he wrote them in English, whereas previously the scribes had generally used Latin.[78] Latin accounts still tended to rely on a fairly extensive English vocabulary when describing items received, purchased, and bought on behalf of the parish. For example, the Bridgwater account for 1418 records "In spikenaill et bordnaill emptis pro scafelt firmando—xvjd." ("For spike nails and board nails bought for fixing the scaffolding—16d.")[79]

Parish records in the vernacular reflected the laity's use of language, making the accounts easily comprehensible when read aloud. The vernacular also reflected the scribe's greater facility with English than with Latin. The vernacular employed qualities inherent in oral ways of communicating, such as recitation or memorization.[80] Use of English also constitutes a negotiation between the bishop's writing-based expectations and the oral nature of parish interaction. But although parish clerks came to use English in record keeping, episcopal ones generally did not. Witness depositions might be in English, but written records of diocesan administration were in Latin. Variation in language also signals the changing roles that records played within the parish. Regardless of the language, the accounts provided the parishioners with ecclesiastical and legal protection for the parish's property.[81] It seems unlikely, however, that records kept only in Latin allowed many parishioners to gain intimate knowledge of their contents. Switching to English made the records more than a means of legal protection now that communities could comprehend their contents.

The switch from Latin to English thus furthered the parishioners' co-optation of episcopal expectations. It granted them greater access to written documents.[82] The accounts from St. Mary the Great in Cambridge demonstrate this point quite clearly. This parish was appropriated by the royal foundation of King's Hall in 1343.[83] This meant that King's Hall collected the tithes and appointed a priest to attend to the parishioners. Immediately upon acquiring St. Mary the Great, King's Hall began making payments for the parish's maintenance. These payments, which continued up to the Reformation, are recorded throughout the fourteenth, fifteenth, and the first half of the sixteenth centuries in the King's Hall accounts, which were kept in Latin until 1529.[84] The first surviving churchwardens' accounts for St. Mary's do not appear until 1504; they are, however, always in English.[85] From 1504 to 1528, two sets of accounts addressed, among other things, the financial relationship between these two institutions in two different languages. Both sets of accounts reflect the needs and languages of the communities that generated them. By hiring scribes, having them recite the accounts out loud, and switching to English, parishes employed strategies that enabled the membership to participate in the writing-based administrative process that had been imposed on them by the bishops. These strategies allowed parishioners to keep track of their churchwardens, observe one another's contributions to the parish's activities and upkeep, and make plans for the next year. Running the parish in such a communal fashion did not ensure everyone's participation in the parish, but it did ensure that everyone *could* participate.

We can, thus, view a recitation or presentation of the annual accounts or, in fact, any presentation of written material, as creating a drama about the previous year, drawing on the more typically oral ways in which the parish operated. The connection between local issues and parish drama has been made before. In her work on East Anglian drama, Gail McMurray Gibson has shown how local interests and parish politics often helped shape parish plays.[86] Her observations provide useful insight into the performative aspects of a parish's interactions with texts.[87] This process is at work in the Robin Hood revels for the parish of Yeovil. Each year a former churchwarden assumed the role of Robin Hood at the annual fundraising revel. His appearance provided many opportunities for local jokes about the parish's administration, the churchwardens, both past and present, and the nature of parish involvement.[88] Reciting or summarizing the accounts reenacted and recounted the communal activities and behavior specific to each parish, giving the annual meeting many of the characteristics of a dramatic performance. The effect was not only to create documents for posterity but also to identify those wanting or needing access to writing. The whole production or communal drama drew the parish together and helped define it as a textual community as well as a spiritual one.

Hearing the financial accounts read out loud probably was not as entertaining or as exciting as hearing a poem or play, but there was precedent for this kind of "listing" performance within parochial culture. Clerks read out bede rolls, lists of gifts given to the church and their donors to the community, at least four times a year. It is against this cultural backdrop that we must analyze the production of churchwardens' accounts. Whatever its legal and monetary purposes, the reading was a ritual designed to further define local history, belonging, and parish membership.

Implied in the terminology of some churchwardens' accounts is evidence of this local interactive drama that produced them. Most accounts record simple statements of how money was raised or spent to maintain the church and its contents, such as "Received for the Easter taper—5s. 7d." or "For a rope to the bells—2s."[89] Generally no personal pronouns identify the agent receiving or spending the money. The assumption was that the wardens, acting on behalf of the parish, had received and spent the money in the manner explained by the account. As the wardens recited their activities to the scribe, however, some personal pronouns crept into the record keeping. When this happens, we are reminded of the oral practices that informed their composition. The scribes who wrote out the accounts for the parish of Yatton frequently included this kind of language, making the account read almost as a dialogue between the clerk and the wardens. For example, in 1474, in the receipt half of the account, the clerk records: "Item—they [the wardens] have received 8 rings." Further on an entry reads: "Item—received of the wardens for their ale—5 marks 8s. 8d."[90] In the expense section, however, we read of the wardens recounting their activities to the clerk: "I paid to a plumber—3d; Item—I paid to the glazier—6s. 8d." and so on.[91] The use of pronouns preserves the different relationships that the clerk and the wardens had to the process of administering the parish and creating accounts. If we look to a set of London churchwardens' accounts from the parish of St. Botolph, Aldersgate, we see a different method of recording this sort of dialogue. In the accounts' left margin, the clerk has listed the category of income or expense as a heading which is subsequently elaborated upon in the body of the account. The elaboration of each category frequently begins with the phrase "they answer" or "they respond." Depending on the circumstances, "they" refers to either the wardens or the parishioners. Drawing up the accounts involved some form of verbal exchange, giving the contents a script-like quality.[92] Creating and using the accounts required the clerk to adapt the parish's oral practices to a literate context and vice versa. Recitation or a performative reading provided a means of accommodation; the residue of this process is preserved in some accounts.[93]

The dialogue embedded in many churchwardens' accounts brings us back to the paradox of the situation: parishes had to keep written records, but parishioners themselves generally could not read or write. The accounts embody the processes of dictation, transcription, recitation, and reception involved in their creation and subsequent performance before the parish.[94] They show that oral and literate modes were not completely distinct and utterly opposed to each other.[95] Rather, the two modes were interactive.[96] Thus the whole process of rendering churchwardens' accounts shaped community interaction and made the parish a textual community; creating the accounts brought the parish together and reminded them of their collective identity.

Access to writing, not literacy itself, organized and assembled the community. If parishioners could not read, they negotiated and co-opted the practice of record keeping through listening to oral recitations and then responding to them. These strategies were meaningful to them and reflected their daily forms of communication. In one instance, the laity even acknowledged the importance of the multiple ways of accessing the contents of written records. The 1524 bylaws of the Bristol parish of St. Stephen, which was just outside the diocese of Bath and Wells, dictated that the annual audit would start promptly at eight o'clock in the morning.[97] Refusal to attend on the churchwarden's part brought a fine of 40s., and the parish penalized any parishioner absent from the meeting 40d. The senior warden was charged with rehearsing the accounts to the whole parish community, so that they might "receive, hear and see" the final reckoning, the very words reflecting the different ways that the laity would comprehend the accounts' contents.

Local Authority

In the middle ages nonliterate individuals, such as churchwardens, frequently depended on the written word in their social and political dealings.[98] This activity placed them within the realm of what Franz Bäuml terms the quasi-literate.[99] "*Litterati* and 'quasi-literates' are acquainted with the oral tradition, but both are functionally dependent on the written word."[100] The office of churchwarden (the individuals who were ultimately responsible for the churchwardens' accounts) was a text-based office, but the interaction of wardens with their parish and with texts of their own creation (in part) drew on strategies which were meaningful to nonliterate parishioners, making the churchwarden's position a performative one as well. Separating the accounts from the office that generated them results in an incomplete understanding of each and drains from them the dynamics that made them meaningful to the medieval parish. [101]

The social role of churchwardens' accounts within a parish was twofold: (1) their status as legal documents relating possession of goods and the acquittal of debts and obligations and (2) the method in which they conveyed and commented on this information. To understand this second role, we must also consider the locus of parish authority. The fact that a parish could not incorporate itself legally, as a town could, complicates this issue. The power of the parishioners with respect to either their churchwardens or their accounts varied according to the administrative structure of each parish. As we will see in the next chapter, some parishes had strong wardens, whereas others had weak ones; some had a vestry that governed the wardens and limited parishioner involvement, whereas others were influenced by local patrons who took an interest in the activities and health of the parish. These variations in parochial administration produced different kinds of accounts. In Lydeard St. Lawrence, a vestry of four men received the accounts.[102] Other parishes, such as Axbridge, Tintinhull, and Banwell, audited the accounts at a gathering of the whole community, at which the assembly also elected new wardens.[103] St. Michael's in Bath marked the occasion for writing and auditing the accounts with a feast for those conducting the audit.[104] The menu and amounts spent on it suggest that only those directly involved in the audit attended. At Bridgwater's audit in 1449, the parish even bought the auditors new woolen cloaks.[105]

A parish's initial accounts often coincide with a new building project.[106] The resulting accounts often show an evolution in parochial record keeping and create the impression of a parish learning how to administer itself. When the Croscombe accounts began, in 1474, they provided information only on sources of parish income. In 1480, the parish built a church house and noted the expenses incurred in this endeavor.[107] By 1485, expenses have become a much more regular part of the accounts, but they never seem detailed enough to include all the expenses of one parish for a whole year.[108] Thus, some of the parish's accounting remained in the realm of oral interaction and was not written. In contrast, the parish of Stogursey kept different kinds of records which they ultimately consolidated into a single account including both fundraising and expenses. The earliest ones began as audit accounts, with some information about sources of income. Two repeated memoranda in the audit record show that the wardens kept separate reports on expenses and receipts: "Whereof they also allow after the preparation of the church and other necessary things done as it appears by a bill as here in the account showed and rested."[109] Later is added: "Item received of diverse persons within our said year of account as by a bill before the auditors showed and rested and also in the book of receipts more plainly does appear."[110]

What survives as this parish's churchwardens' accounts is not the total amount of original documentation kept by the church officers. By 1519, the scribes or the wardens had consolidated their bookkeeping into one place.[111] The accounts are reasonably detailed from this point on until the end of Henry VIII's reign. The records from the parish of St. Cuthbert's, Wells, offer another system of parochial administration. Although churchwardens' accounts of some kind were likely kept, what survives is not a separate account book or series of rolls but the final audit in the city's corporation books.[112] The churchwardens, along with various guild wardens, keepers of the peace, and rent collectors all rendered their yearly accounts to the city council, who then appointed new officers for the following year. All that survive of the parish records are these annual totals and a few references to large sums of money for major projects.[113] The surviving records from both Wells and Stogursey were part of a larger accounting system. These sources reflect the importance of the final totals, the part of the record about which the churchwardens cared. If the parish ended up in debt, they could, as we have seen, be held responsible for making up the difference.[114] In Yatton, the wardens were careful to list parish debts for which they were not responsible.[115]

Just as the variety of organizations makes it difficult to assign a single meaning or role to churchwardens or their accounts, so too does the variety of formats followed by scribes when keeping accounts. Some parishes kept their accounts in bound volumes, and there is clear evidence that scribes used the preceding year's account as a model for the current one. The corrections and ink in Banwell's accounts show that the clerk keeping the records finished up the yearly accounts and then wrote out a portion of the next year's account using what he had just finished writing as a model.[116] In other parishes, the accounts are on individual rolls that were easily lost. Whether churchwardens or their scribes kept their accounts in rolls or books, the choice of format seems to affect the rate of the survival of documents. The fourteenth-century accounts, those from the parishes of St. Michael's in Bath, St. Mary's in Bridgwater, and St. John's in Glastonbury, are all on parchment or paper rolls (see Table 2.1, #1–3). In general, each roll holds one year's account. Survival is sporadic, with the earliest and longest set of accounts coming from Bath. The accounts span 1349 through 1572, but there are only seventy-seven in all. The accounts on rolls, such as those for Bridgwater or Glastonbury, display tremendous variety in format and organization from year to year. Categories of income change and are not listed in the same order from year to year. This variation speaks not only to the skills of individual wardens and scribes, but also to the process of keeping accounts on rolls. Because it might not have been easy to locate an earlier roll to see how it was written, scribes recorded the information as the wardens dictated it to them. By the middle to late fifteenth century, most parishes started putting their accounts in books. The use of books resulted in fewer missing accounts and records covering longer sequences of years. It is easier to keep track of a few books than hundreds of separate rolls. This of course begs the question of how parishes organized their archives. The impression left by the records themselves and by antiquarians is that they were sometimes kept in parish chests with other important documents such as deeds and endowment charters.[117] In other instances, someone, such as one of the churchwardens, took them home for safekeeping.[118] Although not in Bath and Wells, the opening statement at the beginning of what was a new set of records for the Sussex parish of Rotherfield explains that

This is the book of Rotherfield church ordained by the consent of the whole parish . . . and . . . parson to the intent that it shall always remain in the store house of Rotherfield church and never to be taken home to the churchwardens' houses. [F]or by negligence of taking away bills and stories of stuff, rents, stocks and accounts of churchwardens in times past, the said church has been to great losses.[119]

The statement makes it clear that the parish understood recordkeeping both in terms of recording information and as a source of power to control the community through its economic and liturgical resources. For some parishes, the public audit was what mattered, and for others, it was the ability to refer back to earlier accounts as the need arose. The position of collective memory and the intersection of oral and literate practices within the parish records continually shifted depending on where authority was constituted in each parish. Placing the role of writing within the context of social interaction, however, lets us see how some of these shifts took place.

Although there is a shift in authority when a text is present, dependence on memory and oral testimony does not disappear despite the regular creation of accounts. Parishes clearly (re)structured themselves around the need to keep records, but the records also illustrate the prominence of nonliterate strategies for using writing and show how parishioners gained access to and meaning from the accounts when they were read out loud. Thus, the social role of vocalization is as pertinent to our understanding of the records as it was for the parishes using them. The court cases and churchwardens' accounts show the conscious manipulation of these divergent ways of acting and the strongly held assumption that, although parishes operated within the context of literate administrations, they still could rely on nonliterate methods of operation. The literate demands of the legal system and the ecclesiastical hierarchy meant that these accommodations were increasingly important.

The process of using churchwardens' accounts was in some respects analogous to the laity's relationship to the liturgy. The words of the services were recorded in books which the priest read or recited to the assembled congregation. The presence of service books is important, but they alone did not produce the mass or any other liturgical service. The priest's actual performance of the liturgy is important in itself. It is during the mass that the priest turned the bread and wine into the body and blood of Christ. Yet, without the service books, the priest might not know the proper words to say to perform the rite correctly. Most laity did not directly rely on their own personal liturgical books to follow the mass, instead they responded more to visual and aural cues, but behind their interaction was a written text. The service had to be read/performed, and the assembled parishioners had an important role to play in the enactment. The parish as a ritual unit would also be in a position to relate to other written works in a similar manner.

Record keeping not only maintained ecclesiastical authority, but also played a role in establishing or undermining local authority as well. The requirement to keep records became meaningful to the parish community as an account of their own possessions, activities, and, therefore, identity, and not just as a way to assure compliance with episcopal authority. The need to keep records had taken on a significance for the parishioners that differed from the motivations that inspired episcopal mandates in the first place. Parochial administrations became more than a way of safeguarding ecclesiastical property and wealth; they became a means of expressing local concerns and designating priorities for the parishes—how the buildings were to be furnished and decorated, how elaborate the liturgy was to be, and how each community would pay for these things.

In the Axbridge case cited at the beginning of this chapter, where the previous wardens would neither render their accounts nor turn over the parish's goods, their behavior had denied the parish the opportunity for reviewing the previous year. The resulting court case implicitly addresses the connection between record keeping and parish activities; without written confirmation of parochial property and goods, ecclesiastical authorities could not be sure that the church was adequately supplied and that the parishioners could provide appropriate religious activities in their proper setting. For the incoming wardens, the missing accounts should have provided the necessary record of church money and goods; in addition, the accounts' absence represented the outgoing wardens' abuse of authority and the incoming wardens' inability to assume authority. The loss of the accounts deprived the parishioners of their recitation, and consequently, parishioners had no means of assessing the wardens' actions. Repeated problems of this kind would result in an alienation of the membership from the community. The creation and recitation of a local drama out of the process of rendering the accounts served to trigger a community-defining process, providing a frame for the annual cycle of activities and the parochial leadership that governed them. The churchwardens' accounts have power and legitimacy within both a local and ecclesiastical setting, although the type of power and legitimacy varied with the setting. Writing, even if one could not read, became as much a source and symbol of authority as it was a means of recording data. Axbridge was suffering not only a financial crisis but a social one as well. It is not surprising, then, in the chaos that resulted from Henry VIII's split with Rome and the subsequent removal of saints' days from the calendar and images from the church, that parishes often did not know what to do or how to act. This state of affairs is often reflected in the churchwardens' accounts themselves. The format and writing in the accounts from Stogursey, Nettlecombe, and Trull literally disintegrates, making them unreadable.[120]

Churchwardens' accounts must be understood as reflections of not only the episcopacy's growing desire to regulate parishes and ensure their proper management, but also the priorities and interaction of the laity. We can see these concerns, if we read back into the records the literate and oral practices of late medieval parishes. Voice and personal honor played as important a role in business dealings as written contracts. Thus, around the construction of written accounts, the parish formed a textual community, where local power came from the ability to constitute these records, not necessarily read and write them. A final Chancery Court case concerning stolen parish records addresses many of these same issues. This time, however, the issue of power and control rises not between the wardens but between the parish and a local member of the gentry. According to a Chancery petition, the parish church of St. Michael's, Penkevil in Cornwall, received most of its financial support from a single gentry family. Some time around 1529, ten years prior to bringing the suit, two parishioners (churchwardens?) stole the church's records from the plaintiff. The petition for the case states that the two men "of their own extortion and power without any manner or right title or authority have obtained & taken into their hands & custody the book & writings of the said church & also taken upon them to be chief rulers & governors of the said church and without the will, commandment license & authority of . . . your said suppliant."[121] He does not explain why he waited ten years to file suit. Perhaps he had tried other legal venues with limited success; perhaps he had not felt his authority challenged until this moment. Whatever the reason, when he lost the account books, the plaintiff John Carmynowe felt he could no longer control the parish. It did not matter that he remembered exactly what his family had given to the parish, nor did it matter whether or not the wardens could read the records. Carmynowe states three times in the petition that the two men seized control of the parish by taking the parish documents. Without the books, Carmynowe could not collect the rents from the parish-owned property or keep the parish's goods and ornaments. He had also lost his say in how the parish should spend its money, and, according to him, the parish was falling into decay as a result. Acquiring the church books switched control of the community to the two men, showing just how much writing was an avenue to local authority and community identity. Concerning this "book & writings," however, literacy was not at issue. Access, and the performative authority it conveyed, was.

3 "A SERVANT OF THE PARISH"

The Office of Churchwarden and Parochial Leadership

The Rise of Churchwardens

Within a hundred years of the thirteenth-century requirement that the laity maintain and furnish their parish churches, parishes throughout Bath and Wells had organized offices and procedures to oversee their obligations. Leading this organization was the churchwarden. The churchwardens of Bath and Wells are especially interesting for a number of reasons. Fifty percent of England's surviving fourteenth-century churchwardens' accounts come from Bath and Wells.[1] Combined with the large number of fifteenth- and sixteenth-century churchwardens' accounts that survive for the diocese, we can explore the rise of the office and the range of local custom that shaped it. Also of note was the relative willingness of Somerset parishes to allow women to serve as churchwarden. According to the surviving records, women served as churchwardens in greater numbers in Bath and Wells than in any other diocese in England. Similarly, although most wardens came from the middling classes, we can find people from both the gentry and the lower social orders filling this office. The medieval parish was not a proto-democracy fostering a sense of egalitarianism between the classes or the sexes, but greater participation in parish governance by different social groups does show the parish to be a religious community that accepted broad participation from its members. The different ways in which the laity organized their parishes further illustrates varying expectations for parish involvement. Their unique parochial administrations framed their interaction with orthodoxy. Thus, the local customs surrounding the office of churchwarden are another manifestation of community identity.

In the nineteenth and early twentieth centuries, scholars discussed church-wardens largely in terms of selection process. Many believed the medieval election of churchwardens to be one of the origins of Europe's democratic traditions. The parish was a place where all members, regardless of status, participated equally (democratically) in a benevolent church that encouraged and fostered this religious commitment.[2] More recently, scholars interested in the process of the Reformation have focused on this office, because it was often a conduit for reform policies from the government or Church to partic-ular localities.[3] However, this scholarship has tended to focus on the relations between the churchwarden and a central power, be it the crown or the bishop. The array of local records in Somerset makes it possible to study the relations between the churchwardens and their parishes and the tremendous range in power and local influence individual wardens could wield.[4] The office had different meanings and implications in different parishes. Despite a general consensus regarding the duties of churchwardens, some parishes saw this office as desirable and prestigious, others as a duty and a burden.

Charles Drew has pointed out in his important work on the origins of the English churchwarden, "the fact that lay parishioners had become responsible for the provision of the instruments of worship was not immediately regarded as conferring on them any right to take such things into their own custody."[5] Transition from provision to custody of the church's liturgical furnishings developed in a piecemeal fashion through a process of legislation and litigation during the thirteenth and early fourteenth centuries. Initially, the laity did not have much financial investment in their parish churches. There was as yet no reason for them to feel that they, and not the clergy or the parish patron (person or institution with the advowson), would control the goods they gave to the parish. Until they developed feelings of responsibility for what they provided, the laity had no incentive for developing or sustaining a parochial administration.

Although the 1287 statutes for the diocese of Exeter include the first de-scription of a churchwarden's duties, this office already existed in some par-ishes. The first actual mention of a churchwarden predated Exeter's diocesan statutes by twenty-six years. In 1261, Alice Halye left the churchwardens of her parish of All Saints, Bristol, a house for the maintenance of a light in that church.[6] There were also churchwardens in two Oxford parishes of St. Peter-le-Bailey and St. Mary's by the 1270s.[7] Something of the process by which the laity took control of their parishes and developed an office of churchwarden is visible in the earliest parish accounts from Bath and Wells.

The level and permanence of lay organization in parishes was not consis-tent throughout the diocese in the mid-fourteenth century. Some parishes achieved a permanent lay administration by the end of the fourteenth century;

for others, it came much later. In 1318, the parishioners of Bridgwater raised money and collected scrap metal for the founding of a new church bell.[8] Four men oversaw the process and left an account of their activities. The account records a parish collection and several gifts to finance the bell. The parish guild of the Holy Cross, which already existed, lent financial support to their efforts. The four men, however, have no title. They acted on a seemingly ad hoc basis for the benefit of the parish. At this point, the laity of Bridgwater focused on purchase and upkeep of components of the church, such as the high cross and a bell. The liturgy associated with the high cross warranted a permanent organization. The bell had no such needs and thus required minimal attention. As yet no overarching organization had taken responsibility for the entire church and its contents. In 1366, when the church needed a new tower, the parishioners again rallied together. Again they contributed to collections and proffered gifts in support of the project. This time one man with the title of "the receiver concerning the work in the parish church" (*receptoris nomine operis in ecclesia parochiali*) was in charge of the accounting.[9] His title of receiver suggests the involvement and supervision of the town bureaucracy acting on behalf of the parish. A receiver's account from 1375 confirms this relationship.[10] At this point, the town oversaw the parish church, just as it did the roads, bridges, and ditches. The town's bureaucracy handled money from a testator for his burial, alterations on the new tower, and installation of the new church clock. The building account for the tower reveals an intermediate stage between the parishioners' occasional organization to help facilitate a specific project and an independent parish administration. Although the parishioners appear quite capable of organization and collective action, they contributed to this effort under the auspices of the town's government. By 1385, however, separate churchwardens' accounts for the parish of Bridgwater begin to survive. Two men designated as churchwardens (*procurator bonorum ecclesie parochialis*) supervised the raising and spending of money on the parish.[11] Although the town government retained an interest in the parish, it no longer attended to it in the manner of the town's bridges or roads. The parishioners had been able to create a permanent parish organization, largely separate from the borough government.

Not all town parishes achieved this level of independence from the town's government. As early as 1377, the borough council for the city of Wells elected the churchwardens for the parish of St. Cuthbert, along with other city officials.[12] The churchwardens presented their accounts to the council, not to the parish as a whole. The council, in turn, oversaw major financial expenditures and parish fundraising. We can speculate that this situation grew out of the burgesses' desire to separate themselves from the cathedral's authority. By controlling the churchwardens and the parish's finances, the city council prevented the cathedral from usurping the parish's resources by co-opting the churchwardens.

Although parishioners of Bridgwater and Wells did not have a separate organization to oversee the parish in the 1360s, other parishes at that time, or earlier, did. The development of parochial organizations at such an early date might be related to the relatively young age of the parishes. St. Michael's without the North Gate was founded in the thirteenth century to accommodate the city's population, which had expanded beyond the city walls.[13] By 1349, when its first account appears, the parish of St. Michael's had two churchwardens (*procurator ecclesie*), who were already responsible for collecting rent on parish-owned property, collecting money for the Christmas and Easter candles, and receiving and managing bequests from parishioners who had died.[14] The wardens had also overseen the purchase of new torches and new lamps, the washing of the ornaments and vestments, and the purchase of a new missal. St. John's, Glastonbury was another relatively new parish; the abbey had only founded it and the town in the thirteenth century.[15] The first account, which dates from 1366, shows a situation similar to St. Michael's. The two churchwardens (*custodum bonorum ecclesie*) supervised the parish's property, conducted collections for candles, and administered testamentary bequests.[16] Compared to their counterparts in the late fifteenth century, these fourteenth-century wardens had relatively few responsibilities, yet these first accounts clearly do not document either parish's first experiences with lay administration or with churchwardens. Lay administration of the parish existed prior to the first surviving churchwardens' accounts. Neither parish had a history that predated the episcopal statutes, making it that much easier to initiate lay organization. Although we have no comparable information for the rural parishes, the process was probably similar, albeit maybe starting later in the century.

Drew argues that, in general, when religious foundations served as parish patrons, they accelerated the laity's taking up of responsibility for their parish church. The Church actively sought to acquire the patronage of benefices in order to limit the number of secular patrons. Patrons had responsibility for providing the parish with clergy, but other than that they generally left the community alone. By the mid-thirteenth century, religious foundations had appropriated between one-third and one-half of all parishes.[17] The episcopal statutes clearly stated that the nave belonged to the laity, and ecclesiastical patrons were quick to enforce this responsibility. For those parishes with lay patrons, however, the process was less clear-cut. The statutes do not delineate the status of laity who were to care for the nave. Although some lay patrons, typically local nobles or gentry, continued to play a prominent role in parish support, others turned these financial obligations over to their dependent laity. Initially, the laity's fulfillment of these obligations did not require permanent organizations. But as their donations to the parish expanded and as their expectations for the parish as their own local religious forum increased, temporary organizations ceased to be practical.[18] Most of the parishes in this study, including those parishes with the earliest evidence of lay organization, had been appropriated by religious foundations. The parish patron of St. Mary's in Bridgwater was the Hospital of St. John in the same town. St. Cuthbert's in Wells was appropriated by the cathedral, while St. Michael's in Bath and St. John's in Glastonbury were held by the bishop and the abbey of Glastonbury, respectively.[19]

As Drew points out, when lay administrations eventually did develop, the result was not "a standard pattern of parochial organisation. [The process of developing lay parish administrations] produced a norm to which there were throughout the Middle Ages, and later, plenty of exceptions—nowhere did 'approved local custom' play a greater part than in the parish."[20] The rest of this chapter focuses on these "approved local customs" and their implications for religious practice and lay parochial involvement. Parish organization did not happen in a vacuum. Parishes had to interact with local economies and local political organizations, both of which shaped lay administration of the parish and the office of churchwarden. One way of understanding the importance of local variation in religious practice is to consider the role of the churchwarden in different parishes and the ways in which this office shaped lay involvement in parish life.

Local Customs

Broadly speaking, a churchwarden administered the parish's goods and property and served as the parish's representative at visitations. This was true for both England and the rest of Europe.[21] In practice, these obligations gave churchwardens a wide variety of responsibilities that varied, according to a parish's resources and needs. In giving an account to the bishop or his deputy for the parishioners' moral and religious behavior and seeing to the maintenance of the parish's goods and property, churchwardens had to be fundraisers, general contractors, politicians, and arbitrators.[22] When the laity desired new forms of worship, whether related to church seating, new devotions, new cult images, or dramatic performances, it was the wardens' responsibility to make them happen. Their duties involved them in both the secular and the sacred aspects of parish life.

The wardens' control of the parish's goods and property potentially gave them access to wealth. Failure to conserve that wealth could have a detrimental effect on the liturgy and ultimately on the souls of the parishioners. Thus, parishes did not want their wardens to formulate policy or act in any way that compromised the religious activities of the parish, an all too likely possibility given their broad responsibilities and financial authority. What is less clear is whether a small group of elite within the parish or a broad selection of the membership initiated the policies designed to limit a churchwarden's authority. As one embattled churchwarden explained, when called upon to justify his actions, he was but "a servant of the parish" and must serve the community.[23] Evidence from court records and churchwardens' accounts suggests that the office of churchwarden was a subservient one, despite the respect and status granted to those who kept the parish goods. The continual attempts to contain their influence, however, further implies that many used the office to further their own ambitions or those of their family and friends.

A Chancery case from sometime between 1538 and 1544 for the parish of Kilmersdon in Bath and Wells shows how this desired subservience might look in action.[24] In his testimony, the warden emphasized his duty to consult with the laity and comply with their demands. The parish church had become too small, and the community decided it needed to add a new aisle. The plaintiff (one of the churchwardens at the start of construction) explained that, in a general meeting, he had solicited pledges from the members. Later, Thomas Rychmonde refused to pay the money he had promised, although he did not deny his financial commitment to the new aisle.[25]

About the said time a convocation was had among the good men of the said parish for the enlargement of their said parish church. At which time one Thomas Rychmonde otherwise shepherd husbandman said in convocation with your said supplicant to know his mind that he would give toward the building and making of a new aisle for the enlarging of the said parish church saying that he would be contributing to charge of the said church of your said orator [and] would be a helper to the same . . . and then and there guaranteed to give £6 13s. 4d.[26]

When Rychmonde tried to back out of his responsibilities, the warden had to rectify the situation. We see, in this case, the wardens acting in an ideal fashion. They facilitated decisions, attended to administration, and, when necessary, brought suit on behalf of the parish.

Not all wardens were so solicitous of the parishioners' concerns. During a disagreement over a new wall painting in 1467 and 1468, the parishioners of Yatton reprimanded their wardens for acting independently of community opinion.[27] Although the parishioners were satisfied with the picture of St. Mary, they were less than pleased with the one of St. Christopher. The accounts do not say whether it was the image in general or just this particular execution that disappointed them. The artist repainted it the following year, and in 1470 the parishioners made the old wardens reimburse the parish, out of their own pockets, for the cost of the original St. Christopher painting.[28]

The churchwardens' accountability to the parish becomes even more obvious after 1497, when the scribe changed the wording at the beginning of each new account. When the incoming wardens received the parish stock from the outgoing ones, the accounts begin to explain that they did so "in the name of the parish of Yatton."[29] Previously, the practice had been to list only the names of the new and old wardens and the amount of money that changed hands. The parish's position in this transition had been assumed but not made explicit. Now it was spelled out clearly.

If the problem was serious enough, the laity could seek outside help. In Nynhead Flory, a former clerk had stolen some of the church's goods.[30] The wardens filed an action of general acquitance for common fraud, but the action expired without the wardens actually recovering the missing goods. The wardens refused to pursue further action, so the laity petitioned the chancellor to make the wardens do their job. They were to serve the parish, and failing to protect the parish's property was a dereliction of their duties. If parishioners could not control their wardens, perhaps outside authorities could.

Some of these churchwardens' problems arose over issues of what constituted the will of the parish. Discerning the parish's will presented a further task for the churchwarden, a task sometimes more or less perplexing depending on the circumstances. Even in the most placid of times, the parish's will was not always obvious or self-evident. When there was a difference of opinion, which group of parishioners should the warden serve? "The parish" was often an amorphous and ill-defined group, making the wardens' job very political. For some parishes, "the parish" referred to the male property holders; in other situations, it was not as clear.[31] A case from Tavistock, Devon, in the diocese of Exeter, addressed this very issue. Although the case is from outside Bath and Wells, it is worth considering in detail because of the frankness of the churchwardens' testimonies. This case illustrates how individual wardens could have very differing opinions about the nature of their job and their relationship to "the parish."[32] The feuding churchwardens could not agree on who constituted "the parish." The issue that brought this case to trial was payment for a new silver cross. The conflict, however, highlights preexisting tensions and factionalism within the parish.

Originally, one of the parishioners, John Amadas, had agreed to buy a new cross for the parish, taking the old one in partial payment. Amadas delivered the new cross to the wardens, but he claimed he received neither the old one nor the outstanding £62 4d. they owed him. In the course of trying to settle this dispute, the court petitions provide many details about parish decision making and the warden's role in this process. A number of issues made it difficult for Amadas to collect his money. First, no one was quite sure who had made the decision in the first place. The churchwarden at the beginning of the process, John Williams, stated that

at the which time Nicholas Yeo, esquire, William Hawkyns, Richard Hawke, & Richard Mayeo, & the more part & most substantial men of all the said parish were contented to have the same cross & to pay for every ounce thereof 5s. 1d. & that the said John Amadas should have in payment a cross of silver not gilt at the price of 3s. the ounce.[33]

John Williams was willing to regard a decision made by the "most substantial men of the parish" as a parish-wide decision. His successor, John Guscote, had a different perspective. He claimed it was not a parish issue because "if any such request or desire were made, it was made by certain persons to the number of 6 or 8 & not by the whole inhabitants & rulers of the said parish." John Guscote resented the influence of a small group of parishioners and sought, during his term as warden, to undo it. To make this situation more complicated, Amadas described yet a third decision-making process:

that upon admonition & warning of the vicar of the said church of Tavistock openly in the pulpit to the parishioners of the same and also where the most substantial men of the same parish were warned by the warden of the said church to assemble together and make answer to the said John Amadas whether they would have the said cross or not.[34]

His description of events shows consideration of the two factions—perhaps to ally himself with both sides, so that he would be paid regardless of the outcome.

The second major problem in this case was that the decision had been made while John Williams was warden, but John Amadas delivered the cross to the parish when Williams's successor, John Guscote, occupied the office. "Also the said John Williams said he was not warden at this time of the said church of Tavistock but the said John Guscote . . . is now warden."[35] The lack of communication between the two wardens, perhaps because of their differing views, made Guscote unwilling to assume the debt when it was not clear to him that the parish owed it.

This case provides unusually specific information about the processes of parish decision making and the different kinds of leadership a churchwarden could provide. Decision making and local leadership came from many places within the community, and the laity did not always agree on whose input should be acknowledged. The two testimonies show different leadership styles and even political agendas. The warden's position varied according to the individual serving in it—did he lead the entire parish, meaning all the membership, or did he simply do the bidding of the wealthy members? Who, in fact, was meant by "the parish"? Williams appeared more inclined to work with those he considered to be prominent parishioners. His successor, Guscote, was less tolerant of this practice. Dealing with the influence or interference of wealthy families was a constant part of being a churchwarden, but individual wardens could try to choose the way they thought best to handle it. Although each warden could argue he was acting as a servant to the parish, who comprised the parish was not always clear or consistent.[36]

Attempts at curtailing the influence of the churchwarden did not usually involve litigation. Parishes usually relied on local custom or bylaws to define the warden's daily and annual responsibilities. Some parishes strictly limited the term of office and the number of times a warden could serve. This prevented a single person or family from dominating the parish. Other parishes set no such limits and allowed their wardens greater influence and authority. These differences tell us a great deal about how laity understood their parish communities and the relationship between parish involvement and local piety.

Most parishes in Bath and Wells seem to have had two wardens to share the work and to keep each other honest. Yet as soon as we try to establish general rules, there are interesting exceptions that should be addressed. Pilton had only one warden until 1530, when the community began to appoint two. The prominence of parish guilds in this parish may have aided the warden, making two unnecessary. On the other end of the scale, we find that Trull had three wardens.[37] With more people to share the running of the parish, no one person carried the sole burden. The officers could share duties, and embezzling church funds would be much more difficult.

A common leadership practice in the borough parishes of Bath and Wells was to have a junior and a senior warden.[38] This system required the parish to elect one new warden each year, for a two-year term. Staggered terms of office allowed the senior warden to train the junior one, to help ensure smooth transitions from one warden to the next. Yeovil employed this administrative system at least as early as 1456. As late as the early seventeenth century, the parish still elected wardens in this fashion. The parishes of Bridgwater and St. Michael's without the North Gate in Bath also employed this sort of arrangement, but neither followed it rigidly. In Bath, the senior warden "carried the purse," meaning that, having proved his trustworthiness and reliability, he was responsible for the parish's money.[39] The responsibility given to churchwardens in these town parishes made the junior-senior warden system a practical arrangement. As we will see in the next chapter, town parishes relied on property rents for income. Administration of this income would be more successful if an experienced warden oversaw the process. Continuing the practices of former wardens could be complicated and confusing when the details of parish finance eluded new wardens. Managing property did not involve most parishioners, so most would have been ignorant of the details of parish business. Knowledge of leases, contracts, and other business arrangements was less likely to be lost under a regime that encouraged or required a junior and a senior warden. This system of organization suggests a strong corporate identity for the town parishes. As a collective, town parishes owned more property and used writing more often than their rural counterparts. The position of a senior warden brought some consistency to these business arrangements.

Other tenure patterns appear in rural parishes, and they offer alternative visions of the churchwarden's community service and parochial leadership. In Banwell, the wardens served for two years, but there was no junior-senior warden system.[40] The parishioners elected two completely new wardens every other year. For the duration of the pre-Reformation accounts (1515–47), no individual repeated his term of office. Such consistent adherence to a pattern is unusual. Although we cannot determine the antiquity of this practice, most parishes did not maintain such structured administrative systems for even this brief length of time. Banwell is also unusual in that until 1521 it paid its churchwardens a nominal salary of 4d., the price of a mass for one's soul.[41] It is difficult to see the advantage of Banwell's tenure system. The small stipend, however, suggests that serving as a warden for this large rural parish was somewhat onerous but beneficial to one's soul. A short term of office, no expectations of future service, and some financial compensation may have helped make the job tolerable enough to attract qualified parishioners. The parish also tried to have a warden from one of the two hamlets that were also in the parish, as a way of integrating this large parish.

The rural parish of Nettlecombe had yet another pattern of officeholding, again apparently designed to share responsibility for the office among a wider group of people. The office rotated among thirty families, taking fifteen years to complete the cycle (see Table 3.1). The community maintained this system of rotation into the eighteenth century.[42] The late medieval accounts do not explain the basis for the rotation, but other similarly organized parishes and Nettlecombe's own eighteenth-century records show that it was related to landholding.[43] A rotating wardenship clarified who would serve each year and prevented the same individuals from dominating the office. This rotation also permitted a widow to serve as churchwarden after her husband's death, a practice that kept a family's place in the cycle.[44] With the death of James Mychell, sometime between 1508 and 1522, his widow, Eleanor, took over his duties for what would have been his next term of office in 1523. She again served as warden in 1537 and died while in office.[45] Alison Fermer replaced her husband as churchwarden in 1540; he had previously served in 1510 and

Table 3.1. Rotation of churchwardens at Nettlecombe, Somerset (rotation shown in bold, women's names underlined)

1507: Thomas Ynglyche John Stavyn	1522: John Goodenow Robert Westlake	1537: **Eleanor Mychell** **Thomas Herres**
1508: **James Mychell** **Thomas Herres**	1523: **Eleanor Mychell** **Thomas Herres**	1538: John Goodenow Henry Knyghte
1509: **Robert Nycholle** **John Wever**	1524: **Robert Nycholle** **John Wever**	1539: Robert Tarbell John Gage
1510: **George Fermer** Nicholas Burgys	1525: **George Fermer** **William Sollay**	1540: **Alison Fermer** **William Sollay**
1511: **John Thorn** **John Bulworthe**	1526: **John Thorn** **John Bulworthe**	1541: **Alice Thorn** Robert Cross
1512: **Thomas Goher** **William Baker**	1527: **Thomas Goher** **William Baker**	1542: **Anne Goher** John Hurford
1513: **John Darge** **Philip Mellyn**	1528: **John Darge** **Philip Mellyn**	1543: John Solley John Phelipp
1514: **Thomas Goodgrame** John Paris	1529: **Thomas Goodgrame** **Robert Clarke**	1544: **Thomas Goodgrame** **Robert Clarke** Alice Harper
1515: **John Chirghay** Thomas Goodgrame	1530: **John Chirghay** Thomas Baker	1545: John Yar John Somer
1516: **John Gadworthe** John Baker	1531: **John Gadworthe** John Sclade	1546: John Harper
1517: **John Goodenow** William Cross	1532: **John Goodenow** Robert Lando	
1518: **John Fermer** **John Mores**	1533: **John Fermer** **John Mores**	
1519: **John Syndon** **John Hayn**	1534: **John Syndon** **John Hayn**	
1520: **Conand Ynglyche** **Robert Sella**	1535: **Conand Ynglyche** **Robert Sella**	
1521: **Robert Westlake** John Sella	1536: **Robert Westlake** Walter Cont	

1525.[46] The deaths of John Thorn and Thomas Goher also afforded their wives the chance to assume places in the rotation.[47] As we will see, other parishes had the occasional female warden, but no other parish records this level of female involvement in parochial leadership. Allowing widows to serve as churchwardens suggests that the parish viewed the office as a family honor and responsibility that should be preserved, even when it required the unusual step of having widows take over for their deceased husbands.

The large rural parish of Yatton shows no tenure pattern and no obvious clique of ruling families in the more than one hundred years of available accounts. Family names appear repeatedly but not in heavy concentration.

The laity selected their leaders from among a wide group of parishioners and did not seek to regulate their length of office or frequency of service. The boundaries of the parish also included the hamlets of Claverham and Cleeve. Like Banwell, the community seems to have intentionally included one warden from either area, again as a way of keeping the parishioners in the hamlets identified with the parish of Yatton.

The different ways of structuring wardens' terms of office suggest that parishes expected very different things of their leaders. Parishes with a junior-senior warden system, such as St. Michael's in Bath or Yeovil, understood their churchwardens to be facilitators of the parish's business. The wardens were to be businessmen. Banwell's strict term limits suggest that this parish saw the office as a burden to be shared among the qualified men of the parish, so that no one would be saddled with the responsibility for more than one term. In Nettlecombe, the office of churchwarden rotated among thirty families. The willingness of the parish to allow widows of former churchwardens to serve in their husbands' place implies that this position was a family honor that must be preserved. Finally, Yatton had a large number of men, including men from the hamlets of Claverham and Cleeve, who served as warden for short terms. Although some repeated their term, no single family dominated the office. The seemingly wide range of individuals serving as Yatton's churchwarden does not meant that there was no elite. The parish had six hundred members in the mid-sixteenth century, and not everyone would have had equal access to this office. Still, the parishioners seem to have encouraged wide participation, in an almost "quasi-democratic" fashion.[48]

Although most parishes were concerned with limiting the warden's influence and power, not all parishes succeeded in this effort, and others never seem to have tried. In two communities in particular, a few individuals served repeatedly, showing the development of a parish oligarchy.[49] In the small rural parishes of Croscombe and Tintinhull, parish leadership was concentrated in the hands of a few families. Comparing these two communities is instructive, because they reacted differently to this situation. Tintinhull tried, on different occasions, to end an oligarchic administration, whereas in Croscombe sequential one-family rule ended only with the Reformation.

At Croscombe, the run of pre-Reformation accounts seems to chronicle the development of an oligarchic administration. One warden held office for life; he was aided by another warden who changed almost every year.[50] When the accounts start in 1474, the office of churchwarden was in the hands of two men, John Hille and John Harper, who served together for four years. After Hille's retirement, William Branche took over and served for more than twenty years (1478–98 and 1502–6). Edward Bole then succeeded him and remained as warden for the next twenty-five years (1506–31), having previously served with Branche in 1493. Edward's son, John, became church-warden in 1532, after Edward's retirement or death. John was not able to hold on to the office as firmly as his father had. His tenures were short and intermittent (1532, 1534–37, 1546, 1552–53), due in part to the religious changes in the sixteenth century.

In addition to their long tenures as churchwarden, both Branche and Bole held other positions within the parish hierarchy. Croscombe had several parish guilds that sponsored fundraising activities to support the parish fabric. Both men served as wardens to various guilds. William Branche's name first appears as one of two men organizing the King's Revel in 1474. From 1474 to 1506, he also gathered money for St. Michael's light. On three occasions (1478, 1480, and 1482) he worked for the Holy Cross endowment, and twice (1485 and 1495) he helped oversee the Christmas collection and accompanying celebrations. Branche also tended the church clock and made the wax, thus effectively monopolizing most parish responsibilities. This hold on the parish hierarchy apparently extended to his family. Two female relatives (daughters?) served as wardens for the maidens' guild in 1491 and 1503. Like Branche, Bole had held other parish offices, although he was not as ubiquitous as his predecessor. He first appears as one of the two wardens for the tuckers' (fullers') guild, a position he held from 1480 to 1501.

With the onset of Henry VIII's religious reforms, a shift occurred in Croscombe's parish leadership, shortening the warden's time in office. The parishioners did not accept change easily, and parish tensions surfaced in two Star Chamber petitions from the mid-sixteenth century. In 1540, John Bole (alias Middle), the former churchwarden, brought suit against the parish priest, paying for the litigation with parish funds.[51] This case was apparently part of a long history of problems between the two men that had surfaced during Bole's tenure as churchwarden. While churchwarden, he had accused the priest of chopping down box trees in the churchyard that the parish had used for decorations on Palm Sunday. In a second Star Court case, Bole served as a witness against the same priest, who was too reformed for the plaintiff's taste.[52] These court cases help to relate John Bole and Croscombe's parochial leadership to the theological divisions created by the early stages of the Reformation. The priest had accused one of his parishioners of heresy and treason, along with disobedience and libel. Many parishioners aligned themselves against the priest, accusing him of similar deeds. John Bole was sympathetic to the traditionalist faction. These upheavals explain Croscombe's abrupt change in administration and the curtailment of John Bole's tenure as warden. Those parishioners loyal to the reformers' cause began replacing old leaders who were unwilling to change the parish's religious observances. Interestingly enough, Bole came back as churchwarden in the last year of Edward VI's reign and again in 1556–57 during Mary Tudor's reign, when she had reintroduced Catholic practices into England.[53]

With such long-serving and strong wardens, most of the laity did not take part in parish leadership and were, like the parishioners in the Tavistock case discussed earlier, excluded from some of the decision-making processes in parish life. Instead, they participated in parish life through the many parish guilds. These guilds earned much of the money the churchwardens used to maintain the parish. Guild membership, which was based on occupation, life cycle, and veneration of particular saints, channeled lay participation so that it did not interfere with the churchwardens' duties and decision making. This arrangement, while a common feature of Devon and Cornish parishes, was unusual in parishes in Bath and Wells.[54] The guilds created another layer of bureaucracy; when they reported to the churchwarden, they turned over all the money they earned. Their subservience to the warden enhanced his authority.

Tintinhull, another rural parish with a lengthy run of churchwardens' accounts, also consolidated parish administration in the hands of a few parishioners, but the parish, or factions within it, resisted this situation. These accounts run from 1433 through the Reformation. During this one-hundred-and-thirteen-year period, the parish underwent four reorganizations of its administration. The death of the older members and the rise of their children into positions of authority account for only some changes. For twenty-four years, between 1433 and 1457, only eleven men served as churchwarden, although no one served for longer than nine years.[55] In the late 1450s, this administrative pattern changed subtly, with new men becoming churchwardens more frequently and serving shorter terms. Instead of five- to seven-year terms, this new group often served for only one or two years. The average term of office dropped from 2.2 years to 1.9 years. Although this meant that a greater number of men served as churchwardens in the last half of the fifteenth century (twenty-two men for forty-two years), this is only a minor shift.[56] Parish administration was still in the hands of a select group of people. Many churchwardens served more than once, and many members from the prominent Stacey family served repeatedly.[57]

By maintaining tight control on the leadership, an elite few could realize some of their desires and expectations for the parish. The rest of the laity appear to have had little formal or official input into how the wardens handled financial resources. Specifically, this meant that decisions about whom to hire for building projects and interior decorations and who could lease the parish church house were in the hands of a few individuals. These churchwardens could choose which artisans and clients would benefit from the parish's corporate wealth. The clique of men who served as warden could also regulate to some degree the level of lay involvement with the parish. For example, in 1452, two women, Isabel Wilmot and Margaret Stacey organized and ran the church ale held on the feast of St. Margaret (20 July).[58] Although women occasionally took on such responsible positions, it was unusual. However, Isabel's husband, Thomas, served as churchwarden twice, once in 1447 and then again in 1463, and Margaret's relative by marriage, John, was the local bailiff and served as warden on a regular basis, as did other members of her family.[59] It seems likely that these women gained such visibility because of their familial relationship with members of the elite who ran the parish.

For reasons that are never explained, a sudden and dramatic change occurred in the way the wardens served the parish, starting in 1500. From 1500 to 1518, Tintinhull strictly observed the practice of having junior and senior wardens.[60] The men who served during this period were mostly new to parish administration, and they did not repeat their service. The accounts show other signs of community stress at this point; they were often incomplete, omitting expenses and including only a few receipts, and the day that the community audited them had changed from the feast of St. Margaret (July 20) to Palm Sunday.[61] The accounts from 1519 to 1523 are missing from the account book, and the reappearance of the accounts in 1524 signaled yet another change in parish administration.[62] Tintinhull maintained the shorter terms of office— two to three years—but eliminated the offices of junior and senior warden. There was also greater repetition in the men who served as wardens, but it never returned to the level of the early fifteenth century. In the sixteen years between 1524 and 1540, thirteen men served as warden, giving them an average term of office that added up to slightly more than a year (1.2). By the end of the 1540s, the parish had successfully limited the churchwardens' terms and expanded the pool of men serving. The missing accounts and abrupt change in tenure practices imply a power struggle similar to the one in Tavistock, Devon. Two factions had different visions for parish leadership; one sought to limit access to decision making, whereas the other sought to share it among a larger group of men. We can only speculate about the role of the Reformation, but attempts at changing parish administration predate Henry's split with Rome or other religious reforms. The internal dynamics of the laity who lived within the parish of Tintinhull remain a mystery, as do the reasons behind the shift in leadership. The changes in the administration, however, speak to new priorities and perhaps a new group of laity within the parish able to shape these priorities through new administrative policies. By the sixteenth century, financial stability had returned to the parish, perhaps as a result of changes in administration.

In a period of growing lay activism and increasing parish self-consciousness, choosing an oligarchy to run the parish seems counterintuitive. Oligarchies limited the involvement of most of the community. Susan Reynolds, however, has made the important observation that the term "oligarchy," as used by historians, usually implies a way of addressing moral failings.[63] Oligarchies were common in town government as a way of ensuring unity and security, constituting an obvious model for parishes to follow.[64] Nonetheless, parishes are not towns, and the parishes of Bath and Wells generally developed less restrictive forms of parish administration. Among parishes with surviving churchwardens' accounts, Tintinhull and Croscombe are unusual in the way they limited access to the position of churchwarden. The unity and security that oligarchy could provide, however, eluded Tintinhull and as a result it changed its leadership structure. The size of both Croscombe and Tintinhull may have been a factor in shaping their form of lay administration. Like Banwell and Yatton, they were rural parishes; however, they had smaller populations and were not as spread out. Banwell and Yatton had populations of over five hundred living in more than one village; Croscombe and Tintinhull each had around two hundred parishioners.[65] Geographic size and distance between settlements may have made it much harder for Banwell and Yatton parishioners to develop an oligarchy, whereas the small size of Croscombe and Tintinhull made it easier. In addition, a strong churchwarden could manage the tensions that often developed in small communities and prevent them from overwhelming the parish.

Although the accounts themselves are generally silent on the process of appointing churchwardens, differences in tenure practices imply that parishes employed a number of election procedures to appoint wardens. At most, a statement at the bottom of the account declares that the following people were elected to be the next wardens. We find a similar vagueness in elections for manorial offices.[66] Although this entry is common and suggests some sort of democratic process, it does not reveal exactly how parishes selected their leadership.[67] In part, this is because the Latin word *eligere* could mean either "to elect" or "to choose." For accounts written in English, the wording is frequently "elected or chosen," which is just as unclear.[68] Because of this sort of wording, nineteenth-century historians assumed that the election of a churchwarden was a democratic process. Some parishes regulated the selection of churchwardens with bylaws or parochial ordinances. None of these regulations survive for parishes in Bath and Wells, but the existence of tenure patterns implies that they had them. Two sets exist from nearby Bristol, one from the parish of St. Stephen and the other from All Saints.[69] These statutes suggest that all (male) members were expected to serve their time as churchwardens. These city parishes legislated a junior-senior system of wardens. At All Saints, a fine of 6s. 8d. was levied for refusing to serve. The ordinances also outlined additional fines for wardens acting without parish consent or failing to attend the audit of their accounts.

In Nettlecombe, the rotation made elections only minimally important. Similarly, in Croscombe, with the office of the warden virtually in the hands of one man, elections would probably have been a formality, if, in fact, they were ever held. There is no indication as to how the other warden gained his position. In parishes such as Yatton, Lydeard St. Lawrence, or Banwell, where a large number of men served for short periods, we are less certain about the process for appointing the wardens, although the lack of an obvious tenure pattern suggests that the parish held some sort of elections. In the borough of Wells, the borough council had charge of the selection of the churchwardens and guild wardens. At election time, all out-going wardens and city officers rendered an accounting of their financial activities to the assembled burgesses and master (office similar to that of a mayor).[70] The earliest entries (1378) in the *Wells Convocation Book* show that, in addition to the churchwardens, the burgesses also elected the master, constables of the peace, rent collectors, wardens of the shambles (butchery area), and warden of the vicars' choral in the cathedral.[71] The burgesses rewrote the city ordinances in 1437; these state that after the burgesses have "elected and chosen" the master, two constables, and two rent collectors,

> they shall choose 2 Trinity Wardens, 2 Churchwardens, and 2 Wardens of our Lady's Altar; and likewise they and every of them to be sworn upon a book by the clerk, true proctors to be, and truly to keep the goods of the church, and true reckoning and account to give of their receipts unto the Master and his Fellows when they be duly warned.[72]

As the parish formed new guilds, the city council added their wardens to the list of officers they elected.

Variations in churchwardens' tenure created a spectrum of community dynamics and reflect a range of priorities. As the parish's representatives to the bishop, the wardens mediated one level of interaction between the laity and the Church hierarchy. On another level, wardens influenced the laity's religious practice. Although churchwardens could not legally keep parishioners away from the church, they could, through their management of the parish's goods, influence their religious experience once they arrived. In parishes where the wardens sold seats, they influenced how close or how far from the host one sat. This in turn determined in what order one received the pax bread or kissed the pax, the wooden board carved with a cross and passed around during mass. In a world where proximity to the sacred was important, a churchwarden could wield some influence over a parishioner's religious experience. Abuse of fellow parishioners could be turned back on offending wardens once they left office.

Parishioners brought differing levels of experience and competence to the office of churchwarden. Some were quite skilled and dedicated, drawing on personal connections and experiences to help their communities. Others were less interested and less successful. Most earlier scholarship has assumed that the position of churchwarden was an office for the local elite, whether wealthy landlords or rich merchants.[73] Although this background would bring useful knowledge to the role of churchwarden, closer research on specific parishes calls these assumptions into question. The local gentry usually did not fill this office; instead, parish leadership generally rested in the hands of the non-elite. The churchwardens' influence in parish affairs was potentially substantial; however, the status of those who served as warden suggests that the prestige the role conferred within the larger social and economic world of the town or manor was relative.

It is difficult to assess the status of individual churchwardens in Bath and Wells, because little corroborating documentation exists on these men and women. Not enough of them left wills to make generalizations about their status, wealth, or occupation, although the importance of both agriculture and the cloth industry to Somerset is apparent in the brief list of churchwardens' occupations. Of the few who did leave wills, two described themselves as citizens of Bath, another was a husbandman from Yatton, another a yeoman from Yatton, another a husbandman in Tintinhull, and the last a clothier from Croscombe.[74] The churchwardens' accounts provide similarly fragmented information. The Yatton accounts list one warden as a weaver and another as a carpenter.[75] Another weaver served the parish of St. Michael's in Bath in 1441.[76] Chancery and Star Chamber petitions from Bath and Wells mention three churchwardens who were husbandmen, two who were weavers, one who was a fuller, and one who was a clothier.[77] Edward Bole, one of Croscombe's long-serving churchwardens, was a guild warden in the local fullers' guild before he was a churchwarden. The data from the city of Wells are more complete. Gary Shaw has found that, of the wardens who served the parish from 1377 to 1500, most were weavers (19.3 percent) and merchants (18.2 percent), none were from the gentry, and less than 10 percent were tailors (9.1 percent), tuckers (6.8 percent), or employed in any of the building trades (4.5 percent).[78] This sort of fragmentary evidence suggests that those who served as churchwardens in Bath and Wells were not generally rich individuals but were prosperous in business. Their prominence in the parish came from something other than wealth, such as interest, piety, and general respectability. This evidence also shows that, even though churchwardens routinely dealt with the problems of fixing and maintaining a building, parishioners did not perceive experience in building trades as a qualification for the office. One did not need specific technical knowledge to be a churchwarden.

Studies of other dioceses with stronger documentation support these findings. Beat Kümin's study of ten parishes throughout England shows a similar preponderance of wardens coming from the artisan class.[79] Judy Ford's study of four parishes in Kent also shows that the churchwardens from those parishes were of lower-middling status.[80] Unfortunately many of the subsidy rolls from Somerset, which could be used for assessing status or wealth, are missing or are mutilated. Only partial records remain for Yatton, Nettlecombe, and Tintinhull, and none exist for Banwell, Pilton, or Trull.[81] With the possible exception of Nettlecombe, churchwardens identified on the lay subsidy rolls reflect the same range of status as that identified by Kümin and Ford and as turned up by the anecdotal evidence. Nettlecombe's rotating office of churchwarden seems to draw mostly, but not exclusively, from parishioners assessed in the top-third income bracket, but does not involve the two wealthiest families of the parish.[82] Those families in the lower income bracket might have been wealthier in previous generations when the rotation scheme developed.

Mid-fifteenth-century collection reports from both the borough and the parish of Bridgwater reveal a similar profile of churchwardens.[83] Individuals, either as heads of households or on their own, gave money in the annual collection to support the parish in an amount commensurate with their wealth. The churchwardens who are listed on the collection sheets come from the lower end of the economic spectrum; they were not the largest contributors, they did not have servants, and they did not live in the best parts of town.[84] They also had different economic backgrounds from the men who served in the town's civic offices. In Bridgwater, those who ran the town did not directly administer the parish. Members of the merchant guild filled town offices, while the keepers of smaller shops and artisans served as churchwardens.

A similar situation prevailed in Wells, where the records cover a longer expanse of time. From 1377 to 1545, only 6.6 percent of those men who served as churchwarden of St. Cuthbert's went on to become master of the city. However, this low percentage hides a subtle change in the early sixteenth century. In the nineteen years between 1499 and 1518, twenty-nine men served as churchwarden, and six of them (21 percent) went on to become master.[85] This change suggests a modest increase in the prestige of the office and a shift in the ambitions of those who filled the office of churchwarden; earlier burgesses did not view it as an avenue to the top leadership position in the city, whereas in the sixteenth century this began to change.

One other group of churchwardens from Bath and Wells merits some additional comment. In the West Country—the counties of Cornwall, Devon, and Somerset—women also served in this office. Unlike most public positions in the middle ages, the office of churchwarden was not closed to women.[86] Although this should not be taken as the norm, at least in this part of England, the parish was more accepting of women's leadership than were other medieval institutions. At least five parishes in Bath and Wells had female churchwardens in this period: Yatton, Trull, Tintinhull, Nettlecombe, and Halse. Even though women appear as churchwardens infrequently, and generally at the end of the late medieval period, women churchwardens are more common than earlier scholars had assumed.[87] The relatively high number of women churchwardens in the West Country appears to be part of a broader regional pattern of including women in parish administrations. The West Country was also home to the majority of all-women's parish guilds.[88]

Women took up the position of churchwarden under a variety of circumstances. The earliest recorded female churchwarden in Bath and Wells is Lady Isabel Newton of Yatton, widow of John Newton, a local knight. She served as warden in 1496–97.[89] Her status as a member of the local gentry overrode the usual limitation of her sex with respect to the office of churchwarden. Her involvement speaks more to the privilege of her family's status than it does to her interest in parish affairs. Her election allowed her to supervise a parish project that was important to her. While she was warden, she oversaw construction of a new parish chapel dedicated to St. John the Evangelist, where she and her husband were buried.[90] Serving as a churchwarden was a means of honoring her deceased husband (he died in 1487) and filling her role as a widow intent on furthering her family's honor.

As we have already seen, Nettlecombe maintained a family's place in the rotation of the office of churchwarden by relying on the service of widows of former churchwardens. The religious turmoil in the 1540s created yet another opportunity for women to serve as churchwarden. With so much tension surrounding the office, men could not always be convinced to serve.[91] It is within this context of religious uncertainty that most of the women churchwardens held tenure. Perhaps the West Country's greater willingness to see women in this office made it an alternative to have them serve during these difficult years. Certainly, other parts of England did not follow this practice. Nettlecombe added a third warden in 1544 from outside the rotation—Alice Harper.[92] Trull, a small parish next to Taunton, found itself in the same situation. Generally this parish elected three churchwardens, but in 1542 only two served—Master Cogwyll and Agnes Shorter.[93] Two years later, in 1544, Christine Voyse served as one of the three churchwardens.[94] Additionally, in 1547, Maryn Bone served as warden for that parish's guild of St. Mary.[95] Like Yatton, Trull showed no prior pattern of women serving in such capacities. Tintinhull

also had a female warden, Sibyl Smith, at this time.[96] At Halse, three different women held office as churchwardens during this period. Joanne Wassher
served with William Blayke in 1543, when they conducted a very profitable ale,
raising over £5 as opposed to the more usual £3. Five years later, William Ylary
and Jane Raxworthy were listed as the wardens. Another woman, Joan Lawrence, served with Thomas Notte in 1550.[97] Unfortunately, the extant accounts are late, starting only in 1541 and containing few details; it is, therefore,
impossible to establish particular patterns of administration characterizing
the women's tenure or the women's precise roles. As Halse is only about
eight miles from Nettlecombe, it may have had a similar method of choosing
churchwardens, and the women serving in the 1540s were in fact the widows
of earlier churchwardens.

The little information available on the women who served as churchwardens makes it difficult to know much about them. They were all widows from
reasonably prosperous families, where status helped mitigate the concerns of
gender. As noted, Isabel Newton came from the local gentry. In Nettlecombe,
Alison Fermer's husband George was assessed at £8 in the 1524 lay subsidy,
and John Thorn, whose widow Alice served as warden in 1541, paid taxes on
£10 of goods.[98] This amount of wealth would place the family in what Julian
Cornwall described as the upper bracket of the lower middle class.[99] Similarly,
Sibyl Smith, who served as Tintinhull's churchwarden during the early phases
of the Reformation, was well enough off to appear on the lay subsidy roll; she
was assessed at 40s. We can only speculate on what her status was twenty years
later when she became churchwarden; it is unlikely, however, that it had increased. The other identifiable churchwardens generally paid taxes on between £4 and £12 of goods or income, which suggests that Sibyl was not as
well off as the majority of individuals who had served before her.[100] Her tenure
reflects the stress caused by religious reforms and perhaps the unwillingness of
others usually tapped to serve in this position.

The lifestyle of this middling rank of individuals who became churchwardens gave them many of the necessary skills for administering the parish's property. Managing one's private property was a good background for a
churchwarden. There were other ways, however, to acquire applicable experience. Parish offices such as guild warden, ale warden, or rate collector developed skill and allowed individuals to gain visibility and community trust. A
parish would seek a warden with willingness to serve; an ability to motivate,
lead, and cooperate with others; and knowledge of the area and of capable
people who could perform the work needed by the church at an affordable
price. Churchwardens' accounts suggest that some served their time not only
with enthusiasm and commitment but also with effectiveness and skill. Judy

Ford's study of four Kentish parishes shows that the churchwardens there left larger bequests to their churches than did others of similar status; their service was perhaps also motivated by piety.[101]

One example from the parish of Bridgwater illustrates how an individual gained the experience and visibility necessary to becoming a warden. William Snothe appeared first in 1444 as a collector for the parish assessment, then as a warden for St. Katherine's guild, and finally as a churchwarden for three terms (1447–50).[102] No other individual held so many positions during this period. Snothe left unusually detailed, organized, and thorough accounts. The only surviving parish inventory also comes from his tenure as churchwarden.[103] It is not a quick addendum to the year's account, but a separate and detailed listing of all the church's ornaments and vestments. His year in office was a big one for the parish; he helped oversee the construction of two chapels—one to St. Mary and the other to St. George. To finance these projects, he conducted a very successful parish-wide collection.[104] Snothe's earlier work in the parish shows how one man gained the necessary experience to serve his parish as churchwarden. He had demonstrated his skills in less important capacities and his fellow parishioners then trusted him enough to serve as churchwarden during the important project of enlarging the church. The character of his accounts and the work completed during his tenure suggest that he was a skilled administrator.

In both town and country parishes, service in parish guilds became a common way for individuals to train to be churchwardens. In the parish of St. Cuthbert in Wells, the number of parish guilds suggests that in addition to acquiring skills or knowledge, the parishioners also observed a hierarchy of service. Some guilds were more prestigious and more clearly on the path to advancement than others. In 1456, the city council began electing wardens for the altar of St. Mary; in 1473, they started electing wardens of the guild of Holy Trinity; and finally in 1487, 1500, and 1501, they began electing wardens to the altar of the Name of Jesus, the altar of St. Erasmus, and the Holy Cross respectively.[105] Between 1456 and 1547, when the guilds closed, 30 percent of the wardens for St. Mary's altar went on to become churchwardens. Only 12 percent of the wardens from the Name of Jesus and 8 percent of the Holy Cross wardens ever became churchwardens. The Trinity guild had a more prominent place in the city. Whereas 15 percent of the Trinity wardens became churchwardens, 11.5 percent became the city's master. There was a much greater likelihood of becoming city master after serving in the Trinity guild than any other guild. In Wells, the guilds clearly provided experience and greater visibility. Between 1455, when the accounts list the first guild warden, and 1547, 41 percent of the churchwardens had previously served as a guild warden.

In the country parishes, where the responsibilities of the warden were generally less complicated, other parish offices such as guild warden or collector did not serve as obvious training grounds for the churchwardens. In Trull, only 23 percent of the churchwardens served first as warden of the parish guild of St. Mary. In Banwell, only 22 percent had first served as parish collectors.[106] Yatton presents an exception, as 44 percent of the wardens had previous experience in parish office. Yet, for much of the fifteenth century, this parish was rebuilding its entire church. Managing this project made the wardens' job far more complicated, and experience in parish administration would have been helpful. This does not stay constant, however. The frequency with which the parishioners chose men with previous administrative experience declines slightly in the late fifteenth century, and by the beginnings of the Reformation the men who served as warden had little obvious experience in running the parish. As we saw in Croscombe, the uncertainty surrounding the break with Rome moved a new group of men into parish offices. With the exception of Yatton, the differences between town and rural parishes suggest that rural parishioners thought that individuals were knowledgeable about the job without extensive prior experience. As we will see in the next chapter, the financial apparatus supporting these parishes was less corporate and more open to member scrutiny.[107]

Studies of other parts of England also reveal a connection between manorial and parochial offices. It was common for an individual to turn his experiences as a guild or churchwarden into manorial offices such as reeve or bailiff.[108] We cannot test to see if this is true for Somerset, because there is no overlap in Somerset of the kinds of records necessary to show this practice.[109] In one instance, as we have already seen, John Stacey, who was frequently a churchwarden in Tintinhull, was also the bailiff.[110] There is no real reason, however, to believe that Somerset residents did not follow this practice.

The visibility of the churchwarden, and the fact that in many communities the position was a stepping-stone to higher office, conferred a level of prestige that did not go unnoticed by the clergy. John Mirk in his *Instructions for Parish Priests* warned priests to be on the lookout for parishioners who took pride in the offices they had held.[111] He was anxious that what should be a manifestation of piety did not become a source of sin. Mirk echoes his dubious opinion of local officials in his sermon for the feast of the dedication of a church.[112] In an *exemplum*, he tells the story of an angel who instructs the churchwarden to ask the bishop to remove a corpse from the churchyard; the corpse is possessed and is haunting the parish. The angel warns the warden that he will die within thirty days, if he does not do this. The warden refuses and dies. This story shows how far-reaching the churchwarden's responsibilities were. The office needs to be viewed as much more than a means to local visibility; the wardens had control of wealth that shaped religious life. Failure to care for the community was a serious breach of trust.

Not all wardens took pride in this office; some were in fact ineffective or downright incompetent. Variations in year-to-year income depended on the economy, but they also depended on a warden's skill. Despite the availability of training, not all wardens were skilled or competent. Nettlecombe's system of rotating the churchwardens allows us to compare the competency of individual wardens. Nettlecombe had a very diverse parish economy. It raised money from church ales, had some rental property it occasionally leased, sold goods, and collected money during an annual revel. In certain years, some sources of income disappear from the accounts, suggesting that some wardens were better managers than others. Two years, 1513 and 1528, stand out particularly (see Figure 4.5a). They coincide with the tenure of John Darge and Philip Mellyn. The parish experienced a drop in both income and in the number of fundraising activities.[113] Compared to those of other years, Darge and Mellyn's administration appears decidedly less vigorous. In 1513, the parish received money only from the church ale, and it was not a particularly profitable one at that. There was no Christmas collection (a mainstay of the parish's income), no income from rental property or sale of goods. In their second term as wardens in 1528, Darge and Mellyn had the collection and an ale but nothing else appears among the receipts: no gifts, no produce, and no rents. Their accounts do not record any expenses either. These less-detailed records are symptomatic of Darge's and Mellyn's lack of interest. Although other factors could have contributed to these poor accounts, the quality of the preceding and succeeding accounts, and the fact that these two wardens report noticeably less income than other wardens do suggests that it was a failure of these particular men and not of the scribe. The rotation exposes a pattern of behavior for these two that would not otherwise be obvious. The drop in parish income does not appear to have been serious, but their successors do show increased income in all categories, perhaps to make up for the previous year. Both the decline during Darge and Mellyn's service and the subsequent increase the next year point to the conclusion that Darge and Mellyn were either incompetent or apathetic. In 1543, which would have been their next year of office, two new wardens served.[114] Both men may have died in the intervening fourteen years, but the rotation was maintained, at least in part, in both preceding and succeeding years (see Table 3.1).

John Darge and Philip Mellyn's apathy or incompetence presents an alternative view of the churchwarden's office. Although some may have viewed it as an honor and a privilege, others may have found it burdensome, time consuming, and potentially expensive. Instead of demonstrating piety, managerial skills, and an understanding of community dynamics, some may have tried to ignore their official responsibilities. If enough parishioners felt this way, parish leadership could easily fall into the hands of a select few; this may explain why some communities imposed stiff fines on those who refused to serve.

Local Gentry

Bylaws and local customs that regulated the length of a churchwarden's term of office were not the only way that wardens found their authority limited. In addition to dealing with different groups of parishioners from their own class and lower, churchwardens had to respond to the interests and concerns of wealthy patrons and local gentry. By and large the nobility were uninvolved in the local parish, preferring instead to make their household a center of religious practice. They also tended to choose monastic houses as the recipients of their largess.[115] The local gentry had less lofty aspirations. Although these powerful individuals were technically and legally members of the parish, their social position and wealth allowed them a different relationship with local parish life from that of the majority of parishioners. Many had more than one home and were at best part-time members of a parish.

The gentry's wealth and military presence made them difficult to ignore, even though they rarely assumed the office of churchwarden or took an obvious role in the daily life of the parish. There has been a great deal of debate over the extent of the gentry's interest and involvement in their local parishes. Many scholars looking at the condition of late medieval lay religion believe that the large landholders were withdrawing from public religious life during this period.[116] Based on examination of wills of the Warwickshire gentry, Christine Carpenter believes that the fifteenth-century gentry were very committed to their parishes.[117] Colin Richmond disagrees, stating that parish life was not "gentlemanly" enough, and "fear of Purgatory" motivated testamentary bequests.[118] Another way of thinking about this debate concerns not whether, but in what ways, the gentry participated in local religious life. Their greater financial resources gave them different religious options. They involved themselves in parish life in ways that distinguished them from other levels of society and bolstered their status. Although they often gave elaborate and generous legacies to their parishes, the gentry often removed themselves from regular contact with their parishes by building private chapels in their manor houses and elaborate and secluded stalls and pews in the parish church. Yet their interest combined with their status, rather than status alone, seem to have determined their impact on parish affairs; some were quite interested and others less so.

Somerset gentry took advantage of their wealth and status and frequently sought episcopal licenses for private chapels, so that they could worship at home. For example, the bishop granted Sir Robert Coker of Lydeard St. Lawrence a license for one year to hear mass privately in his home.[119] Typically, licenses add that on high holy days the gentry had to attend church. The gentry's absence from many services highlighted their ability to afford a private chapel. Licensing private chapels did not necessarily remove the gentry from the parish on a permanent basis; rather it gave them another way to display themselves. On those occasions when they did attend the parish church, their presence was that much more noteworthy and served as a reminder to the rest of the congregation that they did not usually attend, because they could afford a private chapel or a second (or third) home in another parish.

Although it is likely that the gentry were often absent from weekly services, they did not altogether abandon their parish churches. Many had a deep interest in parish worship. In Nettlecombe the local lord and parish patron, Sir John Trevelyan, was very regular in his church attendance and generous in his financial support. In a petition for the Court of the Star Chamber, he claimed that ten men lay in wait for him while he was at evensong.[120] He was attacked again on another occasion while marching in a parish procession.[121] A land dispute spawned these attacks, but Trevelyan's habit of attending church made him easy to find. At his death, he left money for a new parish chapel to be built onto the nave.[122] Trevelyan's regular attendance would have made him familiar with some parochial issues. Construction of his legacy of a new chapel and aisle, however, added to the wardens' responsibilities, since they had to oversee the project, along with its future maintenance.

Even while attending mass at home, the gentry still demonstrated to the parish their greater wealth and status in a variety of ways. They had better seats and bigger tombs, and they gave larger gifts. Their family arms usually decorated the nave, windows, and family chapels. The provision for the souls of the local gentry through donations of tombs, chapels, windows, and memorials could be intensive enough to turn some parish churches into extensions of the gentry's family chapel. Indeed, some gentry probably thought of the parish church as a family church. Local lords sometimes provided for church expansion, taking financial responsibility for new construction out of the parishioners' hands and presumably influencing the style and presentation of the project.[123] When the gentry stepped in to build new additions, however, they assumed many of the duties of the churchwardens. This complicated the position of the churchwarden and restructured his (or her) relationship to the parish. They had to be attentive to the desires of the benefactor, seeing to it that his or her work was completed or that the rest of the laity did not interfere. One Chancery case from Suffolk is particularly illustrative of these sorts of problems and worth recounting because it clearly illustrates how the presence of a wealthy patron could make a churchwarden's job difficult. Sometime in the 1530s, a wealthy cloth maker from Essex, named Richard Darnell, left £100 in his will to "the edifying and building of the north aisle of the parish church of East Bergholt (Suffolk)."[124] His son, Jakes, paid the bills, and Robert Cole, the churchwarden, oversaw the project. The mason he hired was one Richard Pepyrton. Shortly after the project started the churchwarden, Robert Cole, died, and Jakes Darnell took over the project but not the office of churchwarden. Not knowing anything about how to judge good stone from bad, Jakes and the parishioners relied on the mason Pepyrton's advice and expertise to provide them with material of sufficient quality for the project. Part way into the construction the parish consulted with some other masons and discovered that Pepyrton was using poor quality stone; the whole aisle would have to be rebuilt at the cost of an extra £40. Because the mason was too poor to make up the loss, Jakes simply withheld the remaining £9 16s. 10d. from his salary. Pepyrton sued the churchwarden at the time, Nicholas Ffryer, for the rest of his salary in the mayor of Colchester's court and won. Ffryer then countersued in Chancery, maintaining that, although he was church-warden, he was not involved in the project and not responsible for Pepyrton's remaining salary. As with most Chancery cases, we do not know the outcome, but the case illustrates how once the money and aspirations of a wealthy patron entered the picture, they compromised the wardens' duties. It removed the warden from his usual obligations but did not absolve him, or so the mayor believed, of his administrative and financial responsibilities.

Some parishes benefited greatly from the piety of local lords. Walter Lord Hungerford completely rebuilt the parish church of Farley Hungerford in the fifteenth century.[125] Elizabeth Lady Botreaux, intending to found a college of priests in the parish church of North Cadbury, had the entire parish church rebuilt on a grand scale in the early 1400s.[126] Most involvement was not on this grand scale; typically the gentry only added new aisles and family chapels. When Sir Richard Chocke of Long Ashton died, he specified in his will that he be buried "in my chapel . . . and that there be made a sculpture making mention of the day, month, and year of my decease."[127] But even a new tomb or chapel could potentially add to the wardens' responsibilities. A chapel needed to be furnished and maintained, and even if there was an endowment to support it, the actual work often fell to the parishioners. It may have been the recognition of this reality that led Yatton to take the unusual step in electing Isabel Newton churchwarden in 1496. Having her serve as churchwarden united her position as wealthy benefactor with the duties of the churchwarden.

In some parishes the local lord was a religious foundation. The nearby Cluniac priory of Montacute held the manor of Tintinhull along with the ad-vowson.[128] This meant that the priory held regular manor courts and had the right to appoint the parish clergy. The parish leased a bake house from them, but the priory generally had little involvement in the daily administration of the parish. As long as the laity paid their tithes, the priory seems to have left the parish alone. In the parish of Croscombe, the local gentry were no longer in residence by the middle of the fifteenth century. The Paltons were the hereditary patrons of the parish. William Palton had left money for a chapel in the south chancel which the parish completed in 1459, but the family had not lived in Croscombe since the death of William Palton in 1449.[129] They continued to hold the advowson, and thus appointed the parish priest, but played no other obvious role in late fifteenth and early sixteenth parish affairs.[130]

The lack of involved gentry might be another explanation for the fact that Tintinhull and Croscombe had such strong churchwardens. With no outside authorities challenging their leadership decisions, the office of churchwarden became a way for a local elite to realize their ambitions and promote their concerns. Resident local gentry, however, wielded more power and influence than any churchwarden of middling status. Their presence helped mitigate the potential authority of the churchwarden. He (or she) needed to attend to their desires and see to the fulfillment of their projects.

Although potentially responsible for a great deal of wealth, churchwardens did not generally act as supreme rulers of their parish. The late medieval parish, situated within a nexus of religious and secular interests, made the churchwarden accountable to a number of concerned parties. Even with specifics about local dynamics missing from the records, we can see that wardens occupied a political position that required the skills of arbitration and negotiation as much as financial acumen and management know-how. The presence of the gentry added to this situation, because their social status gave them a different kind of relationship to the parish community that the wardens could not ignore, and indeed had to accommodate, should the need arise.

Vestries

Throughout the middle ages, lay organization of the parish continued to deal with two pressing issues of leadership: containing their wardens' influence and ensuring the continuity of administration. In the sixteenth century, a new level of parish bureaucracy, called the vestry, began to develop in order to address these issues. The creation of vestries placed the wardens in a position similar to that of some guild wardens. The vestry was a supervisory group of parishioners who oversaw the annual audit. Their exact makeup, function, and development are open to debate. They were not a common part of late medieval parish organization. Edmund Hobhouse, the nineteenth-century editor of many Somerset churchwardens' accounts, describes the vestry as a group of parishioners who elected or appointed the wardens, audited the accounts, oversaw the transfer of parish property from one set of wardens to another, determined the parish's needs, and decided on new projects and repairs.[131] Hobhouse, however, mistakenly assumes that the phrase *coram parochianis* (before the parish) always denoted an institutionalized vestry, when, in fact, it was merely descriptive of how the parish acted. Cox's survey of churchwardens' accounts provides several examples of parishes developing what he called select vestries around the time of the Reformation. He does not, however, specifically link them to the Reformation, nor does he discuss how they affected the churchwardens' position.[132]

Recent research links vestries with the government's post-Reformation use of the parish as both a governmental and an administrative unit.[133] With the increased expectations for the parish and the reformers' disapproval of many parochial fundraising practices, parishes needed to shift their fundraising from activities such as ales to mandatory payments such as church rates. In the late sixteenth and early seventeenth centuries, the vestry in the parish of St. Olave in Southwark, outside London, not only oversaw the churchwardens but also controlled and maintained four pumps that supplied the parish with water.[134] Trends identifiable in London are also at play in Bath and Wells. As early as 1524, Lydeard St. Lawrence had a vestry that operated at a level above the churchwardens. The churchwardens' accounts simply refer to them as "the four men." The accounts provide no description of who they were or how they came to this position. They audited the account each year to ensure that the wardens had managed the parish properly.[135] The existence of a vestry probably explains why the wardens in Lydeard St. Lawrence had such short terms of office. The wardens served the parish through the vestry and appear to have had limited influence or authority. No family or individual appeared overly eager to monopolize the position. Stogursey also developed a vestry of some sort toward the middle of the sixteenth century. It is a shadowy organization, not named specifically. An undated entry, from around 1540, records that "an order taken by the 24 present of the whole parish" rescheduled the date of the St. Mary's Ale to "the Sunday seven nights after [the] ascension of our Lady."[136] Somebody charged the twenty-four with deciding when the wardens would hold their annual ale, an important source of parish income.[137] As in Lydeard St. Lawrence, no group or individual dominated the office of churchwarden, although several families had more than one member who served. In the 1560s, in St. Thomas parish, one of the Bristol parishes in the diocese of Bath and Wells, the parishioners no longer attended the annual audit. The vestry supervised it, and the curate published the accounts after the fact.[138]

The development of a vestry distanced relations between the churchwarden and the parishioners. Creating such a supervisory body that represented the parish in some fashion further defined the churchwardens as servants to the parish. The vestry also served to contain local apathy. Although this is not obvious from the surviving records, many members were probably only too glad to turn over parish decision making to a small group. In some parishes, the formation of a vestry may have institutionalized how business had actually been conducted, with a select few making many of the decisions. Once constituted, the vestry could formulate or distill parish opinions and desires. In the face of apathy, vestries helped ensure continuity and stability in the parish.

Conclusion

Although churchwardens characterized themselves as servants to the parish, the meaning of this role in individual parishes depended upon individual capabilities as well as local constraints and resources. The canonically defined position gave them potentially a great deal of power which they could use to garner further local influence and prestige. Yet their position was continually mediated by conscious attempts to limit their power and by the social and economic realities of late medieval society. The involvement of local elites, uninterested in serving as churchwardens but wanting their concerns addressed and their families' status and honor displayed in the church, could control a churchwarden more effectively and more thoroughly than bylaws and court cases. On the other hand, some parishes appeared to lack the ability to limit their wardens' authority.

The religious practices of the parish reflected the official and unofficial power structures of the parish. As we will see in subsequent chapters, the wardens' abilities to influence the character and quality of parish life and worship depended on local circumstances almost as much as it depended on canon law. Directives from many places regulated lay involvement in the parish. The wardens provided the first contact with the ecclesiastical hierarchy overseeing the morals and liturgical practices of the parish. But their position vis-à-vis the bishop's administration did not give them a free hand. Neither should we see the parish as a bastion of early democracy or proto-democracy. Although town or manor government may have provided models for community regulation and participation, parishes did not completely adopt them. Parish governments developed their own unique structures that sought to address the financial and religious concerns of the laity. This understanding of leadership shows the parish as more than a coercive unit responding only to outside administrative demands. The laity constituted a body with the ability to express a will.

The variety of local customs surrounding late medieval churchwardens reflects different priorities, but these priorities also raise questions about whose priorities they were. Who constituted "the parish"? It seems clear that in Bath and Wells some parishes relied on a local elite to formulate priorities but expected the churchwarden to achieve them. How this elite coalesced, we can only guess. To some extent it was based on wealth and social status, but not exclusively. The very rich used the parish in very different ways from the rank and file. Their wealth gave them many more religious options and much greater visibility. Local elites might also have depended on interest. If the range of individuals who served as warden is any indication, those interested in shaping parish life came from a broad spectrum of the membership that even included some women. Whatever the case, the churchwarden embodied many of the local customs that marked his or her parish as different from those surrounding it. Although perhaps only marginally accountable to the poorest and most disenfranchised members such as most women, children, servants, and wage laborers, the office of churchwarden was another manifestation of the community identity of the parish.

4 "RECEIVED BY THE GOOD DEVOTION OF THE TOWN AND COUNTRY"

Parish Fundraising

Forms of Fundraising

The financial demands of maintaining a parish were too large and too important to depend solely on parishioners' occasional generosity.[1] Altars needed candles, sacred images required repainting, and priests, for the often numerous side altars, demanded salaries and vestments. Additionally, roofs leaked, gutters corroded, and walls and windows cracked. The parish thus came to need permanent and reliable ways of providing a steady flow of income for these and the hundreds of other expenses relating to the care and fitting of a building.[2] Over the course of the fourteenth and fifteenth centuries, parishioners, led by their churchwardens, developed different fundraising strategies. Just what form these methods of fundraising took was largely at the community's discretion. They depended upon local resources, shrewd advertising, and peer pressure, and they exploited popular activities and community concerns.[3]

Unlike tithing, that portion of a family's income which all laity had to pay, parish fundraising involved a measure of choice. Tithes went to the clergy, quite often distant clergy, such as the rector who lived off the parish as a benefice, whereas parish maintenance stayed within the parish. When discussing fundraising, we must use the most inclusive meaning of "parish" to include more than the clique of householders influencing the leadership. Fundraising could involve much more of the membership, becoming a means of integrating men and women into the community of the parish. Comparing fundraising strategies exposes further differences between parishes, showing that financial obligations were not just another burden imposed on the laity by a remote clergy, but an expression of local, communal, and spiritual expectations. Fundraising helped to determine the relationship of the parish as an institution to its members.

Parish participation involved much more than receiving the sacraments or attending the liturgy. The sociology of fundraising allows us to expand our notion of religious culture. It involved more than belief; it included action and behavior. Never far from any parish project was the idea that it was for God. A pious bequest could help ease a soul from Purgatory.[4] Fixing the church made the building a worthy home for the host, and candles, altar cloths, and vestments added to the liturgy's splendor and furthered the veneration of the saints and the worship of God. Making contributions to meet the parish's financial needs became a local expression of religious faith rather than simply a response to the demands of church doctrine or polity.

Over the course of the late fourteenth and fifteenth centuries, parishioners developed several successful financial strategies for parish maintenance. The surviving churchwardens' accounts from the fourteenth century show that parishes already had some means of supporting themselves. As we saw in a previous chapter, collecting house rents on parish-owned property predates the earliest churchwardens' accounts. As a parish's liturgical needs grew, so did fundraising. At the same time, as the laity realized the successes of their efforts, they expanded their religious and liturgical activities. Part of the process of the laity's learning to administer their parish was learning how to raise money to meet the needs of the community. By the beginning of the sixteenth century, most parish communities had several entrenched means of fundraising that had become part of local culture.

One way scholars have looked at financial support of the parish is to distinguish between income from the living, such as profit from an ale, and income from the dead, such as property left as a bequest by a deceased member.[5] This approach exposes differences between urban and rural settings. In this chapter, I want to refine this model even further to show the different roles fundraising could play in the lives of parishioners and how it influenced the quality and character of local religious life. By recognizing the different ways in which parishes involved their members, we can further understand the ways in which a parish created its community identity.

There were essentially five categories of fundraising: gifts, rents, sales, collections, and entertainment. Each involved its own set of administrative concerns. On its own, this taxonomy oversimplifies parochial fundraising; the categories are not always distinct, and they do not always account for unusual circumstances that required or brought in money.[6] Each year brought a variety of regular and irregular financial demands. Parishioners needed to supply the numerous candles and oil for the many altars, along with ensuring that someone did the cleaning, decorating, and repairing. The laity sought not only to repair their churches but to embellish and expand them, and an unexpected disaster, such as a tree falling on the church roof, could seriously strain even the most well-endowed budget. Any given year combined both the usual fundraising methods and attempts to meet unforeseen expenses. Contextualizing the five basic ways of fundraising shows that parish communities developed a sense of financial planning and were often able to accommodate the changing needs that confronted them. By considering the geographic, social, and economic context of these strategies, we can add to this taxonomy and explore how fulfilling episcopal requirements to maintain the parish church helped create a unique religious culture intimately connected to the local setting.

Regional and local economies influenced parish fundraising. In the Levels and the coastal plain of Somerset, agriculture predominated, and parishioners commonly left barley, wheat, and sheep to their parishes in their wills. The wardens usually sold these items, but some parishes rented out their livestock. This is what William Kyppng of the parish of Buckland Dinham expected when he left the parish of nearby Frome two cows in 1538.[7] In the coastal parish of Minehead, where livelihoods depended on the ocean, Thomas Braye left the parish a quarter-interest in his fishing boat the *Patrick* in 1513.[8] If churchwardens' accounts had survived for this parish, we might find that as in Walberswick, which lay on the coast of Suffolk, fishing comprised an important part of the parish's revenues.[9] In this way, local resources and regional economies helped shape local religious life. Most pronounced, however, are the differences between urban and rural parishes.[10] Rural parishes employed a greater number of fundraising methods than town parishes did. These different methods not only aided the parish but also benefited the individual parishioners. Their fundraising activities directly involved the parishioners in parish affairs and addressed some of their expectations for parish life. Conversely, town parishes, such as those in Bath, Glastonbury, Bridgwater, and suburban Bristol, had more investments in rental property and relied less on direct parishioner participation as a means of raising money.[11] These differences allow us to see how each local economy influenced the particular social and religious expectations of the parishioners. These differences are another way the laity created and experienced community identity.

How parishes raised money largely determined the role that the parishes played in the town or manor. Fundraising required parishes to involve themselves in local markets and cope with the economic fluctuations of the late fifteenth and sixteenth centuries. How a parish raised money also demonstrates a close connection between religious practice and social interaction. Fundraising brought the laity together in different ways for a common goal.

Many fundraising activities tried to foster the same charity that the mass promoted. They also encouraged neighborliness, shared experiences, and spiritual well-being that added to a sense of community membership and local identity. Fundraising strategies determined many of the duties of the parish's churchwardens, many of the parish's activities, and the relationship between members and the institution of the parish.

Gifts

Individual donations, although erratic, are the most ubiquitous of the fundraising categories. All Somerset parishes depended on them to some degree, although their prominence in the annual receipts varied greatly. Small gifts such as clothing or livestock enhanced the parish receipts, if they could be sold. Large donations such as land or houses usually became part of the permanent parish endowment. If the wardens did not sell the property outright, they could lease it to provide the community with an annual source of money. In order to circumnavigate royal prohibitions against giving land to the church, and thus removing it from the tax rolls, parishioners made use of trustees called feoffees in order to give land to their parishes. This practice essentially set up a trust to control the land, and the money earned from the land went to the trust and was forwarded to the parish by the trustees. For the most part, however, donations of land seem to have declined throughout the late middle ages because the crown, through the statutes of mortmain, made it more difficult to give land to ecclesiastical institutions.

Most individual gifts came at the time of death in the form of testamentary bequests. The uncertainty and the fear of Purgatory, or worse, could be financially lucrative for a parish, but we should not view these gifts in only financial terms.[12] The laity left money and goods in their wills for masses and other good works to help ease their souls out of Purgatory. This money often found its way into the parish coffers, which helped perpetuate the parish's spiritual and communal life and created a permanent bond between the living and the dead. As the parish was a community largely run by the laity, they had initiated many of the extra trappings surrounding death rituals, such as special vestments and altar covering and special masses, as a way of dealing with the emotional and spiritual wounds left in the wake of a death. The larger institution of the Church might exploit this vulnerability by encouraging the practice of paying for masses, but, to a significant extent, the local parish and its liturgy provided comfort.

The Church encouraged the laity to understand giving as a good work through practices such as bede rolls. A bede roll was a list of parish benefactors. A contribution to the parish earned the benefactor's name or the name of a specified person, living or dead, a place on the roll. The priest or clerk read the entire list from the pulpit four times a year and maybe an abbreviated list every Sunday; the congregation would pray for those named.[13] Over the course of the fifteenth century, bede rolls become increasingly popular. In some parishes the bede roll was a source of income for the laity's portion of the church. In other communities, the clerk or vicar took the offerings as part of his salary. An episcopal inquiry into the vicar of Dunster's living revealed that part of the vicar's annual salary came from the bede roll offerings.[14] Tintinhull introduced its bede roll sometime in the late 1470s. The account from 1477–78 records, for the first time, that the parish paid the priest 12d. to read the bede roll four times that year.[15] In Bridgwater, the bede roll appears as early as 1441 as part of the All Saints celebrations, which included a procession around the parish.[16] Neither community, however, recorded the proceeds as parish income. In contrast, the churchwardens' accounts for both Yeovil and Stogursey included bede roll offerings as part of the annual receipts. In Stogursey they appear as a source of income in eighteen of the thirty-eight accounts, contributing anywhere from 3 to 20 percent of the annual income. Yeovil's bede roll appears for the first time in 1519. It contributed 8 percent of the income and continued to be a significant source of money until the Reformation.[17] The different financial uses that parishes made of their bede roll offerings reflect the broad conception of good works. Whether supporting either the clergy or the laity's half of the church, they brought spiritual benefits.

Money recorded for the bede roll was by no means the full extent of individual financial support. Wills and churchwardens' accounts record a variety of legacies for various specified and unspecified purposes. People left money for permanent endowments, funeral expenses, anniversary masses, and obits, all with the hope of easing their souls out of Purgatory.[18] Parishioners also left money and goods to maintain the parish fabric. In 1537, Joan Tedbury of St. Mary Magdalene's in Taunton left 40s. to the parish to help build a new church house.[19] Most of the Somerset laity who left wills remembered their parish in some manner. Sixty-five percent specifically left money to the parish church. This might be a somewhat inflated number because not all wills specify the purpose of the bequest. Some of these gifts might have been for forgotten tithes instead of parish support. Other testators left money to specific endowments within the church and not to the general fund. Taken together about eighty percent left some sort of bequest to their parish.

The kinds of gifts parishes received varied somewhat according to location and the donors' status and gender. Looking at pious bequests in terms of gender and status is one way of seeing different levels of parish involvement. Contributions were not determined by piety alone, but also by what money or goods one had to give. Although the local gentry were not particularly involved in the daily running of the parish, they did not ignore the parish in their wills, especially if supporting the parish eased the pains of Purgatory and further promoted their family's honor.[20] For example, in 1484, Dame Margaret Chocke of Ashton required that her executors oversee the construction of a window in the church which would portray "my husband's arms and mine underneath the images, and Saint Sunday will be one of the images and Saint Gregory is to be the other."[21] Failure to accept a gift that memorialized a family could mean the loss of the gift. The Taunton merchant John Tose left money in his 1501 will for a blue velvet cope which was to have his marks. If the parish did not agree, he declared that another parish would receive it instead.[22]

Large gifts from the well-off are relatively easy to see. Their pious concerns were not, however, the only ones that inspired parish bequests. Far less obvious are the ways in which women and the less financially secure contributed to their parishes. The ways parishioners raised money and the ways that scribes and churchwardens drew up their accounts frequently masked individual participation. Accounts do not necessarily make distinctions between an individual's or a household's gifts. This practice especially hides women's bequests. Because a women's family identity often overshadowed her individual economic and social roles,[23] the accounts often credit the head of the household, the husband or father, with the gift which the community would have recognized as coming from a family. The wardens might not know which family member prompted the donation. There is no reason to believe that the money a Banwell father gave in memory of his dead child was only from him, even though the accounts name only him. The mother's role in this memorial, although invisible in the documents, is easy to surmise.[24]

Wills are the most obvious source for tracking individual gifts, but they are biased towards the better-off members of society who typically left them. Although the Church wanted everyone to leave a last will and testament, many did not. Churchwardens' accounts, however, record gifts received often from a much wider range of individuals. Looking at the bequests recorded in churchwardens' accounts demonstrates how gift-giving and parish support varied according to sex and class. The poorer members might not have left a will, but they still remembered their parish with smaller amounts of cash or gifts of grain. Gender differences, however, shaped patterns of giving in other ways. These differences are more pronounced when we look at gifts of goods. Men had more money at their disposal, but even though married women could not by law own property, they could still dispose of small household items which were likely part of their dowries. Gifts to individuals, rather than the parish, tended to follow similar patterns.[25]

The difference in legal status between men and women meant that they participated in the parish differently. Women were more likely to give jewelry, domestic objects, or clothing. Both were equally likely to offer liturgical items to the church, except that women did not typically give books.[26] In the borough parishes, cash was the preferred gift, which typically rendered men more visible. Gifts of goods, however, suggest patterns similar to those found in the countryside. Bridgwater's churchwardens' accounts list only three gifts of articles of clothing; all three, however, came from women. In Yeovil, women and men gave clothing equally, but male parishioners gave precious objects or jewelry twice as often. Differences between borough and rural giving patterns reflect something of the local economy. Bridgwater's was based on trade, whereas Yatton's was based on agriculture. Even though the late middle ages had a cash economy, rural communities still had less available money. [27]

Gender-based giving patterns became more pronounced in the late fifteenth and early sixteenth centuries, suggesting the solidification of a culture of giving and a growing place for women in the parish on the eve of the Reformation.[28] The differences in gift-giving depended, in part, on the availability of money. When town women did give to their parish, they gave money more often than their rural counterparts, but they were named as benefactors less often. In the rural parishes, such as Croscombe or Yatton, women typically gave jewelry and clothing—personal or individualized property rather than household or familial property controlled by their husbands.[29] The boroughs' more moneyed economy, combined with women's lack of control of personal income, may account for what appears to be a scarcity of individual women as donors in the market towns. Women, as part of a household, participated in supporting their parishes, but since the medium of support was cash, they do not appear as individual donors as frequently as the rural women. Rural areas were not as heavily dominated by currency, and parishes relied more on donations of goods that they could sell at larger area markets. Rural parishes had built into their local administration an expectation of receiving and converting goods, which allowed for more individualized giving and greater visibility for women. The economic structure of rural areas allowed women to personalize their parochial support and gave them a more observable role in their parishes than their urban sisters had.

Evidence from wills duplicates these subtle differences between men's and women's gift-giving.[30] Women's roles as wives and housekeepers shaped much of their parish participation. These differences imply that gender and status influenced one's relationship to the parish. We cannot see sincerity of belief, but we can see how legal status and wealth framed religious involvement. Women and the poor had less. When women did give, it reflected their lack of legal status and what they could give that had meaning to them. The community of the parish was by no means composed of equals, equally participating.

Selling Goods and Services

Some gifts a testator expected the churchwarden to sell. Other items the parish received were not immediately appropriate or needed. The churchwardens' sale of these good made the parish a clearinghouse for items that other members might find useful. Under these conditions, selling goods was not a constant or necessarily lucrative feature of any parish's annual receipts; it depended largely on what the wardens or parishioners had available for sale, which in turn usually depended on the donations and bequests accumulated throughout the year. The accounts for Tintinhull, Yatton, and Croscombe regularly report money received from selling donated items. In 1479, the wardens of Tintinhull sold a dress left by Peter Prettyll's wife as a bequest for 5s.[31] The same year, the Yatton wardens sold for 12d. a sheep left to them by the will of one Margaret Knight.[32] Storing unnecessary goods and feeding livestock cost money, so selling them served a practical purpose. Churchwardens also sold off old furnishings. This not only made money for the church, but also solved the problem of disposing of old materials. When Tintinhull built new pews, it sold the old ones for 5s. 4d.[33] In Yatton, where fifty years of accounts detail the construction of a new nave, the wardens regularly sold limestone, lead, old boards, nails, and even the old church doors and gate.[34]

What parishes sold often reflected the local economy. The churchwardens received and sold local produce. Trull supplemented its income by selling apples and grass gathered in the churchyard, and Pilton and Tintinhull parishes owned some milk cows.[35] Sales and lease of cattle appear regularly at the beginning of the Tintinhull accounts but gradually become less important, disappearing altogether after 1453. When a cow died, the parish sold off the hide.[36] The distinctions between rural and town life are not as pronounced when comparing smaller towns with the countryside. Even the borough parishes in Somerset could be influenced by rural concerns. Although clearly not an important revenue source, even the city parish of St. Michael's in Bath had a flock of sheep that occasionally produced wool for parish income.[37]

Although town parishes did not generally market goods, they often sold seats or pews. In the fourteenth century, most parishioners either stood during the liturgy or brought their own stools or benches. In the fifteenth or sixteenth centuries, parishes began installing permanent seats for the laity to use. Seating was not open on a first-come-first-served basis; rather some form of system allotted a family or individual a seat for life use. In the town parishes of Bath, Bridgwater, Glastonbury, Yeovil, and St. Thomas in Bristol, the churchwardens sold seats. Sale of seats never constituted a major source of income, appearing more as a convenience offered to those who could pay rather than a serious attempt to increase revenue.[38] Bridgwater parishioners started to build pews in a haphazard fashion in 1428, but their sale did not become a regular feature of the accounts until 1453. At this point, the parishioners hired two carpenters for two weeks to outfit the church further with pews. The wardens subsequently reported revenues for selling them; the first year they were available in large numbers, 17 percent of the annual income came from seat sales.[39] They did not continually earn this much money, but still remained a part of the fundraising scheme. Rural parishes installed pews at about the same time, but they were not a source of income.[40]

Sale of goods or seats never constituted a major portion of any parish's income. The presence of sales, however, shows something of a parish economy's flexibility. Through resourcefulness and attention to what people had or wanted, churchwardens could earn their communities some extra income along with providing a service. Selling extra items and goods also reflects the various roles the parish church played in the local area. It was a connection to the outside economy, able to turn pious bequests of goods into necessary funds for parish maintenance. The parish economy could also occasionally provide its members with needed items. In 1519, the town parish of Yeovil took advantage of this function and held a rummage sale.[41] Parishioners supplied all manner of goods from pots and pans and petticoats to anvils, hammers, and a hen roost. When the wardens had finished selling these items they had realized a profit of £5 8s. 9d. for the parish.

Renting Property

Differences between town and rural parishes become more pronounced when we look at property leases as a source of revenue. These differences also speak to the ways in which parishioners constructed their community identity. From the earliest churchwardens' accounts in the fourteenth century, leasing property, services, or goods was a source of parish revenue. Over the course of the fifteenth century, it became an increasingly common and important way of raising money. Like selling goods, the items a parish leased helped determine the churchwardens' duties and the parish's position within the area. Property ownership by the parish turned churchwardens into de facto landlords. They spent time negotiating leases, collecting rents, fixing houses, and dealing with the problems associated with being a landlord. Comparatively few parishes in Bath and Wells owned enough property to make rental property the major source of revenue. Those that did were the town parishes of St. Michael's in Bath, St. Mary's in Bridgwater, St. John's in Glastonbury, and the suburban Bristol parishes of St. Mary Redcliffe and St. Thomas. Burgage tenure (the ability to own and sell property), practiced only in boroughs, made it much easier for the parish to own property, which the wardens then rented out on behalf of the community.[42] Those parishes with only a few fields or tenements used rents as just one of many income sources.[43]

Although town parishes shared in their reliance on rents as a source of income, these did not play the same role in every parish's finances. The parish of St. Michael's in Bath began acquiring property before the extant records, and it continued to do so throughout the late medieval period. As property holdings increased, so did its overall income. According to the first account of 1349, the parish earned 5s. 9½d. in old rents and 10s. 9d. in new ones. By 1400, as the amount of parish property increased, the annual income from rents rose to £6 6s. 8d. and had nearly doubled by 1503 to £11 19s. 8d. After 1380, rental property was the parish's primary source of income, comprising between 60 and 100 percent of its receipts[44] (see Figure 4.1). The parish of St. John's in Glastonbury operated in a similar fashion. By the fourteenth century it too earned more than eighty percent of its income from its rents.[45] In contrast, St. Mary's in the borough of Bridgwater did not begin to rely on rents until the early fifteenth century. The switch to rents begins to appear in 1428 and is part of a larger change in parish administration that I will discuss later. From 1428 onward, rents were a regular feature of the accounts, though their significance to the overall income is never more than about 50 percent.[46] Rents were never as important to Bridgwater as they were to St. Michael's, Bath (see Figure 4.2). Although the data are much less complete, evidence form the suburban parishes of St. Thomas and St. Mary Redcliffe, outside of Bristol, show that they also supported themselves largely through rents. In comparison to the 20s. that Bridgwater collected or the £10 earned by St. Michael's in Bath, St. Mary Redcliffe was far wealthier. A miscellaneous account from around 1530 shows that all the parish's income came from leasing property, and the wardens collected £47 2s.[47] The income for St. Thomas parish was comparable to that of St. Michael's in Bath. In 1544, it earned £11 7s. from its leases.[48]

The smaller borough parishes of Stogursey and Yeovil also owned land, but on a much more limited scale. Sometime between 1457 and 1516, Yeovil parish acquired two houses that the wardens continued to rent out well into the reign of Edward VI (r. 1547–53). This money never amounted to more than 6 percent of the parish's total income.[49] In Stogursey, rents constituted only about one-tenth of the receipts, and they declined in value. In 1507, the accounts record income from two tenements, two workshops, and two acres of land. By 1521, there were only five properties of unspecified type.[50] The real drop, however, was not in the number of leases but in the amount of money they earned the parish. Rental income had stabilized in 1524 to between 10s. and 12s., but this was a decrease from the first years of the sixteenth century when they had earned over £1. Because these parishes owned so little property, they were compelled to turn to other forms of fundraising such as parish-wide collections and church ales.

Throughout the fifteenth century, borough parishes continued to acquire property, making rents an ever-increasing portion of their total income. Parishes appear to have received most of their property as testamentary bequests. For example, in 1498, Richard Vowell of St. Cuthbert's in Wells left to the master and burgesses of the city of Wells three tenements for the celebration of masses in honor of his soul and the souls of his wife, parents, and children.[51] The close tie between this parish and the town administration meant that parish property was in the hands of the town. In general, however, most testators alienated property to the church prior to making their will. What property is transferred in the will is more likely, according to Clive Burgess, to be a last-minute change.[52]

The reversal of fortunes that many English towns suffered in the sixteenth century affected property values and reduced some parishes' income. Starting in 1427, St. Michael's in Bath regularly reported lost revenues from defaulted rents.[53] As for farmland, low rents and the high cost of labor discouraged rural parishes from acquiring property.[54] Although burgage tenure made it easier to own property within a borough, urban land was not necessarily profitable. In general, it seems that the smaller boroughs, such as Stogursey, were in the most difficult position. They needed their rents, but could not acquire enough property to offset the effects of the stagnating late medieval economy. Thus, their finances were an amalgam of different fundraising strategies designed to keep the parish running and giving them more in common with rural parishes than the other borough parishes.

Rural parishes generally did not rely on property rents or on a policy of acquiring land; Yatton and Trull owned no property. For those rural parishes that did, it was, at best, a minor source of income.[55] Nettlecombe owned one tenement in nearby Taunton, which first declined in value and then disappeared from the accounts altogether, although in 1541 the parish paid to repair a house there.[56] Banwell, a large parish in northern Somerset, owned eight fields, which had contributed roughly 10 percent of the annual income. In 1521, this property also disappeared from the accounts without explanation, but the parishioners made up for it by building a church house, which they then leased for private ale brewing.[57] Rents from the church house were not as consistent as those from leases of land, but the parish more than recovered the lost income (see Figure 4.3). Tintinhull had more success with its few parcels of land. Sometime between 1490 and 1496 it acquired some pasture, which earned 9d. a year. The rent rose to 12d. in 1528 and to 15d. three years later. By 1536 the parish added a cottage to its properties, increasing its

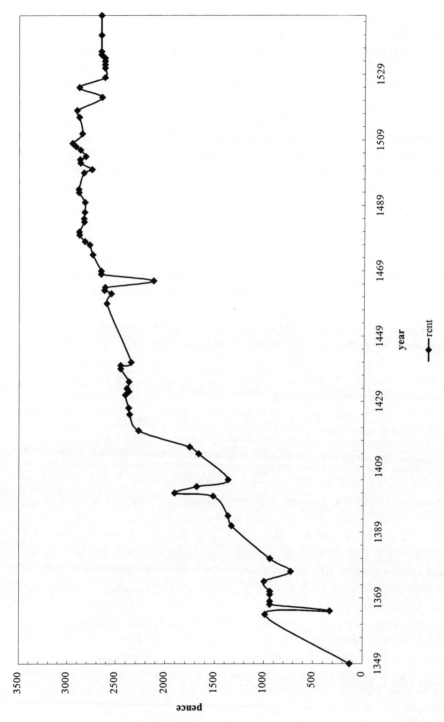

Figure 4.1a. Income from rents, St. Michael's, Bath.

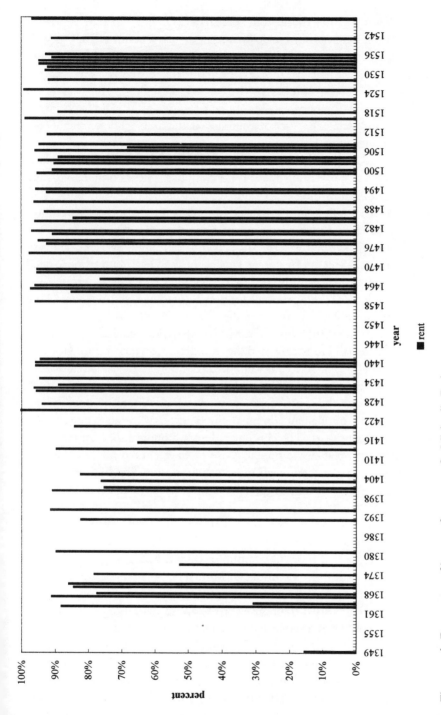

Figure 4.1b. Percentage of income from rents, St. Michael's, Bath.

income by another 15d. Although the parish occasionally added to its posses-sions, it does not appear to have deliberately pursued a policy of land acquisi-tion. In 1547, William Smith left the church a field, which the wardens imme-diately sold for 6s. 8d.—a wise move, considering that the Crown was about to confiscate most Church property.[58] In general, agricultural land was not a sound investment for parishes. The price of agricultural labor rose in the fifteenth century, while the price of grain stayed the same.[59] Thus, it might cost the parish money to own the land.

Parishes found other things to lease besides houses or fields. A particularly common practice was renting out the church house. These outbuildings were especially common in the West Country.[60] Parishioners typically built them adjacent to the church to provide space for their gatherings and celebrations. They were generally rectangular in shape and only gradually came to have a second floor.[61] Like the modern parish hall which might also be a nursery school, a meeting place, and a storage facility, the medieval church house filled a variety of functions. Inventories from Nettlecombe and Yatton both suggest that the parishes used them primarily for brewing, storage, and meetings of the parish administration.[62] Another common arrangement was for the church-wardens to rent the church house from a parish guild. The guild of St. Law-rence in the parish of Dunster owned the church house which it leased for 3s. a year to the parish.[63] The proceeds went back to the guild to help it maintain its chapel.[64] Parishes began to build church houses in the late fifteenth century. [65] This coincided with the consolidation of many parish administrations and the recognition that a permanent administration and yearly events required both storage and activity space. The churchwardens' accounts also show that once parishes began to realize the potential use of their church houses, they ex-panded them to make them even more useful. Yatton first built its church house in 1445/6, and in 1470 the parishioners added a second story, a kitchen, and a chimney.[66]

The rural parishes of Nettlecombe, Croscombe, Trull, Yatton, and Tin-tinhull all leased their church houses, but only Tintinhull's earned a significant and regular amount of money. Tintinhull's church house, which the parish itself leased for 13d. from the priory of Montacute, first appears in the war-dens' records in 1436, three years after the first surviving account.[67] One individual generally leased the house for the entire year, using it for baking. With a fixed rent, it was a stable and dependable source of revenue when the parish had few others. Rent from the church house contributed anywhere from 20 to 60 percent of the receipts. Some years it provided the only income. By the late 1470s, the parishioners had developed other ways of raising money and had come to depend on it less. In 1497, they built their own church house, which allowed the parish to expand its activities even further. The wardens began renting it out for private brewing. They still maintained and rented the old house, now referred to as "la old bakehouse," although after 1459 the parish no longer seems to have paid rent for it[68] (see Figure 4.4). In 1530, the parish expanded its church house again.[69] By this point, however, much of the parish's income came from other sources and income for the two church houses only comprised about 30 percent of the annual revenue.

The prevalence of church houses, particularly in rural parishes, reflects the importance of parish gatherings. Use of the church house and its contents enabled householders to expand their income by means of small-scale brewing without having to purchase the necessary equipment.[70] Leasing the church house was a service the parish could provide its members, helping to set up the parish as a community resource. The church house could also be rented for private parties, wedding receptions, or charitable ales.[71] Some scholars have argued that the church house was a way of extending the liturgical demands for community and charity.[72] The appearance of church houses in the fifteenth century suggests an attempt to classify and then relegate non-liturgical activities to outside the church. Although church houses helped raise money that ultimately benefited the liturgy, the clergy officially disapproved of such activities, even though individual clergy frequently attended church ales.[73] However, we can look at these houses as a sign of how much the laity had come to accept and value the collective nature of parish life and support.[74] They were also eminently practical because they eliminated the need to depend on individuals to store (and perhaps lose) valuable books, vestments, and other liturgical items. The need to maintain the church fostered pride and commitment that had helped the parish become a community, albeit in a way unanticipated by the clergy.

Even communities without extensive property could add to their annual income by lending miscellaneous items to individuals who could not otherwise afford them. The service was in many ways analogous to the sale of goods. Parishes seemed to do this, however, less for economic reasons than as a service to parishioners. Like Tintinhull, Stogursey leased the church oven located in their church house.[75] The accounts for Yeovil provide the best example of the variety of services and items that parishes could offer for hire.[76] In addition to funeral items, the parish rented out space in the churchyard on market days, weights and measures, and an anvil; they also loaned vestments, linens, and liturgical items to a nearby but poorer parish. [77] In 1457, these rentals provided a quarter of the parish's income. By 1516, the date of the next surviving account, the parish had ceased renting the churchyard and weights, but loaned instead various vessels and other large pots and pans, which they continued to do up to Edward VI's reign.[78]

The experiences of these parishes show that rents varied in their importance to a parish's economy. For the larger town parishes, dependence on leases grew throughout the fifteenth century, eventually excluding other sources of income. Unlike their rural colleagues, churchwardens in Bath, Glastonbury, and Bridgwater did not have to depend on unpredictable and variable revenue sources such as ales and revels or selling and leasing goods. Although rising inflation threatened this stability, property rents, nevertheless, offered parishes greater wealth. Reliance on rents also had implications for a community's identity. Rent collecting concentrated financial responsibility in the hands of the churchwardens in larger towns, separating the rest of the parishioners from the business of supporting the parish. Parish property was not always within the parish boundaries or leased to members. The wardens, as representatives of the community, negotiated the contracts, and parishioners were uninvolved in the transaction. This meant that non-officeholders had fewer financial exchanges with the parish than their rural counterparts and probably were less aware of their parish's financial well-being. Yet reliance on endowments of property also had spiritual significance. Given as bequests for the benefactor's soul, they linked town parishioners more firmly to deceased members. The community of the parish extended through time, incorporating the dead.[79]

The rural or poorer parishes, with only a few leases, used them to create a different kind of atmosphere. The parishes' corporate wealth was used to benefit members. Here we see a greater number of parishes renting church houses for baking and brewing. These communities also provided ovens, anvils, and other tools that parishioners occasionally needed but might not be able to afford. Leasing out brewing or baking tools allowed parishioners to supplement not only the church's income but their own as well. The rural parish operated less as a local landlord than as a source of goods and services.

Parish Collections

Community-wide collections or gatherings, as the accounts often called them, served as a prominent and widespread fundraising strategy in all parishes. Parishes used them to meet a variety of regular and special expenses. Collections paid for ad hoc needs such as new vestments or building projects, or they contributed to the general fund or supported specific items within the church. Contributions to these collections were probably not voluntary, although the exact means that the wardens used to enforce payments depended on whether they could bring the defaulters to the archdeacon's court.[80] Frequently a parish held more than one collection in a year, the most common ones being for money for candles at the font and for the Easter and Christmas liturgies. Although some parishes, such as North Curry, paid for wax out of the general fund, most had specific collections for wax.[81] The parish could postpone a new tower or wall, but the liturgy required candles. In Glastonbury, the wardens collected between 10s. and 12s. annually for the Easter taper, whereas in Banwell the wardens received somewhat less, between 6s. and 8s. Throughout the late medieval period this amount remains relatively stable, implying a continuing commitment to the liturgy.

Collections could bring in large sums of money for rebuilding a church or buying new ornaments. In 1325, the hamlet of Wembdon in the parish of Bridgwater levied a church rate to rebuild their ruined chapel.[82] When Bridgwater used this method to raise funds for a new spire in 1367, the collectors had to go out twice to raise enough money. [83] The wardens in Tintinhull used collections for both large and small projects that fell outside the scope of usual expenses. In 1437, the parishioners collected 36s. 10d. in order to buy a new cross and chalice, and three years later 38s. 1d. for four processional torch holders. One wonders if a visitation found these items missing from the parish inventory, and the only way the wardens could rectify the situation quickly was with a collection. When the parishioners wanted to rebuild the church house in 1530, the wardens again solicited money in this manner, and from 1539 to 1541, they paid for an addition to the bell tower with yet another collection.[84]

Although most parishes had only small or occasional collections, Bridgwater used an annual parish-wide collection as the source of most of its income until the mid-fifteenth century.[85] The surviving collection reports suggest it operated more as a tax.[86] Each household paid an amount based on its income. Parish enthusiasm for the collection declined in the mid-fifteenth century, and the wardens increasingly relied on income from newly acquired rental property and individual gifts. Whereas in 1415 money from the collection constituted 97 percent of the total income, by 1445 it had dropped to only 23 percent. The intermittent scheduling of collections in the 1440s and 1450s suggests that they were for particular projects and not the general fund. Antipathy towards the collection appears to have increased, and after 1455 the parish stopped using it altogether despite having paid £1 10s. ½d. for the collectors' new robes.[87]

The switch in fundraising strategies suggests that the parishioners had changed their expectation for their parish. The amount a Bridgwater parishioner had contributed to the collection depended on his or her wealth. It was, therefore, a more egalitarian way of supporting the parish. The community ultimately rejected this method in favor of individual gifts and rental property, methods that limited the number of people directly supporting the church and in fact lowered the income. The preference for rents over the more profitable collection suggests that the parish came to value its role as a source of spectacle—liturgy and decorations—more than its role as an inclusive and more broadly supportive institution. It is also possible that the merchant guild was assuming greater financial responsibility for the parish, and the wardens thought the collection unnecessary. Unfortunately no accounts survive after 1471 to show the long-term results of this decision (see Figure 4.2). However, the economic downturn that hit Bridgwater in the early sixteenth century must have made life difficult for the parish.

Although the wardens in Bridgwater kept records of who contributed, how much they gave, and where they lived—which no doubt made it more difficult for parishioners to avoid payment—there is evidence that Bridgwater's parishioners often tried to resist the collection.[88] Possibly some collections might have been in response to a visitation's injunction to repair the church. In this instance, external rather than internal imperatives compelled the parish to act, and perhaps raised the level of resistance. In 1373, the parish posted a debt of £48 5s. 4d. from parishioners who did not pay.[89] When some parishioners refused to pay for the rebuilding of their chapel at Wembdon, the wardens appealed to the bishop, who warned that canonical sanctions would be used against defaulters.[90] Again in 1415 the parishioners living in the outlying hamlet of Horsey protested against the assessment by withholding 6s. 8d. They claimed that because they maintained their own chapel, they should not have to pay the same amount as other hamlets without chapels. Specifically they were referring to the hamlet of Bower, which had no chapel and was assessed at the same rate of 26s. 8d.[91] The Bridgwater churchwardens started legal proceedings in the archdeacon's court, but they apparently failed to carry them to a conclusion.

Banwell, Nettlecombe, Pilton, and Croscombe also used parish-wide collections, but they tied them to a parish entertainment called hogling and relied on community dynamics very different from Bridgwater's collection.[92] What exactly hogling entailed is something of a mystery. It was apparently a Christmas or New Year's celebration carried out by the men.[93] According to a witness deposition in 1630 from Keynsham parish, during "their hogling they have used to sing songs & be very merry & have good entertainment at such houses they went to."[94] Another witness declared that he was hospitable "to those of Keynsham that came a hogling to him, & afforded them good cheer & beer."[95] Although we should recognize the likelihood that forms of entertainment had probably changed between the fifteenth and the seventeenth centuries, hogling at the very least seems to be a door-to-door collection conducted in the spirit of good cheer and neighborliness. In the nineteenth century, Edmund Hobhouse thought that hoglers were "the lowest class of hand-worker."[96] More recent work by James Stokes has shown that the men of Banwell who served as hoglers were from the more middling segment of society.[97] Scholars had also thought that this celebration was unique to southwestern England, but more systematic study of churchwardens' accounts reveals that many parishes all over England had hogling collections.[98]

Whatever the exact nature of the entertainment, hogling collections played different roles in each parish's annual budget, although all the annual collections show a sustained level of income for the duration of the accounts. For Banwell, the hogling collection was the primary source of income, making up on average 60 to 70 percent of the annual receipts. It brought in the most money between 1529 and 1535 when the parish was building its church house and installing new pews and an organ in the church[99] (see Figure 4.3). Nettlecombe's hogling collection was a much less important source of income. Before it disappeared from the accounts after 1541, proceeds ranged between 3 and 19 percent of the annual receipts in 1514 and 1528, respectively, contributing an average of 10 percent of the annual income. The Nettlecombe wardens seem to have used the collection to make up for other losses rather than as a means of financing a new project (see Figure 4.5). Success in these hogling collections depended on membership good will and amenability to the associated activities.

Differences in the financial significance of hogling belie subtle variations among hogling activities. In Nettlecombe the annual collection of money revolved around something called "hogling bread." The Banwell accounts describe the parish's collection process as hogling and the men who collected the money as hoglers. Here, the entertainment was part of the winter observances. In 1588, the churchwardens in Banwell wrote in their accounts: "the hoglers shall pay their money always the Sunday before Saint Nicholas' day (December 6) according to the old order."[100] Croscombe also received money from the hoglers, who apparently constituted a parish guild. Pilton, Glastonbury, and Tintinhull parishes all had hogling lights in their churches, which particular individuals or groups supported[101] (see Map 4). Incorporated into the annual cycle of festivals, collections involved the men and women in a parish in a way different from a parish rate. Revels were more than inducements to coerce payment; the surrounding festivities immediately assembled the community and bound them together. Such active involvement was both a religious and a social experience.[102]

Parishes linked other entertainment to their fundraising. Croscombe's accounts show the connection between collections and entertainment particularly well. In this parish, the guilds, rather than the churchwardens, oversaw fundraising. Each guild conducted its own collection. At the annual audit, the guild wardens turned most of their proceeds over to the churchwardens to support the church fabric. Some of the proceeds then went to the guild's light, and the churchwardens returned 4d. to the guild to finance the next year's activities. Two guilds, the weavers and the tuckers (fullers), drew their member-

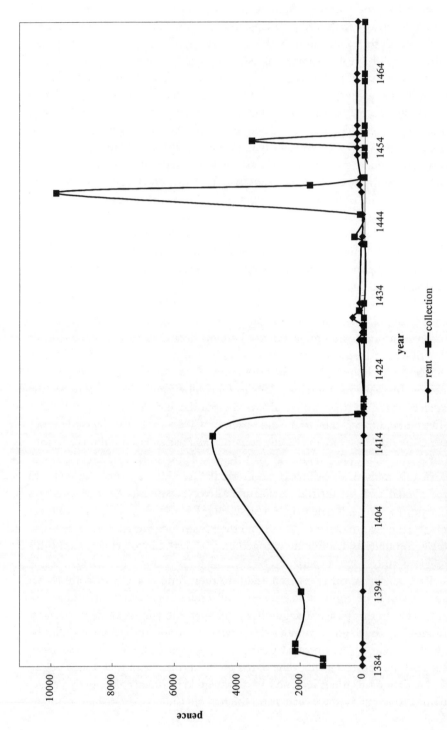

Figure 4.2a. Income from rents and collections, Bridgwater.

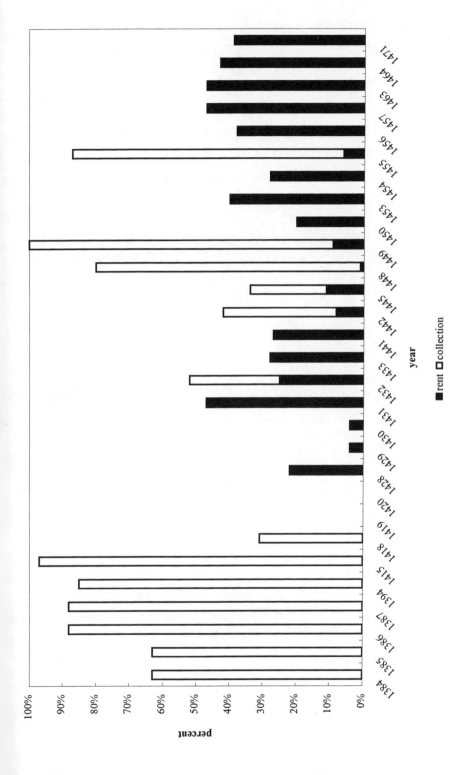

Figure 4.2b. Percentage of income from rents and collections, Bridgwater.

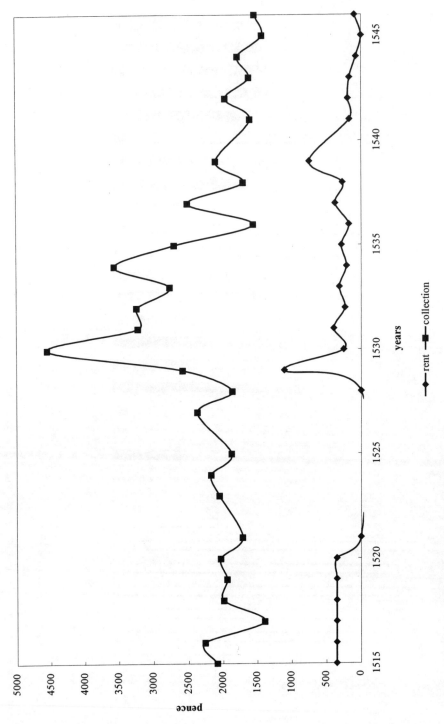

Figure 4.3a. Income from rents and collections, Banwell.

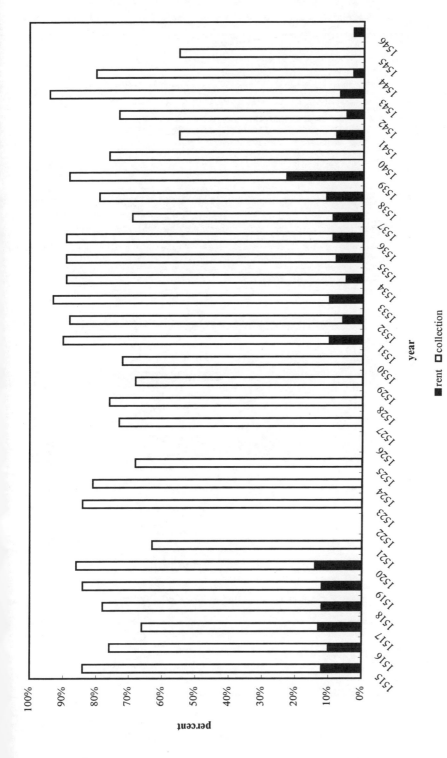

Figure 4.3b. Percentage of income from rents and collections, Banwell.

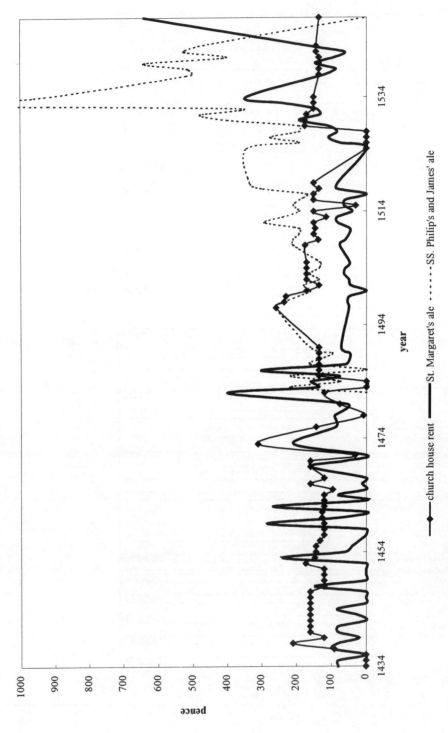

Figure 4.4a. Income from rents and ales, Tintinhull.

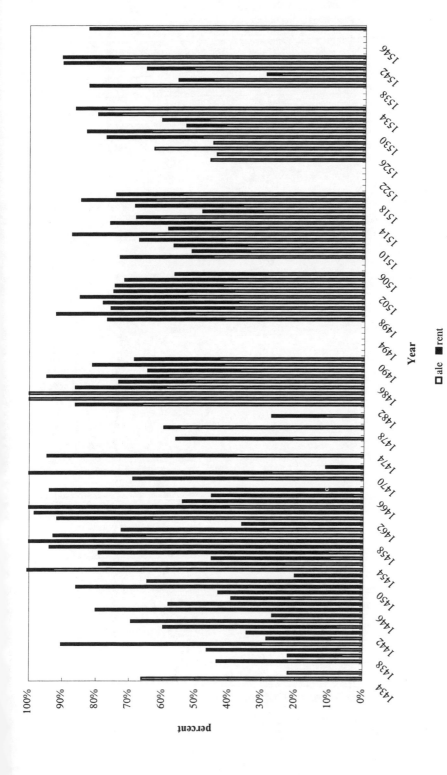

Figure 4.4b. Percentage of income from rents and ales, Tintinhull.

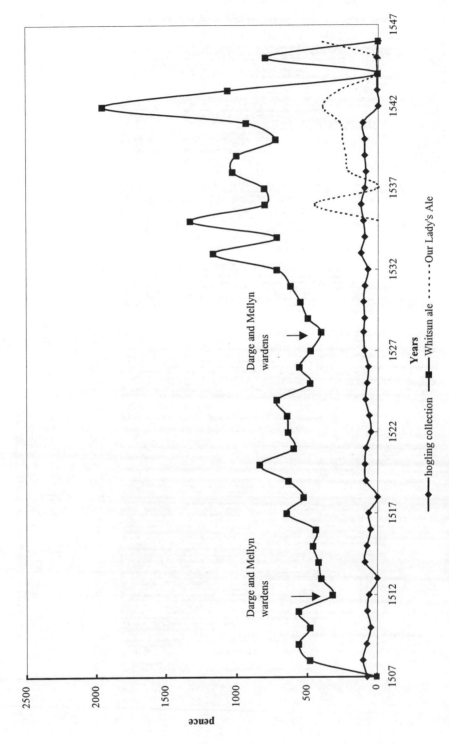

Figure 4.5a. Income from collections and ales, Nettlecombe.

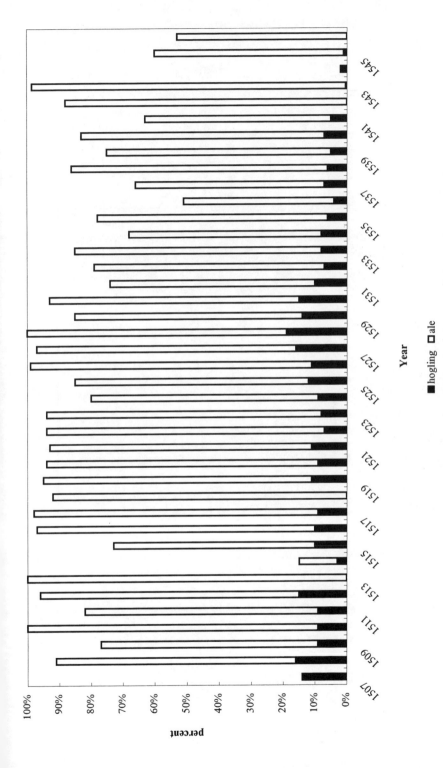

Figure 4.5b. Percentage of income from collections and ales, Nettlecombe.

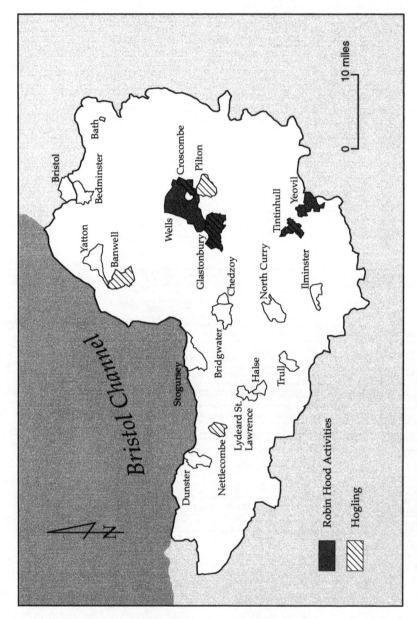

Map 4. Parishes celebrating Robin Hood revel and hogling activities.

ship from local trades; two others were dedicated to saints—the guilds of St. Michael and St. Nicholas. The latter disappeared from the accounts in 1477. The remaining four guilds (the maidens, the younglings, the hoglers, and Robin Hood and his company) provided entertainment to accompany the fundraising exercises. They supported the church by sponsoring revels or dances. Croscombe's biggest and most successful fundraiser was the Robin Hood collection. The parish only held it when they had a major building project or other significant expenditure such as the church house. The youth guilds, particularly the maidens, held their activities on Hocktide. Hocktide fell on the second Monday and Tuesday after Easter. The guilds earned money by hosting Hocktide games. This entailed the women capturing the men on Monday, and the men paying a forfeit for their release. On Tuesday the men and women reversed roles.[103] The maidens usually contributed more money than the younglings. By capturing men who had more money, the women could reap higher profits for their collection. Together the parish youth usually contributed between 20 and 30 percent of the parish's total income, although the maidens alone raised that much in 1493[104] (see Figure 4.6). In some years, the lack of a contribution from the maidens would have caused a tight parish budget. Maidens' and younglings' guilds provided an opportunity for the parish youth to demonstrate their piety, to learn some economic management, and possibly to meet potential spouses.[105] The holiday allowed for a moment of gender role inversion whereby the participants, by capturing and releasing a member of the opposite sex, expressed sexual tensions and concerns about gender roles that operated in the parish. Although there were other women's guilds in parishes throughout England, this is the only one recorded for Somerset. It presented a rare opportunity for Somerset women to act collectively to support their parish.[106] Nearby Pilton also had a younglings' guild, but there was no female counterpart.[107] Without a maidens' guild, it was more likely that they conducted their merrymaking on Plow Monday (the first Monday after Epiphany when plowing started) or May Day.[108]

The differences between the Bridgwater parish collections and those of Banwell, Croscombe, and Nettlecombe involve the larger issue of how parishioners integrated fundraising into community activities. By adding entertainment, Nettlecombe, Banwell, and Croscombe changed the nature of the collections and perhaps minimized local resistance. Although individuals may have stayed away from the games or refused to contribute when the collectors came around, the accounts do not hint at the problem of resistance to collections found in Bridgwater. Collections combined with entertainment helped parishioners to think about their parish in broader terms. It was a religious unit to be sure, but entertainment helped incorporate men and women into the parish in other ways than an overt tax did.

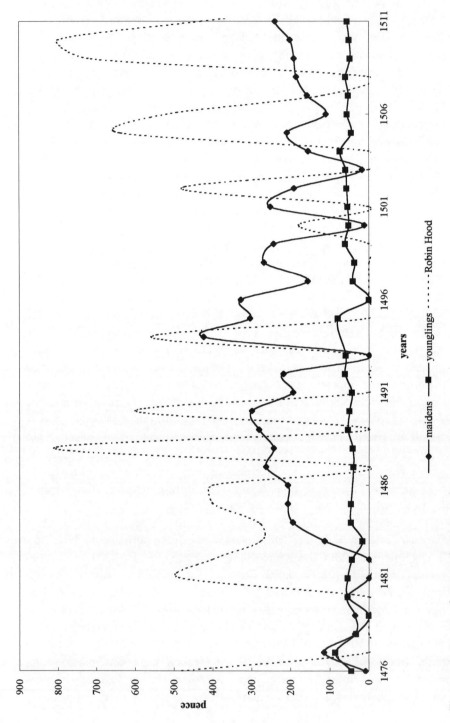

Figure 4.6a. Income from revels, Croscombe.

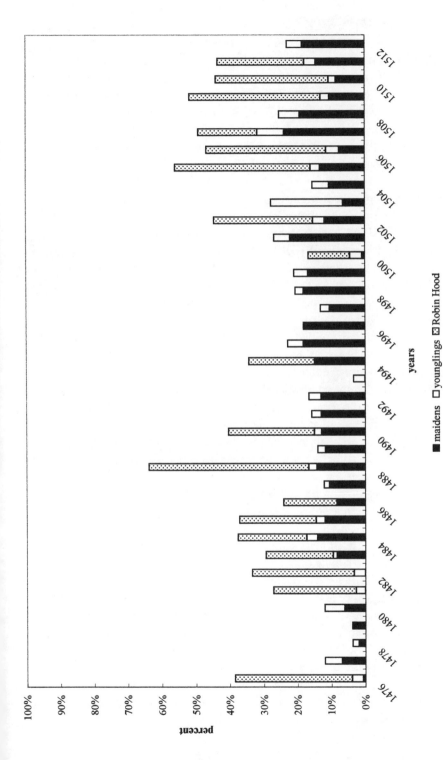

Figure 4.6b. Percentage of income from revels, Croscombe.

Other entertainment used in fundraising included a variety of activities such as revels, ales, and plays, which are historically associated with the pre-Reformation parish.[109] Although they are found in some form in most Somerset accounts, their use by rural parishes as fundraising activities is another way of distinguishing these from their more urbanized counterparts.[110] The forms of entertainment staged by parishioners also express some of their attitudes toward ecclesiastical duties. Although the sums earned over the fifteenth and sixteenth centuries suggest a continuing interest in the Church at the local level, the specific themes and figures invoked at parish gatherings provide some insight into the laity's feelings about parish involvement.

Robin Hood, a figure who accompanied some parish collections, is the most obvious example of social commentary.[111] There is a certain irony in linking Robin Hood with parish collections. Since he was an outlaw known for using his criminal activities to help those in need, what could be more worthy than convincing parishioners to support their church, even if it did feel like a shakedown? Giving the role of Robin Hood to the warden or some other prominent local figure added further bite to the revel by playing upon themes of inversion.[112] Through the Robin Hood revels, popular festivals linked up with local and national politics. The role-playing transformed the warden from an upstanding member of the parish into a bandit. The revel became a form of commentary on the growing financial needs of the parish and the wardens' continuing insistence that members offer their financial support. The laity generally supported their parish, but they did not do so blindly and submissively, and in some years it may have been with more resignation than outright enthusiasm.

Although Robin Hood's appearance at springtime festivals might harken back to ancient fertility rites, he is not an ancient figure dating back to pagan times. The earliest references to him date only to the fourteenth century.[113] The frequency of Robin Hood revels in Somerset provides a good example of how parishes used similar practices for different purposes. In some places, the character of Robin Hood appeared regularly as part of parish fundraising and entertainment, whereas other parishes used him intermittently to raise money for major projects. Robin Hood appears in the records of five parishes, all located in the southeastern portion of the county between the Parrett and Axe Rivers (see Map 4). Yeovil introduced this revel as part of a springtime collection at some point between 1458 and 1515, with a former churchwarden playing the role of Robin Hood.[114] Robin Hood organized the Whitsun ale and its accompanying entertainment and collected the money that the ale earned. He presented his earnings to the current churchwarden. James Stokes points out that "those integrated duties required a person who could be trusted, who could organize . . . , who knew the traditional entertainments . . . , and who could persuade parishioners to give him their hard-earned money."[115] The celebrations enveloped the entire parish, not just the core settlement around the town. The account for 1519 describes the activities: "Received of Richard Hacker that year being Robin Hood, by his good provision & diligent labors and by the good devotion of the town and country he presented to God & holy church £6 8s. ½d."[116] In 1516, the "good devotion of the town and country" that Robin Hood tapped brought in nearly 50 percent of the parish's total receipts, and these revels never earned below 20 percent of the total income in each subsequent appearance. It was a festival in which everyone could participate, not just the parish elite.

Robin Hood was also a frequent, but not annual, figure in Croscombe. In fact, the parish provides the earliest known "impersonation" of the character.[117] Here his May Day activities alone contributed anywhere from 12 to 47 percent of the parish's income (see Figure 4.6). The few notes provided by the accounts suggest that the Robin Hood revel included some sort of dress-up, with the cast of characters expanding over time. There was likely some sort of play or reenactment of a Robin Hood story, perhaps with a competition between dressed-up members of the parish. Initially two men, as representatives of the games, presented their money to the churchwardens. Sometimes we are given their real names; at other times only the revel characters are mentioned. The 1480/1 account records: "Comes John Halse and Roger Morris for Robin Hood's revel, presents in 40s. 4d."[118] In 1499/1500, the account states: "comes Robert Hode & Little John & presents in 15s."[119] Still later the accounts tell of Robin Hood and all his company presenting money from their sport.[120]

There is far less information about the other three Robin Hood revels. In the parish of St. Cuthbert in Wells, Robin Hood appeared with dancing girls in some sort of procession or pantomime. We cannot ascertain from the records how regular or important this activity was to the parish's finances, because we only hear about it when the festivities ran into trouble. In 1498, the money raised at the event disappeared. [121] The burgesses, in their capacity as parish overseers, apparently had subsidized the event and had lost track of the proceeds. The town council had to authorize an investigation into what had happened to the money. Two other parishes staged Robin Hood activities, but, in both cases, it was a singular occurrence that helped to raise money for a major renovation project. In 1512, the rural parish of Tintinhull received 11s. from "Robin Hood's Ale" that helped pay for new pews.[122] St. John's in Glastonbury held a Robin Hood revel in 1500 that earned the parish £8 7s. 8d., a handsome profit considering the 14s. they paid for costumes.[123] The parishioners were specifically raising money for new seats and for extensive restoration of their image of St. George.

The interplay of Robin Hood and St. George is another instance of lay commentary on parish life and is not unique to Glastonbury. As Robin Hood appeared less and less frequently among Croscombe's fundraising revels, the churchwardens replaced him with an ale held in honor of St. George. Like the figure of Robin Hood, St. George was a popular figure in spring festivals.[124] St. George was an eastern import to England and by the fifteenth century had come to be viewed as the protector of the English nation. Towns and parishes commonly recounted in plays and processions the story of his slaying the dragon to save the princess and town of Silene.[125] By juxtaposing these two characters, the parishioners comment on their relationship to the Church. Both figures serve as metaphors for parish activities and address the tension between the seemingly secular world of the churchyard and the sacred space of the nave. There was a tension between the parishioners' appropriation of folk images and celebrations for parish fundraising and the religious goal of maintaining the church and providing for the mass. The revels and other festivities parishioners held to raise money had long troubled the episcopal administration. In his statutes, Bishop Bitton had specifically called for an end to "dishonest games" or fights within the confines of the churchyard.[126] In the fifteenth-century didactic work *Dives and Pauper*, the clerical figure Pauper complains to the worldly character Dives about parishioners whose interests in the Church were more social than spiritual and who would "rather to hear a tale or a song of Robin Hood or of some ribaldry than to hear mass or matins or anything of God's service or any word of God."[127] The figures of Robin Hood and St. George help to reconcile this tension by defining "the carnivalized authority" of Robin Hood in terms of the devotional image of St. George.[128] We might even consider St. George an inversion of Robin Hood. They both have distinctly masculine behavior, but Robin Hood was of an indistinct social class, used a bow and arrow, and relied on trickery to achieve his goals. St. George, on the other hand, was presented as a noble of military bearing who used a sword and directly confronted his enemies. St. George also had more legitimacy because of his sainthood and royal patronage.[129] When the Croscombe wardens switched the springtime figure from Robin Hood to St. George, they were also symbolically representing their appropriation of fundraising obligations. Robin Hood was not a religious figure and his revel had taken place outside the direct control of the wardens and the parish. Individual parishioners in the guise of Robin Hood had collected money, which they turned over to the churchwardens, but the wardens had not apparently sponsored the revel. St. George, however, was a religious figure, and the Croscombe wardens ran the ale held on his feast day.[130]

The parishes that held Robin Hood revels in Bath and Wells lie in close proximity to each other. Wells, Croscombe, and Glastonbury are situated in the central part of the diocese, within easy traveling distance. Tintinhull and Yeovil are both on the southwestern edge of Bath and Wells. Thus, within one diocese we can identify a smaller area that shared certain practices. The earliest Robin Hood celebration took place in Croscombe, but interest could have spread from here to other parishes in the region, where different parishes adapted the revel to their specific needs.[131] The celebrations in the towns of Wells and Glastonbury were much larger affairs, whereas Tintinhull only held an ale. To be sure, the Tintinhull accounts are silent on what actually went on at the ale, but the wardens did not lay out money for the ale, and their accounts record only limited profit. Adopting the fundraising strategies of nearby parishes speaks to the laity's awareness of each parish's uniqueness. Local variation was part of community identity, but it did not mean that parishes did not learn from each other or imitate each other.

Only three parishes in Bath and Wells used other forms of dramatic activities, such as plays, to augment their annual income. Their infrequent use as fundraisers suggests that this role was of secondary importance. Much of what we know about medieval drama comes from the big mystery plays performed in cities such as Coventry and York. The large city productions, as part of a conscious celebration and demonstration of civic power and pride, were quite different from the smaller productions staged by parishes.[132] The plays that parishes sponsored were generally not as elaborate and involved more than local pride; the parishioners were often trying to raise money.[133] Plays earned money when the parish either charged admission or held a collection during the performance. The use of drama to raise money marks a shift in the use of public theater. The producers of the cycle plays, to our knowledge, meant to instruct and inspire but not to create profits.[134] Five parishioners in Tintinhull put on a Christmas play in 1451 that earned the parish 6s. 8d., which helped defer the extra expenses for a new rood screen.[135] In 1428, St. John's in Glastonbury was still paying off the debts incurred by the construction of the new parish church eight years earlier.[136] That year the parish hired William Doeret and "his society" (suis sociis) to put on a Christmas play. It earned the parish 8s. At midsummer, Walter Brewderer and "his society," put on a St. John's Day play that earned the parish 26s. 8d.[137] This second play was in honor of the parish's patron saint and appears to have been the more popular of the two. The better weather in June might also have attracted laity from surrounding parishes as well as pilgrims visiting the shrine at Glastonbury Abbey. Yeovil also turned to drama to raise its receipts. From its earliest account in 1457, this parish had held a Corpus Christi procession around the town which in 1540 they turned into a play that earned £3 5s. 11d.[138] The accounts provide no information as to why the parish produced a play this particular year or what financial concern they hoped it would cover.

The importance of theatrical activities to parish culture lay not only in their power to raise extra sums, but in their ability to assemble the parish and re-create its bonds and fissures. Revels such as Robin Hood, hogling, or Hocktide provided an opportunity for parishioners to examine social and gender issues that bound and divided the parish and were a part of the community's identity. A far more common combination of entertainment and fundraising was the church ale. In general, parishes that relied on rental property for their income did not hold ales, these were more of a rural than a town occurrence.[139] Not only were they financially successful, but they also demonstrated the close tie between sociability and religious experience on the local level. The ale might have had some major attraction such as a play or dance, but it also offered a chance to gossip, tell stories, and possibly compete in athletic competitions. People who worshipped together drank and socialized together.[140] An ale re-created the bonds of charity and community that ideally the laity had forged at mass. Churchwardens and other parishioners frequently attended a neighboring parish's ales. Such visits provided opportunities for local comparisons and community solidarity, while showing community conviviality and a spirit of neighborliness among parishes.[141] The parish of Yatton regularly contributed to the ales held at the nearby parishes of Ken, Kingston, Wrington, and Congresbury, which all supported Yatton in return.[142] Tintinhull's wardens went to nearby Stoke's ale, and Nettlecombe supported Monksilver's ale.[143]

Parishes generally held their ales in the spring and summer, on the feast days clustered around the first of May. This scheduling suggests links to old fertility religions and the importance of spring to an agrarian culture, but it was also when the weather improved, making it easier for visitors to come to the ale. Many parishes had ales at Pentecost or Whitsun (the seventh Sunday after Easter).[144] This holiday could fall anywhere from the beginning of May to the beginning of June (May 10—June 13). The ales falling after Easter picked up on the themes of charity and reconciliation that were so much a part of Lent and Easter. In Lent, the laity went to confession, and, once shriven, they could receive the Eucharist at Easter. Additional occasions for ales included the feasts of St. Philip and St. James (May 1), St. Margaret (July 20), St. Peter and St. Paul (June 29), Roodmas (May 3) and Hocktide (second Monday and Tuesday after Easter). Trull held its ale quite late in the season, on the feast of All Saints (November 1), but it was also its dedication day.

In general, Somerset parishes were very successful with their ales. Most parish ales retained or increased their income levels over the course of the fifteenth and sixteenth centuries. The one exception is Banwell, which had held an ale in the mid-fifteenth century, but by the time the churchwardens' accounts begin to survive in 1515, the parish had ceased to hold it.[145] For parishes holding ales, entertainment was their major source of annual income, so the success or failure of the festivities was crucial to the support and maintenance of various parish activities and projects. One ale a year was not usually enough to earn adequate funds; consequently, many parishes held multiple ones. The permanent or occasional addition of an extra ale demonstrates a sense of economic rationality on the part of parochial administrators. In 1499, Yatton had to hold two extra ales because Davy Gibbs had stolen the church plate the year before.[146] The parishioners not only had legal expenses but also had to replace the missing items.

Tintinhull began with only one ale, on the feast of their patron St. Margaret of Antioch (July 20). In 1447, after two years of low receipts, the parish held an additional ale on the feast of St. Philip and St. James (also May Day). For undisclosed reasons, the parish had held no St. Margaret's day celebrations for the previous three years (1445–47), and the parish cow, which had earned the parish upwards of 8s., became sterile.[147] The drop in income made these lean years for the parish.[148] The financial straits were not completely alleviated by a one-time extra ale, but when the Philip and James ale became an annual event in 1481, income levels returned the parish to prosperity (see Figure 4.4). This ale was so popular that it quickly outstripped the Margaret ale in profits. By the 1490s, the St. Margaret ale earned less than a pound, compared to the £2–3 earned by the St. Philip and St. James ale. In 1532, after the king deleted the feast of St. Margaret from the ecclesiastical calendar, however, the St. Margaret ale began earning more revenue and by 1547 the parish collected £3.[149] The ale allowed the parish to continue honoring their patron saint, even though she was no longer officially sanctioned. Similarly Nettlecombe, which already had a successful Pentecost ale, introduced a second one in 1536, which was held on one of the Virgin Mary's feast days.[150] The date of the new ale was probably not a coincidence either. Scheduling the new ale on a feast of the Virgin Mary was a way of commenting on, or protesting against, Henry VIII's religious policies that had rearranged the liturgical calendar and would eventually require the removal of the saint images from the churches (see Figure 4.5). The relatively small amount of money that the St. Mary's ale earned, compared to the increasing profits from the Whitsun ale, would seem to support the idea that there was more than a financial motive for holding it.

The cycle of successful ales at Yatton made good use of the parish's large population. Usually there were three ales a year—on Whitsun, Hocktide, and midsummer—each sponsored by one of the three hamlets of the parish: Yatton, Claverham, and Cleeve.[151] Dividing up the fundraising among the three villages helped to integrate this large parish, and the large population assured a good turnout and good profits. As in Tintinhull, income from Yatton's ales grew throughout the whole period, as did the parish's dependence on them for its income. Claverham's decision to hold its ale at Hocktide implies that they included Hocktide's accompanying activities. The midsummer ale at Cleeve might also have included a bonfire. In both cases, these activities would have helped increase attendance and profits. In 1521, the wardens added a minstrel to the Whitsun ale to add to the attraction, and income increased[152] (see Figure 4.7). The sums earned by these ales were substantial enough to pay for the construction of a large and elaborate nave, a new south porch, and a stone rood screen.[153] The ales provided a way for the whole parish to support the church in a convivial and active way that was expected and appreciated, unlike the "tax" imposed by Bridgwater.

At the same time that Tintinhull, Nettlecombe, and Yatton were having success with their ales, revenues from Stogursey's Whitsun ale stagnated in terms of both the absolute amount of money earned and of its importance to the parish's overall income. The financial problems of this small borough are reflected not only in the declining rents we saw earlier, but in diminished ale revenue as well. In difficult economic times, the parishioners perhaps had less money to spend at ales, but also by this point they may have been losing interest in parish activities. Stogursey's falling income could also be related to the increase in apathy and ambivalence noted by Whiting in his study of the Reformation in the diocese of Exeter. He argued that, although there was little outright interest in religious reform, the amount of money raised and spent by the laity on behalf of their parishes had declined.[154]

The reformers, like the bishops before them, condemned church ales as drunken, violent affairs. Reformers argued that holding ales on Sundays kept parishioners away from divine services.[155] Medieval church authorities had leveled this criticism as well.[156] During the Reformation, Protestants forced parishes to find alternative ways of supporting the parish. They could no longer rely on what the reformers defined as un-Christian behavior. Despite these problems, the Somerset ales did unite the community in the common purpose of supporting their parish.[157] The festive atmosphere added further incentive to come to the celebration.[158]

Financial Success

Fundraising shows the uniqueness of each parish and how it adapted to its setting. Geographic, legal, and economic differences played a major role in determining the parish's financial structure and the subsequent social and religious experiences of men and women. Fundraising helped create social bonds between the laity and their church that had underlying religious goals. Through the financial options available to each community, the parishioners themselves created a particular kind of parish life. Raising money at an ale was a substantially different experience from paying a tax or renting out houses to people who may not have been members of the parish. For rural parishioners, the parish was one of the primary forms of association. It served not only as a religious and liturgical center, but also a social and economic one as well. The diverse forms of fundraising reflect this central position. The town offered urban parishioners far more diversions. Town parishes competed with other forums of social life and activity and other venues of religious expression. Thus, borough parishes relied upon the experience of the wardens and raised money in a way that minimized their parishioners' direct participation. Their fundraising practices reflect the advantages offered by a borough economy and minimize the liability they would incur if they had to directly compete with the other entertainment offered by the borough and associations within it.

Lay organization had important social and material consequences for the men and women of a parish. Over the course of the fifteenth and early sixteenth centuries, fundraising strategies multiplied and parish income grew. Parish administrators became more comfortable in organizing lay religious life, and this confidence translated into larger projects that required more income. Although not all parishes had the same level of financial success, from the fourteenth through the early sixteenth centuries most parishes showed an overall growth in their receipts. We can see this growth especially in communities with long runs of churchwardens' accounts, such as Tintinhull, Bath, and Yatton, whose accounts all span more one hundred years. Overall, Tintinhull's income in the 1430s was £1–2; by the end of the century it had doubled. This growth continued through the 1530s and 1540s (£5–7 a year). This is not a large amount of money, but Tintinhull was a small rural parish; its growth shows both the commitment of its community and the skill of its administrators. The income for St. Michael's in Bath grew even more rapidly, from only £4–5 in the fourteenth century to £11–12 in the sixteenth (see Figure 4.8). All three parishes kept up with inflation.

The expansion of parish economies in Bath and Wells contrasts with the experiences laid out by Robert Whiting in his study of the Reformation in Exeter. Although decline is visible in Stogursey, and probably happened in Bridgwater, it does not appear to be typical of all parishes, especially the rural ones. To be sure, the Reformation changed parish celebrations and made financial success quite difficult for many parishes. Reformers curtailed their traditional entertainments and fundraising events, making it difficult to meet the community's financial and social needs.[159] These changes to parish finances do not appear in Bath and Wells until the reign of Edward VI; until then, the laity appear very willing to participate in parish fundraising.

The criticism that parish activities received from religious authorities is,

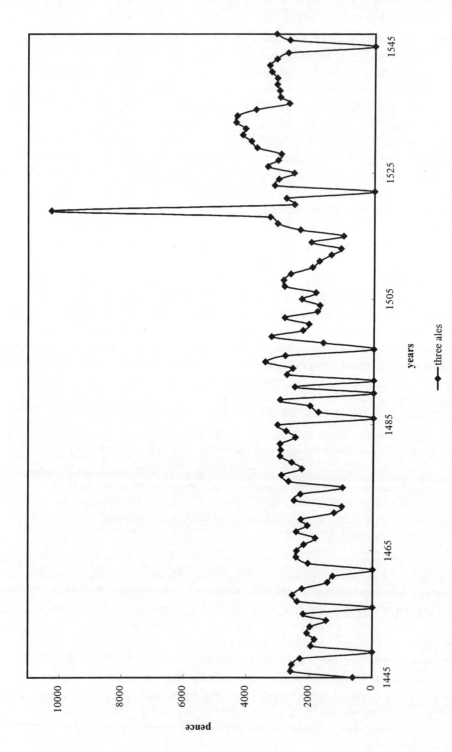

Figure 4.7a. Income from ales, Yatton.

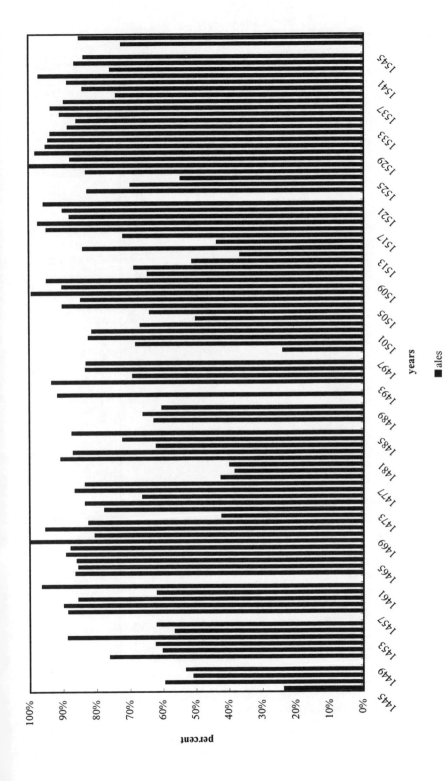

Figure 4-7b. Percentage of income from ales, Yatton.

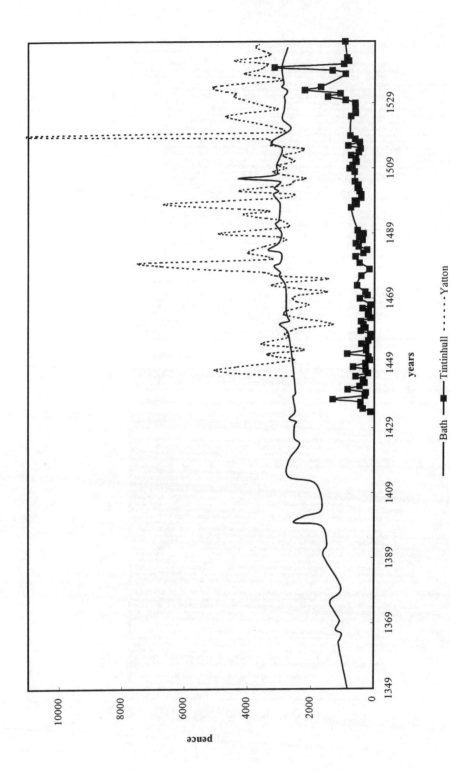

Figure 4.8. Total income, Bath, Tintinhull, and Yatton.

——Bath ——■——Tintinhull ----- Yatton

then, perhaps ironic. Certainly, the commercial, and often alcoholic, behavior displayed at parochial activities in and around the church brought about scandal, violence, and sacrilege.[160] The thirteenth-century episcopal statutes for Bath and Wells warned about clerical involvement in parish ales, lest the priest get drunk and set a bad example for the rest of the parish.[161] In the fifteenth century, John Mirk echoed these concerns when he warned parish priests of the dangers of gluttony at ales. He specifically instructed the priest to ask his parishioners during confession whether they had been guilty of this sin at these occasions.[162] Yet, despite these concerns, it was the requirements laid down by the bishops that the laity maintain their parishes which initiated such social and economic activities. These in turn perpetuated the blurred distinction between secular and sacred activities that worried many religious authorities. As far as parishioners were concerned, their ales and rents served for the greater celebration and decoration of the church and manifested the sense of community that their priests so strongly encouraged. Glastonbury's use of Robin Hood to help pay for the St. George statue suggests not only a shared folklore and oral heritage, but also a close connection in the minds of the parishioners between the activities in the church and those in the churchyard.

$\int$ "CURIOUS WINDOWS AND GREAT BELLS"

The Architecture of Community

The Parish Church

In the anonymous fifteenth-century work *Dives and Pauper*, the author sets up a conversation between the clerical character of Pauper and the worldly Dives about the ten commandments. The ensuing discussion is a rich source of information about what the clergy understood to be the tensions and concerns of late medieval religious behavior. One concern was that pious observances would become sources of pride. All too often, Pauper warns, the tradition of collective worship inspires competition, because the laity imbued their worship with local concerns. We see something of this tension in their discussion of churches. Those building the church might be tempted to spend large sums of money on church adornment, which might be better spent on feeding the poor. Dives tells Pauper, "I think that it would be better to give money to poor folks: to the blind and the lame whose souls God bought so dearly, than it is to spend it in solemnity and pride on building a church or rich vestments or curious windows and great bells."[1] Pauper counters by explaining that one should not spend money on a church for prideful reasons, but rather with the intent of glorifying God. He goes on to explain that both the Old and New Testaments justified the expense of building a beautiful place of worship.[2] Even the widow's mite, given in support of the church, was a valuable and pious contribution, more important in the eyes of God than the rich man's gift. Pauper argues that a beautiful church should be a source of comfort and succor to all, and the support of the church was for all Christians, not just the rich. As we will see, these concerns are not misplaced. Parishioners built into their churches and their churches' furnishings all manner of local and personal priorities.

Throughout the late middle ages, many parishes within Somerset and throughout England rebuilt or expanded their parish churches with community worship in mind. The resulting buildings embody both sacred and profane motivations and both collective and individual concerns. Although the church was a sacred space where men and women received the sacraments, it was also a gathering place for social functions. The parish church was thus much more than a place for the liturgy; it played a role in the local economy and the social life of the area. The design of a church made it unique, as did the location, the method of financing it, and the means of administering it. The parish church concurrently reflected local aspirations and the shared Christian life.[3] Inscribed into each building were a parish's ideas about its place in the village or town. In the church and churchyard the "supernatural and the every-day overlapped."[4]

The church building itself was a parish's biggest expense. The damp English weather was hard on stone buildings; the freezing, thawing, and constant moisture eroded the masonry and its fittings. Parish churches required only walls, a roof, a floor, and effective gutters, but because the ultimate goal was the proper performance of the mass, parishioners and clergy alike wanted a suitable home for the host and a worthy monument to God. What constituted proper and suitable, however, continually evolved as fashions changed, fortunes grew, and communities redefined the boundaries between honor and God. Over the course of the late middle ages, parishioners updated their stained glass windows and rood screens and installed pew benches, new bells, new clocks, and sometimes an organ. Reaching this goal involved both collective action and individual wealth.

The resulting architecture and interior furnishings reflect a parish's evolving ideas about its community identity. Building and furnishing the parish church bound the parishioners together through shared discussions of expectations, fundraising, work, and building use. The entire process required cooperation. The number and tone of the bells, the height of the tower, and the overall size and splendor of the church and its decorations provided different focal points for celebrating the glory of God and for advancing local pride. As they built and repaired their own unique church building and supplied the items for the mass that regularly assembled them together, the parishioners continually confronted what it meant to belong to the parish. Thus, the parish church's layout reflects what it meant to be both a Christian and a parishioner, and what role the parishioners expected their parish to play in their lives. As with other aspects of parish life, however, it is easier to see the priorities of the wealthy than those of the poor.

At the same time that church architecture projected an identity and image to all who viewed it, the parishioners sought to affirm the distinctions that comprised the membership. The parish included men and women of all ages from a variety of social classes. Parishioners not only wanted their building to reflect these distinctions, they incorporated them into their religious behavior. Social and sexual differences determined one's place in religious processions, seating arrangements, and the cemetery.[5] As the laity both expanded and furnished their churches, they inscribed into the building and displayed in the liturgy their competing ideas of self-aggrandizement and charity. When we consider how the church's space reproduced the parish's social and gender hierarchies, we see that parishes were far from egalitarian and not always harmonious.[6] This realization, however, should not distract us from thinking of the parish as a community, or of parish involvement as less than a collective concern. Parishioners brought multiple identities to their status as parishioner. These identities in turn became a part of the community's identity. How a parish chose to use the space in and around the church expressed to members and visitors alike a public image and a community identity.

Construction and Maintenance

As we have already seen, episcopal statutes from the thirteenth century had mandated that the laity provide certain liturgical items such as a chalice, candlesticks, and a sacring bell for an acolyte to ring at the consecration. The statutes also explained that the laity were responsible for the nave and the clergy for the chancel. Otherwise, the bishop was silent on what a church needed to look like. Tradition, however, helped parishioners decide how they should lay out their churches and what they should contain. The churches in Bath and Wells developed their own regional style of church architecture, and the churches in this area constitute some of the most spectacular examples of perpendicular gothic architecture.[7] The tall west tower often distinguishes Somerset churches; as a rule, these towers are rectangular, without spires, and crowned with pinnacles.[8] Art historians of Somerset churches identify eight separate classifications or schools of towers, which not only reflect the work of individual artisans working in particular regions of Somerset, but also the fact that parishioners imitated each other and sought to copy successful designs.[9]

Somerset possesses several types of building stone, but four types dominated church building.[10] England's "geological backbone," a belt of oolite, runs along the eastern portion of the diocese starting in the north, near Bath. This oolite belt supplied both the gray stone out of which the parishioners in the Mendip region built their churches and the yellow stone common in churches in the southern part of the diocese. The best and most famous of this yellow stone comes from quarries at Ham Hill. To the west of the oolite belt lies softer and coarser lias stone and to the west of that, in the area encompassed by Bridgwater and Taunton, is red sandstone. Neither material is suitable for fine, detailed carving, and the parishioners in the south-central part of the county either imported stone for this purpose or left it off their churches altogether. Because of the difficulty of transport, builders sought to use as much local stone as possible, thus giving churches distinctive regional colors.

Parishioners themselves provided much of the basic labor needed to maintain the parish church on a day-to-day basis. Men carried out most of the trade-based labor, such as masonry, carpentry, plumbing, and glazing, necessary for regular maintenance. Women did work similar to what they did at home. They cleaned the church, washed the altar cloths, and sometimes mended the old ones or made new ones.[11] In Yatton, Joan Beme mended the altar cloths, and for many years the clerk's wife did the parish laundry.[12] For the specialized work needed to build or renovate a church, parishioners looked to the larger towns of Bridgwater, Bristol, Taunton, Bath, and even Exeter. When the parish of St. John's, in Glastonbury, built new pews in 1500, they hired a carver all the way from Bristol.[13] When rural Yatton set out to rebuild its nave, it drew upon the resources of communities throughout the northern half of the diocese as well as the cities of Bristol and Southampton.[14] Artisans from outside the parish were part of the network that spread artistic trends from one parish to the next. Along with the mendicants who moved from parish to parish preaching sermons and hearing confessions, artisans' experiences in other parishes helped to introduce new ideas. The parishioners may have outlined what they wanted, but there was still room for individual artists to influence style and presentation.

Architectural historians have identified post-plague England as a boom time for parish church construction. The reasons for this expansion are both economic and cultural. Many scholars look to a crisis of faith brought on by the Black Death and the rapid social and economic changes that followed the fourteenth century as helping to explain this development.[15] The doctrine of Purgatory, which became much more important in the late middle ages, held that living Christians could act to help save the souls of their departed loved ones through intercessory prayers and good works. For some Christians, this also became a way to add extra security for their own salvation. Whatever the motives, the parish church was often the recipient of such actions, because, as we saw in the last chapter, work on the church was a good work that benefited the souls of the community, both living and dead.[16] The combination of increased concern for one's salvation and the availability of money for patronage, on either an individual or a communal level, encouraged the expansion and decoration of local churches. Also, by the late middle ages, many churches were simply old and decrepit and needed rebuilding, regardless of the community's religious or economic situation. Decrepit or not, many parishes rebuilt their churches during this period, and the resulting buildings reflect an exuberance and commitment to the parish and all that it represented.

As often the largest building in the village or town, the parish church did far more than simply house the liturgy; it symbolically represented the community of the parish both to its members and to outsiders.[17] The buildings did this in many different ways. Most obvious are Somerset's tall "liturgically useless" west towers, which announced that the church was much more than a place to celebrate the mass.[18] Their domination of the landscape made them beacons to local travelers coming up to the town or village from a distance. One gets a sense of this scene from John Leland's *Itinerary* when he describes the town of Minehead, a parish on the north coast of Somerset. He writes: "the fairest part of the town stands at the bottom of an hill. The rest runs steeply up a long hill, at the top there is a fair parish church."[19] In 1484, the merchant adventurers of Bristol took advantage of the local penchant for tall towers and financed a new tower for the church of Dundry, a parish on the Somerset coast of the Bristol Channel. According to an inscription in the church, the tower served as a "seamark" for mariners coming into the port at Bristol.[20]

Housed in the towers were as many as eight bells. Both the bells and the tower served as forms of self-promotion. Although canon law required only the sacring bell, which was often a hand bell, the money and care lavished on both bells and towers shows them to be important features of the parish church.[21] A traveler might hear the church bells before seeing the tower. Parishioners worked to have distinctive bells, and the quality of their sound was a source of local pride.[22] The bells marked the hours, summoned the community to worship or for an emergency, and drove away the devils present during thunderstorms. [23] They came to symbolize individual parishes. We get a sense of this feeling in two Chancery cases from outside Bath and Wells. In both instances the plaintiffs make the connection between local pride and the church bells' sound. The problem confronting both parishes was that the bell founders were unable to fulfill the parishioners' requirements for the bells' tone. The plaintiffs, probably the churchwardens, from the parish of Basingstoke in Hampshire, stated that in 1506 they had contracted with a bell founder who "agreed . . . that the said bells should well truly & sufficiently accord, agree, & ring in good perfect tone with other bells then being within the said parish church of Basingstoke."[24] The parishioners from Harlington, Middlesex, sometime in the 1530s, also wanted the sound of the new bell to match the old one so they "delivered . . . unto one John Fford citizen & bell founder of London one bell . . . weighing eight hundred pounds weight to the purpose & intent that the said John Fford should newly caste & make the said bell to agree in the treble note & sound to four other bells in the same parish yet hanging."[25] After consideration, the Basingstoke parishioners decided that "that the greater bell of [the] 2 new bells did not accord nor agree in perfect tone with the other bells" and they wanted their money back.[26] The peal, unique to each community, was part of what identified a parish, and a mismatched sound was unpleasant and humiliating. The sentiments expressed in these two cases do not appear to be particularly regional ones. Although no similar court cases survive for Bath and Wells, parishioners there still manifested pride in their bells as markers of their community. The men and women of Shepton Mallet all remembered the church bells in their wills.[27]

So strongly did some identify with their bells that conflicts erupted over the bell-ringing schedules of adjacent churches. In 1424, after much controversy, the bishop of Bath and Wells had to regulate when the Bath parish of St. Mary de Stalles and the abbey of Bath could ring their bells, so they would not interfere with each other.[28] The bells of the abbey and those of the parish marked out different worship schedules, and the monks claimed that the parish's bells interfered with their liturgy. Competition could be especially fierce when the laity and monks shared the same church building, as was the case with the priory of Dunster. A fourteenth-century ruling made the priory responsible for most of the building, including the roof and tower. Nevertheless, in 1442, the parishioners, acting alone, contracted with a stonemason to build a new bell tower.[29] The contract makes no mention of the priory's earlier responsibility to "repair and roof the tower suitably and without defects."[30] Sometime between 1484 and 1494, the priory brought suit against the parishioners in the Court of the Star Chamber.[31] The prior requested "remedy of certain great and grievous injuries and hurts ministered unto the prior [and] cell of Dunster . . . where the inhabitants there being right riotous and people of full erroneous disposition."[32] The parish's rebellion included parishioners consecrating holy water without monastic permission, withholding funeral and wedding offerings, and refusing to pay the fee for a license to bury their dead in the churchyard. As a final insult, the parishioners also stole the bell ropes and said that "the prior and convent there should have no bells there to ring."[33] Without the ropes, the monks could not mark their hours and call the monks to worship. Stealing bell ropes was not the most serious offense, but the bells symbolized the different schedules, priorities, and lifestyles of the two feuding parties. The bells, which hung in the tower that the parishioners had built, had become a symbol of the dispute. They and the tower defined the opposing interests of the two groups.

Because the church edifice represented an important manifestation of a community's identity as well as a sanctified place where one could receive sacramental grace and pray for one's soul and the souls of one's family and neighbors, parishioners spent a great deal on the building and furnishing of their church. Although they were responsible only for the nave and churchyard, these two spaces encompassed other elements of the church building such as the bell tower, side altars, and aisles. The churchwardens' accounts often chronicle the rebuilding or renovation of the parish church.[34] When we read this information against the economic and administrative conditions surrounding such building projects, we can see how each church building has its own local significance. When parishes chose to alter or expand their nave, aisles, or chapels, they also declared what was important to the parish socially, economically, and liturgically.

The motives behind rebuilding and expanding a parish church varied. Some, like St. Mary's Bridgwater, were adapted and modified in bits and pieces over the course of a century (Figure 5.1). Others, such as St. John's, Glastonbury or St. John's, Yeovil, were rebuilt all at once (Figures 5.2, 5.3). The end results are churches with differing appearances. When we compare the processes of rebuilding these churches we can see how the final product reflects specific local circumstances and organizations. The church of St. Mary's in Bridgwater is essentially of twelfth- and thirteenth-century construction, but attached to various points in the nave are numerous chapels of later construction. Starting in 1364, the parish paid Bristol mason Nicholas Waleys and his two helpers, John Aleyn and John Beter, nearly £100 to build a steeple onto the twelfth-century tower.[35] Whereas the tower was made of the lesser quality red sandstone quarried in nearby Wembdon, Waleys used the more desirable yellow Ham Hill stone for the steeple.[36] Prosperity from the wool trade meant that the parish could now afford higher quality building materials from farther away.[37] Bridgwater's location as a port on the Parrett River made transportation of the stone that much easier. Until the modern period, this steeple was the focal point for the surrounding landscape. Nine years after the steeple's construction, in 1373, the merchant guild paid for additional tower repairs, as well as a new roof and a clock.[38] Over the course of the next century, the parishioners added numerous chapels to their thirteenth-century nave. In 1385, the parish built a charnel house with an All Saints chapel on the second floor.[39] Sometime around 1414, the guild merchant loaned the parish money to build a new Holy Trinity chapel.[40] Between 1415 and 1420, the parish planned and built a chapel to St. Anne.[41] Six years later, the parish built another new chapel dedicated to St. George and expanded and renovated the St. Mary's chapel.[42] By 1471, the last surviving pre-Reformation account, there were eight identifiable chapels in this church. The continual addition of chapels reflects the town's economic prosperity and growing interest in new devotions; both St. Anne and St. George became very popular in the late middle ages.[43] By exploiting this prosperity with their collection system, the parish administrators could afford to adapt their church to changing devotional fashions.

Although pride and changing devotional fashions inspired many an addi-

Figure 5.1. St. Mary's, Bridgwater. Photograph by Katherine L. French.

tion, practical considerations also came into play, and they often produced different architectural results. St. John's in Glastonbury underwent complete reconstruction in the fifteenth century because of a series of disasters. The surviving medieval church attests to the community's willingness to deal collectively with its difficulties. The parishioners completely rebuilt their church

Figure 5.2. St. John's, Glastonbury. Photograph courtesy of Dr. Christopher Wilson.

Figure 5.3. St. John's, Yeovil. Photography courtesy of National Monuments Record Centre.

and arrived at a far more integrated style of architecture than the church of St. Mary's in Bridgwater. The first crisis came in 1407, when a fire destroyed the St. Nicholas aisle.[44] Whether this served as the impetus to rebuild the entire church is not clear, but in 1428 the accounts refer to expenses made around the new church and the need to acquire more stone from the quarry at Doulting.[45] Glastonbury's building woes did not end here. Around 1465, a pinnacle fell from the roof into the nave, causing further damage. The parish took this opportunity to outfit at least a portion of the nave with new seats.[46] When the parish finished its renovations, it had built the second-tallest west tower in Somerset, possibly as an attempt at rivaling the powerful abbey with whom they shared their town (Figure 5.2).[47] The parish's misfortune required a collective response, and the parishioners made that response an opportunity to work out some of their competition with the abbey.

Population growth was another practical concern that motivated building expansion. St. Michael's in Bath underwent major renovation at the end of the fourteenth and early fifteenth centuries because the original church could no longer accommodate the growing number of worshipers who were moving to this portion of the city. In the 1390s the community extended its nave, possibly rebuilding most of the church.[48] In 1425, the parish enlarged its St. Mary's chapel. Finally, sometime around 1442, William Philyps, a parishioner, began building a new St. Katherine's chapel, and he left money and instructions in his will for his executors to finish it.[49] The guild of St. Katherine had its own chapel in the center of town, and it enjoyed the membership and patronage of many prominent members of the city. Building a chapel to a saint held in high esteem by the burgesses brought this parish into line with the city's larger civic culture. It might also have reflected the increase in prominent parishioners now living in the parish. The medieval church no longer remains. St. Michael's has been entirely rebuilt twice since the Reformation.[50]

When we consider the history of this particular parish combined with the way it raised money, we can see that the new building did not reflect the same kind of group effort that Bridgwater's did. St. Michael's was a relatively new parish, founded only in the thirteenth century and, therefore, was not a parish with an ancient heritage.[51] As we saw in the last chapter, this parish raised money quite successfully by leasing out property. Taken together, these characteristics suggest that the parish was not particularly integrated. Rather, the new and expanding building seems to have reflected the interests of a few, such as William Philyps. At St. Michael's, when new families moved into the area, they interacted with a building with which they had no common history and which they did not build. The liturgy performed in this space, with its message of charity and reconciliation, thus had to do more work of incorporation than it would have in other parishes, where incorporation and association also grew out of other activities such as ales and long-term interaction.

Rebuilding a church was not only a town parish concern. Many rural parishes rebuilt their churches in spectacular style. The parish of Yatton rebuilt their nave on a large and elaborate scale that is well out of proportion to the tiny chancel (Figure 5.4). This awkward arrangement highlights the division of responsibility between the parishioners and their clergy.[52] Here, the parish's interest outstripped that of the rector. Constructing it required economic sacrifice, commitment, and the resources that a big population could muster. In this former minster parish, with a population of 500, the churchwardens could look to larger numbers of parishioners rather than a few individuals with great wealth for the success of this project. Funding came almost exclusively from the cycle of church ales and not from wealthy patrons. A general chronology of construction would seem to indicate that the community rebuilt the chapel of St. James in 1447.[53] The tower and porch were built in the 1450s and the nave probably in the 1470s.[54] At the end of the century, the local gentry

Figure 5.4. St. Mary's, Yatton. Photograph courtesy of Fren H. Crossley and Maurice H. Ridgway F.S.A.

family, the Newtons, built their second family chapel, while Isabel Newton served as churchwarden. This chapel they dedicated to St. John the Evangelist.[55] The finished church had a large and elaborate perpendicular gothic nave with a central tower.

Not all parishioners had to work so hard to rebuild their church. Some had wealthy patrons who wished to turn the parish church into their own private memorial. The church at Yeovil serves as just one of many such instances. Here the local patron was the rector, Robert Samborne, a canon of Wells. He rebuilt the parish church probably as a personal memorial, but also perhaps as a way of either reconciling or confronting the town's burgesses with whom he had quarreled for several years. Samborne and the townspeople had fought over his rights as rector and lord of the town, and Samborne had won.[56] Rebuilding the church continued to show his influence, wealth, and power in the town, but it also might have ameliorated the situation. As rector he had responsibility only for the chancel, but by rebuilding the entire church, he not only achieved a unified architectural design, he offered a gift to the parishioners (Figure 5.3). He started rebuilding the church in the mid-fourteenth century. When he died in 1382, he left most of his goods to pay for finishing the church.[57] Construction apparently was finished without incident, suggesting some residual good will on the part of the parish. As a canon of Wells, Samborne occupied a position where he could know of and hire a noted architect. The church at Yeovil, with its body of lais and its fittings of Ham Hill stone, was possibly the work of master mason William Wynford, who had previously designed the nave of Winchester Cathedral, New College in Oxford, and the western towers at Wells Cathedral.[58] St. John's Yeovil, like St. John's Glastonbury, is all of one uniform and integrated style.

The size of the nave had implications for liturgical practices. In large churches, with large populations, those in the back stood or sat farther from the priest's activities in the chancel and perhaps paid less attention to him. When he elevated the host, it was more difficult for the parishioners to see. Proscriptive literature often complained about inattentive worshippers who, oblivious to the liturgy, carried out conversations during the mass. In the fourteenth century, John Mirk in his *Instructions for Parish Priests* writes that the priest must teach the laity how to behave in church. They are not to talk to each other and lean against the walls or pillars, ignoring what the priest is doing in the chancel.[59] The experiences of those attending smaller parish churches such as Trull, Tintinhull, and Croscombe might dampen some of this criticism, because the smaller naves made the mass a more intimate experience. It was possible for those in the back to have a better idea of what the priest was doing, and it was more difficult to ignore the sermon.

The laity's expectations for their parish went beyond the liturgy, and they demonstrated these expectations in their parish architecture—both the church and its outbuildings. Whether the parishioners of Bath and Wells were expanding their church or building a church house, they built their local priorities into the structure. To some degree they reflected local interpretations of the liturgy and what they as a community wanted to emphasize and facilitate. A large church held many people and presented an imposing edifice to the outsider. It showed that the parish had money, raised either on its own initiative or with the generosity of a patron.

Lay and Clerical Space: Rood Screens

The appearance of the church's exterior of the church reflected the importance of collective action to the parish community. The layout of the interior reflected this as well, but it also reproduced the organization and interaction of the men and women who made up the parish. The most obvious demarcation of space was between the nave and the chancel, which were the separate purviews of the laity and clergy, respectively. Beyond that, however, the laity further divided the nave: the gentry had private chapels and chantries that were off limits to the rest of the membership, men and women sat in their own sections for the liturgy, and parish guilds carved out places for their chapels, lights, and other venerations, effectively assuming control of these areas. Looking at how parishes divided up their naves shows something of how the various parts of the parish membership came together to form a community and how a community's identity incorporated status and gender into it.

The locally-specific floor plans and interior arrangements of chapels, seats, and side altars worked to make the liturgy a unique experience for each parish. The celebration of the Christian liturgy can never be removed from the specific locale and all its attendant resources and limitations.[60] Played out in an arena with its own history and social composition, the liturgy was a site for the interaction of local and universal concerns. Part of what made each liturgy unique were the processions. Prior to the start of the mass, a procession of the parish clergy prepared the church by sprinkling all the altars with salt and holy water.[61] Another procession preceded the reading of the Gospel, and during the evening service of vespers, there was a final procession.[62] The route of the procession imitated as closely as possible the route followed in the cathedral. The clergy in order of rank walked out of the chancel through the south chancel aisle, down the south aisle, up the central aisle, down the north aisle, and back up the central aisle to the chancel. Parish churches without all these aisles had to adapt their processions.[63] In small churches without any side aisles or chancel aisles, the clergy presumably walked out of the chancel and up and down the central aisle of the nave. In churches with only a north or south aisle, the procession incorporated it into its peregrinations. As the laity filled their nave with pews, chapels, and side altars, they shaped the route of the liturgical processions and compelled the clergy to acknowledge their social concerns, while caring for their spiritual ones.

By the late middle ages, a rood screen dominated the interior.[64] Rood screens are a good place to begin to see how the laity's control of the nave shaped the liturgy in locally specific ways. This elaborately carved fence divided the nave from the chancel; its position in the church defined the status of those attending mass as either clerical or lay. The rood screen supported the crucifix, with statues of St. Mary and St. John on either side.[65] Also on top of the screen there was often a loft which housed the organs and possibly a chapel. The parishioners covered the solid bottom half of the rood screen, called the dado, with paintings of saints. There also might be some side altars against the dado dedicated to the saints. The upper half they left open, so that those in the nave could see what was happening in the chancel. As a divider of the church into nave and chancel, and as a backdrop for side altars, the rood screen holds in tension the laity's relationship to the mass. On the one hand, it separated the laity from the sacred space housing the host and the priest; on the other, its side altars familiarized the laity with the mass and the liturgy. The elaborate carvings and decorations on the screen seem to express the awe and admiration with which the laity regarded the host regardless on which side of the screen they saw it.[66] As a feature in the liturgical process, it served to integrate as well as separate the high altar from the rest of the church and its accompanying side altars. The priest had to walk through this barrier to start his procession. If the loft had an altar, it and its priest had to be incorporated into the processional route. If there were altars along the dado, they too had to be integrated into the procession. In this way, the reasons behind the foundation of these altars became integrated into the liturgy.

Today, most surviving screens remain in either East Anglia or in Devon. Each area has its own style. That portion of Somerset that borders Devon also has a number of surviving screens, and they share many of the characteristics of Devon screens. The West-Country-style screens, such as those still found in Minehead, Trull, Halse, and Dunster (see Figure 5.5) are intricately carved with fan vaulting, canopies, and long projecting cornices that supported the loft.[67] They span the width of the church in an unbroken line, separating not only the chancel from the nave, but also any chapels in the east end of the north and south aisles. West-Country screens often had doors with locks, a reminder of where the laity's responsibilities began. Somerset also has another style of screen, which is plainer and has no fan vaulting. These simpler styles are also found in screens from the Midlands.[68] In these screens, represented by those that still survive in Nunney, Mells, and Congresbury, the panels are square-headed, and the screen dividing the laity from the chancel is separate from the lower ones dividing off the north and south aisles from their chapels. The variation in style speaks as much to parish wealth and vision as it does to artistic networks.

The construction of a rood screen attracted pious bequests from individual parishioners, from groups such as guilds, and from the parish as a whole. In Croscombe, Richard Maudley, a wealthy clothier, contracted to build the church a rood loft, which would have housed an altar or chapel for a guild or as a memorial to Maudley and his family.[69] The size and presentation of this gift powerfully demonstrated individual piety. The saints, lights, and altars along the rood screen also attracted bequests. A Frome weaver, William Jorden, left money in his will to ten different lights dedicated to different saints. It is likely that at least some of these saints were paintings on the dado of the rood

Figure 5.5. Rood screen, St. George's, Dunster. Photograph courtesy of National Monuments Record Centre.

screen.[70] Unfortunately, these screens and their decorations no longer survive, so we cannot see the specifics of each man's pious interests.

Most rood screens were wooden, and parishes had to replace them periodically. Information survives detailing the construction of nine rood screens in Bath and Wells.[71] Not only do the records show the time, effort, and expense that went into making the screens, but also they note the artisans who built them. Rural parishes had to look to the towns for artisans capable of doing the delicate carving typical of West-Country screens. When the parish of Trull built a new screen for its church between 1536 and 1539, both the carver and much of the expensive oak timber and wainscoting came from Bridgwater.[72] When the parishioners of Banwell wanted a new rood screen in 1521, they drafted the plans themselves but hired a carver from Bristol.[73] He apparently built it in his workshop and then moved it in pieces to the church for installation. [74] The painter also came from Bristol, but as his work at this point was largely cosmetic, he only received 2s. 8d. for his efforts.[75] He probably did the major painting and gilding in Bristol, where he was perhaps working as a subcontractor to the carver. To celebrate the new rood screen and venerate the images on it, the parish decorated it with branches on its first All Saints day in 1521.[76]

The conflict between the monks and parishioners at Dunster shows how important the rood screen could be as the demarcation point for lay and clerical space.[77] In this case the concern was not with the parish clergy, but with the monks who also used the church. Some fifty years after the parishioners built their tower, and only a few years after they stole the bell ropes, the laity again came into conflict with the priory. As we saw in Chapter 1, this was not the end of the story. In April 1498, the monks and parishioners assembled before the court of the bishop of Bath and Wells.[78] The two sides disagreed over the schedule of services, control of the offerings and tithes, and maintenance of the building. The vicar, William Bonde, wanted more clarification of his rights and privileges with regard to the monastery. The monks felt that the parochial processions in and around the choir interfered with their services. In the end, a six-part agreement addressed the vicar's relationship with the priory, but the settlement, which also divided the church, dramatically reorganized relations between the monks and laity. The division of the church gave the monks the chancel and choir and gave the parishioners the nave. Now that each group controlled half of the building, they modified each section to suit their respective needs. The parishioners erected a new rood screen to create a new chancel, and the monks expanded the old choir and chancel, making it comparable in size to the ninety-foot section now controlled by the parishioners (Figure 5.5).[79] When both groups adapted architectural features to ensure the proper performance of the mass, they inscribed in the building itself their rivalry and antagonism. The church was no longer just a place to act out hostilities, but a physical representation of the antagonistic relationship that characterized and organized the two religious communities. The conflict became more than a part of their shared history; it was now always present in the church's construction, floor plan, and new rood screen.[80]

The changing prescriptions for how the two groups were to use the building renegotiated their relationship, not just legally and financially, but also physically, liturgically, and ritually. The vicar and his successors were to celebrate divine services without the prior's interference at the altar of St. James. This meant that the vicar could now perform high mass for the parishioners, whereas before the prior had been the main celebrant. The vicar was also to bless all the bread, wine, and candles for the feast of the Purification, ashes for Ash Wednesday, and flowers and greenery used by the parishioners for decorations. He also could consecrate both the holy water and all the offerings received by the vicar from the parishioners on behalf of the prior and monks. The vicar and his parishioners could conduct any procession in the nave or churchyard on all feast days except the thirteen major ones.[81] On these occasions the monks and parishioners would march together in a joint procession around the church interior or, weather permitting, the churchyard.

With changes in the liturgy came changes in the processional order. Before the bishop's court divided the church, the parishioners and monks joined in a common liturgy and procession. The fourteenth-century attempt to mediate between these two squabbling groups had required that the prior and the monks, followed by the vicar, "unite in one procession to begin Mass."[82] The order of the procession and the way that the clergy conducted mass affirmed the parish's subservience. "On festivals the vicar may begin mass privately at the altar of the Holy Rood for the parishioners after the Gospels have been read at High Mass."[83] The prior presided over the major services. Although the groups shared space and shared support of the building, their relationship was organized hierarchically, with the prior as the dominant cleric. The 1498 agreement specified a new processional order. Instead of placing the parish clergy at the end of the procession in the position of least importance, the new order integrated the two groups, alternating personnel from the priory and the parish. This new order expressed a new understanding of the balance of power. First came the priory's crucifer, then the parish's crucifer, then the vicar and the parish clerks, followed by the prior and monks. Finally, came the parishioners in order of status. The processional order kept the parish and priory in opposition, but neither side dominated the other. The priory's crucifer came before the parish's, but the vicar came ahead of the prior. The old procession had taken place at every high mass, stressing monastic superiority within a shared enclosure. The new processional order reflected the parish's increased importance as a social, economic, and religious unit, providing structured contact only on the major holy days, when all Christendom was united in celebration. The route the united procession followed reinforced the themes of unity and separation. The monks walked down the center of their choir through the parishioners' chancel and out into the nave, where the parishioners joined them. The whole procession then exited through the north door, circled the churchyard, and returned participants to their respective areas of worship for the rest of the mass.

By specifying the organization of sacred space and the liturgical procession's order, the ecclesiastical hierarchy used rituals to try to control a community. Specifically, the decision used ritual performance to promote social integration, but integration of a specific and local form. Although these compromises may have temporarily masked the ruptures and conflicts within the group, they did not heal them.[84] The Dunster processions tried to integrate the two groups, but the competing issues and priorities of two kinds of religious communities infused Dunster's liturgy, as it took place in the newly organized building. In this church, the rood screen divided the parish clergy from the laity, but it also served as a reminder of the divisions between the parish and the priory. The social healing that the mass promoted did not transcend parochial or monastic identity.[85]

The rood screen could provide the physical expression for community dynamics, but building one also shaped community interaction. The rood screen for which we have the most detailed construction records was in Yatton. Once the parishioners had rebuilt the nave and the south porch, they went on to erect a new rood screen with a loft. This rood screen, which the parish removed in the Reformation, was unusual, because it was made out of stone.[86] The project was started in 1446 and took fourteen years to complete. Unlike the Banwell screen, which the carver constructed in his workshop, this one had to be built in place. In 1446, as the parish worked on a design for their new screen, various parishioners and the stone carver, John Crosse, made trips to the parishes of Easton-in-Gordano, Bruton, and Selwood to view their rood screens.[87] The accounts describe the final product as having a covered loft that housed a chapel and some organs. It also had a painted loft, and carvings covered the entire structure. An entry in 1455 states that sixty-nine images adorned the loft, probably made elsewhere and installed and painted at Yatton. This part of the work was not done until 1455, after John Crosse had completed the basic structure.[88]

The Yatton rood screen is a good example of the interplay of local and regional input into a parish project. The parishioners had researched rood screens by visiting other churches, and many of the materials came from outside the parish. Stones came from different quarries throughout Somerset, and the paint came from Bristol.[89] The very act of seeking out new designs and comparing proposed plans with existing screens defines this project in terms of local competition and prestige. Because Crosse built it in place and did not assemble it in a workshop elsewhere, parishioners, particularly the wardens, could supervise its progress. Perhaps because of their excessive enthusiasm for supervising or perhaps because Crosse had a difficult temperament, the wardens had some problems with their stone carver. During the course of the project, Crosse disappeared several times, and the parish had to send someone to find him.[90] But for an illuminating comment made by the scribe keeping the churchwardens' accounts, we might assume that Crosse went to do further research or oversee another project. The account records 2½d. for "ale given to Cross in certain times in his work to make him well willed."[91] Despite these difficulties, the parish retained Crosse, and he finally finished his work. Although not originally from Yatton, he retained his connection with the parish; in 1465 he gave the parish 3d. worth of candles, and an Alice Crosse left a bushel of wheat to the parish as a testamentary bequest.[92] In 1477, when John himself died, he left a gift of 20d. to the church.[93]

The patience of the community and of the many wardens who served during this lengthy construction project demonstrates the commitment of this parish to a specific kind of rood screen. Whether this represented purely pious motivation is doubtful, but the intertwining of status and spirituality was a staple of parish life. The elaborate rood screen said much about the parish's collective wealth, but it was also the feature that dominated the interior, facing the parishioners as they heard mass. The carvings, paintings, side altars, and organs were all expressions of lay piety.[94] The screen, in both construction and existence, united the parish while hearing mass. That they were willing to spend nearly fifteen years on this project demonstrates the level of involvement in and commitment to parish life. It was a community project dependent on community finances and not the wealth and spiritual concerns of one family or donor.

The construction of rood screens, particularly the one at Yatton, raises questions about the laity's relationship to the activity in the chancel during the mass. There has been much discussion of whether the screens hid or framed the mass and whether the laity were paying any attention to the activities in the chancel.[95] We should note that the laity, whether as parishioners or as artisans, designed these screens with their saints, lights, and altars; they are monuments to lay pious concerns. Furthermore, because Yatton's screen took such a long time to build, and because it was built on site, the vicar must have celebrated several masses without a rood screen, or with only portions of it, separating him from the laity. Although this was not the common experience of parishes replacing their screens, thinking about their construction disturbs the image of the medieval laity as always removed and isolated from the mass. Most laity at some point in their lives would have attended a church without a rood screen. The practical matters of construction, refurbishment, and expansion make the laity's relationship to the chancel more complicated and the role of the rood screen more complex. It simultaneously decorated and obscured the mass, but this was not a timeless or constant situation as religious reformers would have had us believe.

Church Seating: Men's and Women's Spaces

Although families and individuals might display their devotion and wealth through patronage of individual screen panels, the screen as a whole primarily emphasized the division between the laity and the clergy. Since parishioners were not a homogeneous group with all the same concerns, the laity's arrangement of the nave manifested, and in some ways facilitated, their differences. Seating arrangements were one of the most obvious ways of marking social and gender differences. In the fifteenth century, naves did not commonly have pews.[96] Their introduction began gradually, in an unorganized fashion, becoming more prevalent in the late fifteenth century. Once there were seats in the nave, status and sex became important features of seating arrangements. Men and women typically sat in their own sections and not together as a family. The well-to-do bought good seats, those less well off bought seats farther from the altar, and the poor probably had no seats at all. Seating arrangements shaped the laity's experience of the liturgy and show that they did not consider themselves to be an undifferentiated or homogeneous group.

The town parishes of Bath and Wells appear to have been the first communities to put pews in their parish churches. Eventually, specific building programs superseded earlier ad hoc arrangements and provided urban parishioners with more seats. The parish of Bridgwater was selling seats as early as 1418, but installed a more extensive set of pews in 1453.[97] St. Michael's in Bath started building seats in 1425.[98] The parishioners of Glastonbury had had seats built twice before 1530.[99] Rural parishes added seats later. With the exception of Yatton, which began building seats in 1445 as part of the expansion of the nave, it seems that rural parishes did not install seats until the beginning of the sixteenth century.[100] Trull, which still has its medieval benches, installed them in bits and pieces over the course of the sixteenth century. One bench-end bears the date 1510. The accounts state that in 1527 the wardens hired carvers to add some more, and a later carver dated his later work in 1560.[101] Although Tintinhull had some seats, starting in 1511 the wardens began refitting the nave with new ones.[102] This two-year project cost the parish a considerable sum of money, which the parishioners offset with their one-time-only Robin Hood ale.[103]

The installation of permanent seats helped foster a new genre of decorative carving by providing new surfaces on which carvers could display their artistic skills.[104] Like rood screens, the best surviving examples of medieval pews come from the West Country and East Anglia.[105] Artists decorated them with a variety of abstract designs, pictures from everyday life, and religious symbols. Carved into five of the bench-ends that still survive in Trull is a religious procession (Figure 5.6). In Brent Knoll, scenes from the story of Reynard the fox appear on three bench-ends. They include Reynard's preaching to geese while wearing a miter, Reynard on trial, and finally Reynard swinging from a gibbet. Although this is recognizable as part of an old and popular folk tale, depicting the execution of either a bishop or an abbot also offers a critique of the Church and the clergy. Although Brent Knoll was not appropriated to Glastonbury, some have suggested that these bench-ends comment on the Abbot of Glastonbury and his less than charitable relationship with his parishes.[106] Perhaps the carver came from one of Glastonbury's parishes.

We know the name of one such artist who worked in Somerset, Simon Warman. The wardens of Nettlecombe had him look at their seats in 1544, perhaps because they were thinking about hiring him for future work.[107] In 1560, the wardens of Trull hired Warman to add more seats to their church. Although he is not named in the accounts, he signed and dated his work, making it possible to link him to some of the benches still in the church.[108] Warman also made the seats in Broomfield, where he again signed his work (Figure 5.7).[109] His benches are notable for their carved edge moldings, while most other Somerset carvers favored plain moldings. When we compare his known work to other surviving medieval bench-ends, his unique stylistic features suggest that he or his workshop provided some of the benches in nine other Somerset parishes.[110] Based on the location of these remaining pews, his workshop was probably in or near Taunton. Warman worked through the Reformation and died in 1585. He must have seen much of his work destroyed by iconoclasts. His later work, still extant in Trull, favors uncontroversial leaf and flower patterns with little obvious religious significance, but still calling for artistic skill.[111]

The design of bench-ends not only gave space for a carver's imagination, but also for that of the occupants as well. Some owners dictated that their benches have their family crests or trade implements. In both Bishop's Lydeard and North Cadbury, there are benches with windmills (Figure 5.8), while in Donyatt a bench-end sports carved initials tied together, probably connoting a marriage that united two families. Below the initials are four yokes

Figure 5.6. Bench-end with carving of a crucifer, All Saints, Trull. Photograph by Katherine L. French.

Figure 5.7. Bench-end with carving of Simon Warman's name, All Saints, Broom-field. Photography courtesy of the Conway Library, Courtauld Institute of Art.

Figure 5.8. Bench-end with carving of a windmill, St. Mary's, Bishop's Lydeard. Photograph courtesy of the Conway Library, Courtauld Institute of Art.

and a plow, which may represent the families' occupation.[112] The variety of designs shows how seats carried more than just concern for the liturgy; the decorations and the arrangements of the pews reflected community dynamics. They illustrated who was a member of the parish and where he or she fit into the local hierarchy. As we have seen in the last chapter, town parishes were more likely to sell seats as a way of augmenting parish income. In these communities, the parish itself through the distribution of seats was in some measure responsible for articulating local prestige. A good seat gave a better view of the host, and testimonies from pew disputes show that parishioners took their seating privileges very seriously.[113] The physical proximity to the host gave affirmation to social status.

In rural parishes, landholding often determined one's right to a seat. In 1533, in a pew dispute from Minehead, Giles Dobell explained that because he held land in Minehead, he and his wife could also have seats in the church.[114] Here, seating was not up to the churchwarden, but to local tradition and oral agreement. The parish reflected the larger environment in which the parish was situated. As the Minehead case shows, however, regulations according to landholding did not make seating any less contentious in rural parishes than in borough ones. Whatever the parish custom, seating arrangements were an easy way of identifying status and position within the community. The practice of separating men and women would also make women more visible and easy targets for violence directed against their families. Margaret Dobell bore the brunt of the injuries in the fight between her husband Giles and Walter Soley over Giles's right to a pew in the church.[115] Her use of a pew made her an easy victim of Walter Soley's violence. In contrast to sitting or standing in a random fashion, permanent seats ordered the congregation. Everyone knew where particular parishioners sat, making it more difficult for them to escape attack. In three other disputes appearing before the Court of the Star Chamber, the defendants all explained that their attackers found them while they worshiped in their pews.[116] Even though these cases did not involve seating issues, they do show how parish seating made individuals visible.

Survival of family chapels and manor pews suggests that sitting together as a family was a privilege of wealth. For those without private chapels, sex determined part of the seating arrangements. Women sat in their own section, usually on the north side of the church, while men sat on the south side. Another way of separating the sexes was to put the men in the front and the women in the back. Where men and women sat during services was a physical demonstration of gender relations within the parish. Individuals went to mass as members of a community governed by different roles for men and women. Removing men and women to their own sections served to strengthen these differences and fostered local subcultures dependent upon gender. Although men had plenty of public opportunities to gather in all-male groups, attendance at church became one of the few sanctioned places where women could gather in all-female groups.[117]

Scholars have speculated about the significance of separating men and women.[118] Separating the sexes during worship goes back to the early church, where it may have stemmed from ideas about women's impurity and the need to keep them as far as possible from the altar and the host.[119] The clergy also believed that women distracted men and that separating the two groups would help direct everyone's attention to the liturgy. The north side (or the left side as one faced the chancel) was, according to folk tradition, the devil's side, and associated with things dark and damp. Women sat on the north because of their role in the Fall. There is, however, another way of looking at this situation. Above the rood screen was the great crucifix with Mary on the left and John the Baptist on the right; the north is also Mary's side and women sat on Mary's side. When facing the assembled congregation, as the priest did for his sermon or blessing, Mary and the women were on the right-hand side of God—a much more positive position than the "devil's side."[120] This ambiguity in the significance of seat location reflects the ambiguous position of women within the church. Condemned for their supposed sinful and lustful natures, they, nevertheless, shared the same sex as Mary and comprised half of the parish membership.

Segregated seating began to disappear in some parishes by the end of the middle ages. Parishioners took advantage of church re-pewing and bought or rented seats as a family. Between 1457, the date of Yeovil's first surviving account, and 1516, the date of the next surviving account, the wardens had re-pewed the nave in three sections: north side, middle range, and south side; this plan remained in effect through the end of Henry VIII's reign.[121] With the creation of a new section of seats, segregated seating began to die out. In 1516, the churchwardens received "1s. 4d. of John Gelat for a seat for his wife or himself whichever it shall please him in the middle range."[122] By the next surviving account, 1519, women also sat with men in the south section. And in 1541, the next surviving account, men finally took seats with the women in the church's north side. Sitting together as a family seems to have become an option in the early sixteenth century, growing in popularity on the eve of the Reformation. The north side, however, had retained its association with women longer and was the last part of the seating plan to be integrated.

The different status issues that seating arrangements could highlight come together in the changing seating plans of Bridgwater. With these changes, the nave became a place to demonstrate the public status that men gained from service in town office. As we saw in the last chapter, the wardens started selling seats in 1418, and between then and 1471, the last surviving pre-Reformation churchwardens' account, there are the names of fifty-nine people who bought seats from the wardens. There is even a rudimentary church seating plan from 1454, after the parish had outfitted part of the nave with new seats the previous year.[123] Those individuals listed in both the churchwardens' accounts and the seating plan can be cross-referenced in the borough records to assess their occupation or relative status.[124] The result is that we can see how seating changed with the installation of new pews.

When Bridgwater's wardens started selling seats, there were only a few, and they did not cost very much. They appear to have been for the elderly or infirm. Neither the men nor the women who had purchased pews appeared frequently in the municipal records; the women were not part of prominent families, nor were their husbands holders of civic or parish offices or major landholders. The same is true for the men buying seats. Prior to the installation of new seats, only two bailiffs and a churchwarden purchased seats. After the parish built new pews, however, the profile of those purchasing seats changed substantially. They were men of substance; several served in civic offices in the borough, and one was even a member of Parliament. The men buying pews were more active in the town's administration than in the parish's. A correlation of those who bought seats, both before and after 1454, with the amount they were assessed for the annual parish rate, shows that those buying seats after 1454 were also better off financially.[125] They contributed more to the annual upkeep of the parish and lived in wealthier neighborhoods than those who bought seats before 1454.

While the Bridgwater records list many important public officials as purchasers of parish seats, they do not show a similar correlation for parish officeholders. It is of course possible that the churchwardens automatically received a seat upon assuming their office. Yet even if this is true, it does not significantly change the profile of the group. Furthermore, former churchwardens and guild wardens did not buy seats after they finished their time in office. As the seats built in 1454 were now for the town's socially prominent, the lack of men who *both* bought seats and held the parish offices of either churchwarden or guild warden suggests that running the parish did not impart the same level of social prominence as the town offices did. Status and prestige appear to have come from serving in town offices and not parish ones; this status could then be demonstrated by how much one gave to the church and where one sat in the nave. The new seating arrangement attracted wealthier and more prominent parishioners, while the previous arrangement had reserved seats for those in physical need.

Adding new seats to the nave also altered the ratio of the men and women who held seats, and this change reflects other changes in the role of women in this community. Prior to the installation of new pews, women, either on their own or through their husbands, had purchased 50 percent of the seats. With the introduction of more pews, the percentage of women purchasing seats declined to 37 percent. Although there is no indication of how complete the plan is, it only lists men. The plan itself also shows how men had begun to dominate the nave, even in those areas traditionally used by women. According to the plan, seating was in four parts of the nave: the church (probably the central part), the northern part, the southern part, and by the chapel of St. George. Men sat in all parts, even the north side. Male domination of both sides of the nave further suggests that the women might have been relegated to the back (the west end) of the church, as far away from the chancel as possible. However incomplete the plan, its existence and the lack of women in it further indicates how the significance of seating had changed.

The installation of new seats appears to have been part of a fundamental rethinking of the parish's position in the town and the role of the parishioners in the parish. Re-pewing the church came at the same time that the parish dropped its annual rate as a form of fundraising. As we saw in the last chapter, all heads of households, which sometimes meant women, had supported the parish through the annual collection.[126] Now the household was no longer a unit of parish support. The parish began to finance itself exclusively through the collection of rents from houses it owned and from pious gifts. Unless Bridgwater women rented property or left a testamentary bequest, they do not appear in the churchwardens' accounts as directly supporting the parish. These changes also affected the men of the parish. However, unlike women, men could serve in parish offices and work to maintain the parish as individuals. As individuals some men might be excluded from parish offices, but not as a sex.

Although seats themselves could be a source of contention, they more often exposed pre-existing tensions within the community. The laity might all join together at the liturgy, but, theological demands for charity notwithstanding, social distinctions did not disappear at church, nor were they expected to. In borough parishes, these dynamics seemed to play a greater role in community interaction and identity. The town parishes sold seats, and in Bridgwater particularly, they took on new meaning as the parish shifted its priorities. In Bath and Wells, parishes that depended on inclusive forms of fundraising, such as ales, did not sell seats. Although this should not suggest that social hierarchy or conflict did not exist in rural parishes, their parochial administrations did not facilitate internal divisions as much as town parishes did.

Side Altars and Social Status

Arrangement of the nave, like parochial dynamics, involved more than simply juxtaposing men and women. Social status and personal ambition that grew out of familial and business networks also shaped parish life and influenced the internal space of the parish church. Other groups within the laity—parish guilds and trade guilds—proclaimed their existence with the construction of side altars and chapels. As markers of both social status and religious affinity, side altars further configured the liturgy in terms of a variety of lay interests. Membership in the parish was just one of many possible religious affiliations available to late medieval parishioners. Guilds were another popular form of religious association that fit into the existing structure of the parish. Guilds often developed their own chapels and religious devotions and in the process further divided the space within the nave according to local priorities. In similar ways, the local gentry made its presence known. A local gentry family's patronage of the parish may have helped it during some difficult financial moments, but patronage had its consequences. Those entering the church would recognize the parish's dependency on their wealthy patron through the presence of family chapels, private pews, and family coats of arms adorning the walls, memorials, and windows of the church. Guild endowments combined with family chapels made much of the nave a hodge-podge of private or quasi-private spaces reflective of the parishioners' myriad interests, concerns, and identities In this way, the nave held in tension local and universal Christian priorities.

Most parish churches had their complement of private chapels and family acknowledgments. When Sir George Speke wrote his will, just before his death in 1528, he outlined how he wanted to be memorialized in his parish of Dowlish Wake. He left instructions for an elaborate tomb for himself and his wife, which was to have "our pictures there upon in copper, [and] resting above the said tomb is scripture of copper [listing] who lies there."[127] He further specified that this tomb should be placed in a new chapel in an aisle that he would build. The resulting sixteenth-century addition stands in contrast to the rest of the thirteenth-century nave.[128] Furthermore, Spekes endowed the chapel with enough lands that it could support an "honest and discrete priest, not beneficed, to sing and say mass for my soul within the said new aisle and for the souls of my wife, my father, my mother, my brother, my sister, all our friends, and for all Christian souls."[129] The family chantry with its attendant chapel served as a reminder to all that this family held power and prestige in the area. Far from this example being unique, most knightly families throughout Somerset behaved in similar ways.[130]

The construction of family chapels reordered the interior of the nave and changed how the parish clergy celebrated the liturgy.[131] George Speke's new chapel meant that the parish priest had to incorporate the new altar and the new chantry priest into the liturgical processions. Speke's addition, like those in countless other parish churches throughout the diocese and throughout England, meant that the liturgical procession now had another aisle through which to move and another altar to bless. The dedication of this particular altar is lost, but that too would have shaped the local liturgy, possibly by introducing a new saint to the list of saints venerated in this church. The addition that memorialized a family or individual gave the benefactor the opportunity to adapt the liturgy so as to remind observers of the gentry's role in the parish. [132] Speke further emphasized this message by a statement on his tomb that explained that he had built this portion of the church.[133] The family also displayed its status by placing its heraldic devices on the chapel walls and windows. When John Newton of Yatton married Isabel Chedder (the future female churchwarden of Yatton), her father commemorated the match with a window in the Chedder parish church. The window has an image of St. John the Baptist and includes the Chedder arms impaled by the Newton arms.[134]

In addition to family chapels, many parish guilds supported and maintained chapels, altars, and lights that were scattered throughout the nave. Through guild membership, parishioners were able to incorporate their differences into a community of the parish. Guild membership created further hierarchies and avenues for local advancement that defused the multiple ambitions and egos present in each parish. Because guilds were voluntary associations, historians have argued that they met the needs of late medieval Christians more readily than the parish itself, where membership and boundaries were set and immutable.[135] These scholars often portray relations between guilds and parishes as competitive. However, being a member of the parish did not mean that one could not join several groups simultaneously and support and participate in them all. Relations between guilds and parish administrations in Bath and Wells appear to be mostly supportive. As we have already seen, in Pilton and Croscombe, the parish guild did most of the fundraising. We might view guilds as a way for individuals to share an interest with like-minded members of the parish; guild membership did not undermine the parish but rather helped address the many differences that it contained. Duffy also points out that, although many scholars perceive guilds to be more interesting because they were voluntary associations, ecclesiastical courts regulated both parish and guild activities. "Membership of the gilds might in principle have been voluntary, but membership contracted or promised clearly was held to have much the same binding character as membership of the parish."[136]

Some parish guilds catered to specific interests within the parish community. The clearest examples are Croscombe's numerous guilds, which defined their membership according to occupation and gender. Along with the maidens' and young men's guilds, Croscombe had a fullers' and a weavers' guild that also supported endowments within the church. Pilton and Stogursey also had younglings' guilds, and Stogursey's St. Mary's guild seems to have drawn much of its support from the parish women.[137] Although the wardens were men, only women rented the guild's property. The fraternity of St. Mary in the priory of St. James in Taunton drew its support from the townsmen.[138]

Sex was not the only factor in determining admission to a guild; sometimes wealth or status was a defining feature of membership. The hoglers of Banwell attracted the wealthier men of Banwell, and in Bridgwater the merchant guild founded and supported the guild of St. Mary and appointed the wardens of the Holy Trinity guild.[139] The Trinity guild in Wells attracted a similar sort of town elite. Leadership in this group often served as a stepping-stone to civic leadership rather than to parish leadership. There is also some suggestion that this exclusivity became more pronounced as the fifteenth century drew to a close.[140] In contrast to these more restricted guilds, rural parish guilds tended to be more inclusive. In the small parish of Trull, the guild of St. Mary seems to have drawn its membership from most of the parish's men and women.

Parishes had multiple guilds that usually supported a side altar, a chapel, and a light. (See Appendix.) Indeed, the variety of ways in which parishioners venerated the saints suggests that church interiors were crowded to the point of being cluttered. Bridgwater's extensive building campaign, which resulted in eight different chapels by the end of the fifteenth century, might be unusual in its scope, but not in practice. Only interest and money limited the number of chapels and other venerations within a nave. Yeovil had two chapels dedicated to St. Mary, one in the churchyard and one in the church.[141] The church of Banwell had four chapels located throughout the church and a guild chapel dedicated to St. George some distance from the church.[142] Smaller guilds had their endowments as well. The maidens of Croscombe had a light somewhere in the nave, as did their male counterparts. Although the exact placement of these and other foundations have been lost over the course of successive redecorations and "restorations," we can still view them and the parish church as providing particular sacred spaces for groups within the larger body of the parish. Even without knowing how parishioners arranged guild foundations in their nave, we can see that their creation would rearrange the liturgy in ways similar to that of new family chapels built by the gentry. When liturgical processions in these parishes stopped at each guild altar to sprinkle it with holy water and bless it, the parishioners were also reminded of the groups in their midst that supported and maintained these endowments.

Conclusion

Building and furnishing a church required piety and organization; the final product revealed much about the self-definition of the parish community. The church building and its furnishings organized both space and behavior, allowing the community to represent itself in a variety of ways.[143] The building itself was a major investment for the parishioners and brought the parish together not only for the liturgy, but also for fundraising and maintenance. It required organization, commitment, and long-term planning. The community had to agree on the various projects and their financing, decide on a master artisan and the style, and finally contribute time and effort to ensure its completion. The parish church not only provided a forum for community gatherings, but also a focus for community pride and concern. The building itself demonstrated that the parish was a cooperative organization. The men and women of the parish worked together for the common goal of salvation, but their work incorporated and reflected their many similarities and differences. Although the work of raising money and hiring artisans was done to ensure the proper performance of the mass, the parish simultaneously defined itself, and the community's place within the borough or manor, with the choices it made in how to expand or rebuild the nave and arrange the space within it. The seats, rood screens, family chapels, and guild endowments both united and divided the community in the very ways that the laity understood their parochial involvement.

6 "THE WORTHIEST THING"

Liturgical Celebrations and the Cult of the Saints in Place

The Liturgy

The clergy and laity shared the same goal in building, maintaining, and furnishing the church. They sought a proper space for the celebration of the liturgy. Although many aspects of parish life fell under the rubric of religious practice, formal worship consisted of the liturgy. Parishioners typically attended three services on Sundays: matins at around six or seven o'clock in the morning, high mass at around nine or ten o'clock, and finally evensong between two and three o'clock in the afternoon.[1] Although the laity might go to church only on Sunday, their parish priest, along with the stipendiary priests, said a daily mass and the other canonical offices. When and how depended largely on local custom; he might say the hours privately or fold them into the beginning and end of the daily mass.[2] The mass, as the reenactment of the Last Supper and Christ's passion and resurrection, provided the most important access to sacramental grace. *The Lay Folk's Mass Book* declared the mass to be "the worthiest thing, [and] most of the goodness in all this world."[3] The doctrine of transubstantiation held that the bread and wine of the Eucharist were turned into the body and blood of Christ. As such, the Church expected the laity to worship the host as the very body of the Lord. Punctuating the year of Sunday services came special holy days that commemorated the life of Jesus and the martyrdom of the saints. On these days, called *festa ferianda*, the laity were to leave off work and attend church.

Parish life promoted and facilitated the celebration of the mass and this cycle of holy days. Their celebration by the parish holds in tension the demands of orthodoxy and local practices. Through visitations and educational programs, the church hierarchy worked to keep each parish within the bounds of acceptable Christian practice; yet, as we saw in the last chapter, liturgical performances cannot be removed from the specific place or lay organization that facilitated them.

In addition to the formal celebration of the liturgy within the church, the laity moved celebration into the churchyards and church houses in the form of processions, ales, and revels, and these celebrations continued throughout the year in the form of the cult of the saints. In this way, local concerns shaped orthodox religious practices, and through liturgically sanctioned celebrations, a parish further articulated its community identity. The differences and similarities in the scale and form of the parish liturgy highlight the parameters of orthodox liturgical practice, while at the same time showing worship to be a creative enterprise for the laity. Unlike the local variations in parish administrations, greater uniformity resided in liturgical calendars and the actual liturgical observances. The primary reason is that orthodoxy by its very nature limited deviation. Although the episcopacy tolerated a variety of practices, there were set boundaries that delineated the acceptable from the unacceptable. In 1464, Bishop Beckynton asked his commissary-general to investigate reports of a spring within the hamlet of Wemdon, in the parish of Bridgwater, that had alleged healing powers.[4] It was not the fact of a holy spring per se that worried the bishop—there was biblical precedent for that—but rather the idea of uncontrolled religious enthusiasm and erroneous worship.[5] In the end, parish religious practices were essentially conservative in nature, but conservatism does not mean stasis.

In this chapter, we will explore how the church hierarchy's educational programs tried to instill orthodox religious practices and beliefs into the parish. Then, as a way of seeing how parishes practiced orthodoxy, we will look at the parishes' celebration of holy days that celebrated the life of Jesus and the cult of the saints. Throughout the late middle ages, parishes expanded their liturgical celebrations to include extra-liturgical activities that increased the laity's participation in the holy day. This expansion expressed the anxieties and affirmations of the parish's growth as a forum for lay initiative and religious expression.

Learning About Christianity

One way in which the Church worked to maintain orthodoxy was through education. In the wake of the Fourth Lateran Council of 1215, the papacy and the episcopacy worked to increase lay knowledge of Christianity. Without proper and regular instruction, the laity could fall into error and heresy. At the same time, bishops also worried about the quality of the clergy and their preparedness for the cure of souls. Ultimately, lay and clerical education went hand in hand. The laity learned about Christianity in a variety of ways. In 1281, the archbishop of Canterbury, John Pecham (1279–92), outlined what the laity and the parish clergy were to know in an educational program known as the *Ignorantia Sacerdotum*. This program blended specific knowledge of Christianity with behavior. Specifically, Pecham called for parish priests to explain four times a year the fourteen articles of faith, the ten commandments, the two precepts of the Gospel, the seven works of mercy, the seven deadly sins, the seven principal virtues, and the seven sacraments.[6] Not only should regular attendance at mass instruct the laity, but so should their annual confession during Lent. Here, the priest quizzed them on their religious knowledge and behavior.[7] Mirk's *Instructions for Parish Priests* explains that the priest was to inquire about the penitent's knowledge of the Lord's Prayer, the Ave Maria, the Creed, the articles of faith, the ten commandments, and whether they had behaved in accordance with these precepts.[8]

By the late middle ages, preaching had become another increasingly important method of education. The laity had access to a variety of preachers; mendicant friars moved around England, and bishops increasingly encouraged the local parish clergy to preach to their flocks.[9] Sermons might be part of the Sunday mass, or they could be a separate event happening after mass on Sunday afternoons. Those laity living in towns also heard itinerant preachers in their market places on weekdays.[10] Several vernacular sermon collections still survive. Scholars assume that these collections served as models for preachers to imitate or copy. One of the most popular collections was John Mirk's *Festial*, a sermon cycle he wrote at the end of the fourteenth century, that enjoyed its greatest popularity in the fifteenth and sixteenth centuries. It included sermons for the different feast days and saints' days that came throughout the year.[11] Other sermon collections include two unique fifteenth-century manuscripts, the *Speculum Sacerdotale* and British Library manuscript Royal 18 B. xxiii, known as the Ross collection.[12] Elements from the *Ignorantia Sacerdotum*, along with the lives of the saints, formed the core of most of these and other late medieval sermons. At the beginning of the fifteenth century, Archbishop Thomas Arundel (1352–1414), in his provincial constitutions, limited the content of what preachers could tell the laity and required all bishops to license all preachers working in their dioceses. Only the beneficed clergy could preach on scripture; the unbeneficed had to confine themselves to the topics outlined in Pecham's *Ignorantia Sacerdotum*.[13] As a result, writes Leith Spencer, preachers focused on the "lukewarm" Christian, who fell into acts of "uncharity, inconstancy, and levity," not those who were well outside the bounds of orthodox Christian life.[14] In 1435, John Stafford, Bishop of Bath and Wells (1425–43), translated the *Ignorantia Sacerdotum* into English, helping to make this educational program widely known in southern England.[15] Stafford opened his translation by stating:

We ordain and command that every curate and priest having cure of soul of the people 4 times in the year, that is to say once in every quarter of the year, the Sunday or the Holy Day, declare openly in English to the people without curious dissembling first the particulars of the belief whereof, if consideration be had to them that made the Creed, then the articles of the faith be 12 to the number of 12 apostles.[16]

He concluded by ordering all parishes to acquire a copy of this work and by requiring the clergy to read it to their parishioners four times a year. In this manner, the bishop hoped to address both clerical and lay ignorance. This syllabus formed the basis for pastoral care in the late middle ages; it set the process both of hearing confessions and of preaching. In 1413, Bishop Nicholas Bubwith of Bath and Wells found that Robert Rouse, the candidate for the vicarage of Henstridge, lacked sufficient knowledge to perform his job. At his institution, Rouse had to promise "to procure as soon as possible a book containing the seven sacraments of the church, the ten commandments, the seven deadly sins, the seven works of mercy, the five senses, the cardinal virtues and the articles of the faith, and learn and understand the contents of the same."[17] This syllabus promoted Christian conventions and presented them as codes of behavior and community values.

Bishops could also address the problems of clerical education and, thus, lay education, in more structural ways. By taking advantage of the papal constitution of 1298, *Cum ex eo*, bishops could send their clergy to school, without worrying about accusations of nonresidency. This constitution gave bishops the power to release beneficed clergy from their obligations to reside in their cures. As long as they pursued an education, clergy could be away from their benefice for up to seven years.[18] John Broun, rector of Hardington, received a license from Bishop Stafford to absent himself from this parish for the year of 1431 so as "to attend schools in England wherever in England there is a *generale studium*."[19] Of all the bishops in Bath and Wells, Thomas Bekynton (1443–65), the humanist, appears to have been the most concerned with the issue of Christian education.[20] The crown's continued order that bishops hunt for Lollards and his own earlier contact with Italian humanism may have inspired his efforts. Bekynton's register shows that he put this commitment into practice by increasing the parochial clergy's knowledge of scripture, theology, and Latin. On numerous occasions, he or his chancellor extracted oaths from clerks being presented for benefices that they would resign if, after a specific period of time, the bishop or his chancellor still found their education lacking. Sometimes Bekynton prescribed extra years of study, with another episcopal examination awaiting the candidate at the end of this time.[21] The new vicar of Banwell, John Gernesey, "swore on the Gospels that for a whole year he would study every day to understand his divine office and daily service, literally and grammatically at least, and during that year maintain in his house at his own expense a young man well-learned in grammar to instruct him."[22] In three instances, the bishop simply rejected the candidate for lack of education and provided one of his own.[23]

Another way bishops sought to increase the level of learning was to increase the number of clergy preaching in the diocese and to license better-educated clergy to serve the diocese. Archbishop Arundel had required his bishops to license all preachers working within their dioceses. In this way, he sought to prevent heretical preachers from working in the dioceses and to keep the clergy and parish life orthodox. Sermons served as an important way of countering heresy and educating the laity, and sermon cycles such as Mirk's *Festial* specifically dealt with issues such as the priest's sacerdotal efficacy, which the Lollards attacked.[24] As Bristol was both on the fringes of the diocese of Bath and Wells and a local source of Lollardy, licensing preachers, and any other cleric who performed any liturgy or sacrament outside the confines of the parish, became an important means of combating heresy. Mendicant or other non-beneficed clergy needed permission not only to preach, but also to hear confessions, and the wealthy had to seek licenses to have either their own confessors or a private oratory within their houses. Over the course of the fifteenth century, bishops increased the qualifications of those preaching in the diocese on either an itinerant or an occasional basis. Monks from the local houses in Glastonbury, Bath, and Muchelney received licenses in increasing numbers, as did unbeneficed clerics with theological degrees living outside the cloister.[25] To leave little room for confusion, the licenses stipulated that clerics could preach in either Latin or the "vulgar tongue."[26] The overall increase in number and quality of licensees is especially apparent in Bekynton's register. Of the twenty-seven licenses appearing in his register from between 1444 and 1464, eleven went to masters of theology and nine to bachelors of theology.[27] This afforded the bishop an opportunity to patronize the scholars who interested him, while also shaping the quality of instruction and preaching at the parish level.

The Franciscans in particular had an impact on late medieval spiritual practices.[28] The friary in Bridgwater was one of the earliest in England.[29] The friars' popularity among parishioners can be seen in the churches themselves; the devotions they promoted, such as the rosary, the five wounds, the host, and Mary as Our Lady of Pity, became common images in parish church windows, carvings, and shrines.[30] Banwell had an altar dedicated to the five wounds and Frome had a light dedicated to Our Lady of Pity.[31] These examples suggest that the policy of licensing better-educated clergy, and the prominence of friars in this group of preachers, had helped with the process of lay education and influenced parochial spirituality. The will of Agnes Burton, alias Bascombe, from Taunton illustrates their continuing impact on lay worship. She was especially interested in liturgies popularized by the Franciscans. She specified that, after her death, her heirs should find a priest to pray for her soul and the souls of her friends and family, "which priest shall sing daily about the hour of 9, if he be disposed, and that the said priest shall say every Wednesday in the year, the mass of the Five Wounds, and every month Dirge and commendations with the Psalms of the passion."[32]

The mendicant orders were well represented in the West Country. Generally the Franciscans working in Bath and Wells came from convents in Bridgwater, Bristol, and Dorchester; the Dominicans from their houses in Bristol and Ilchester; and the Augustinians and Carmelites from their houses in Bristol. Parish priests often saw the growing popularity of the mendicants and the number of their convents in the region as a threat to their livelihood, fearing the loss of revenue and influence when their parishioners sought out confession with a mendicant or requested burial in mendicant or monastic churchyards.[33] From the parishioners' perspective, however, confession to a mendicant priest offered more privacy; he would be less likely to stay in the area once he was finished and remind them of their sins, or worse, leak the contents of their confession. In 1445, the bishop had to warn the vicar of Yeovil to desist in his practice of driving off properly licensed friars who had come into the diocese from their convent in nearby Dorchester.[34]

Many reformers and scholars of the Reformation have accused the late medieval church of supporting an undereducated clergy and encouraging superstition among the laity.[35] They argue that patrons gave preference to relatives and to individuals to whom they owed favors, rather than appointing the most qualified candidate. As Peter Heath has pointed out, however, this view is the direct result of the polemics of the Reformation itself. Heath found little evidence of an apathetic or badly trained parish clergy. Furthermore, bishops also encouraged their parish clergy to have more than a minimal knowledge of Christianity so that they could instruct their flock.[36] The desire for improvement does not necessarily mean that the status quo had failed. The fifteenth-century growth in vernacular manuals for priests suggests that, although knowledge of Latin might have been declining, the desire for knowledgeable and literate clergy was not.[37] At the same time, parishioners also wanted qualified, honest, and committed clergy who would perform their jobs with sincerity.[38] The numerous side altars, chantries, and parish guilds that the laity ran, meant that they themselves could expect to hire and fire many clergy, largely at their own discretion.[39] Thus they could employ clergy who would offer specific liturgical and spiritual practices and fulfill the laity's spiritual needs. The problem, Heath argues, was that the clergy were unable to keep up with the growth in literacy or the laity's increasing interest in religious matters.[40] Bishops may not have established consistent programs of study to facilitate the clergy's role in pastoral care, but they cared about the quality of their clergy. In Bath and Wells it seems that the episcopal hierarchy, especially under Bekynton's leadership, did try to accommodate the laity's growing interest in religious affairs, that their administration of their parishes had helped foster. They did seek more and better qualified clergy, even if their attempts were sometimes haphazard or incomplete.

Another way the Church promoted orthodoxy was by setting the liturgical calendar and prescribing the liturgy. The ecclesiastical calendar consisted of days that commemorated the life of Jesus and days that honored the saints. Together these days comprised nearly 50 holidays, in addition to Sundays, when the laity ceased working and attended church. The dioceses of England observed a variety of different feast days.[41] Prior to the 1530s, clerics did not strive for nationwide uniformity; they focused instead on following what the bishops had mandated, while tolerating a wide divergence in celebrations from diocese to diocese.[42] Thus, responding to a variety of local and national concerns, the liturgical calendar continued to expand throughout the late middle ages.[43] In 1318, the bishop of Bath and Wells, John de Drokensford, in conformance with the pope's mandate of 1234, introduced Corpus Christi to the diocese's religious calendar; he was the first to do so.[44] His successor, Ralph of Shrewsbury, listed forty-three *festa ferianda*, including Corpus Christi, when the laity were not to work but to go to church.[45] On these days, neither agricultural work nor any other kind of work could interfere with religious observance.[46] With the exception of local saints who had chapels and parishes dedicated to them, and those holy days outlined in "ancient canons," the laity must reject all other spurious festivals. [47] This list of holidays was not the sum total of those celebrated by the parishes, but these were the ones for which the laity could leave their work.

In the fourteenth century, a move toward more ceremonies and public processions simultaneously strengthened the church's position and inspired local devotion.[48] In the wake of the nationalist sentiment growing out of the Hundred Years' War, the Church added several new saints' days to the calendar. They helped to promote the image of King Henry V as *miles Christi* and England as a chosen and favored land.[49] These new feasts appear in the registers of the bishops of Bath and Wells. In 1415, in accordance with orders from the archbishop of Canterbury, Nicholas Bubwith called for the perpetual observance of the political saints George and David, along with St. Chad and St. Winifred.[50] Two years, later as a result of Henry V's victory at Agincourt, Bubwith mandated that the diocese celebrate the feast of the Deposition and Translation of St. John of Beverly.[51] In 1445, Bishop Thomas Bekynton added the feast of the Translation of St. Edward the Confessor to the calendar.[52] As we will see, only St. George left any obvious mark on parish life. In a similar fashion, bishops periodically ordered parishes to hold processions and prayers for the health of the state or nation. Wars, droughts, and floods all prompted calls for national penance.[53] These public celebrations tapped into parishioner interest and enthusiasm for involvement in ritual celebrations.

Occasionally parishioners sought to rearrange their own local calendars in accordance with local needs. Prior to the Reformation Act that switched all church dedication days to the first Sunday in October, ten different parishes in Bath and Wells petitioned the bishop to change their parishes' dedication days.[54] As the vicar of Combe St. Nicholas explained, "The dedication of their church, falling as it does on the eve of St. Laurence, namely 9 August, cannot be celebrated with due devotion on account of the harvest and the necessary occupations of the autumn and other reasonable causes."[55] The liturgical calendar was by no means fixed or constant, but was continually adapted to reflect both local and national concerns. Yet it is difficult to know how many parishes adopted these new feasts or how much variation existed from parish to parish. Most parish liturgical books have long since disappeared, and churchwardens' accounts do not give a consistent description of either books or liturgical practices, nor do they necessarily account for all innovations and changes; they list only those things that cost the parish money. In addition, as Richard Pfaff has pointed out, adopting a new saint's day into the national, diocesan, or local calendar was a piecemeal and imprecise process.[56] Papal or provincial legislation did not mean that bishops automatically adopted a new devotion, and a diocesan promulgation did not mean that a new saint's day found its way into a parish's liturgical cycle. New holidays required new liturgies, which in turn required new books, or at least new folios inserted into those that the parish already owned.[57] Pfaff concludes that " 'the introduction of a feast', then, cannot mean that each new feast established by authority was immediately observed in every church in the kingdom. Reformation and counter-Reformation ideas of liturgical uniformity simply do not fit for the middle ages."[58]

Over the course of the fifteenth century, English bishops in the province of Canterbury further regularized the liturgy by promoting the use of Sarum in all churches. This effort, however, did not eliminate the other uses. The diocese of Hereford, the most remote English diocese in the province of Canterbury, maintained its own use, as did the province of York.[59] Even among those areas where the Sarum Use prevailed, there was no way to assure complete uniformity; until the advent of printing, liturgical books continued to vary.[60] The Church held out an ideal of eight books a parish needed to own and thereby tried to assure a general standard for liturgical performance. According to the statutes of the diocese of Bath and Wells, a parish had to supply eight different liturgical books: an antiphoner (musical parts of the services), a gradual (choir music for the mass), a psalter (psalms for the different days of the week), a troperium (sequences sung after the epistle at mass), an ordinal (instructions on the administration of the liturgy and sacraments), a missal (the whole office of the mass), a manual (occasional services of baptism, marriage, churching of women, and last rites), and a breviary (text and office of divine service, including music).[61] These were by no means the total possible number of liturgical books.[62] Provincial legislation, such as Lynwood's *Provinciale* and Archbishop Winchelsea's constitution, required a legenda or a book of readings from the Bible and saints' lives. As the middle ages progressed, however, some books absorbed the contents of others, making it difficult to know from inventories just how well or poorly equipped a parish was. For example, a fifteenth-century breviary might also contain the psalms, hymns, and readings, making the legenda, antiphoner, and ordinal not strictly necessary. [63] Similarly, missals of the fifteenth century also contained music, readings, and other elements of the liturgy, making the gradual, processional, and Gospel book somewhat redundant.[64] As local scribes and bookbinders often rebound the parish books more than once, they could combine any number of the liturgical texts.

Churchwardens' accounts demonstrate that the parish spent money on the purchase and repair of their liturgical books, but just what books a parish owned is less clear. The names given to liturgical books were not standardized until the advent of printing.[65] Accounts sometimes give generic names such as "mass book," which could refer to either a breviary or a missal. When we compare the two surviving inventories of Bridgwater and Glastonbury with the detailed accounts of Tintinhull, we find that all three parishes were reasonably well supplied with liturgical books (see Table 6.1). In the case of Tintinhull and Glastonbury, however, this may have been due to proximity to a monastery. The thirteenth-century episcopal statutes for the diocese directed that monasteries should give away their old copies of liturgical books to parishes under their patronage, so Tintinhull's large collection of mass books probably came from Montacute Priory, and likewise St. John's Glastonbury may have received their collection from Glastonbury Abbey.[66] Evidence from clerical wills also suggests that sometimes the parish clergy provided their own books. About 26 percent of the clerical wills from this diocese mention books, and of these, 66 percent left them to either a parish or a member of the parish clergy. Out of the 18 wills from vicars, 6 (or 33 percent) gave books to either their parish or local clergyman.[67] For example, John Caudbek, vicar of Wellington, who died in 1498, left his parish "one antiphon not bound containing in it a suitable legenda."[68] Of the 19 wills from cathedral canons, 7 (or 37 percent) did the same thing, although they often chose to give books to their birth parishes, which sometimes lay outside the diocese.[69] Rectors tended to be less generous; of the 32 wills from self-identified rectors, only 6 (or 18 percent) gave books to

Table 6.1. Liturgical books owned by parishes

Books	Tintinhull	Yatton	Croscombe	Trull	Banwell	Pilton
mass book	1509	1483(2–3) 1501	1499 1521(3)		1523	
breviary/portiforium	1440 1510	1463	1496			
antiphoner	1457					
psalter		1480				
ordinal	1433					
collects						
missal	1440					
gradual/grail	1509		1496			
troperium						
manual			1500			
processional	1447		1496			1512 printed
epistolary						
legenda		1484	1475			
sermon book						
Bible	1541	1538		1540	1541	
service book in English						

their parish.[70] John Ganvill, rector of Yeovil, who died in 1407, wrote explicit instructions in his will for the care of the books he gave to the parish.

> I bequeath a missal and my great breviary to the perpetual use of the said church of Yeovil and I will that they never be removed therefrom as I trust in my faithful parishioners that they keep the said breviary forever for three chantry priests and their successors serving within the said church on the side of the choir, and the said missal for the perpetual use of the high altar, and that the said book remain where the other books of the said church are accustomed to be kept.[71]

Nettlecombe	Bridgwater	Glastonbury	Yeovil	Bath	Stogursey
1508	1447(3)				1531
	1447	1418	1407	1371	
		1421	1519	1427(2)	
				1430	
	1447(2)	1418(3)	1516		
		1421(3)	1544		
1507		1418			
		1421			
	1447	1418		1427	
		1421			
	1447	1418			
		1421			
1507	1420		1407	1427(2)	
	1447(2)	1418		1427	
		1421			
	1447	1418(2)		1439	1545(2)
		1421(2)			
	1447(2)	1418	1519	1364	1543
		1421	1544(Eng)	1427(2)	1544(5)
	1447				
	1447	1418		1349	
		1421		1427	
	1415	1418(2)	1547		
		1421(2)			
1540			1540		
			1547	1547	

The interest that some parish clergy felt for their parishes helped the church-wardens provide for their parishes, and at the same time suggests a certain level of knowledge and education about the liturgy among the clergy. When we look at the information gleaned from the accounts of other parishes, they appear less well supplied, but the accounts may be deceiving. Repairs to books might be folded into other expenses, or simply listed as repairs to a book; some sets of accounts, such as those from Banwell or Trull, may not have coincided with the years when parishes needed to mend or purchase liturgical books.

Nevertheless, in general, the parishes for which we have churchwardens' accounts appear to be well stocked with liturgical books.

Celebrating the Life of Jesus

The ecclesiastical calendar was organized to celebrate events in the life of Jesus, with additional saints' days and other commemorations added as necessary. The churchwardens' accounts show that, beyond the Sarum Use, parishes shared a common culture and liturgical structure that was flexible enough to allow for local variation and local concerns.[72] Although the occasion and the liturgy might be virtually the same from parish to parish, local details infused the processional route, location of the celebration, and lay participation with additional significance. Not all holy days appear in the churchwardens' accounts, nor did every parish celebrate them in the same fashion. Wealth and interest played a crucial role in the scope of observances. Poorer parishes could not afford large quantities of wax, elaborate vestments, or valuable liturgical items. Small parishes did not have lengthy processional routes and crowds of laity in attendance, while town parishes might attract visitors from all over England. We can also assume that in some cases, parish guilds added to the ceremony of those feast days that honored their patron saint. The surviving records do, however, give some picture of the most important holidays for particular parishes and the local variations in community celebrations. Beyond the specified liturgy, both large and small parishes added to their celebrations by increasing the amount of spectacle and drama, and in this way they increased their participation.

The Christian calendar started four weeks before Christmas with the season of Advent, which receives no mention in the churchwardens' accounts. Medieval sermon collections admonish listeners that this was a season of preparation and repentance. The author of the *Speculum Sacerdotale* says that parishioners had to ready their hearts for the coming of Christ, and to this end, there must be no marriages and couples should refrain from sexual relations.[73] Christmas itself was much more obvious. In most parishes, the wardens bought, or had made, a Christmas candle that stood before the rood. It would have burned during the three masses for the feast of the Nativity as specified by the Sarum Missal.[74] Again turning to the *Speculum Sacerdotale*, the preacher explains that the three masses are for the three ages of the world. The first mass on Christmas eve was for the first age (Adam to Moses), the mass on Christmas morning was for the second age (Moses to Advent) and the midday mass was for the third age (Advent to the end of the world). The three ages are the time of natural law, of written law, and of grace.[75] How large the candle was varied according to each community's wealth. At St. Michael's in Bath, the earliest account of 1349 says that the candle contained one pound of wax.[76] By 1377, the amount had increased to ten pounds, and in 1420 both Christmas and Epiphany vigils required still more wax.[77] In Banwell, the parish spent a great deal on wax for the many candles placed throughout the church. There were two for the chancel, one for each of the four side altars, one before an image of the five wounds of Christ, and a trendal (a circular candle holder suspended before the rood). On average, they used 37 pounds of wax for Christmas.[78] This sort of fragmentary information is typical of how parish accounts recorded holy days. We have to infer that the increase in the amount of wax coincided with elaboration in observances. The increasing size of the candles also suggests that the laity took an interest in expanding their liturgical celebrations. Increasing the number and size of the candles was a way for them to participate in the parish's liturgy.[79]

Only the accounts for Bridgwater regularly record extra Christmas celebrations. This is perhaps to be expected with a Franciscan convent in town. St. Francis had popularized the manger scene as a Christmas celebration. Although the details emerge only gradually, it appears that Bridgwater developed some sort of Christmas or Epiphany pageant. There are expenses for repairing and washing the "starred suit" and for a man to hang a star inside the church.[80] In addition, in 1432 the parish paid someone to paint a picture, perhaps a movable one, of the three kings for Twelfth Day (Epiphany).[81] E. K. Chambers, in his work on the medieval stage, writes that many communities, especially on the Continent, had Christmas or Epiphany plays.[82] Although there is no direct mention of a play, perhaps the clerk, dressed in the star-covered robe, raised and lowered the star over a Christmas pageant or manger scene, where the painting served as scenery.

The Easter season, preceded by Lent and followed by Whitsun is far more evident in parochial records. During Lent, the wardens had all the images in the church covered with cloths; a Lenten veil also hung before the rood screen, hiding from view the high altar and the priest's celebration of mass.[83] Tintinhull bought a new veil in 1435 that cost 14s. 2d., a significant investment; Bridgwater recycled its old one as a cover for their image of St. George.[84] Most veils appear to have been attached to pulleys, so that they could be raised quickly for the right dramatic tone at the moment of the Resurrection on Easter. The author of the fifteenth-century didactic work *Dives and Pauper* explains that parishioners must cover the images in their church "in token that while men are in deadly sin they must not see God's face or the saints in heaven, and that God and all the court of heaven hide their faces from men and women while they are in deadly sin, until they will amend themselves by sorrow for their hurt and shrift of mouth (confession) and amend making."[85] As part of this concern with repentance and the health of the souls of the parish, Banwell's Lenten observances included reading the bede roll on each of the four Sundays, for which the clerk received extra payment.[86]

For both parishioners and the clergy, Easter was the highlight of the ecclesiastical calendar. As the commemoration of Christ's resurrection, it was a celebration of renewal and rebirth. Extensive preparations made this a busy season. The Easter sermon from the *Speculum Sacerdotale* admonished that, because Easter was the most important feast of the year, the church had to be cleaned and prepared.

On the wall curtains and hangings are to be hung and raised. In the choir are to be set dosers [ornamental hangings], tapits [ornamental hangings] and bankers [tapestry chair coverings], and a veil that was before the crucifix shall be removed and a pall put behind him, because that which was hidden before the passion of Christ is now opened and showed. The banners that symbolize the victory of Christ are raised up high. The altar is honored with his ornaments and with crosses set in order and in a row with the corporas case, the box with God's body, texts of the Gospels, and the table of the commandments.[87]

Typically a parish woman had cleaned the church, washed the linens, and scoured the candlesticks clean of old wax. Someone came in and covered the floor with fresh rushes, and the wardens had special large candles made. Tintinhull's Easter candle used between four and seven pounds of wax, while Banwell's used about 14½ pounds on average. Easter was also the one time of the year that most people received the Eucharist. During the rest of the year, they watched from the nave, received a piece of blessed bread, and perhaps kissed a wooden board carved or painted with a cross and called a pax, which a clerk passed through the nave.[88] To prepare for their annual Eucharist, the laity went to confession and received absolution. In the weeks leading up to Easter, the parish clergy spent a great deal of time listening to confessions and prescribing penance.

Easter ceremonies became increasingly elaborate in the later middle ages. In the fifteenth and sixteenth centuries, many parishes in Somerset began to reenact the Resurrection using an Easter sepulcher.[89] In most communities, such as Yeovil, the Easter sepulcher was a temporary wooden structure that the wardens paid someone to set up each year.[90] It usually stood along the north wall of either the chancel or a chapel, often the Mary chapel. Some parishes even built permanent niches into their church walls. In small rural Pilton, the sepulcher was a recess in the wall about five feet long and three feet high, probably the tomb of a clergyman or member of the local gentry. In contrast, the wealthy parish of St. Mary Redcliffe, in the suburbs of Bristol, built a particularly elaborate sepulcher in 1470. The vicar and churchwardens took delivery of the sepulcher on the fourth of July. It was covered in gold, silver, and brightly colored paint and adorning the wooden structure was an Image of God almighty rising out of the same sepulcher . . . Heaven made of timber & stained cloths . . . Hell made of timber & iron-work thereto with Devils to the number 13 . . . 4 knights, armed, keeping the sepulcher with their weapons in their hands; that is to say, 2 axes & 2 spears & 2 pikes . . . 4 pairs of angel wings for 4 angels, made of timber & well painted . . . the Father, the Crown, & Visage, the ball with a cross upon it, well gilt . . . the Holy Ghost coming out of Heaven into the Sepulcher.[91]

Parish records also suggest that a variety of other activities accompanied the Easter sepulcher. In the parish of St. Mary Magdalene in Taunton, a parish guild sponsored a play about Mary Magdalene as part of the sepulcher activities.[92] In some parishes, such as Yeovil, the wardens and the vicar performed the weekend vigil. By 1540, the Yeovil wardens concluded their vigil with an Easter breakfast.[93] Like their Christmas celebrations, Bridgwater's spectacle included a painting of the Resurrection.[94] A bell rang as the cloth dropped from the sepulcher, signaling the Resurrection. One account reads, "for cords & lines about the sepulcher & to the bell at the church door—14d." [95] Dropping the cloth may also have revealed the painting.

The sepulcher, with its attendant drama culminating in the Eucharist, became the centerpiece of the Easter celebration, linking the community with the mystery of the Resurrection.[96] On Good Friday, the priest placed the host in the sepulcher and covered it. A candle burned in front, and members of the parish kept a vigil in the church until Easter morning; then the host could be removed, and Easter mass celebrated.[97] When Redcliffe parishioners watched this reenactment, the decorations made the Easter message explicit. There was little confusion about what the laity were watching. In Pilton, however, the message of the Resurrection was relayed in other ways. Even if the wardens heavily decorated the tomb, using one of a deceased local cleric or noble personalized the message. This was the tomb of a former member whose fate was in God's hands.

There is some suggestion that this Easter drama came relatively late to western England, becoming popular only in the latter part of the middle ages.[98] Even when it begins to appear in the West Country parishes, it is a gradual process. In the boroughs of Bath, Bridgwater, and Yeovil, trade brought parishioners into contact with people and customs from all over England, and in these parishes, Easter sepulchers appear first. The accounts for St. Michael's, Bath, first report one in 1391, and the accounts for Bridgwater and Yeovil in the middle of the next century.[99] However, Glastonbury, which also had contact with the rest of England, does not record one in its churchwardens' accounts until 1500.[100] As we might expect, rural parishes adopted such practices somewhat later. As parishioners traveled to towns, they saw or heard about new devotional practices and introduced them to their home parishes. In this instance, diffusion of religious practices started in towns and gradually spread out to the countryside. Pilton's Easter sepulcher still survives, yet the accounts do not refer to it until 1517.[101] Banwell's church-wardens' accounts do not mention an Easter sepulcher until 1537, twenty-two years after the appearance of the first account.[102]

Following Easter, parishes celebrated a series of lesser holidays defined by their distance from Easter: Rogation, Ascension, and Whitsun. The activities conducted at this time of year addressed the parish's financial, social, religious, moral, and regulatory aspects, thus obviously infusing these seasons with local concerns. The parishes in Bath and Wells marked these days with added candles and processions with special banners. Rogation involved the parish-ioners processing around the parish boundaries (beating the bounds) to de-marcate exactly where the parish was. In Mirk's Rogation Sunday sermon contained in his *Festial*, he describes the procession as a noisy and boisterous affair. He writes: "Thus therefore put away all danger and mischief, holy church ordains that each man fast these days and go in procession, in order to have help and succor of God and of his saints. Wherefore in procession bells ring, banners are carried first, the cross comes after and the people follow."[103] In practice, this celebration appears more often in urban churchwardens' accounts than in rural ones.[104] St. Michael's in Bath annually paid someone 1d. for carrying banners during its rogation procession.[105] In 1457, the Yeovil wardens bought new banners for its rogation celebration. All the attendant activities served to define one parish from another and identify who belonged to which community.[106] Whitsun was also the season for ales and other fund-raising entertainments, as well as a common time for parish visitations and the churchwardens' presentments at the archdeacon's court. In one way or an-other, this season reminded parishioners of their duties and obligations to the parish, and those elements of parish life that distinguished them from sur-rounding parishes.

On the ninth Thursday after Easter came Corpus Christi. This holiday ex-tended the mystery surrounding the Easter sepulcher drama by honoring the host—the body of Christ. Mirk's sermon for the occasion worked to develop the mystery of the Eucharist with an *exemplum* about the host. He told the story of a woman who made the bread used at a mass being said by Pope Gregory the Great. When he gave her a piece of the bread, she smiled. When asked why she smiled she replied "you call that God's body which I made with my own hands."[107] Gregory, saddened by her disbelief, prayed that God might work a miracle to convince her otherwise. Instantly, the bread turned into raw and bleeding flesh, which he showed to the woman. She cried out "Lord, now I believe that you are Christ, God's son of Heaven in the form of bread."[108] Then Gregory prayed again and the flesh returned to bread form.[109] This story, which is not original to Mirk, does a number of things. It reaffirms the doctrine of transubstantiation and the importance of the priest's role in this doctrine. It also shows something of the relationship that the Church wanted the laity to have with the host; they should believe that it was the actual body of Christ and worship it as such. Yet by the fifteenth century this *exemplum* took on extra meaning because it also assumes the laity's role in preparing for parish celebrations. Their work for the parish was religious work.

Corpus Christi celebrations developed into more than a series of church services. The highlight of the celebrations included a procession that could become quite elaborate.[110] Corpus Christi was usually more a town celebration than a parish one. Glynne Wickham suggests that its prevalence in towns and cities, rather than the countryside, comes from the greater opportunities of patronage and financing that urban areas offered.[111] In larger towns, processions included plays or pageants dramatizing Bible stories that artisan guilds had sponsored.[112] As we will see, however, the parish still had an important role to play in the festivities; especially in smaller towns the form of these celebrations furthered the processes of community identification.[113]

Corpus Christi celebrations have attracted much attention from historians. Using the methodologies that anthropologists employ to study ritual, historians such as Charles Phythian-Adams, Mervyn James, and Miri Rubin have studied the social composition of such displays as a way of understanding what communities hoped to accomplish with their ever-expanding celebrations.[114] Phythian-Adams, whose work on early modern Coventry looks at the relationship between the city's ritual life and its economic prosperity, believes that the procession reflected an elite male view of the urban society.[115] James is more generous. In his often-cited article, "Ritual Drama and the Social Body in the Late Medieval English Town," he states: "the final intention of the cult [of Corpus Christi] was, then, to express the social bond and to contribute to social integration."[116] Later he adds that it was "a symbol of social wholeness [. . . providing] an essential and generic human bond without which there would be *no* society."[117] Rubin responds to this somewhat optimistic claim by reminding us that trying to view Corpus Christi as a mirror of the polity hides and ignores many of its components. While articulating a desired order for society, it does not resolve contradictions or ease local tensions.[118] Town organizations were by no means open to all. In the case of Coventry, where Phythian-Adams estimates that only 20 percent of the city's population was involved with the celebration, we can view the processions as a means of articulating order and hierarchy. These celebrations built into their procession a stratified image of their world. Coventry's claims that such celebrations contributed "to the wealth and worship of the whole body" does not negate an elitist view of the city.[119] More recently, Sarah Beckwith has looked at these festivals in terms of contemporary theological debates. The conflict between the Lollards and orthodox Christians make the host itself "a forum for social conflict."[120] Corpus Christi was a political statement of religious orthodoxy at a time when some challenged this orthodoxy. The presence of Lollards in Bristol and Taunton makes this interpretation especially relevant. Processions reinforced a specific town's governance system, but they were also a manifestation of orthodox Eucharistic doctrine. Taken together, these two views of Corpus Christi defined the town and its government as orthodox.

Evidence of Corpus Christi processions in Bath and Wells survives for only the larger boroughs of Bath, Glastonbury, Bridgwater, and Yeovil,[121] where the city oligarchies controlled the celebrations. Parishes provided the host, priests, and attendant torches—the physical signs of Christian orthodoxy—for the procession. The churchwardens' accounts for St. Michael's in Bath are the earliest to list Corpus Christi among their celebrations, as we might expect from a parish in a cathedral town. Here close contact with the bishop and his administration brought this holiday into the parish's calendar as early as 1370, although direct reference to a procession does not appear until the 1460s.[122] In 1462, the churchwardens carried a cross in the town's procession, the following year the parish also paid for the torchbearers, and by the 1470s, the parish also supplied banners.[123] A more centrally located parish, or perhaps the abbey, provided the host. Lack of documentation makes the town's exact contributions unclear. We do know that corporation funds paid for "drink and bread" on Corpus Christi eve every year.[124] The will of alderman John Jeffreys, alias Cocks, also suggests the prominence of civic authorities in this festival.[125] When Cocks died in 1511, he left £20 for an endowment to provide alms to the poor at Corpus Christi. Rather than have his parish's churchwardens or vicar oversee his bequest, he made it the mayor's responsibility. By putting his bequest in the hands of the mayor, he acknowledged that Corpus Christi was a town celebration and not strictly a parish one.

Although St. Michael's had the earliest reference to a parish celebrating this holiday, the first actual evidence for Corpus Christi processions in the diocese comes from Glastonbury. Its Corpus Christi procession started sometime between 1421 and 1428. The 1421 parish inventory makes no mention of it, but the 1428 one lists "1 canopy with 2 hangings of fine gauze for Corpus Christi."[126] In 1500 the parish paid one Master Hampton for the pageants and one play that he provided in the churchyard during Corpus Christi.[127] The Corpus Christi celebrations in the parish of St. John's in Yeovil followed a similar pattern. From the earliest records, the parish helped the borough celebrate the holiday.[128] Each year the parish rang the church bells during the procession and provided the host and a canopy to cover it. In 1540, the parish paid £3 5s. 11d. for a Corpus Christi play.[129] This was the last time the accounts mention this holiday; whether the town took it over completely, or it was a victim of Henry's reforms, is not clear.[130]

Bridgwater had another early procession. Here we can see something of how the town and parish worked together to put on the procession. Their cooperation delineates the relationship between them and picks up on the themes expressed in the seating arrangements discussed in the last chapter. Celebrations first appear in 1418, when the parish provided the shrine or fertour to carry the host and fortified the chaplains who prepared it with wine.[131] The parish continued to repair and adorn the fertour each year.[132] The parish also prepared the route by strewing the road with rushes to prevent the processioners from slipping.[133] The town provided food and drink to the marchers and supplied wine to the hospital and the Franciscans also resident in the town.[134] Both the amount of wine and the volume of spectacle increased over the years. In 1443, the town needed only one gallon, but by 1462, the corporation was providing five gallons. In 1431, the bailiff's accounts first recorded a shepherds' pageant, which was to be a regular feature until the mid-sixteenth century.[135] In 1449, the town hired pipers for the procession.[136] Eventually the town also had a feast, presumably for the merchant guild, who had marched in the procession, and their invited guests.[137] Bridgwater's celebration became large enough that members of the nobility favored the town with visits. In 1457 the duchess of Exeter was on hand, and in 1494 the king's mother, the earl of Arundel, and the mayor of Bristol watched the festivities, while the king's minstrels marched in the procession.[138]

Despite the sparse information, we can still interpret the Bridgwater celebration as a community-defining exercise for the parish. Although we do not know the order of the procession, we do know something of how the parish and the town worked to create it. The parish, as the town's religious center, provided the religious objects around which the town corporation built the procession. Yet even here, we can see a tension between what the clergy and the laity contributed. Specifically, the parish clergy supplied the host and the clerics to carry it, while the laity provided and maintained the fertour, the men to carry the torches which marched next to the host, and the rushes to cover the road. The town, not the parish, hosted the visiting dignitaries. The town also sponsored the pageant, and finally, the town, whose wealth came from the port and its trade in goods, such as wine, supplied the food and liquid refreshment. The different institutions of Bridgwater collaborated for the success of the procession by contributing their own specialties. Giving wine to the hospital and friars, who also had an interest in the civic proceedings and good order of the community, further consolidated the different parts of the town. The hospital was the parish's rector, and it had had a bitter and acrimonious relationship with the town in the past. In 1380 and 1381, relations degenerated into violence, becoming engulfed in the larger Revolt of 1381. Grievances stemmed from the burgesses' unhappiness at the hospital's privileged position. By the fifteenth century, however, tensions had eased, thanks in part to the growth of the burgesses' wealth and prosperity.[139] Nonetheless, it is not hard to imagine that town harmony concerned all involved. This relationship served as one of many backdrops for the Corpus Christi procession in Bridgwater.

The annual Corpus Christi procession recreated the town-parish relationship discussed in the last chapter. Social status came from wealth and involvement in town government, which both attendance at church and religious procession reproduced. Religious behavior clearly extended beyond the nave of the church, but the parish's position with respect to the town was implicated in this religious behavior. Although information on the other Somerset Corpus Christi processions is less complete than what we can see in Bridgwater, we can assume that they too recreated tensions, concerns, and local relationships.

The Cult of the Saints

Catholic concepts of the holy and ordinary shaped time for the medieval community. Christ may have been the most important expression of this shaping, but the ecclesiastical calendar also commemorated the saints. Since the beginning of Christianity, saints have been important to a personal understanding of Christianity, and by the late middle ages, veneration of the saints constituted a large part of local religion.[140] Medieval Christians viewed saints in a variety of different ways: as intercessors to God and Christ on behalf of the supplicant, as helpers in times of trouble, either in this world or in Purgatory, as models for behavior, and as examples of the power of faith and good works.[141] The laity expected to bargain, plead, and encourage the saints through prayers, offerings, and pilgrimages.[142] In a sermon about patron saints, Mirk likens veneration of the saints to the relationship between a lord and his vassal. "For just as a temporal lord helps and defends all parishioners or tenants, just so the saint that is patron of the church helps and defends all who are parishioners to him and have worshiped [and] hallowed his day and [made] offerings to him."[143] Local devotions to the saints multiplied throughout the middle ages. Increased interest in the saints brought a concomitant increase in a parish's financial commitments and obligations. As with holy days that marked out the events of Christ's life, the wealthier parishes had more elaborate and more numerous devotions, and the laity spent more money to enhance them.

Saints had dominion over particular interests, concerns, and desires. Patron saints watched over the activities of groups and individuals and people at different life stages. According to *The Golden Legend*, one of the most popular collections of saints' lives in the middle ages, St. Margaret of Antioch at her death asked that any woman invoking her name during childbirth be protected.[144] Women during and after childbirth also prayed to other female saints, such as Mary, Anne, or Elizabeth.[145] The parish of Bruton had a red silk girdle, a relic of St. Mary's, "which is a solemn relic to women travailing which shall not miscarry *in partu*."[146] In general, however, images played a more important role in these devotions than relics of the saints.[147] The parish of Bridgwater had some of St. Stephen's blood in a silver reliquary, but it only appears in an inventory; there is no associated veneration of St. Stephen.[148] Instead, the laity filled their churches with images. These could be wall paintings, free-standing statues, or windows. Care of an image involved cleaning and repair, but more often it involved decorating it, dressing it, and leaving it items when one died. Dressing the saint seems to be a particularly female form of devotion.[149] Sybil Pochon bequeathed "her best silk robe" to St. Katherine, which she seems to have expected the statue to wear on special occasions, such as her feast day.[150] More common were gifts of wedding rings. Agnes Petygrew of Publow directed that her executors give her wedding ring to the St. Mary "at the pillar."[151] In the churchwardens' accounts of Yatton, the churchwardens recorded as part of the parish's goods the rings given to the parish by women.[152] Whereas in 1468 the parish had only two rings, the gifts of Christine Hycks and Joan Prewett, by 1480 the parish held twenty rings, and the number continued to grow.[153] Such interaction with the saints shows the fundamental importance of their veneration to the late medieval Christian.

Preachers expounded on the importance of such images, sometimes describing them in their sermons. Mirk in his sermon for the Feast of St. Margaret explains that "Margaret is painted. . . with a dragon under her feet and a cross in her hand, showing how by virtue of the cross she had victory over the fiend [devil]."[154] The author of the early fifteenth-century *Dives and Pauper* explains the different ways that images aided memory and inspired religious commitment. Pauper explains that one was not to worship the image but worship before it. [155] The viewer would be better able to identify with and contemplate the suffering of Christ when looking at an image of him.[156] This work also provides a lengthy description of the saints and their symbols to remind the viewer of the saints' special relationship to God. [157] Pauper does not tell Dives to empathize with the saints' suffering, merely to know their symbols and be humble in the face of their great feats of faith.[158] Such an ideology gave artists a strong incentive to maintain conventional iconography and standard depictions of their subjects.[159]

The range of saints venerated in parishes shows how originality and conformity play off against each other. There was some latitude for personal and local preference in deciding which saint would appear in the church. Here, the

Table 6.2. Popularity of Saints and Guild Endowments

Saint	No. of appearances in Appendix	No. of parish guilds	Saint	No. of appearances in Appendix	No. of parish guilds
St. Mary	86	53	St. Peter	2	0
St. Katherine	24	11	St. Rosmi	2	0
Holy Trinity	22	11	Holy Spirit	1	0
Easter Sepulcher	19	1	St. Anthony	1	0
St. George	14	3	St. Blasé	1	1
St. Christopher	11	0	St. Congor	1	0
St. John the Baptist	11	7	St. Culbone	1	0
St. Michael	9	2	St. Cullani	1	1
St. Andrew	8	2	St. Dubricius	1	1
St. Anne	8	2	St. Elizabeth	1	1
Name of Jesus	7	7	St. Ellen	1	0
All Saints	5	0	St. Etheldrede	1	1
All Souls	5	0	St. Gonthal	1	0
St. Erasmus	5	1	St. Joseph	1	0
St. James	5	2	St. Lucy	1	0
St. Leonard	5	1	St. Martin	1	1
St. John (not specified)	4	1	St. Olave	1	1
St. Mary Magdalene	4	1	St. Radegund	1	0
St. Thomas	4	0	St. Savior	1	0
St. Giles	3	0	St. Sebastian	1	0
Corpus Christi	2	0	St. Sitha	1	0
Five Wounds	2	0	St. Savior	1	0
St. Clement	2	1	St. Thomas Becket	1	0
St. Gregory	2	0	St. Wolfrygs	1	0
St. John the Evangelist	2	0	Unknown guilds		21
St. Lawrence	2	1	Total		147

spiritual concerns of particular groups and individuals could be addressed. In general, the saints venerated in Somerset parishes were conventional. According to the evidence from wills and churchwardens' accounts, few local saints, such as St. Dunstan or St. Joseph of Arimathea, attracted the support of the parishioners[160] (see Table 6.2). The most popular saint in Somerset, as in England at large, was the Virgin Mary. Medieval Christians honored her with a number of feast days. Her four major celebrations were her purification (2 February), annunciation (25 March), assumption (15 August), and nativity (8 September). Parishes celebrated them with special masses, processions, and candles. The Church also commemorated her various aspects, such as Our Lady of Pity or Mercy.[161] She was also the most prevalent patron saint for parish churches and parish guilds; all churches seem to have practiced some form of devotion to her.[162] Of the 126 known guild dedications for Bath and Wells, 42 percent were dedicated to Mary (see Table 6.2 and Appendix). Nettlecombe added to the festivity of one of her feast days by adding a second ale in 1536.[163] The next most popular saint was St. Katherine. She was the most honored saint in a group of saints known as the virgin martyrs. Of this group, the most commonly portrayed ones were SS. Dorothy, Margaret, Katherine, Cecilia, Appollonia, and Lucy. Their images appeared on rood screens, windows, and wall paintings. Among the many popular male saints, St. Christopher stands out because of the number of images of him. Unlike Mary and Katherine, however, devotion to him did not take place under the auspices of a guild. Of the eleven devotions to him none are guilds, yet he was the most commonly portrayed saint in wall paintings.[164] An example still survives in Ditcheat. Parishioners popularly believed that seeing him would protect one from harm the rest of the day. Situated typically opposite the door, this placement facilitated a quick peek at him, before one went on one's way.

Many collections of saints' lives appeared in the middle ages. Although some were intended for elite literate audiences, many were written for preachers and parish priests to help them with their sermons. Like the *Ignorantia Sacerdotum*, their composition was part of the post-Fourth-Lateran-Council efforts to educate the laity into the ways of Christianity. The two most influential collections of saints' lives in England were the *Golden Legend*, written by Jacobus de Voragine, and the anonymous *South English Legendary*. De Voragine wrote his *Golden Legend* in the middle of the thirteenth century to help the clergy of his native Lombardy learn the saints' lives. Its popularity soon spread beyond Italy and numerous manuscript copies still exist. The *Golden Legend* was one of the first books that Caxton printed.[165] Although de Voragine originally intended his work for the clergy, copies found their way into the hands of interested and literate laity all over Europe, including Bath and Wells. In 1491, William Stenyng left his copy of the *Golden Legend* to his parish of Selworthy, so that they might pray for his soul.[166] Although only an English phenomenon, the *South English Legendary* was also quite popular. With over fifty copies still extant, particularly from the southwestern and northeastern parts of England, it is one of the most common medieval English manuscripts.[167] The audience of the *South English Legendary* is more of a mystery. There is evidence for well-to-do merchants owning it as well as clerics.[168] Thomas Heffernan argues that clerics read it out loud to peasant audiences.[169] The difficulty in pinning down an audience may come from the fact that the anonymous author was not aiming for a particular social group, but rather sought to make his (or her) work useful in a parish liturgical context, and a parish would have had a wide range of social classes. No specific evidence from Somerset will solve this quandary, but both the wills and the churchwardens' accounts record the existence of many legenda in the diocese. When William Stourton drew up his will in 1410, he left his son his "legend of the saints in English."[170] Vague terms like "legenda" or "legends of the saints" do not explain which versions the churchwardens or the testators meant, if in fact they knew themselves.[171] In the fifteenth century, sermon collections such as Mirk's *Festial*, which retold the stories of the saints' martyrdoms, became popular. The abbreviated stories of the saints that appear in the *Festial*, and also in the unique manuscripts of the *Speculum Sacerdotale* and the Ross collection, provide further examples of how the laity would have learned their saints' lives. As with the case of the legenda, we know that sermon collections proliferated throughout the diocese. St. John's, Glastonbury includes two sermon collections, one large and one small, among its inventory of books.[172] Yet whose sermons they were remains unknown.

Karen Winstead in her book, *Virgin Martyrs: Legends of Sainthood in Late Medieval England*, shows how the literary characterizations of the very popular virgin martyrs did not remain consistent in the late middle ages.[173] This shift in portrayals of virgin martyrs that Winstead identifies is also apparent in parish manifestations of the cult of the saints and has implications for understanding attitudes towards the parish as a unit of lay involvement. The authors of the *Golden Legend* and the *South English Legendary* portrayed the virgin martyrs as triumphant, defiant, heroic, and confrontational. Winstead describes their world as topsy-turvy, where "women were on top."[174] Although the *South English Legendary* dwelt in vivid detail on the torture of the saints, the author did not depict them as suffering. Instead they are triumphant in the face of their tortures and tormentors.[175] Winstead argues that the clergy saw these women as metaphors for clerical authority within society and the authority of the Church in the larger world.[176] Yet she goes on to point out that the overturned gender hierarchies of the *Golden Legend* and the *South English Legendary's* virgin-martyr stories might have attracted those living in post-plague England for different reasons. The decline of serfdom and the new economic opportunities that towns and trade offered to men and women of the lower classes challenged notions of social order. She writes, "virgin martyr legends, with their simultaneous celebration and punishment of the socially disruptive saints, could play to the divergent, and perhaps ambivalent, views that readers would have harbored toward the socioeconomic changes that were occurring in late medieval England."[177]

In Mirk's *Festial* and the *Speculum Sacerdotale*, the saints lose their defiance and suffer during their tortures. For Mirk, one of the big attractions of the saints is their suffering. In his sermon for the feast of St. Andrew, he explains that the laity were to venerate Andrew specifically, but saints more generally, for three reasons: their holiness, miracles, and passion or suffering.[178] In his account of the life of St. Margaret, Mirk goes so far as to eliminate Margaret's confrontation with Olibrius.[179] The author of the *Speculum Sacerdotale* dwells on St. Katherine's suffering and teaching, not her defiance of Maxentius.[180] By shifting their focus to the virgin martyrs' suffering, the preachers emphasized what Winstead describes as " 'transferable' qualities—courtesy, patience, diligence, humility, piety, charity—which would make the saints suitable models for laywomen as well as for consecrated virgins."[181] These fifteenth-century versions, such as those offered in Mirk's *Festial*, but also those saints' lives which were largely unavailable to the rank and file of the parish, such as Lydgate's life of St. Margaret and St. Petronilla and Osbern Bokenham's *Legendys of Hooly Wummen*, provided models for lay behavior. Now they were "heroic examples of gracious comportment."[182] Winstead believes that this shift came about because of an increase in the consumption of books by an essentially conservative bourgeois audience. Authors wrote for paying customers and had to give them what they wanted. They wanted saints' lives, but not ones that would, even inadvertently, challenge their social positions. The ongoing threat of Lollardy also made authorities suspicious of all vernacular learning and literacy. Provocative and rebellious saints might be too threatening.[183]

Winstead directs her discussion to the social elites who hired private confessors to guide their spiritual lives and could and did purchase books and manuscripts. I believe, however, that the changes in what elite audiences expected and wanted from their saints' lives were also played out in different ways in parishes. These literary changes coincide with the growth of lay parochial organization. Although the parish enjoyed increased prominence in the religious and social landscape of medieval England, its growing significance did not come easily. The parish was in many ways an ambivalent space. Something of this ambivalence shows up in the parish's lack of legal status before the common law, which I discussed in Chapter 1. Although the laity acted as a corporation when they worked on maintaining their parishes, they were not, in fact, incorporated. Conflicts such as the ones we saw in the last chapter, between the monks and parishioners in Dunster, or the reorganization of the relationship between the town and the parish of Bridgwater, all speak to the growing pains of the parish as an institution. The lines of tension were not always the parish versus another group; sometimes tension lay internally between groups of laity. This may be, in fact, why we find relatively few men in the town hierarchies of either Bridgwater or Wells who also served in the parish administration. The heroic and confrontational image of the virgin martyrs might have appealed to those inhabiting the ambivalent space of the late medieval parish. The message of social unbalance that Winstead read in these legends might also apply to the rise of the parish and its newfound role as a forum for community identity.

The parish as a forum for lay involvement and community identity came of age in the fourteenth and fifteenth centuries, the time when presentations of the virgin martyrs shifted from heroic and confrontational to submissive and courteous. In a community of many groups and many interests, those with conservative social agendas would have met up with those who benefited from these social changes. The parish accommodated these differences. Well-to-do burgesses and yeomen sought to consolidate and affirm their status through support of the parish. This also meant inculcating their families with proper notions of behavior. Yet these same individuals might also fight to preserve what they understood to be their parish's community identity in the face of competition, be it from another parish, a nearby monastery, or a faction within the parish itself. The same people could hold competing ideas: on the one hand, they wanted to promote the interests of the parish; on the other, they wanted to uphold their own social position. The parish embraced this jumble of opinions through the performance of the cult of the saints and the different ways it portrayed them.

The many different versions of the saints' lives that parishioners heard or read shaped the artistic presentations of images of the saints.[184] Images were part of an elaborate votive structure that contributed to a parish's cult of the saints. As we have seen in the last chapter, the realities of building renovation meant that parish churches could be a jumble of architectural and artistic styles. Initially, wall paintings were the primary form of art, but as perpendicular gothic architecture became more popular, the balance between stained glass and wall paintings tipped in favor of glass.[185] Smaller decorative paintings and depictions of individual saints between the windows replaced the large murals.[186] Scholars have grouped wall paintings into five categories based upon their subject matter: decorative schemes, last judgments, narratives of the life of Christ (especially the nativity or the crucifixion), lives of the saints (including the apostles and the Virgin), and moralities, especially the seven deadly sins and the seven works of mercy.[187] Stained-glass windows followed a similar iconographic program.[188] In general, however, wall painting survival is poor for Somerset; there are no examples of morality paintings and only a fragment of a doom.[189]

The images and *exempla* that preachers used in their sermons appeared in parish wall paintings and other religious art. Yet, despite the similarities between sermons and wall paintings, the two media did not always present the same message. Differences in emphasis and focus between what was represented in art and what the sermons said show the different ways in which the clergy and parishioners understood their Bible stories, saints' lives, and moral exhortations. Paintings and other art work grew from both individual and collective decision-making. In this way, the laity influenced the content and form of the images that adorned their walls and filled their chapels. The windows in several Somerset churches portray St. Katherine crushing Maxentius under her feet rather than with her wheel.[190] This is how the *Golden Legend* and the *South English Legendary* characterized her. At some point in the artistic history of Somerset, this image of St. Katherine was meaningful. Yet it is unlikely that this image remained constant. As we saw in the last chapter, several parishes rebuilt their rood screens in the late fifteenth and early sixteenth centuries. Although the paintings of the saints that adorned the dado no longer survive, we know that in Devon and East Anglia, where they do, the same saint stood demurely in contemporary clothing holding her wheel, the instrument of her passion, like a toy.[191] The very real likelihood of competing portrayals of the same saint picks up on the same tensions as those outlined by Winstead, yet within a parish context these changing images of the saints can also reflect issues of growing parish autonomy and community identity.

We can see something of the process of negotiating the content of these images in an incident in the churchwardens' accounts for Yatton. In 1467, the parishioners instructed their wardens to hire a painter to paint a picture of the Virgin Mary. The wardens then received donations from individuals. In an unusual acknowledgment of lower-class female patronage, the churchwardens' accounts record that two women gave money to help pay for this image.[192] As we have seen in an earlier chapter, when the wardens added a picture of St. Christopher, they incurred the disapproval of the parish. Either the wardens acted without the community's leave, or the painting was not in a manner or location pleasing to the parishioners. Whatever the reason, the wardens had to reimburse the church for the cost of the second painting and the painter had to repaint it.[193] In another example from 1470, we find that when the guild of St. Mary in the parish of St. Cuthbert's in Wells wanted a new carving behind the altar, the guild wardens, in conjunction with the master of the town, negotiated the substance of the new carving with the stone carver. It was to have "imagery such as can be thought by the master and his brothers most according to the story of the said front: in the lowest part of the [first] stage shall be a Jesse. The which Jesse shall lineally run from image to image through all the aforesaid front and course as skillfully as it can be wrought."[194] The contract makes it clear that the guild had a great deal of say over the content of the carving (Figure 6.1). In the same parish, some twenty-eight years later, Richard Vowell left 40s. for the painting of the St. Mary's chapel and altar.[195] It is possible that, having left so much money, Vowell also influenced the iconographic scheme. As the contract between the guild wardens and carver shows, there was a great deal of room for both the carver's and the wardens' interpretive ideas about how to portray the genealogy of the Virgin Mary. And, as the conflict in Yatton shows, there was more than one way to paint a saint.

Figure 6.1. Tree of Jesse carving behind altar in St. Mary's chapel, St. Cuthbert's, Wells. Photograph by Katherine L. French.

Parishioners venerated the saints in a variety of ways. Although the clergy expected the laity to fast on the eve of the saint's day, attend church, and, on the actual day of the feast, attend two more services (morning prayer and high mass), local venerations involved much more than this. By far the easiest and oldest form of parish devotion was a candle or light.[196] Sometimes that was all there was, but often the light was part of a chapel or side altar (see Appendix). As we saw in the last chapter, large endowments could include a chapel complete with stipendiary priest, vestments, and liturgical items. Parish guilds often maintained these chapels. Guilds were the next most common way of honoring a saint, with 42 percent of the known endowments involving guilds. For example, Tintinhull, a relatively poor and rural parish only had one guild and chapel which they dedicated to St. Mary. Banwell, also a rural parish, but with more money, had several guilds, many lights, and multiple chapels. Whatever the form, even in the smallest parish churches, the cult of the saints played an important role in local religious life.[197]

Evidence for the veneration of St. Nicholas shows something of the differences in how the laity and the episcopacy expected to venerate the saints. St. Nicholas' day was one of the 43 *festa ferianda* listed by Ralph of Shrewsbury in 1342. Christians throughout Europe and in England had long venerated him, but in 1503 Bishop Oliver King still felt it necessary to re-promote his feast day.[198] Apparently during a recent visitation he found, or had reported to him, that many parishes did not celebrate the liturgy of his feast day.[199] This mandate is somewhat surprising as 7 percent of the parishes with traceable saint devotions had either lights, chapels, or guilds dedicated to St. Nicholas; this makes him was one of the most popular saints in the diocese (see Table 6.2). Like St. Mary, but unlike St. Christopher, St. Nicholas and his cult inspired a level of collective activity among parishioners. Glastonbury had a side altar and image dedicated to him by 1366.[200] Croscombe had a guild dedicated to him by 1474. Banwell did not have an endowment dedicated to him, but the men of this parish held their hogling activities around his feast day (December 6), and there was a window with scenes from his life somewhere in the church.[201] Although this evidence shows that some parishes knew this saint and kept his feast day, none of it proves that the parishioners attended church on his feast day, or that there were even special services. His image appeared in several churches and his cult became part of some fundraising strategies; this was not, however, the kind of veneration the bishop required. These activities were acceptable only when accompanied by a special liturgy that the laity attended. It is difficult to know how far to take the bishop's complaint, but when read against how parishes actually celebrated the saint, it is easy to see the gap between lay and episcopal religious practices.

Although episcopal promotion might introduce a new saint into parish liturgy, without personal or collective interest to promote the saint he or she would never become part of local religious life. Some new saints, such as David or Chad, made little impact on Somerset parish life. The cult of St. George, however, caught people's imaginations, and he quickly became one of the more popular saints in the diocese.[202] We have already seen something of how some parishes juxtaposed him with Robin Hood, but the growth of his cult also shows how noble interests percolated down to the local level. His role as patron saint of England may have helped to attract the nobility to this cult. Bishop Bubwith introduced the cult of St. George to Bath and Wells in 1415. Already by this point, King Edward III's (r. 1312–77) interest in chivalry had led to the foundation of the Royal Order of the Garter. This order promoted St. George as its patron and associated him with the ideals of loyalty and chivalry.[203] Later, King Henry V (r. 1413–22) and King Edward IV (r. 1461– 70, 1471–83) were also particularly devoted to St. George.[204] Both Glastonbury and Bridgwater quickly integrated St. George into their parishes' venerations. Although there are no reports of plays and processions in his honor, such as were held in Norwich and other areas, St. George became quite popular.[205] By 1418, an inventory for St. John's in Glastonbury includes a painted banner with St. George's image on it.[206] It presumably hung in the newly renovated St. George's chapel within the church. Evidence of a parish veneration, so closely on the heels of episcopal promulgation, suggests that Glastonbury already had a cult of St. George. Eventually, Glastonbury's celebration of his feast day (April 23) involved not only the particular liturgy, but also a special collection for good works. In 1428, the parish distributed money to the poor. In 1500, when the image of St. George needed gilding, Robert Page collected 33s. 4d. from the children, and Robert Hendy collected 13s. 4d. from the women, to finance this project.[207] Bridgwater also developed its St. George veneration in the mid-fifteenth century. The 1447 inventory mentions that the parish had a statue of St. George, and the following year, during an extensive building program, the parish added on a chapel for St. George, further increasing the prominence of his cult within the parish.[208] By the middle of the sixteenth century, a guild supported this chapel.[209] Perhaps Bridgwater's role in trade and the prominence of Glastonbury Abbey gave the laity in these two parishes more contact with national religious fashions than those elsewhere.

Other parishes in Somerset did not become interested in the cult of St. George until the beginning of the sixteenth century, by which point the gentry in particular seem to have promoted it. Because the kings of England particularly favored St. George, local patronage of the saint allowed for the local elites to demonstrate their allegiance to the king and their interest in his pious concerns—an important consideration during and after the turbulent Wars of the Roses and the start of the new Tudor dynasty. In 1485 Sir John Saint Maur,

a member of the local gentry and parishioner of Bekynton, left one cow to ensure that a candle burned perpetually before that church's St. George statue.[210]
Nettlecombe's parish patron, Sir John Trevelyan, did more than that; he left
money in his will, written in 1518 and proved in 1522, to build a chapel
dedicated to both St. Mary and St. George:

Immediately after my decease make a chapel of Our Lady & S. George in the north
part of the chancel of Nettlecombe in length of the said chancel & breadth of 11 or 12
feet, after the cast and proportion as is contained in a bill for the making of the same
signed with my own hand.[211]

His dedication to this cult spread beyond Nettlecombe; he also left St. George
banners to five Cornish parishes. In 1535, the parish started construction on a
new aisle for the chapel.[212] To make room for the new addition the workers
had to take down the preexisting statues of St. Christopher and St. George.
The bequests of John Trevelyan show how his spiritual interests, perhaps
learned by imitation of the court and other nobles, influenced local devotions.[213] Because of this new chapel, Nettlecombe had another priest and altar
to incorporate into its processions and a new image to dress and adore. Introducing a new cult required more than pious interest; it also took money. In
1524, the wardens of Stogursey paid a carver £23 13s. 5d. to make an image of
St. George.[214] Part of the carver's job was to travel to Wells and to Bristol to
view other such statues for comparison. When he finished his job, the statue
had a line attached to a bell that was rung during the appropriate moment in
the service. When Croscombe developed a local cult to St. George, the wardens, as we saw in an earlier chapter, eventually tied it into their fundraising
activities. In 1508, the churchwardens paid John Carter, "the George maker,"
30s. to make a statue of the saint.[215] By 1515, the wardens set up a collection
box by the statue, and in 1522 they turned this collection into an ale that
eventually replaced the Robin Hood revels as a regular source of income.[216] By
the 1530s, St. George was one of the more popular saints in Somerset, with
many parishes honoring him with chapels, lights, and guilds. (See Appendix.)
   The rise in popularity of the cult of St. George shows a different pattern of
cultural diffusion from the one we saw in the spread of Easter sepulchers.
Although Glastonbury and Bridgwater had early St. George cult sites, the
parishioners' interest in St. George did not lead to a greater interest in the saint
in the rest of the diocese. His popularity appears later at the behest of the local
elites. Even in Croscombe, where the gentry were not obviously involved in
either the parish or this cult, the wardens' use of St. George's feast day to hold
an ale mimics, in a limited way, royal use of this cult. In the fifteenth century,
parish guilds had raised most of this parish's money. Over the course of the
sixteenth century, the wardens assumed control over more of the fundraising.

As they did so, they used St. George to legitimize their changing role in the parish. They did not turn over care for his image to a guild; it remained under the control of the churchwardens. Similarly, Edward IV used St. George to legitimize his claim to the throne and the establishment of his new dynasty.[217]

The celebrations surrounding St. George and St. Nicholas show how local concerns intermingled with the liturgies that parishes across England and Europe observed. The laity did not just venerate them on their saints' days, but they built chapels, statues, and altars to them and supported them with guilds. The guilds in turn promoted their cult all year long. What is more, the parish celebrations of these and other saints were not limited to special liturgies; they inspired extra-liturgical celebrations that raised money for the parish and further bound the saint to local religious practice.

* * *

The men and women of Bath and Wells accepted new venerations and religious practices, but they do not appear to be in the forefront of religious innovation. Analysis of these celebrations, however, reveals many of the same expectations that we saw when comparing fundraising strategies. Parishioners used their liturgical calendar and the cult of the saints to articulate the relationship between the parish and the larger world of the manor or town. Urban parishes were a source of spectacle in a way that rural parishes were not. The bigger budgets from rental properties that characterized urban parishes such as Bath and Bridgwater gave them funds to finance productions such as Corpus Christi processions, Christmas plays, or Easter sepulchers, and more money to maintain side altars and devotions to saints. At the same time, relying on rents for income diminished the members' daily involvement in supporting their parish. The activities sponsored by town parishes emphasized their presence in boroughs already crowded with other communal associations. Such displays also identified which parishioners had money, social standing, and political influence. Events such as plays and processions reminded the town and its inhabitants that they were also parishioners. Rural parishes in Bath and Wells did not have to compete for such attention. The church was already the biggest building and a primary form of association and social life. Even the wealthy rural communities of Banwell and Yatton did not use parish income to stage elaborate productions for the benefit of members. Spectacles were used for fundraising or kept to such a modest scale that they cost very little. In rural parishes, entertainment produced income and fostered parish involvement, whereas in borough parishes such productions provided entertainment, instruction, and a way for individuals to promote their own social position through acts of piety.

Along with the message of salvation, feast days gave parishes a chance to express their community identity. These celebrations ordered the parishioners along status and gender lines, reminding all who participated and all who watched how this particular parish structured itself, and what its relationship to neighboring institutions was. These celebrations also gave parishioners a chance to express the ambivalence they had to the parish. To be sure, parish life could be a place to achieve a level of local influence, but it was also a unit of regulation, taxation, and supervision. With lay organization came responsibility and, perhaps, personal liability.

CONCLUSION

Moving the late medieval parish out from under the shadow of the Reformation makes a number of issues and themes visible. We can see how much medieval Christianity depended on local resources and priorities; religious practices cannot be separated from the location in which practitioners operated. The local nature of religious life means that it is difficult to generalize about religious interests and conviction in England on the eve of the Reformation. Medieval parishioners did not know that the Reformation was upon them, and even when it was, no one knew how far it would proceed. What is hopefully now apparent is that medieval parishioners, at least those in Bath and Wells, were not waiting for the Reformation. The medieval parish was a dynamic and creative place in its own right. One way of understanding this vibrancy is to look at parish religion in terms of community identity. This is not intended to be a romantic vision, but rather it is one that acknowledges the laity's ability to invest in and participate in the parish in ways that reflected both individual and collective concerns. As with all communities, membership comes with obligations and burdens. Sometimes parish life could be confining and onerous, sometimes spiritually and socially comforting and affirming.

It is not then surprising in the conservative world of West-Country parishes that the laity of Bath and Wells dragged their feet in accepting Henry's reforms. Henry VIII's religious reforms, pushed through Parliament as he tried to divorce his first wife, brought visible change to Bath and Wells. Although his break with Rome was no doubt emotionally jarring, Rome was far away. The first legislation actually to have an impact on the parishes was Thomas Cromwell's rearrangement of the liturgical calendar. In 1532, he moved all church dedications to October and abolished the keeping of holidays between

July 1 and September 23 and during Westminster's legal terms. The exceptions were the feasts of the Apostles, the Virgin Mary, St. George, Ascension, St. John the Baptist, All Saints, and Candlemas.[1] Although masses could still be said, people could not take the day off from work. This was followed by the abolition of all lights before images and dissolution of all pilgrimage shrines in 1537.[2] If we look at the parish records, however, we see that even these efforts were only partially effective. Banwell stopped collecting money for its St. Katherine and St. Mary lights, but it kept its Holy Cross gathering, renaming it the Easter collection.[3] Tintinhull still commemorated St. Margaret's day with an ale. Henry also had difficulty in getting parishes to buy the English Bible he mandated in 1538. Most parishes in Bath and Wells did not make this purchase until 1541, when they were in danger of being fined (See Table 6.1), and as we saw in the last chapter, this was not because parishes as a rule did not own books.

Henry left for later religious reformers the social and economic networks that parishes provided for their members. Still remaining were the ales, guilds, plays, bells, pews, and rood screens—many now minus their saints. Although the parish never existed outside the hierarchical organization that invented and supervised it, the institutional strictures were not imposed on blank slates, and the parish assumed a greater role in the lives of the laity than merely that of a convenient unit for paying tithes and receiving religious instruction. Abolishing the images in the church may have left holes in the lives of the laity, but the community of the parish was much more than the sum total of its liturgical practices, just as the reformers feared. There were important cultural dimensions to parochial religion. The parish was a unit that provided its members with responsibilities and support. Henry's reforms did not wipe this all away in his efforts to create an English Church. He created, however, a great deal of confusion over the new liturgical role of the parish in the lives of its members. This is expressed poignantly by the 1549 churchwardens' account from Bridgwater. In it the scribe writes: "to John Fillips for to ride to Wells to know how the church should be used, his horse, hire 3 days himself & for certain songs— 6s. 6d."[4]

APPENDIX

Parish Endowments 1298–1548

Parish (dedication)	Year	Saint veneration	Form	Source
Abbots Isle [Abbotsleigh?] (Holy Trinity)	1548		Light	CC
Aller	1548	St. Mary	Light (2)	CC
(St. Andrew)	1548		Guild	CC
Ashbrittel	1504	St. Mary	Light	Will
(St. John Bapt.)	1548	St. Mary	Guild	CC
Asshton (All Hallows)	1483	St. John Baptist	Chapel	Will
Backwell (St. Andrew)	1548		Light	CC
Bageworth (St. Congor)	1548		Altar	CC
Banwell (St. Andrew)	1548		Guild	CC
	1515 1532	Five Wounds	Light	CWA
	1515 1539	High Cross	Light Guild	CWA Will
	1516 1518 1548	St. George	Altar Guild Chapel	CWA
	1515 1536	St. Katherine	Light Altar Guild	CWA
	1515 1537	St. Mary	Light Altar Guild	CWA

Parish (dedication)	Year	Saint veneration	Form	Source
Barrow Gurney (St. Mary)	1543	St. Mary	Guild	Will
Batcombe (St. Mary)	1543		Guild	Will
Bath (St. Michael within the city)	1548		Light	CC
Bath (St. Michael w/o the North Gate)	1425	All Saints	Altar	CWA
	1364 1441	St. Egidii	Light	CWA
	1510	St. George	Aisle	Will
	1377	St. Katherine	Altar	CWA
	1423		Chapel	CWA
	1450		Guild	Will
	1537			Will
	1394	St. Mary	Altar	CWA
	1506		Chapel	CWA
	1349	St. Michael	Light	CWA
Bath (St. Mary de Stalles)	1389	St. Mary	Guild	GI
Batheaston (St. John Bapt.)	1548		Light	CC
Bathforde (St. Swithun)	1548		Chapel (on Main street)	CC
	1548		Light	CC
Beckyngton (St. George)	1484	St. Christopher	Light	Will
	1484 1535	St. John Bapt.	Light Altar	Will
	1484	St. John Ev.	Altar	Will
	1497 1503	St. Mary	Light Chapel	Will
	1497	St. Sitha	Light	Will
Bedminster (St. John Bapt.)	1548		Chapel	CC
	1548		Light	CC
Beercrocombe (St. James)	1548		Light	CC
Berkley (St. Mary)	1548		Light	CC
Blakedon (St. Gregory)	1548		Light	CC
	1513	St. Michael	Chapel	Will
Bleadon (SS Peter & Paul)	1548		Altar	CC

Parish (dedication)	Year	Saint veneration	Form	Source
Bradford-on-Tone (St. Giles)	1548		Guild	CC
Bratton Seymour (Holy Trinity)	1548		Light	CC
Brent Knoll (St. Michael)	1543	St. Mary	Service	Will
	1548		Altar	CC
Bridgwater (St. Mary)	1481		Guild (at Friary)	Will
	1548		Light	CC
	1310	All Saints	Altar	Will
	1385		Chapel (new)	CWA
	1310	High Cross	Altar	Will
	1373–1420		Guild	GA
	1549			Will
	1428	Holy Rood	Aisle Chapel	CWA
	1487		Guild?	
	1414	Holy Trinity	Chapel	Will
	1483		Altar Guild	
	1548		Altar	CC
	1415	St. Anne	Chapel planned (built by 1420)	CWA
	1455	St. Erasmus	Chapel	CWA
	1483		Altar	Will
	1448	St. George	Chapel	CWA
	1548		Guild	CC
	1483	St. Gregory	Altar	Will
	1385	St. Katherine	Chapel	CWA
	1429		Guild	Will
	1529			
	1310	St. Mary	Altar	Will
	1368–1387		Chapel Guild	GA
	1448		Chapel (new)	CWA
	1548		Guild	CC
Bristol St. Mary Redcliffe (St. Mary)	1440	St. Katherine	Chapel	Will
	c1530		Mathew Medis' Chantry	CWA
	c1530		William Canyng's Chantry	CWA
Bristol (St. Thomas)	1544		Burton's Chantry	CWA
	1544		Cheppe Chantry	CWA
	1544		Stokes' Chantry	CWA

Parish (dedication)	Year	Saint veneration	Form	Source
	1544		Wells' Chantry	CWA
	1544	St. Nicholas	Altar	CWA
Broomfield (All Saints)	1548		Light	CC
Brushford-St. Michael (St. Nicholas)	1548		Light	CC
Bruton (St. Mary)	1442	St. Mary	Guild	Will
	1509		Chapel (new)	Will
Brympton Raffe [Brynpton d'Evercy?] (St. Andrew)	1548		Light	CC
Burnham-on-Sea (St. Andrew)	1543	St. Mary	Guild	Will
	1548		Chapel (old)	CC
	1548		Light	CC
Butleigh (St. Leonard)	1457	St. Mary	Chapel	Will
	1546	St. Leonard	Guild?	Will
	1548		Light	CC
Camerton (St. Peter)	1498	St. Nicholas	Altar	Will
	1524	Holy Trinity	Guild	Will
	1548		Light (2)	CC
Cannington (St. Mary)	1498	St. Katherine	Altar	Will
Carhampton (St. John Bapt.)	1510	Holy Cross	Light	Will
	1510	St. Radegund	Light	Will
	1510	St. George	Light	Will
	1510	St. Leonard	Light	Will
	1510 1532	St. John Bapt.	Light	Will
	1510 1532	St. Christopher	Light	Will
	1510 1532	St. Mary	Light	Will
	1510 1532	St. Nicholas	Light	Will
	1532	All Souls	Light	Will
	1548		Light	CC
Castle Cary (All Saints)	1543		Guild	Will
Chaffecombe (St. Michael)	1548		Light	CC
Chard (St. Mary)	1459	St. Katherine	Altar Guild	Will
	1548		Guild	CC

Parish (dedication)	Year	Saint veneration	Form	Source
	1459	St. Mary	Altar	Will
			Guild	
	1548		Guild	CC
Charlton Makerell (St. Mary)	1548		Guild	CC
Charlton Musgrove (St. Stephen)	1548		Light	CC
Cheddar (St. Andrew)	1548	Holy Trinity	Guild	CC
	1548	St. Mary	Guild	CC
Chedzoy (St. Mary)	c.1500	St. Mary	Guild	Will
	1548		Altar	CC
	1548		Light	CC
Chelworthe?	1548		Light	CC
Chew (St. Andrew)	1491	St. Mary	Chapel	Will
	1498			
Chew (St. Andrew)	1495	St. Nicholas	Altar	Will
Chew Magna (St. Andrew)	1548		Light	CC
Chewton Mendip (St. Mary Mag.)	1548		Light	CC
Clarendon (St. Andrew)	1336	St. Thomas	Chapel	Will
Clutton (St. Augustine)	1548		Light	CC
Cokelyngton ?	1548		Light	CC
Combe Flory (SS Peter & Paul)	1548		Chapel (away from church)	CC
	1548		Guild	CC
Compton Pauncefoot (St. Andrew)	1533	St. John	Aisle	Will
	1548		Guild	CC
	1548		Light	CC
Compton Dundon (St. Andrew)	1548		Light	CC
Congresbury (St. Congor) (now St. Andrew)	1411	St. Congor	Light	Will
	1501			
	1411	St. Katherine	Light	Will
	1411	St. Nicholas	Light	Will
	1503	St. Michael	Altar	Will
	1505		Chapel	Will
	1548		Light	CC
Cossington (St. Mary)	1548		Light	CC

Parish (dedication)	Year	Saint veneration	Form	Source
Cothelstone (St. Thomas of Canterbury)	1499	All Souls	Light	Will
Coulue?	1548		Lights	CC
Creech St. Michael (St. Michael)	1548		Light	CC
Crewkerne (St. Bartholomew)	1520 1546	Holy Trinity	Guild	Will
	1527	St. Martin	Guild	Will
	1548	St. Mary	Chapel (in churchyard) Guild	CC
	1548		Light	CC
Croscombe (St. Mary)	1474 1526	St. Michael	Light Guild	CWA
	1474 1476	St. Nicholas	Light Guild	CWA
	1477 1501	St. Mary	Light Altar	CWA
	1515 1537	St. George	Light	CWA
	1521	St. Anne	Aisle	Will
	1548		Light (2)	CC
Crowcombe (Holy Ghost)	1494 1505	St. Mary Mag.	Chapel	Will
Curry Mallet (St. James)	1520 1548	St. James	Chapel	Will CC
Curry Rivel (St. Andrew)	1423 1457	St. Christopher	Altar Chapel	Will
	1548		Light	CC
Cutcombe (St. John)	1548		Light	CC
Ditcheat (St. Mary Mag.)	1457	Holy Trinity	Chapel	Will
	1457	St. John	Chapel	Will
	1516	St. Mary	Altar	Will
	1548	Altar	CC	
	1548	Light	CC	
Donyatt (St. Mary)	1548		Chapel (with park)	CC
Doulting (St. Aldhelm)	1480	St. Nicholas	Chapel	Will
	1480	St. Giles	Chapel	Will
	1543	St. Mary	Guild	Will
	1546	Light of the Dead	Light	Will
	1548	St. Michael	Guild	CC
	1548		Altar	CC
	1548		Lights	CC

Parish (dedication)	Year	Saint veneration	Form	Source
Dulverton (All Saints)	1546	St. Mary	Guild	Will
Dunster (St. George)	1498	St. James	Altar	Court Case
	1509	St. George	Light	Will
	1517			
	1548		Guild	CC
	1517	Holy Trinity	Aisle	Will
	1548		Guild	CC
	1548	St. Lawrence	Chapel Guild	CC
	1509	St. Mary	Light	Will
	1548		Altar	CC
	1548		Light	CC
East Brent (St. Mary)	1548		Altar	CC
	1543	St. Mary	Guild	Will
East Coker (St. Michael)	1548		Guild	CC
	1500	St. Mary	Chapel	Will
East Harptree (St. Lawrence)	1509	St. Katherine	Light	Will
	1509	St. Mary	Light	Will
East Luckham (St. Mary)	1488	St. Katherine	Light	Will
	1488	St. Mary	Light	Will
	1488	St. Nicholas	Light	Will
East Pennard (All Saints)	1548		Light and Mass (2)	CC
East Quantoxhead (St. Mary)	1548		Lights	CC
Elworthy (St. Martin)	1548		Light	CC
Farley Hungerford (St. Peter)	1548		Light	CC
	1529	St. Leonard	Chapel	Will
Freshford (St. Peter)	1548		Light	CC
Frome (St. John Bapt.)	1487	St. Mary	Chapel	Will
			Light	Will
	1548		Guild	CC
	1489	St. Nicholas	Chapel	Will
	1524		Light	Will
	1548		Guild	CC
	1510	All Saints	Light	Will
	1510	All Souls	Light	Will

Parish (dedication)	Year	Saint veneration	Form	Source
	1510	Holy Cross	Altar	Will
	1524			
	1510	St. Andrew.	Light	Will
	1516	St. Mary Mag.	Light	Will
	1516	St. Christopher	Light	Will
	1524	Our Lady of Pity	Light	Will
	1524	St. George	Light	Will
	1524	St. Giles	Light	Will
	1524	St. John Bapt.	Light	Will
	1548		Guild	CC
	1524	St. Lucy	Light	Will
	1524	St. Mary de Rowe	Light	Will
	1548		Light	CC
Glastonbury	1366	St. Nicholas	Aisle	Will
(St. John)	1418		Altar and Light	CWA
	1501		Chapel	
	1418	St. George	Altar	CWA
	1418	St. Katherine	Light	CWA
	1418	St. Mary	Altar	CWA
	1484		Light	
	1498	Name of Jesus	Guild	CWA
	1540	Holy Trinity	Light	Will
			Altar	
Greinton	1548		Light	CC
(St. Michael)				
Halse	1548		Light	CC
(St. James)				
Haselbury Plucknett	1531	St. Mary	Light	Will
(St. Michael)				
	1531	St. Rosmi	Light	Will
Hawkridge	1548		Light	CC
(St. Giles)				
Henstridge	1524	St. Blasé	Guild	Will
(St. Nicholas)				
	1524	St. Clement	Guild	Will
	1524	St. James	Guild	Will
	1526			
	1524	St. Mary	Guild	Will
	1526			
	1546		Light	CC
Hinton Blewett	1548		Light and Masses (4)	CC
(All Saints)				
Hornblotton	1548		Light	CC
(St. Peter)				
Horsington	1486	St. Mary	Guild	Will
(St. John Bapt.)				
	1548		Light	CC

Parish (dedication)	Year	Saint veneration	Form	Source
Huish (which?) Champflower, Episcopi	1543		Guild	Will
Huntspill (All Saints) (now St. Peter)	1434	St. Mary	Guild	Will
	1548			CC
	1543	St. Nicholas	Guild	Will
Hutton (St. Mary)	1404	St. Mary	Light	Will
Ilminster (St. Mary)	1496	Holy Cross	Guild	Will
	1499		Altar	
	1536		Altar	
	1499	St. Katherine	Chapel	Will
	1501		Guild	
	1548			CC
	1502	St. John	Guild	Will
	1546	St. Clement	Aisle	CWA
	1546	St. Mary	Aisle	CWA
	1548	Corpus Christi	Light	CC
	1548		Altars (3)	CC
Ilton (St. Peter)	1548		Light	CC
Keinton Mandeville (St. Mary Mag.)	1548		Light	CC
Keynsham (St. John Bapt.)	1501	Trinity	Guild	Will
	1507	St. Thomas	Altar	Will
	1548		Light	CC
Kilmersdon (SS Peter & Paul)	1548		Light	CC
King Chrimpton ?	1548	St. Katherine	Guild	CC
Kingston (St. Mary)	1548		Guild	CC
Knowle (St. Giles)	1525	St. Katherine	Guild	Will
Lamyat (SS Mary & John)	1548		Light	CC
Langforde Budville (St. Peter)	1548		Light	CC
Langport (All Saints)	1548		John Heron's Chantry	CC
	1548		Guild	CC
Laverton (St. Mary)	1496	St. Anne	Light	Will
	1496	St. Nicholas	Light	Will
	1548		Light	CC

Parish (dedication)	Year	Saint veneration	Form	Source
Leigh on Mendip (St. Giles)	1513	St. Mary	Chapel	Will
Limington (St. Mary)	1548		Light	CC
	1548	St. Mary	Guild	CC
Littleton [Kingweston] (All Saints)	1548		Light	CC
Long Ashton (All Saints)	1538	St. Mary	Light	Will
	1548		Sir Richard Choke's Chantry	CC
	1548	St. Mary	Chapel (founded by Nicholas and Henry Choke)	CC
Loxton (St. Andrew)	1548		Light	CC
Lydeard St. Lawrence (St.Lawrence)	1548		Chapel	CC
Lympsham (St. Christopher)	1543	St. Mary	Guild	Will
	1548		Altar	CC
Maperton (SS Peter & Paul)	1548		Light	CC
Mark (St. Mark)	1543	St. Mary	Guild	Will
Marson Magna (St. Mary)	1548		Altar	CC
	1506 1512	St. Mary	Chapel	Will
Marston [Magna or Bigott?] (St. Mary or St. Leonard)	1548		Light	CC
Martok (All Saints)	1548		Altar	CC
	1548		Guild	CC
	1548		Light	CC
Mells (St. Andrew)	1495	St. Anne	Altar	Will
	1495 1503	St. Katherine	Chapel Altar	Will
	1495 1521	St. Mary	Altar	Will
Middlezoy (Holy Cross)	1548	Name of Jesus	Guild	CC

Parish (dedication)	Year	Saint veneration	Form	Source
Midsomer Norton (St. John Bapt.)	1502	St. John	Guild	Will
	1502	St. Leonard	Light	Will
	1502	St. Mary	Light	Will
	1524		Chapel	Will
	1548		Guild	CC
Milborne Port (St. John Ev.)	1548		Light	CC
Milton Clevedon (St. James)	1548		Light	CC
Milverton (St. Michael)	1548		Light	CC
	1548	St. Mary	Guild	CC
Minehead	1536	All Souls	Light	Will
	1525	Holy Trinity	Aisle	Will
	1509	St. Mary	Guild	Will
Montacute (St. Katherine)	1548		Light	CC
Nettlecombe (St. Mary)	1507	Holy Rood	Light	CWA
	1507	St. Mary	Light (2)	CWA
	1518		Guild	
	1510	St. Nicholas	Light	CWA
	1525			
	1518	All Souls	Light	Will
	1518	St. Anthony	Light	Will
	1518	St. Erasmus	Light	Will
	1518	St. George	Light	Will
	1535		Chapel	CWA
	1518	St. John Bapt.	Light	Will
	1548		Guild	CC
	1524	St. Mary Mag.	Light	CWA
Newton St. Loe (Holy Trinity)	1548		Light	CC
North Cadbury (St. Michael)	1548		Altar	CC
	1548		Light	CC
North Curry (SS Peter & Paul)	1548		Guild (2)	CC
North Perrott (St. Martin)	1548		Light	CC
North Petherton (St. Mary)	1548		Light	CC
	1548	St. Mary	Guild	CC
Northover (St. Andrew)	1548		Light	CC

Parish (dedication)	Year	Saint veneration	Form	Source
Norton St. Philip (St. Philip)	1548		Light	CC
Nunney (All Saints)	1548		Guild	CC
	1548		Light	CC
Old Cleve (St. Andrew)	1548		Light	CC
Over Stowey (SS Peter & Paul)	1548		Light	CC
Pawlett (St. John Bapt.)	1543	St. Mary	Guild	Will
	1548		Light	CC
Penselwood (St. Michael)	1538	St. Christopher	Light	Will
	1538	St. Katherine	Light	Will
	1538	St. Margaret	Light	Will
	1538	St. Mary	Light	Will
	1538	St. Michael	Light	Will
Pensford (St. Thomas of Canterbury)	1499	St. Nicholas	Altar	Will
	1415 1519	St. Thomas of Canterbury	Chapel	Will
Pilton (St. John Bapt.)	1496	St. John Bapt.	Guild	Will
	1496	St. Mary	Guild	Will
	1508		Chapel and Light	
	1548		Light	CC
Pitminster (SS Andew & Mary)	1548		Altar	CC
Porlock (St. Dubricius)	1527	St. Cullani	Guild	Will
	1527	St. Dubricius	Guild	Will
	1527 1547	St. Mary	Guild	Will
	1527	St. Olave	Guild	Will
	1527	St. Salvatore	Guild	Will
	1548		Guild (2)	CC
Portbury (St. Mary)	1525	St. Ellen	Chapel	Will
	1548	St. Katherine	Chapel	CC
Portishead (St. Peter)	1548	St. Mary	Chapel	CC
Priston (St. Luke)	1546		Light	CC

Parish (dedication)	Year	Saint veneration	Form	Source
Publow (All Saints)	1499	St. Nicholas	Altar	Will
Pylle (St. Thomas of Canterbury)	1548		Light	CC
Queen Camel (St. Barnabas)	1405	St. Mary	Light	Will
Radstock (St. Nicholas)	1548		Light	CC
Redlynch (St. Peter)	1510	All Saints	Chapel	Will
	1510	St. Anne	Chapel	Will
	1510	St. Leonard	Chapel	Will
	1510	St. Mary	Chapel	Will
	1510	St. Peter	Chapel	Will
Rode (St. Lawrence)	1548		Light	CC
Sampford Brett (St. George)	1548		Light	CC
Selworthy (All Saints)	1506	All Saints	Light	Will
	1524	St. Mary	Light	Will
	1546		Light	1548
Sevyngton [which one?] (St. Mary or St. Michael)	1548		Altar	CC
Shepton Beauchamp (St. Michael)	1548		Light	CC
Shepton Mallet (SS. Peter & Paul)	1521	St. Mary	Guild	Will
	1529			
	1548	Holy Trinity	Altar	CC
	1548	St. John Bapt.	Altar and Guild	CC
	1548		Altar	CC
Somerton (St. Michael)	1510	Holy Trinity	Guild	Will
	1543		Guild	Will
South Petherton (SS Peter & Paul)	1510	St. Mary	Guild	Will
	1548		Earl of Bridgwater's Chantry	CC
	1548		Light	CC
Sparkford (St. Mary Mag.)	1548		Light	CC
Spaxton (St. Margaret)	1548		Light	CC

Parish (dedication)	Year	Saint veneration	Form	Source
St. Decumans ?	1548	Holy Cross	Chapel	CC
Staunton Drew (St. Mary)	1488	St. Mary	Chapel	Will
Stawley (St. Michael)	1528	St. Mary	Altar	Will
Stogumber (St. Mary)	1548		Light	CC
Stogursey (St. Andrew)	1507	St. Mary Our Lady of Pity	Chapel	CWA
	1507	St. Mary	Altar and Guild	CWA
	1548			CC
	1519	Holy Trinity	Aisle	CWA
	1520	St. Rosmon	Light	CWA
	1535	St. George	Chapel (new)	CWA
	1548		Light	CC
Stoke Trister (St. Andrew)	1548		Light	CC
Stoke-sub-Hamdon (St. Mary)	1542		Guild and Light	Will
Stowey (SS Nicholas & Mary)	1548		Light	CC
Stowrton (St. Peter)	1502	Holy Trinity	Light	Will
Sutton [which one?]	1501	Holy Trinity	Light	Will
Swell (St. Katherine)	1548		Light	CC
Taunton (St. Mary Mag.)	1486	Holy Cross	Guild	Will
	1547			
	1548			CC
	1488	Holy Sepulchre	Guild	Will
	1547			
	1509	St. George	Chapel	Will
	1500	St. Mary (Mag?)	Guild	Will
	1547			
	1548	St. Mary	Guild	CC
	1548	St. Nicholas	Guild (Bishop's Chantry)	CC
	1548	Holy Trinity	Guild	CC
	1548	Name of Jesus	Guild	CC
	1548	St. Andrew	Guild	CC
	1548	St. Elizabeth	Guild	CC
	1548	St. Etheldrede	Guild	CC
	1548		Swynges' Chantry	CC
Taunton Priory (St. Peter)	1547	St. Katherine	Guild	Will
	1497	St. Mary	Guild	Will

Parish (dedication)	Year	Saint veneration	Form	Source
Thorn Falcon (Holy Cross)	1548		Light	CC
Tintinhull (St. Margaret)	1416	St. Mary	Guild	Will
Trull (All Saints)	1525	St. Mary	Chapel and Guild	GA
	1546			
Ubley (All Saints now St. Bartholomew)	1514	St. Katherine	Altar	Will
Walton (Holy Trinity)	1548		Light	CC
Wanstrow (St. Katherine now St. Mary)	1404	St. Katherine	Light	Will
	1427	St. Mary	Chapel	Will
	1427	St. Nicholas	Light	Will
Wedmore (St. Mary Mag.)	1503	St. Gonthal	Chapel	Will
	1503	St. Mary	Chapel	Will
	1548		Guild	CC
	1548		Altar	CC
	1548	Name of Jesus	Guild	CC
	1548	St. Anne	Guild	CC
Wellington (St. John Bapt.)	1548		Altar	CC
Wellow (St. Julian)	1543	St. Mary	Guild	Will
Wells (St. Cuthbert)	1298	St. Mary	Altar	Will
	1374		Light	
	1401		Chapel	
	1547		Guild close	WCB
Wells (St. Cuthbert)	1407	Holy Trinity	Guild	Will
	1547			WCB
	1482	St. Nicholas	Altar	Will
	1487	Name of Jesus	Aisle and Guild	Will
	1547			WCB
	1498	St. John Bapt.	Guild	Will
	1540		Altar	
	1500	St. Erasmus	Guild	WCB
	1527		close?	
	1540		Altar	Will
	1501	Holy Cross	Guild	WCB
	1540			
	1512	St. Katherine	Guild	WCB
	1516		close?	
	1526		Altar	Will

Parish (dedication)	Year	Saint veneration	Form	Source
	1519	St. Anne	Guild	WCB
	1527		close	
	1526	St. George	Chapel	Will
	1540	St. James	Altar	Will
	1548	St. Andrew	Chapel	CC
	1548		Altars (2)	CC
	1548		Tanners Chapel and Guild	CC
West Buckland (St. Mary)	1548		Guild	CC
West Monkton (St. Augustine)	1548	St. Mary	Guild	CC
West Pennard (St. Nicholas)	1548		Light	CC
Weston (All Saints)	1548	St. Mary	Guild	CC
Whitestaunton (St. Andrew)	1492	St. Mary	Light	Will
	1548		Guild	CC
Wincanton (SS. Peter & Paul)	1528	St. Mary	Light	Will
	1548		Chantries (2) (founded by Lord Zouche)	CC
Winford (SS. Mary & Peter)	1512	St. Mary	Chapel	Will
	1548			CC
	1548		Light	CC
Winscombe (St. James)	1543	St. Mary	Guild	Will
	1548		Altar	CC
Winsham (St. Stephen)	1548		Light	CC
Withycombe (St. Nicholas)	1548		Light	CC
	1532	St. Christopher	Chapel	Will
	1532	St. Mary	Chapel (of the Visitation)	Will
Withypool (St. Andrew)	1519	St. Andrew	Guild	Will
	1519	St. Mary	Guild	Will
	1548		Chantries (2) (founded by Lord Zouche)	CC
	1548		Light	CC
Woolavington (St. Mary)	1548	Holy Trinity	Guild	CC
Woolverton (St. Lawrence)	1548		Light	CC

Parish (dedication)	Year	Saint veneration	Form	Source
Wrington	1502	St. Mary	Light	Will
(All Saints)	1543		Light	
	1502	St. Nicholas	Light	Will
	1548	St. John Bapt.	Chapel (in churchyard)	CC
	1548	St. Katherine	Guild	CC
Yarlyngton	1548		Light	CC
(St. Mary)				
Yatton	1458	St. Nicholas	Altar	CWA
(St. Mary)				
	1466	St. James	Chapel	CWA
	1500		Guild	
	1528		Light	
	1545		closed?	
	1469	St. Katherine	Light	CWA
	1515		Altar	
	1497	St. John Ev.	Chapel	CWA
	1497	St. Mary	Light	CWA
	1529			
	1548		Chapel in churchyard (old)	CC
	1450	St. Mary	Chapels (2)	Indulg.
	1548		Guild	CC
Yeovil	1450	Holy Trinity	Chapel	Indulg.
(St. John)	1455		Altar	Will
	1548		Aisle	CWA
	1506	Name of Jesus	Guild	CWA
	1544		Aisle	
	1548		Guild	CC
	1526	St. Katherine	Altar	Will
	1543	St. Christopher	Aisle	CWA

I have not included references to High Cross lights; all parishes would have had them and there is not uniform mention of them. With respect to the Chantry Certificates, I have not listed obits or free chapels.

Key: CC = chancery certificate; CWA = churchwardens' account; GI = guild inquiry certificate; Indulg. = indulgence; GA = Guild wardens' account

NOTES

Abbreviations

BL—British Library
BRO—Bristol Record Office
CPL—Calendar of Papal Letters
EETS—Early English Text Society
EETS es—Early English Text Society, Extra Series
PRO—Public Record Office
REED—Records of Early English Drama
SRO—Somerset Record Office
SRS—Somerset Record Society
VHC-Somerset—Victoria History of the County of Somerset
WCB—Wells Convocation Book
WCR—Wells City Records

Introduction

1. *Calendar of Inquisitions Post Mortem, 1–6 Henry IV (1399–1405)*, 18, ed. J. L. Kirby (1987), 226–27.

2. John Bedell, "Memory and Proof of Age in England," *Past and Present* 162 (1999): 3–27, esp. 22–25.

3. Robert N. Swanson, *Church and Society in Late Medieval England* (Oxford: Basil Blackwell, 1989), 210–25. By this time, England had no Jewish population; they had been expelled in the 1290s.

4. Ibid., 4.

5. Ibid., 5.

6. Ibid., 4.

7. For a more detailed discussion of this topic and the possible presence of Roman Christians, see Barbara Yorke, *Wessex in the Early Middle Ages* (London: Leicester University Press, 1995).

8. Michael Costan, "The Church in the Landscape: The Anglo-Saxon Period," in *Aspects of the Mediaeval Landscape of Somerset*, ed. Michael Aston (Bridgwater: Somerset County Council, 1988), 49.

9. Ibid.

10. The creation of a new diocese was part of a general reorganization of the church in the southwest. Reformers wanted the dioceses to match the boundaries of the old Anglo-Saxon shires. Out of the two large dioceses of Sherborne and Winchester were created the diocese of Wells for Somerset and the diocese of Crediton for the counties of Devon and Cornwall. Under Athelstan (d. 939), Cornwall was split off as a separate diocese with the bishop's seat at St. Germans. Unable to support itself, it was reunited with Devon during the reign of Edward the Confessor (r. 1042–66). The much-reduced diocese of Sherborne now served the county of Dorset and portions of Wiltshire and Berkshire. Frank Stenton, *Anglo-Saxon England*, 3rd ed. (Oxford: Oxford University Press, 1971), 439–40; Michael Costan, *The Origins of Somerset* (Manchester: Manchester University Press, 1992), 143; Nicholas Orme, *Exeter Cathedral as It Was, 1050–1550* (Exeter: Devon Books, 1986), 13–14.

11. Orme, *Exeter Cathedral*, 13–14; David Gary Shaw, *The Creation of a Community: The City of Wells in the Middle Ages* (Oxford: Oxford University Press, 1993), 22–25.

12. The process began when Bishop Leofric of Crediton moved his seat to Exeter in 1050. Additionally the bishop of Sherborne went to Old Sarum (Salisbury), and the bishop of Litchfield went to Chester. This rearrangement matched continental practices of placing bishops in old Roman cities. Orme, *Exeter Cathedral*, 13–14; Shaw, *Creation of a Community*, 22–25.

13. Shaw, *Creation of a Community*, 34–35.

14. G. W. O. Addleshaw, *The Development of the Parochial System: From Charlemagne to Urban II*, St. Anthony's Hall Publications 6 (York: Borthwick Institute, 1954); Costan, "The Church in the Landscape: The Anglo-Saxon Period," 49–53; *Minsters and Parish Churches: The Local Church in Transition, 950–1200*, ed. John Blair, Oxford University Committee on Archaeology 17 (Oxford: Alden Press, 1988); *Pastoral Care Before the Parish*, ed. John Blair and Richard Sharp (Leicester: Leicester University Press, 1992).

15. Costan, *Origins of Somerset*, 144.

16. Ibid., 153–57; J.H. Bettey, "From Norman Conquest to Reformation," in *Aspects of the Mediaeval Landscape of Somerset*, 56.

17. Yorke, *Wessex*, 196.

18. Costan, *Origins of Somerset*, 145–47; Shaw, *Creation of a Community*, 258–59.

19. Costan, *Origins of Somerset*, 145.

20. SRO D/D/B/ reg. 1 (Register of John de Drokensford), fol. 234b; *Calendar of the Register of John de Drokensford: Bishop of Bath and Wells, 1309–1329*, ed. Edmund Hobhouse, SRS 1 (1887), 251.

21. Bettey, "From Norman Conquest to the Reformation," 57; Martha C. Skeeters, *Community and Clergy: Bristol and the Reformation, c. 1530–1570* (Oxford: Oxford University Press, 1993).

22. Gervase Rosser, "Parochial Conformity and Voluntary Religion in Late-Medieval England," *Transactions of the Royal Historical Society* 6th ser. 1 (1991): 173–89.

23. SRO D/D/B/ reg. 2 (Register of Ralph of Shrewsbury), fol. 426; *Register of Ralph of Shrewsbury: Bishop of Bath and Wells, 1329–1363*, parts 1 and 2, ed. Thomas Scott Holmes, SRS 9 and 10 (1896), 731–32, no. 2788. The petition calls Earnshill both a chapel and a parish, making its previous status vague.

24. SRO D/D/B reg. 6 (Register of Thomas Bekynton), fols. 12–13; *Register of Thomas Bekynton: Bishop of Bath and Wells, 1443–1465*, part 1, ed. M. C. B. Dawes, SRS 49 (1934), 12–13, no. 44.

25. SRO D/D/B reg. 6 (Register of Thomas Bekynton), fol. 301; *Register of Thomas Bekynton*, 412, no. 1567. Two years later the parishes of Hardington and Laverton and of Berkley and Fairoak faced a similar situation and their patrons recommended the same solution to the bishop. D/D/B reg. 6 (Register of Thomas Bekynton), fols. 54–55, 292; *Register of Thomas Bekynton*, 67–68, 403–4, nos. 230–31, 1529.

26. SRO D/D/B reg. 9 (Register of Oliver King), fols. 9a–b; *Register of Oliver King, Bishop of Bath and Wells, 1407–24 and Hadrian de Castello, Bishop of Bath and Wells, 1503–1518*, ed. H. C. Maxwell-Lyte, SRS 54 (1939), 78, no. 103.

27. For more on the ecclesiastical divisions of this diocese see *The Victorial History of the County of Somerset*, ed. William Page (London: Constable, 1911), 2: 67.

28. R. W. Dunning, "The Wells Consistory Court in the Fifteenth Century," *Proceedings of the Somerset Archaeological Society* 106 (1961/2): 57. For a description of the archdeacon's responsibilities see *Calendar of the Manuscripts of the Dean and Chapter of Wells* 1, Historical Manuscripts Commission 12a (1907), 538–39.

29. For more on peculiars see Swanson, *Church and Society*, 18–24.

30. Jane Sayers, "Monastic Archdeacons," in *Church and Government in the Middle Ages: Essays Presented to C. R. Cheney on His 70th Birthday*, ed. C. N. L. Brooke et al. (Cambridge: Cambridge University Press, 1976), 183–85. These parishes were exempt from the bishop's authority except on cases of appeal.

31. St. John's, Glastonbury was in the peculiar of Glastonbury; Ilminster a royal peculiar; St. Cuthbert's, Wells was in the peculiar of the Dean of Wells; North Curry was in the peculiar of the Dean and Chapter of Wells; Yatton was in the peculiar of the Prebendaries of Wells; and Pilton was in the peculiar of the Precentor of Wells. *VHC-Somerset*, 2: 67.

32. For more on York see A. Hamilton Thompson, *The English Clergy and Their Organization in the Later Middle Ages* (Oxford: Oxford University Press, 1947), 73–100; Swanson, *Church and Society*, 20–25.

33. The late medieval bishops of Bath and Wells were: Henry Bowet (1401–7); Nicholas Bubwith (1408–25), John Stafford (1425–43), Thomas Bekynton (1443–65), Robert Stillington (1466–91), Hadrian de Castello (1503–17), Thomas Wolsey (1518–23), John Clerk (1523–41), William Knight (1541–47).

34. The Council of Constance was called by Emperor Sigismund to end the Great Schism and the threat of the heretical Hussites who were challenging imperial control of Bohemia. Jan Huss, the leader of the Hussites, had been a student of John Wycliff and carried his heretical messages back to Bohemia, where he used them in the cause of Bohemian independence. Bubwith's presence at Constance would have made him very aware of the threat that Lollardy posed to England, and the danger of heresy to royal authority. J. Catto, "Religious Change Under Henry V," in *Henry V: The Practice of Kingship*, ed. G. L. Harriss (Oxford: Oxford University Press), 104.

35. *Registers of Thomas Wolsey, Bishop of Bath and Wells, 1518–1523, John Clerk, Bishop of Bath and Wells, 1523–1541, William Knyght, Bishop of Bath and Wells, 1541–1547, and Gilbert Bourne, Bishop of Bath and Wells, 1554–1559*, ed. H. C. Maxwell-Lyte, SRS 55 (1940), ix; *VHC-Somerset*, 2: 30–1.

36. *VHC-Somerset*, 2: 29.

37. Ibid., 30.

38. For more on Beckynton see Arnold Judd, *The Life of Thomas Bekynton: Secretary to King Henry VI and Bishop of Bath and Wells, 1443–1465* (Chichester: Regnum Press, 1961).

39. Robert Weiss, *Humanism in England During the Fifteenth Century* (Oxford: Basil Blackwell, 1957), 57.

40. Ibid., 74. Of Bekynton's humanism, Weiss writes: "Bekynton's role in the development of Renaissance learning in England must be sought chiefly within the province of administration, for it was reserved for him to raise the standards of official epistolargraphy in this country by following classical models, and by a disregard of the formalities of medieval epistolary practice" (71).

41. Thompson, *The English Clergy*, 205. Beckynton handled 67 percent of the ordinations during his tenure, compared to Bubwith, who was on hand for 35 percent, Stafford for only 27 percent, and Stillington for none. Beckyngton also took great interest in the education of his clergy. See Helen Jewell, "English Bishops as Educational Benefactors in the Later Fifteenth Century," in *The Church, Politics, and Patronage in the Fifteenth Century*, ed. Barrie Dobson (Gloucester: Sutton, 1984), 146–67.

42. *Register of John Clerk*, x–xi; *VHC-Somerset*, 2: 31.

43. Thompson, *The English Clergy*, 18–19. Scrope was executed in 1405 for his part in a rebellion led by the Earl of Northumberland against Henry IV.

44. Although it is sometimes difficult to distill Lollard beliefs, they tended to deny the efficacy of the saints and the doctrine of the real presence. Some scholars have described them as "proto-Protestants." See A. G. Dickens, *Lollards and Protestants in the Diocese of York* (Oxford: Oxford University Press, 1959). For more on Lollardy see Margaret Aston, *Lollards and Reformers: Images and Literacy in Late Medieval Religion* (London: Hambledon Press, 1984); Shannon McSheffrey, *Gender and Heresy: Women and Men in Lollard Communities, 1420–1530* (Philadelphia: University of Pennsylvania Press, 1995). Scholars disagree on how much of a threat Lollardy posed. Literary scholars such as David Aers and Sarah Beckwith see Lollards as much more a concern than do historians such as Eamon Duffy. Duffy, *Stripping of the Altars: Traditional Religion in England 1400–1580* (New Haven, Conn.: Yale University Press, 1992); Sarah Beckwith, *Christ's Body: Identity, Culture, and Society in Late Medieval Writings* (London: Routledge, 1993). See also Paul Strohm, *England's Empty Throne: Usurpation and the Language of Legitimation, 1399–1422* (New Haven, Conn.: Yale University Press, 1998), esp. chapters 2 and 3.

45. Thompson, *The English Clergy*, 5–6; Peter Heath, *Church and Realm, 1272–1461: Conflict and Collaboration in an Age of Crisis* (London: Fontana Press, 1988), 278; Catto, "Religious Change Under Henry V," 97; Beckwith, *Christ's Body*, 71–75; Margaret Aston, "Bishops and Heresy: The Defense of the Faith," in *Faith and Fire: Popular and Unpopular Religion, 1350–1600* (London: Hambledon Press, 1993), 73–93.

46. Catto, "Religious Change Under Henry V," 99–101.

47. McSheffrey, *Gender and Heresy*, 72–79.

48. Skeeters, *Community and Clergy: Bristol and the Reformation*, 34–38. Because there was no strong ecclesiastical authority in the city, and because the city straddled two dioceses, it became a haven for Lollards, who could easily cross diocesan boundaries and escape prosecution; SRO D/D/B reg. 5 (Register of John Stafford), fols. 52d–53d, 66d–68, 179–80; *Register of Bishop Stafford, Bishop of Bath and Wells, 1425–1443*, ed. Thomas Scott Holmes, SRS 31 (1914), 76–80, no. 263; 103–9, no. 332; 266–69, nos. 833–34; D/D/B reg. 6 (Register of Thomas Bekynton), fols. 212–13, 249–337; *Register of Bishop Bekynton*, 120–7 nos. 455, 458; 282–84, no. 1044; 334–37, no. 1276; D/D/B reg. 7 (Register of Robert

Stillington), fols. 52a–b, 100a–b; *Register of Robert Stillington and Richard Fox: Bishops of Bath and Wells, 1466–1494*, ed. H.C. Maxwell-Lyte, SRS 52 (1937), 61–63 no. 342; 99–100 no. 63; D/D/B reg. 9 (Register of Oliver King), fols. 42b–44b, 60a; *Register of Oliver King*, 39–43 nos. 236–39, 242–43.

49. Catto, "Religious Change Under Henry V," 103.

50. Ibid., 109. The two other common uses were Hereford and York. Bath and Wells used Sarum.

51. *VHC-Somerset*, 2: 533.

52. Costan, *Origins of Somerset*, 1.

53. Ibid., 1–4.

54. R. Schofield, "The Geographic Distribution of Wealth, 1334–1649," *Economic History Review* 2nd ser. 18 (1965): 504, quoted also in J. L. Bolton, *The Medieval English Economy, 1150–1500* (London: Dent, 1980), 230–31.

55. *VHC-Somerset*, 2: 298, 304.

56. For more on Somerset fairs, see N. F. Hulbert, "A Survey of the Somerset Fairs," *Somerset Antiquarian and Natural History Society* 83 (1937): 83–86.

57. *Somerset Medieval Wills*, ed. F. W. Weaver, SRS 19 (1903), 2: 64.

58. Bruce M. S. Campbell, "Ecology Versus Economics," in *Agriculture in the Middle Ages: Technology, Practice, and Representation*, ed. Del Sweeney (Philadelphia: University of Pennsylvania Press, 1995), 81–90.

59. Joan Thirsk, "The Farming Regions of England," in *The Agrarian History of England and Wales*, ed. Joan Thirsk (Cambridge: Cambridge University Press, 1947), 4: 72.

60. W. K. Jordan, *Philanthropy in England, 1480–1660* (London: Allen and Unwin, 1959); Norman P. Tanner, *The Church in Late Medieval Norwich, 1370–1532* (Toronto: Pontifical Institute of Mediaeval Studies, 1984); J. J. Scarisbrick, *The Reformation and the English People* (Oxford: Basil Blackwell, 1984).

61. For more on the problems of using wills see Clive Burgess, "Late Medieval Wills and Pious Conventions: Testamentary Evidence Reconsidered," in *Profit, Piety and the Professions*, ed. Michael Hicks (Gloucester: Sutton, 1990), 14–33. See also Caroline Litzenberger, *The English Reformation and the Laity* (Cambridge: Cambridge University Press, 1997).

62. Scholars of English local religion have not really used these sources. One exception is William J. Dohar, *The Black Death and Pastoral Leadership: The Diocese of Hereford in the Fourteenth Century* (Philadelphia: University of Pennsylvania Press, 1995).

63. Richard M. Wunderli, *London Church Courts on the Eve of the Reformation* (Cambridge, Mass.: Medieval Academy of America, 1981); Brian Woodcock, *Medieval Ecclesiastical Courts* (London: Oxford University Press, 1952).

64. Beat Kümin, *The Shaping of a Community: The Rise and Reformation of the English Parish, c. 1400–1560* (Aldershot: Scolar Press, 1996), 265–69.

65. *The Survey and Rental of the Chantries, Colleges and Free Chapels, Guilds, Fraternities, Lamps, Lights and Obits in the County of Somerset, 1548*, ed. Emmanuel Green, SRS 2 (1888), 74, 89.

66. Costan, *Origins of Somerset*, 153–57.

67. *Survey and Rental of the Chantries*, 137.

68. Unlike the chantry certificates for Yatton and Banwell, the certificates from Tintinhull and Pilton do not include information on population. The lay subsidy rolls from 1542 that might otherwise help provide an alternative way of deriving population figures are similarly missing.

69. Barry Cunliffe, *The City of Bath* (Gloucester: Sutton, 1986), 109–10.

70. *Bridgwater Borough Archives: 1200–1377*, ed. Thomas B. Dilks, SRS 48 (1933), 1: xxxvi.

71. *Bridgwater Borough Archives*, 1: xvi–xxx.

72. *VHC-Somerset*, ed. R. W. Dunning (Oxford: Oxford University Press, for Institute of Historical Research, 1992), 6: 197.

73. *VHC-Somerset*, 6: 197–200.

74. *The Survey and Rental of the Chantries*, 155, 68.

75. Shaw, *Creation of a Community*, 140.

76. Michael Aston and Roger Leech, *Historic Towns in Somerset* (Taunton: Somerset County Council, 1977), 55–59.

77. *Survey and Rental of the Chantries*, 53, 140.

78. This printed collection also includes the wills proved in the prerogative court of Canterbury. As the editorial quality is high, I have relied on the printed versions.

79. Toulmin Smith, *The Parish* (London: H. Sweet, 1857), 50–60; *Church-wardens' Accounts of Croscombe, Pilton, Yatton, Tintinhull, Morebath and St. Michael's Bath: Ranging from 1349–1560*, ed. Edmund Hobhouse, SRS 4 (1890); J. Charles Cox, *Churchwardens' Accounts: From the Fourteenth to the Close of the Seventeenth Century* (London: Methuen, 1913); J. Charles Cox, *Bench-Ends in English Churches* (Oxford: Oxford University Press 1916); J. Charles Cox and Charles Bradley Ford, *The Parish Churches of England* (London: Batsford, 1937); F. A. Gasquet, *Parish Life in Mediaeval England* (London: Methuen, 1906).

80. Charles Drew, *Early Parochial Organisation in England: The Origins of the Office of Churchwarden*, St. Anthony Hall Publications 7 (York: Borthwick Institute, 1954). See also Swanson, *Church and Society*, 217–19.

81. Drew also edited the churchwardens' accounts for Lambeth. *Lambeth Churchwardens' Accounts, 1504–1645 and Vestry Book*, ed. Charles Drew, Surrey Record Society 18 (1941).

82. He built on his earlier work *The Lollards and Protestants in the Diocese of York*; A. G. Dickens, *The English Reformation*, 2nd ed. (University Park: Pennsylvania State University Press, 1989). He is reacting to A. F. Pollard, *Thomas Cranmer and the English Reformation* (London: Putnam, 1905), A. F. Pollard, *Wolsey: Church and State in Sixteenth-Century England* (London: Longmans, 1929), and S. T. Bindoff, *Tudor England* (Harmondsworth: Penguin, 1950). Rather than seeing the Reformation as an act of state, the position taken by previous scholars, Dickens culled evidence from court testimonies that challenged the prevailing interpretations. His evidence recounted not only unhappiness with the church, but ignorance of the basic tenets and practices it preached. Dickens was arguing for a reformation from below, and implicitly for the failure of parochial life to inculcate a strong identitication with the church.

83. James E. Oxley, *The Reformation in Essex to the Death of Mary* (Manchester: Manchester University Press, 1965); Margaret Bowker, *The Secular Clergy in the Diocese of Lincoln, 1495–1520* (Cambridge: Cambridge University Press, 1968); Christopher Haigh, *Reformation and Resistance in Tudor Lancashire* (Cambridge: Cambridge University Press, 1975); Roger Manning, *Religion and Society in Elizabethan Sussex* (Leicester: Leicester University Press, 1976); Rosemary O'Day, *The Debate on the English Reformation* (London: Methuen, 1986).

84. Scarisbrick, *The Reformation and the English People*, 1–39.

85. Ibid., 60.

86. Ronald Hutton, "The Local Impact of the Tudor Reformations," in *The English Reformation Revised*, ed. Christopher Haigh (Cambridge: Cambridge University Press, 1987), 114–38.

87. Hutton has gone on to look at churchwardens' accounts for what they have to tell us about ritual and celebrations. He argues in his book *The Rise and Fall of Merry England*

(Oxford; Oxford University Press, 1994) that many traditions, such as May Day, are inventions of the late middle ages and not ancient pre-Christian ones (49–69).

88. Robert Whiting, *The Blind Devotion of the People: Popular Religion and the English Reformation* (Cambridge: Cambridge University Press, 1989).

89. Despite an abundance of fifteenth- and even fourteenth-century material for Exeter, Whiting begins his statistical analysis of parish finances only in the 1520s. When he compares his findings from the 1520s with those of the 1530, he concludes that there was a decline in the money that parishes raised and spent. He has interpreted this as waning enthusiasm for parish support. See in particular Whiting, 93–95, where the data provided also call Whiting's conclusions into question. He cites eight new projects completed in the 1530s and '40s, while providing only five examples of abandoned work—and two of the five are questionable, even by his own admission.

90. Duffy, *Stripping of the Altars*. See also my critique of this work in "Competing for Space: The Monastic-Parochial Church at Dunster," *Journal of Medieval and Early Modern Studies* 27 (1997): 215–44. Duffy outlines his critique on pp. 2 (popular religion) and 6 (late middle ages from a Reformation perspective) of *Stripping of the Altars*. See also the earlier critiques of the popular-elite dichotomy in William A. Christian, *Local Religion in Sixteenth Century Spain* (Princeton, N.J.: Princeton University Press, 1981) and Natalie Zemon Davis, "From 'Popular Religion' to Religious Cultures," in *Reformation Europe: A Guide to Research*, ed. Steven Ozment (St. Louis: Center for Reformation Research, 1982), 321–41.

91. "I am well aware of the importance of regional variation in many of the institutions and practices I have attempted to describe, from the parish structures to the cult of the saints, but it was an overview I was seeking. In attempting to provide it I hope I have not imposed a distorted unity on the variety and complexity of the evidence." Duffy, *Stripping of the Altars*, 4; see also 92, 121–22.

92. Robert Whiting has recently synthesized some of this local work on the Reformation in his textbook *Local Responses to the English Reformation* (New York: St. Martin's Press, 1998). In this work he addresses issues of regional location, status, and occupation in trying to assess the level of commitment or resistance to religious change.

93. Kümin, *Shaping of a Community*.

94. Ibid., 260–64. Specifically Kümin is looking at the concepts of "confessionalization" and "communalism." See also Peter Blickle, *The Communal Reformation: the Quest for Salvation in Sixteenth-Century Germany*, trans. Thomas Dunlap (Atlantic Highlands, N.J. and London: Humanities Press International, 1992).

Chapter 1. Defining the Parish

1. David Sabean makes a similar point regarding peasant communities. It is the politics, legal system, and local administrations that create peasant status; they do not exist without it. David Sabean, *Power in the Blood: Popular Culture and Village Discourse in Early Modern Germany* (Cambridge: Cambridge University Press, 1987), 25–28.

2. This is Miri Rubin's critique. See her "Small Groups: Identity and Solidarity in the Late Middle Ages," in *Enterprise and Individuals in Fifteenth-Century England*, ed. Jennifer Kermode (Gloucester: Sutton Press, 1991), 134–36.

3. John Bossy, "Blood and Baptism: Kinship, Community and Christianity in Western Europe from the Fourteenth to the Seventeenth Centuries," *Studies in Church History* 10 (1973): 129–43; "The Counter-Reformation and the People of Catholic Europe," *Past and Present* 47 (1970): 51–70; Gervase Rosser, "Communities of Parish and Guild," in *Parish,*

Church and People: Local Studies in Lay Religion, 1350–1750, ed. S. J. Wright (London: Hutchinson, 1988), 29–55. See also Emma Mason, "The Role of the English Parishioner: 1100–1500," *Journal of Ecclesiastical History* 27 (1976): 17–29 for a similar view.

4. Rubin, "Small Groups," 134.

5. Ibid.

6. David Gary Shaw, *The Creation of a Community: The City of Wells in the Middle Ages* (Oxford: Oxford University Press, 1993), 3.

7. Ibid., 2–4.

8. Eamon Duffy, *The Stripping of the Altars: Traditional Religion in England, 1400–1580* (New Haven, Conn.: Yale University Press, 1992), 151–53.

9. Shaw, *Creation of a Community*, 5–6.

10. John Bossy, *Christianity in the West: 1400–1700* (Oxford: Oxford University Press, 1985), 57; Robert N. Swanson, *Religion and Devotion in Europe, c. 1215–c. 1515* (Cambridge: Cambridge University Press, 1995), 18.

11. Swanson, *Religion and Devotion*, 63; see also Duffy, *Stripping of the Altars*, 92–130.

12. John Mirk, *Mirk's Festial: A Collection of Homilies*, ed. Theodor Erbe, EETS, es 96 (1905), 278.

13. *Dives et Pauper*, ed. Priscilla Heath Barnum, EETS 275 (1976), 196.

14. See also Shaw, *Creation of a Community*, 4, who makes a similar point about the importance of leadership.

15. Christopher Dyer, "The English Medieval Village Community and Its Decline," *Journal of British Studies* 33 (1994): 419–24.

16. Gervase Rosser, "Going to the Fraternity Feast: Commensality and Social Relations in Late Medieval England," *Journal of British Studies* 33 (1994): 444.

17. See also Beat Kümin, *The Shaping of a Community: The Rise and Reformation of the English Parish* (Aldershot, Hants.: Scolar Press, 1996), 1–2 and Maryanne Kowaleski, "Introduction to 'Vill, Gild, and Gentry: Forces of Community in Later Medieval England,'" *Journal of British Studies* 33 (1994): 339.

18. *Somerset Medieval Wills*, ed. F. W. Weaver, SRS 16 (1901), 1: 181–85.

19. Ibid.

20. Parish guilds regularly relied on social pressure and coercion to maintain standards of behavior. Barbara A. Hanawalt, "Keepers of the Lights: Late Medieval English Parish Gilds," *Journal of Medieval and Renaissance Studies* 14 (1984): 21–37 and Barbara A. Hanawalt and Ben R. McRee, "The Guilds of *Homo Prudens* in Late Medieval England," *Continuity and Change* 7 (1992): 163–79.

21. For more on chapels see Nicholas Orme, "Church and Chapel in Medieval England," *Transactions of the Royal Historical Society* 6 (1996): 75–102.

22. *CPL* 5: 587.

23. It seems that the pope granted their petition, because seven of the eight wills from Leigh show the testators asking for burial in the church of St. Giles of Leigh-on-Mendip. *Somerset Medieval Wills*, 1: 234 *Somerset Medieval Wills*, ed. F. W. Weaver, SRS 19 (1903), 2: 158–59, 166, 120, 241; *Medieval Wills from Wells*, ed. Dorothy Shilton and Richard Holworthy, SRS 40 (1925), 47.

24. F. A. Gasquet, *Parish Life in Mediaeval England* (London: Methuen, 1906), 157.

25. SRO D/D/B reg. 6 (Register of Thomas Bekynton), fols. 117, 198–99; *Register of Thomas Bekynton: Bishop of Bath and Wells, 1443–1465*, part 1, ed. M.C.B. Dawes, SRS 49 (1934), 153–54, nos. 539, 257, 944.

26. Between 1360 and 1509, 110 chapels in England petitioned the pope about their dependent status. See *CPL* vols. 1–18.

27. *CPL* 13: 561–62.

28. It is true that midwives and other laity could perform baptisms, it was only in an emergency, when the priest could not get there in time. The preference was for a priest.

29. Christopher R. Cheney, *From Becket to Langton: English Church Government, 1170–1213* (Manchester: Manchester University Press, 1956), 160.

30. Charles Drew, *Early Parochial Organisation in England: The Origins of the Office of Church-warden*, St. Anthony Hall Publications 7 (York: Borthwick Institute of Historical Research, 1954).

31. C. R. Cheney, *English Synodalia of the Thirteenth Century* (Oxford: Oxford University Press, 1941), 7–9; André Vauchez, "The Pastoral Transformation of the Thirteenth Century," in *The Laity in the Middle Ages: Religious Beliefs and Devotional Practice*, ed. Daniel E. Bornstein, trans. Margery J. Schneider (Notre Dame, Ind.: University of Notre Dame Press, 1993), 95–106. For discussions of the quality and character of the English church before 1215 see Charles Duggan, "From the Conquest to the Death of John," in *The English Church and the Papacy in the Middle Ages*, ed. C. H. Lawrence (New York: Fordham University Press, 1965), 95; Marion Gibbs and Jane Lang, *Bishops and Reform 1215–1272, with Special Reference to the Lateran Council of 1215* (Oxford: Oxford University Press, 1932), 94–95; Cheney, *From Becket*.

32. Gibbs and Lang, *Bishops and Reform*, 96.

33. Ibid., 105; Cheney, *From Becket*, 122, 145.

34. Gibbs and Lang, *Bishops and Reform*, 99.

35. Ibid., 3.

36. Cheney, *English Synodalia*, 33–4.

37. Ibid., 36.

38. Ibid., 34–51 for a more detailed discussion of the influence of particular sets of statutes.

39. C. R. Cheney, "William Lyndwood's *Provinciale*," in *Medieval Texts and Studies* ed. C. R. Cheney (Oxford: Oxford University Press, 1973), 158–84; F. R. H. Du Boulay, "The Fifteenth Century," in *The English Church and the Papacy*, 214.

40. Joseph W. Goering, "Changing Face of the Village Parish II: The Thirteenth Century," in *Pathways to Mediaeval Peasants*, ed. J. A. Raftis, Papers in Mediaeval Studies 2 (Toronto: Pontifical Institute of Mediaeval Studies, 1981), 238.

41. Gervase Rosser, "Anglo-Saxon Gilds," in *Minsters and Parish Churches: The Local Church in Transition, 950–1200*, ed. John Blair, Oxford University Committee on Archaeology 17 (Oxford: Alden Press, 1988), 31–34.

42. They are longer than any other preceding set of statutes and establish a well-organized and coherent diocesan administration. They were subsequently adapted by the sees of York in 1258 and Winchester sometime after 1262. For further discussion see Cheney, *English Synodalia*, 97–101. Four later bishops of Bath and Wells republished them. SRO D/D/B reg. 1 (Register of Bishop Drokensford), fol. 105a; *Calendar of the Register of John Drokensford Bishop of Bath and Wells, 1309–1329*, ed. Edmund Hobhouse, SRS 1 (1887), 127; D/D/B reg. 2 (Register of Ralph of Shrewsbury), fols. 84, 132; *Register of Ralph of Shrewsbury: Bishop of Bath and Wells, 1329–1363*, part 1, ed. Thomas Scott Holmes, SRS 9 (1896), 149 no. 579; 250 no. 957; D/D/B reg. 7 (Register of Robert Stillington), fols. 142b–43b; *Register of Robert Stillington Bishop of Bath and Wells, 1466–1494*, ed. H. C. Maxwell-Lyte,

SRS 49 (1937), 145 no. 862; D/D/B reg. 10 (Register of Hadrian de Castello), fol. 36a; *Register of Oliver King, Bishop of Bath and Wells, 1496–1503, and Hadrian De Castello Bishop of Bath and Wells,* ed. H. C. Maxwell-Lyte, SRS 54 (1939), 120 no. 727.

43. For full Latin text see "Statutes of Wells: 1252–1258," in *Councils and Synods II,* part 1, ed. F. M. Powicke and C. R. Cheney (Oxford: Oxford University Press, 1964), 586–626.

44. Ibid., 592–93, no. 5.

45. Ibid., 599, no. 15.

46. Ibid., 600, no. 16.

47. Ibid., 601–2, nos. 19 and 20.

48. Ibid., 600, no. 16; Drew, *Early Parochial Organisation,* 9–11.

49. "Statutes of Wells," 600, no. 16.

50. Ibid., 602, no. 22.

51. Drew, *Early Parochial Organisation,* 8, n. 10.

52. Ibid., 9–10.

53. Susan Reynolds, *Kingdoms and Communities in Western Europe, 900–1300* (Oxford: Oxford University Press, 1984), 79–80. Reynolds argues that it was not the statutes, but episcopal neglect in the wake of the statues that spawned lay organizations.

54. SRO D/P/bw #22; D/P/ba. mi 4/1/1 #1; D/P/gla. j. 4/1/1.

55. "Statutes of Wells," 613–14.

56. Edmund Kern, "The 'Universal' and the 'Local' in Episcopal Visitations," in *Infinite Boundaries: Order, Disorder, and Reorder in Early Modern German Culture,* ed. Max Reinhart, Sixteenth Century Essays and Studies 40 (Kirksville, Mo.: Sixteenth Century Journal Publishers, 1998), 35–54.

57. Herbert Edward Reynolds, *Wells Cathedral: Its Foundation, Constitutional History and Statutes* (Wells: privately printed, 1882), 125–26.

58. *Visitations of the Diocese of Lincoln: 1517–1531,* ed. A.H. Thompson, Lincoln Record Society 33 (1940), 1: xxiv–xxv.

59. Reynolds, *Wells Cathedral,* 126.

60. Ibid.

61. In peculiars, where the bishop had only limited authority, visitations were in the hands of the peculiar.

62. Gasquet, *Parish Life in Mediaeval England,* 218–20; John Moorman, *Church Life in England in the Thirteenth Century* (Cambridge: Cambridge University Press, 1955), 186–96; Roy M. Haines, *The Administration of the Diocese of Worcester in the First Half of the Fourteenth Century* (London: S.P.C.K., 1965), 148–64; Dorothy Owen, *Church and Society in Medieval Lincolnshire,* History of Lincolnshire 5 (Lincoln: History of Lincolnshire Committee, Lincolnshire Local History Society, 1971), 35, 120; Robert N. Swanson, *Church and Society in Late Medieval England* (Oxford: Basil Blackwell, 1989), 163–66.

63. Swanson, *Church and Society,* 165. A few visitation reports from medieval England do exist, see for example "Visitation Returns of Hereford in 1397," ed. Arthur T. Bannister, *English Historical Review* 44 (1929): 92–101; 45 (1930): 444–63; *The Courts of the Archdeaconry of Buckingham, 1483–1523,* ed. E. M. Elvey, Buckingham Record Society 19 (1975); *Kentish Visitations of Archbishop William Warham and His Deputies, 1511–1512,* ed. Katherine Wood-Legh, Kent Records (1984); *Visitations in the Diocese of Lincoln: 1517–1531,* Lincoln Record Society 33, 35 (1940–41). The Council of Trent required regular visitations to investigate and correct the local clergy and educate the superstitious population about Rome's new religious policies. As a result, visitation records become more common, allowing scholars to compare the effectiveness of religious reformers from region to region and over time.

Scholars' primary concern is the effect of clerical mandates on the lay population and its practice of religion. See for example Robert Sauzet, *Les visites vastorales dans le diocèse de Chartres pendant la première moitié du XVIIe siècle* (Rome: Edizioni di Storia e Letteratura, 1975); Keith P. Luria, *Territories of Grace: Cultural Changes in the Seventeenth-Century Diocese of Grenoble* (Berkeley: University of California Press, 1991); Allyson Poska, *Regulating the People: The Catholic Reformation in Seventeenth-Century Spain* (Leiden: Brill, 1998).

64. SRO D/D/B reg. 2 (Register of Ralph of Shrewsbury), fol. 89; *Register of Bishop Shrewsbury*, 153, no. 599.

65. SRO D/D/B reg. 7 (Register of Robert Stillington), fols. 59b–60b; *Register of Bishop Stillington*, 71 no. 393.

66. *VHC-Somerset*, 2:29–30; SRO D/D/B reg. 10 (Register of Hadrian de Castello), fol. 36a; *Register of Bishop Castello*, 120 no. 727.

67. Owen, *Church and Society in Medieval Lincolnshire*, 35; Robert Brentano, *Two Churches: England and Italy in the Thirteenth Century* (Berkeley: University of California Press, 1988), 66–69.

68. SRO D/P/stogs 4/1/1 fols. 5, 5v., et passim; D/P/tin 4/1/1 fols. 5, 70, et passim.

69. SRO D/P/tin 4/1/1 fol. 11.

70. "Statutes of Wells," 613–34, no. 53.

71. SRO D/P/tin 4/1/1 fol. 34.

72. SRO D/P/tin 4/1/1 fol. 35.

73. "Episcopal Statutes of Robert Grosseteste for the Diocese of Lincoln (c. 1239)," trans. John Shinners in *Pastors and the Care of Souls in Medieval England*, ed. John Shinners and William J. Dohar (Notre Dame, Ind.: University of Notre Dame Press, 1998), 93.

74. See for example the 1397 episcopal visitation for the diocese of Hereford. Bannister, "Visitation Returns," 281, 286–87.

75. SRO DD/WO 49/1, fol. 14.

76. The act book for the Dean and Chapter of Wells, which was in charge of its own peculiar, shows similar kinds of visitation findings. *Calendar of the Manuscripts of the Dean and Chapter of Wells*, 1 and 2.

77. Because of the lack of visitation reports and court records, we do not know how prevalent clerical concubines were, or how concerned the bishops were about eradicating them. For one of the few examples recorded in the bishops' registers, see SRO D/D/B reg. 2 (Register of Ralph of Shrewsbury), fol. 138, *Register of Ralph of Shrewsbury*, 260–61 no. 990. For more discussion see also Peter Marshall, *Catholic Priesthood and the English Reformation* (Oxford: Oxford University Press, 1994), 150–63; 175.

78. SRO D/D/B reg. 2 (Register of Ralph of Shrewsbury), fol. 153; *Register of Ralph of Shrewsbury*, 282–83 no. 1069. This was not an uncommon finding; see for example: SRO D/D/B reg. 1 (Register of John Drokensford), fols. 15b, 137a, 181a; *Register of John de Drokensford*, 12, 152, 202; D/D/B reg. 4 (Register of Nicholas Bubwith), fols. 6d, 201d; *Register of Nicholas Bubwith*, 18–19, no. 63; 436–37, no. 1182; D/D/B reg. 6 (Register of Thomas Bekynton), fols. 56, 73, 74, 77–78, 155; *Register of Thomas Bekynton*, 69, no. 237; 90–91, no. 330, no. 332; 98, no. 353; 202–3; no. 739.

79. For example, in January 1310, the bishop asked the archdeacon to check further into the state of East Coker; SRO D/D/B reg. 1 (Register of John Drokensford), fol. 28b; *Register of Bishop Drokensford*, 27. In 1318, the same bishop had inquired after the condition of the parish of Turloxton and ordered that the chancel, books, and ornaments be repaired, D/D/B reg. 1, fol. 15b; *Register of Bishop Drokensford*, 12. In 1410, Bishop Nicholas Bubwith had similar concerns for the parish buildings and lands of Kynewardeston, D/D/B reg. 4

(Register of Nicholas Bubwith), fol. 6b; *Register of Nicholas Bubwith, Bishop of Bath and Wells, 1407–1424*, ed. Thomas Scott Holmes SRS 29 (1914), 18–19 no. 63.

80. SRO D/D/B reg. 6 (Register of Thomas Bekynton), fol. 22; *Register of Thomas Bekynton*, 1: 25 no. 93.

81. SRO D/D/B reg. 6 (Register. of Bekynton), fol. 16; *Register of Thomas Bekynton*, 1: 16–17, no. 59.

82. SRO D/D/B reg. 6 (Register. of Bekynton), fol. 16; *Register of Thomas Bekynton*, 1: 17, no. 59.

83. SRO D/D/B reg. 10 (Register of Hadrian de Castello), fol. 9b; *Register of Bishop Hadrian de Castello*, 105 no. 620.

84. Jeremy Catto, "Religious Change Under Henry V," in *Henry V: The Practice of Kingship*, ed. G. L. Harriss (Oxford: Oxford University Press, 1985), 109–10; Virginia Reinburg, "Liturgy and the Laity in Late Medieval and Reformation France," *Sixteenth Century Journal* 23 (1992): 526–47.

85. SRO D/D/B reg. 7 (Register of Robert Stillington), fol. 13b–14b; *Register of Robert Stillington*, 13, no. 85; similar procedures were followed in other parishes. See for example D/D/B reg. 7 fol. 5b–6a and 30b; *Register of Robert Stillington*, 5–6 no. 29 and 36 no. 176; D/D/B reg. 9 (Register of Oliver King), fol. 90a; *Register of Oliver King*, 76, no. 459. This appears to be a diocesan oddity, as other dioceses relied on the testimony of other clergy or local gentry.

86. SRO D/D/B reg. 2 (Register of Ralph of Shrewsbury), fols. 343–47; *Register of Ralph of Shrewsbury*, 596–603, nos. 2301, 2303–6, 2308–9, 2322–24.

87. SRO D/D/B reg. 2 (Register of Ralph of Shrewsbury), fol. 343; *Register of Ralph of Shrewsbury*, 597 no. 2304; 598 no. 2306.

88. SRO D/D/B reg. 2 (Register of Ralph of Shrewsbury), fol. 346; *Register of Ralph of Shrewsbury*, 602 no. 2322. For women and their participation in riots see Ralph A. Houlbrooke, "Women's Social Life and Common Action in England from the Fifteenth Century to the Eve of the Civil War," *Continuity and Change* 1 (1986): 171–89; Sharon L. Jansen, *Dangerous Talk and Strange Behavior: Women and Popular Resistance to the Reforms of Henry VIII* (New York: St. Martin's Press, 1996), 103–14.

89. SRO D/D/B reg. 2 (Register of Ralph of Shrewsbury), fol. 344; *Register of Ralph of Shrewsbury*, 599, no. 2308.

90. R. W. Dunning, "Wells Consistory Court in the Fifteenth Century," *Proceedings of the Somerset Archaeological Society* 2 (1961–62): 48.

91. Ibid., 57.

92. Ibid., 49; for more on ecclesiastical courts see Colin Morris, "A Consistory Court in the Middle Ages," *Journal of Ecclesiastical History* 14 (1963): 150–59; Swanson, *Church and Society*, 158–90.

93. Dunning, "Wells Consistory Court," 55. The case was unusual in that it lasted 12 years; SRO D/D/Ca 1, fol. 261. The book has been recatalogued, restored, and repaginated since Dunning wrote his article.

94. Morris, "A Consistory Court," 157, n. 4.

95. Ibid., 154; Dunning, "Wells Consistory Court," 48.

96. R. A. R. Hartridge, *A History of Vicarages in the Middle Ages* (Cambridge: Cambridge University Press, 1930); D. J. A. Matthew, *The Norman Monasteries and Their English Possessions* (Oxford: Oxford University Press, 1962), 58–61; Giles Constable, *Monastic Tithes from Their Origins to the Twelfth Century* (Cambridge, Mass.: Harvard University Press, 1964); Marjorie Chibnall, "Monks and Pastoral Work: A Problem in Anglo-Norman History," *Journal*

of *Ecclesiastical History* 18 (1967): 165–72; B. R. Kemp, "Monastic Possession of Parish Churches in the Twelfth Century," *Journal of Ecclesiastical History* 31 (1980): 133–60.

97. Hartridge *A History of Vicarages*, 196–203; Rosser, "The Cure of Souls in English Towns Before 1000," in *Pastoral Care Before the Parish*, ed. John Blair and Richard Sharpe (Leicester: Leicester University Press, 1992), 267–84.

98. Rosser discusses some other similar situations in "The Cure of Souls in English Towns Before 1000," 267–84. Bruton church in eastern Somerset also shared its space with both monks (Augustinian canons) and laity. Although the bishop cited the monks for excessive familiarity with the laity and their lifestyle, there is no report of animosity over sharing the church itself. *VHC-Somerset*, 2: 135–36.

99. The parishioners' willingness to litigate also shows that, while they might act collectively on behalf of the parish, it was not always a harmonious environment. See also Beat Kümin, "Parishioners in Court: Litigation and the Local Community, 1350–1650," in *Belief and Practice in Reformation England*, ed. Susan Wabuda and Caroline Litzenberger (Aldershot: Ashgate, 1998), 20–39.

100. Frederick Pollock and Frederic William Maitland, *The History of English Law Before the Time of Edward I*, 2nd ed. (Cambridge: Cambridge University Press, 1968), 1: 488.

101. Ibid., 490–96.

102. This position was outlined in the 21–22 Edward I yearbook. See Pollock and Maitland, *History of English Law*, 1: 503–4. Just exactly what this overseeing entailed was disputed.

103. For a fuller discussion of this process see Pollock and Maitland, *History of English Law*, 1:499–504; see also Robert E. Rhodes, Jr., *Ecclesiastical Administration in Medieval England: The Anglo-Saxons to the Reformation* (Notre Dame, Ind.: University of Notre Dame Press, 1977), 153–57.

104. Pollock and Maitland, *History of English Law*, 1: 560. Exceptions to this position came in the area of temporal rights. Since the reign of Henry II, the state had asserted that the rights of the landholders who endowed the church were temporal rights and that advowsons were temporal property. Conflicts over these issues had to be tried in secular courts (125).

105. Ibid., 613–14.

106. W. S. Holdsworth, *A History of English Law* (London: Metheun, 1903), 1: 398. In the fourteenth century, executors and administrators of wills were granted rights of action and were liable to be sued in King's Court for debts due to and by the deceased. To some extent this must be related to the lack of enthusiasm and ineffectiveness of particular bishops and their administrations.

107. Brian Woodcock, *Medieval Ecclesiastical Courts* (London: Oxford University Press, 1952), 30–36. Richard Wunderli, *London Church Courts and Society on the Eve of the Reformation* (Cambridge, Mass.: Medieval Academy of America, 1981), 20–23.

108. Wunderli, *London Church Courts*, 2–7. This would seem to be another case of London being different.

109. Ibid., 3–5, discussing Margaret Bowker on Lincoln, Stephen Lander on Chichester, and Brian Woodcock on Canterbury.

110. Dunning, "Wells Consistory Court," 61; for more explanation of the distinction between instance and office cases see Swanson, *Church and Society*, 163.

111. Robert C. Palmer, "Selling the Church: Law, Religion, Commerce, and the English Parish, 1348–1540" (forthcoming). I want to thank Robert Palmer for sharing his unpublished work with me.

112. PRO C1 31/87.

113. For a full discussion of the rise of equity courts see Margaret Avery, "A History of Equitable Jurisdiction of Chancery Before 1460," *Bulletin of the Institute of Historical Research* 42 (1969): 129–30; Margaret Avery, "An Evaluation of the Effectiveness of the Court of Chancery Under the Lancastrian Kings," *Law Quarterly Review* 86 (1970): 84. Holdsworth, *History of English Law*, 198; J. H. Baker, *An Introduction to English Legal History*, 3rd ed. (London: Butterworths, 1990), 115.

114. Avery, "History," 130–32; The primary legal concern focused on feoffment to use.

115. Holdsworth, *History of English Law*, 200–201; Avery, "History," 132–33.

116. Margaret Avery, "History," 132–34; Swanson, *Church and Society*, 186–90.

117. Baker, *Introduction to English Legal History*, 136–38. For further discussion of the Court of Star Chamber see *Select Cases Before the King's Council in the Star Chamber*, ed. Isaac Saunders Leadam, Selden Society 16 (1903); *Select Cases in the Council of Henry VII*, ed. Charles Gerien Bayne and William Huse Dunham, Selden Society 75 (1958); Geoffrey Elton, *Star Chamber Stories* (London: Methuen, 1958); Stanford E. Lehmberg, "Star Chamber: 1485–1509," *Huntington Library Quarterly* 24 (1961): 189–214.

118. Lehmberg, "Star Chamber," 195, 214; Baker, *Introduction to English Legal History*, 136–37.

119. Baker, *Introduction to English Legal History*, 138; *Select Cases in the Court of Requests: 1497–1569*, ed. Isaac Saunders Leadam, Selden Society 12 (1898), xi.

120. *Select Cases in the Court of Requests*, x–xi.

121. For a more thorough discussion of this subject, see Avery, "History."

122. Pollock and Maitland, *History of English Law*, 1: 125; Wunderli, *London Church Courts*, 20–23; Swanson, *Church and Society*, 144. Swanson also states that tithes were spiritual issues and by the late fourteenth century they were only subject to secular oversight if they amounted to more than one quarter of the benefice's income.

123. PRO C1 1014/48–49.

124. PRO C1 1014/48.

125. PRO C1 1014/49.

126. The king's willingness to involve himself in parish issues became especially obvious and important in the 1530s and 1540s as he was trying to push through and enforce the early stages of his Reformation.

127. Dyer, "The English Medieval Village Community and Its Decline," 424–29.

128. Gervase Rosser, "Parochial Conformity and Popular Religion in Late Medieval England," *Transactions of the Royal Historical Society* 6th ser. 1 (1991): 173–89.

Chapter 2. Churchwardens' Accounts and Record Keeping

1. Michael Clanchy, *From Memory to Written Record: England, 1066–1307* (Cambridge, Mass.: Harvard University Press, 1979).

2. Shannon McSheffrey, "Literacy and the Gender Gap in the Late Middle Ages: Women and Reading in Lollard Communities," in *Women, the Book, and the Word*, ed. Lesley Smith and Jane Taylor (Woodbridge, Suffolk: Boydell and Brewer, 1995), 157–70; Malcolm B. Parks, "Literacy and the Laity," in *The Medieval World*, ed. David Daiches and Anthony Tholby (London: Alaus Books, 1973), 555–77; Janet Coleman, *Medieval Readers and Writers: 1350–1400* (New York: Columbia University Press, 1981), 18–57; Jo Ann Hoeppner Moran, *The Growth of English Schooling, 1340–1548: Learning, Literacy and Laicization in Pre-Reformation York Diocese* (Princeton, N.J.: Princeton University Press, 1985); Susan Crane, "The Writing

Lesson of 1381," in *Chaucer's England: Literature in Historical Context*, ed. Barbara Hanawalt (Minneapolis: University of Minnesota Press, 1992), 202–3.

3. F. R. H. Du Boulay estimated that by the fifteenth century 30 percent of the male population could read and that this had grown to 40 percent by 1530. F. R. H. Du Boulay, *Age of Ambition: English Society in the Late Middle Ages* (London: Thomas Nelson, 1970), 118–19; see also Moran, *The Growth of English Schooling*, 20. David Cressy is not as optimistic, especially with respect to the lower classes. He estimates that while 30–40 percent of artisans in the cities of Durham, Norwich, and Exeter might have been able to read by the sixteenth century, yeomen and husbandmen generally could not. He sets the level of male literacy at 10–20 percent, but lowers it for women; David Cressy, *Literacy and the Social Orders: Reading and Writing in Tudor and Stuart England* (Cambridge: Cambridge University Press, 1980), 15–18, 159–63. See also Clanchy, *From Memory to Written Record*, 184–88. For a critique of assessing literacy rates and their impact on society, see Brian Stock, *Implications of Literacy: Written Language and the Models of Interpretation in the Eleventh and Twelfth Centuries* (Princeton, N.J.: Princeton University Press, 1983), 4–7.

4. Stock, *Implications of Literacy*; Walter Ong, *Orality and Literacy: The Technologizing of the Word* (London: Methuen, 1982); Clanchy, *From Memory to Written Record*.

5. Susan Brigden, *London and the Reformation* (Oxford: Oxford University Press, 1989), 16; Stock, *Implications of Literacy*, 9.

6. T. W. Machan, "Editing, Orality, and Late Medieval English Texts," in *Vox Intexta*, ed. A. N. Doane and C. B. Pasternack (Madison: University of Wisconsin Press, 1991), 230.

7. Parks, "Literacy and the Laity," 555–77.

8. Clanchy, *From Memory to Written Record* 37–38, 177–85; Franz Bäuml, "Varieties and Consequences of Medieval Literacy," *Speculum* 55 (1980): 237–65. The mid-fifteenth century is also the point when Court of Chancery petitions start appearing in English, and there is a slow growth in vernacular literature in general. See Malcolm Richardson, "Henry V, the English Chancery, and Chancery English," *Speculum* 55 (1980): 727–28.

9. "Statutes of Wells," in *Councils and Synods II*, part 1, ed. F. M. Powicke and C. R. Cheney (Oxford: Oxford University Press, 1964), 602, no. 22.

10. Charles Drew, *Early Parochial Organisation in England: The Origin of the Office of Church-warden*, St. Anthony Hall Publications 7 (York: Borthwick Institute of Historical Research, 1954).

11. "Statutes of Exeter II," in *Councils and Synods II*, part 2, ed. F. M. Powicke and C. R. Cheney (Oxford: Oxford University Press, 1964), 1008, no. 12. "Precipimus insuper quod de ecclesiarum instauro ipsius custodes coram rectoribus vel vicariis ecclesiarum seu saltim capellanis parochialibus et quinque vel sex parochianis fidedignis, quos ipsi rectores, vicarii, vel capellani ad hoc duxerint eligendos, quolibet anno compotum fidelem reddant; et redigature in scriptis, quam scripturam precipimus loci archidiacono cum visitat presentari."

12. It is an account from 1318 detailing the money raised and spent on casting a new bell for the parish church of Bridgwater. SRO D/P/bw # 3.

13. Clanchy, *From Memory to Written Record*.

14. PRO C1 872/17.

15. PRO C1 872/17.

16. PRO C1 872/17.

17. Charles Drew reminds us that the identification of a document as a churchwardens' account is an archival distinction above all else. *Lambeth Churchwardens' Accounts, 1504–1645*, part 1, ed. Charles Drew, Surrey Record Society 40 (1940), x.

18. Some do not consider these to be churchwardens' accounts, as they were only totals

written out separately for purposes of the annual audit. Ronald Hutton, *The Rise and Fall of Merry England: The Ritual Year, 1400–1700* (Oxford: Oxford University Press, 1994), 263. Five parishes in Bath and Wells have abbreviated records: Wells, Lydeard St. Lawrence, Halse, Ilminster, and Croscombe. There were probably supporting records that accompanied these accounts that no longer survive.

19. Hutton, *Rise and Fall of Merry England*, 263–93. Hutton is interested in those records with enough detailed information to help him in his study of changes in local rituals and celebrations.

20. Beat Kümin, *The Shaping of a Community: The Rise and Reformation of the English Parish, c. 1400–1560* (Aldershot: Scolar Press, 1996), 265–69.

21. I am using Kümin's figure. Audit accounts may not tell us much about rituals and parish activities, but they are still useful for illuminating issues concerning lay parish administration.

22. Edmund Hobhouse calendared and discussed five sets of Somerset accounts in 1890. His introduction and appendices were one of the earliest discussions of these kinds of sources, making some of the Somerset materials well known. His editorial decisions, however, make it necessary to go back to the manuscripts whenever possible. *Churchwardens' Accounts of Croscombe, Pilton, Yatton, Tintinhull, Morebath and St. Michael's Bath*, ed. Edmund Hobhouse, SRS 4 (1890).

23. Bäuml also identifies this apparent contradiction in "Varieties and Consequences of Medieval Literacy," 237.

24. For a survey of work on this subject see D.H. Green, "Orality and Reading: The State of Research in Medieval Studies," *Speculum* 65 (1990): 267–80.

25. This is basically the position that Brian Stock argues when he develops a notion of textual communities. He writes: "the rapprochement between oral and written consequently began to play a decisive role in the organization of experience. The results can be seen in sets of dichotomies based upon linguistic considerations which lie beneath the surface of a number of the period's key cultural issues" (*Implications of Literacy*, 3–4). Mary Carruthers in *The Book of Memory: A Study of Memory in Medieval Culture* (Cambridge: Cambridge University Press, 1990), 16–17 argues that such a rigid separation invariably relegates memory exclusively to a discussion of oral practices, thus neglecting its powerful and important role in literate intellectual life. Paul Zumthor in *Oral Poetry: An Introduction*, trans. Kathryn Murphy-Judy (Minneapolis: University of Minnesota Press, 1990), 25 categorized this situation as secondary orality: "where [orality] is (re)composed based on writing and that is central to a milieu where writing determines the values of voice both in usage and in the imaginary sphere." See also Bäuml, "Varieties and Consequences," 242–49.

26. Stock, *Implications of Literacy*, 90–91; Brian Stock, "Medieval Literacy, Linguistic Theory and Social Organization," *New Literary History* 16 (1984): 13–29, esp. 18.

27. Stock, *Implications of Literacy*, 3–5.

28. Zumthor, *Oral Poetry*, 22 and 46; Stephen G. Nichols, "Voice and Writing in Augustine and the Troubadour Lyric," in *Vox Intexta*, 138.

29. Paul Zumthor, "The Text and the Voice," *New Literary History* 16 (1984): 67–69.

30. Nichols, "Voice and Writing," 138; Paul Zumthor, *Oral Poetry*, 22, 46.

31. Zumthor, *Oral Poetry*, 27–29, 46, 61.

32. PRO C1 1090/33.

33. PRO C1 1090/34.

34. Kümin, *Shaping of a Community*, 96.

35. Clive Burgess in his discussion of the London parish of St. Mary at Hill shows that an elite group ran this parish and that the phrase " the parish" might in fact coincide with this elite group. Clive Burgess, "Shaping the Parish: St. Mary at Hill, London, in the Fifteenth Century," in *The Cloister and the World: Essays in Medieval History in Honour of Barbara Harvey*, ed. John Blair and Brian Golding (Oxford: Oxford University Press, 1996), 268–69.

36. Clanchy, *From Memory to Written Record*, 37–38; Peter Burke, *The Historical Anthropology of Early Modern Italy: Essays on Perception and Communication* (Cambridge: Cambridge University Press, 1987), 113.

37. Clanchy, *From Memory to Written Record*, 38; Burke, *Historical Anthropology*, 113; Adam Fox, "Custom, Memory, and the Authority of Writing," in *The Experience of Authority in Early Modern England*, ed. Adam Fox, Paul Griffiths, and Steve Hindle (London: Macmillan, 1996), 89–116.

38. Margaret Avery, "A History of Equitable Jurisdiction of Chancery Before 1460," *Bulletin of the Institute of Historical Research* 42 (1969): 134; Stock, *Implications of Literacy*, 58–59.

39. W.S. Holdsworth, *A History of English Law* (London: Methuen, 1903), 1: 197–99; Margaret Avery, "An Evaluation of the Effectiveness of the Court of Chancery Under the Lancastrian Kings," *Law Quarterly Review* 86 (1970): 84–95; J. H. Baker, *An Introduction to English Legal History*, 3rd ed. (London: Butterworths, 1990), 114–16.

40. Clanchy, *From Memory to Written Record*, 231–57; Stock, *Implications of Literacy*, 18, 88.

41. PRO C1 307/70a.

42. PRO C1 367/38.

43. PRO C1 1008/51.

44. PRO C1 215/20. The churchwardens' accounts start in 1474 and were transcribed, edited, and published in 1890 by Edmund Hobhouse for the Somerset Record Society. The originals are now missing. See Edmund Hobhouse, "Church-wardens' Accounts of Croscombe," 1–48.

45. The edited accounts make no mention of this donation or the court case.

46. "Church-wardens' Accounts of Croscombe," 22.

47. SRO D/D/Cd 35, not paginated.

48. "Accounts of the Proctors of the Church of Yeovil, Co. Somerset, 36 Henry VI. 1457–8," ed. John G. Nichols, *Collectanea Topographica et Genealogica* 3 (1834): 134–41 (original lost); SRO D/P/yeo.j 4/1/6; T/PH/bm 31 s/1800 (microfilm of churchwardens' accounts from 1516, 1519, and 1540 onwards); BL Add. Mss. 40,729A are the originals. The accounts were on individual rolls and this might explain why they were not checked; they were scattered and perhaps not readily unavailable.

49. PRO C1 962/21.

50. PRO C1 962/22.

51. Clanchy, *From Memory to Written Record*, 249. "Forged charters were often based on earlier authentic documents or on good oral tradition. The purpose of forgery was to produce a record in a form which was acceptable, particularly in courts of law, at the time it was made."

52. John Bossy argues that medieval society was influenced by the Augustinian ideal that lawsuits should be avoided. They were a form of enmity which Christians should avoid as a hindrance to forging charity and social integration. John Bossy, *Christianity in the West, 1400–1700* (Oxford: Oxford University Press, 1985), 60.

53. PRO C1 679/62.

54. PRO C1 679/62.

55. Susan Brigden, "Religion and Social Obligation in Sixteenth-Century London," *Past and Present* 103 (1984): 90–94.

56. Brigden, "Religion and Social Obligation," 92; Clanchy offers a similar view of the relationship between writing and trustworthiness, *From Memory to Written Record*, 233.

57. Ong, *Orality and Literacy*, 32–33.

58. Clanchy, *From Memory to Written Record*, 116–50; Bäuml, "Varieties and Consequences," 57–59; Stock, *Implications of Literacy*, 89.

59. Among the Somerset records, there is evidence that suggests only a very few wardens were even marginally capable of writing. Julia Carnwath, however, has found greater writing skills among the wardens of Thame in Oxfordshire. See her article "The Churchwardens' Accounts of Thame, Oxfordshire, c. 1443–1524," in *Trade, Devotion and Governance: Papers in Later Medieval History*, ed. Dorothy J. Clayton, Richard G. Davies, and Peter McNiven (Gloucester: Sutton, 1994), 183–84.

60. SRO D/P/ban 4/1/1, fol. 68.

61. SRO D/P/tin 4/1/1, fol. 16.

62. SRO D/P/yat 4/1/1, fol. 7.

63. SRO D/P/yat 4/1/1, fols. 55, 63, 90, 97, 135, 247, 253, 268, 271, 276, et passim.

64. SRO D/P/bw #51, #18.

65. *Accounts of the Wardens of Morebath, Devon, 1520–1573*, ed. Erskine Binney, Devon Notes and Queries 2:3 (1904). Because Trychay wrote all the accounts himself, even reconstructing the years 1520–25 before he took up the task, these particular accounts have qualities akin to a personal diary. They are reflective of Trychay's immersion in the affairs of his parish.

66. *Churchwardens' Accounts of Ashburton, 1479–1580*, ed. Alison Hanham, Devon and Cornwall Record Society ns 15 (1970), 1, 2, 3, 7, 24, 26, 35, 38, 89, 98, 101, 110. In fact, we know little about professional writers. Nigel Ramsay, "Scriveners and Notaries as Legal Intermediaries in Later Medieval England," in *Enterprise and Individuals in Fifteenth-Century England*, ed. Jennifer Kermode (Gloucester: Sutton, 1991), 118–31; Kümin, *Shaping of a Community*, 85.

67. Ruth Crosby, "Oral Delivery in the Middle Ages," *Speculum* 11 (1936): 88–110; Clanchy, *From Memory to Written Record*, 38.

68. SRO D/P/ban 4/1/1, fols. 26, 31, 167.

69. SRO D/P/yeo. j. 4/1/6, fol. 5.

70. Bäuml, "Varieties and Consequences," 239; Clanchy, *From Memory to Written Record*, 177–85.

71. Tim William Machan, "Editing, Orality, and Late Middle English Texts," in *Vox Intexta*, 230–32. Steven Justice has argued the opposite position, suggesting that Latin did not remove anyone from writing, since even serfs must have had a rudimentary Latin vocabulary to allow them to participate in documentary practices. Justice is making his argument for the period around the peasants' revolt in 1381, and it could be that the general population's knowledge of Latin had declined by the fifteenth century. *Writing and Rebellion: England in 1381* (Berkeley: University of California Press, 1994), 33–35. John Mirk's fifteenth-century collection of English sermons, however, makes the comment that Latin was not well understood. "It is much more effective and meritable for you to say your Pater Noster in English than in Latin, as you do. For when you speak in English, then you know and understand well what you say." John Mirk, *Festial*, ed. T. Erbe, EETS, es 96 (1902), 282; see also Duffy, *Stripping of the Altars*, 80.

72. SRO D/P/bw #14, 15, 16.

73. *Churchwardens' Accounts of St. Edmund and St. Thomas, Sarum*, ed. Henry J. F. Swayne, Wilts Record Society 1 (1896), 14, 32, (quote) 54.

74. SRO D/P/bw nos. 14, 15, 1057, 13, 12, 11; Dorset Record Office PE/WM/CW 1/33, 1/35, 1/40; *Churchwardens' Accounts of St. Michael's Church, Oxford*, ed. H. E. Salter, Oxfordshire Archaeological Society 78 (1933), 163–64.

75. St. Botolph Aldersgate's accounts start in 1466 and are all in English, as are St. Mary at Hill's, which start in 1420. See London Guildhall Library 1454/1; 1454/2 et passim.; 1239/1 parts 1 and 2.

76. In his introduction to the Somerset churchwardens' accounts, Hobhouse comments that the parish was one of the earliest institutions to use English. See *Church-wardens' Accounts of Croscombe etc.*, xxiii, n. 1.

77. SRO D/P/ba. mi. 4/1/6 #67.

78. Peter Heath does not believe that English literacy was a major problem for the late-medieval English clergy, but Latin learning was not as high as either Protestant or Catholic reformers wished. Peter Heath, *The English Parish Clergy on the Eve of the Reformation* (London: Routledge and Kegan Paul, 1969), 70–75. In this case, the term "vicar" would seem to denote a clergyman generally and not a vicar in the technical sense, as Tintinhull did not have a vicarage instituted until 1528. See *VHC-Somerset*, ed. R. W. Dunning (London: Oxford University Press, for the Institute of Historical Research, 1974), 3: 262.

79. SRO D/B/bw #42.

80. Machan, "Editing, Orality, and Late Medieval Texts," in *Vox Intexta*, 230; Bäuml writes that "the increase in the use of writing in the vernacular, both for literary and documentary purposes, breached the link between literacy and Latin, and vernacular literature from the oral tradition made its appearance in written form" ("Varieties and Consequences," 244). Sarah Beckwith writes that "It became increasingly clear that a God in the vernacular was a different God from a God in Latin, as contemporaries were well aware." *Christ's Body: Identity, Culture, and Society in Late Medieval Writings* (London: Routledge: 1993), 38. This in part explains the hesitancy to translate the Bible into the vernacular, which was one of the sources of contention with the Lollards. Thus churchwardens' accounts in Latin in fact embodied a different meaning from those in English.

81. For a more detailed discussion of the importance of accounting and record keeping see Jack Goody, *The Logic of Writing and the Organization of Society* (Cambridge: Cambridge University Press, 1986), 45–86.

82. "A social stratum . . . which requires and possesses access to literate transmission in a literate society is not disadvantaged in respect to its ability to use the written transmission for the execution of its social functions" (Bäuml, 244).

83. *REED-Cambridge*, ed. Alan H. Nelson (Toronto: University of Toronto Press, 1989), 2: 734, 759.

84. *REED-Cambridge*, 1: 80–100.

85. *Churchwardens' Accounts of St. Mary the Great, Cambridge from 1504–1635*, ed. J. E. Foster, Cambridge Antiquarian Society 35 (1905).

86. "The incarnational drama of the late Middle Ages was transformed by the local likeness at the same time it helped make that local community identity recognizable and coherent. Medieval community theater in this sense both defined the social structure and celebrated it." Gail McMurray Gibson, *Theater of Devotion: East Anglian Drama and Society in the Late Middle Ages* (Chicago: University of Chicago Press, 1989), 41.

87. Ibid., 40.

88. James Stokes, "Robin Hood and the Churchwardens in Yeovil," *Medieval and Renaissance Drama in England: An Annual Gathering of Research, Criticism and Reviews* 3 (1986): 1–25.

89. These examples were chosen at random. SRO D/P/yat 4/1/1, fols. 77, 79.

90. SRO D/P/yat 4/1/1, fol. 114.

91. SRO D/P/yat 4/1/1, fol. 115. Using pronouns was by no means limited to only the Yatton accounts, as those for Ashburton in Devon and St. Mary the Great in Cambridge also show; Hanham, *Ashburton*, 18, 19, 31; Foster, *St. Mary the Great*, 14, 61–63, 69.

92. London Guildhall Library 1454/9, 1454/10 et passim.

93. A.N. Doane, in the introduction for *Vox Intexta*, writes: "Once the songs became texts, stripped of their sonic component and location within and between bodies, the 'written residue' was endowed with all the prestige that has traditionally inhered in the texts studied by classicists and medievalists. . . . On the other side, it is known—though rarely is the knowledge effective—that nearly all vernacular texts and many Latin ones . . . down to the thirteenth century and beyond are merely traces of an existence that was normally vocalized. Texts were written to be heard" (p. xii). For an alternative approach to the relationship between speech and texts, see Goody's discussion of lists and accounts. In discussing early Mesopotamian writing, he states that speech and the writing of accounts are quite separate from each other. Goody, *Logic of Writing*, 92–110, and *Domestication of the Savage Mind* (Cambridge: Cambridge University Press, 1977), 80.

94. Ward Parks, "Textualization of Orality in Literary Criticism," in *Vox Intexta*, 47.

95. John Miles Foley, "Orality, Textuality, and Interpretation," in *Vox Intexta*, 37.

96. James N. Baker, "The Presence of the Name: Reading Scripture in an Indonesian Village," in *The Ethnography of Reading*, ed. James Boyarin (Berkeley: University of California Press, 1993), 103.

97. F. F. Fox, "Regulations of the Vestry of St. Stephen, 1524," *Proceedings of the Clifton Antiquarian Club* 1 (1884–88): 199, 203. Beat Kümin kindly produced this example for me. St. Botolph, Aldersgate, in London also fined parishioners absent from the meeting. London Guildhall Library 1454/7, 1454/8 et passim.

98. Bäuml, "Varieties and Consequences," 237–65.

99. Ibid., 246.

100. Ibid., 246–47.

101. Paul Zumthor argued in his studies of medieval lyric poetry that a shift occurs in the power relationship between audience and performer when a written text is interposed between them; he feels that writing holds more authority than the voice. Because of this primacy given to writing, scholars have usually separated churchwardens from their accounts, rather than studying the relationships between them, including the element of vocal performance and its impact on the parish as a community. Zumthor, *Oral Poetry*, 27–29, 46, 61.

102. SRO D/P/l. st l. 4/1/1, fols. 1 et passim.

103. SRO D/P/tin 4/1/1, fol. 24; D/P/ban 4/1/1, fol. 94.

104. SRO D/P/ba. mi. 4/1/1 #1,2, 7.

105. SRO D/P/bw #7. One wonders if it was a bribe, extortion, or cold. For a particularly vivid description of the audit process see Margaret Aston, "Iconoclasm at Rickmansworth, 1522: Troubles of Churchwardens," *Journal of Ecclesiastical History* 40 (1989): 532.

106. Kümin, *Shaping of a Community*, 83.

107. "Church-wardens' Accounts of Croscombe," 8.

108. Ibid., 13. It is impossible to know how much this impression is due to Hobhouse's

editing. He may have omitted expenses that he considered quite typical, and since the accounts have subsequently been lost, there is no way to check the originals.

109. SRO D/P/stogs 4/1/1, fols. 9 et passim.

110. Ibid., fol. 18v. et passim. The Ilminster accounts also have a similar statement (SRO D/P/ilm 4/1/1).

111. SRO D/P/stogs 4/1/1, fol. 21v.

112. WCR *WCB* I, fols. 4, 11, 17 et passim.

113. WCR *WCB* I, fol. 45.

114. PRO C1 226/31.

115. SRO D/P/yat 4/1/1, fol. 369; 4/1/2, fol.19.

116. SRO D/P/ban 4/1/1.

117. Kümin, *Shaping of a Community*, 89,

118. *Church-wardens Accounts of Croscombe etc.*, 229.

119. "Churchwardens' Account Book of Rotherfield," ed. Canon Goodwyn, *Sussex Archaeological Collections* 41 (1898), 27.

120. This is not uncommon, as Hutton points out. Of the 205 accounts covering the period between 1535 and 1562, only 18 kept records during these turbulent years. *Rise and Fall of Merry England*, 69.

121. PRO C1 623/12.

Chapter 3. The Office of Churchwarden and Parochial Leadership

1. Beat Kümin, *The Shaping of a Community: The Rise and Reformation of the English Parish, c. 1400–1560* (Aldershot: Scolar Press, 1996), 265–69.

2. Toulmin Smith, *The Parish* (London: H. Sweet, 1857); *Church-wardens' Accounts of Croscombe, Pilton, Yatton, Tintinhull, Morebath and St. Michael's Bath*, ed. Edmund Hobhouse, SRS 4 (1890), xi, xv, n. 1; J. Charles Cox, *Churchwardens' Accounts: From the Fourteenth to the Close of the Seventeenth Century* (London: Methuen, 1913), 1–2; F. A. Gasquet, *Parish Life in Mediaeval England* (London: Methuen, 1906), 1–20, 106–7. Women's involvement in the parish is more problematic. All four historians comment in seemingly favorable terms on the many examples of women serving as churchwarden, yet their notion of democracy must be understood as coming from a period when women could not vote.

3. Peter Blickle, *The Communal Reformation: The Quest for Salvation in Sixteenth-Century Germany*, trans. Thomas Dunlap (Atlantic Highlands, N.J.: Humanities Press, 1992), 165. See also Marc R. Forster, *The Counter-Reformation in the Villages: Religion and Reform in the Bishopric of Speyer, 1560–1720* (Ithaca, N.Y.: Cornell University Press, 1992); Kümin, *Shaping of a Community*, 260–64.

4. Eric Carlson addresses these same concerns for the post-Reformation period. His findings suggest that at an earlier time, there was a greater level of organization on the part of the parishioners in Bath and Wells than in Ely. Eric Carlson, "The Origins, Function, and Status of the Office of Churchwarden, with Particular Reference to the Diocese of Ely," in *The World of Rural Dissenters, 1520–1725*, ed. Margaret Spufford (Cambridge: Cambridge University Press, 1995), 164–207.

5. Charles Drew, *Early Parochial Organisation in England: The Origin of the Office of Church-warden*, St. Anthony Hall Publications 7 (York: Borthwick Institute of Historical Research 1954), 9.

6. Ibid., 6

7. Ibid.

8. SRO D/P/bw #3.

9. SRO D/P/bw #23.

10. *Bridgwater Borough Archives: 1200–1468*, ed. Thomas Bruce Dilks, SRS 48 (1933), 1: 220–25.

11. SRO D/P/bw #22.

12. WCR *WCB* I, fol. 4; Thomas Serel, *Historical Notes on the Church of Saint Cuthbert in Wells: The Priory of St. John, College of La Mountery and Chapels Formerly at Southober, Southway, Polsham, and Chilcote* (Wells: Atkins and Beauchamp, 1875), 38; according to Hobhouse, the town council of Chard also elected the parish's churchwardens. Hobhouse, *Church-wardens' Accounts of Croscombe, etc.*, xvii.

13. Barry Cunliffe, *The City of Bath* (Gloucester: Sutton, 1986), 66.

14. SRO D/P/ba. mi. 4/1/1 #1.

15. Michael Aston and Roger Leech, *Historic Towns in Somerset* (Taunton: Somerset County Council, 1977), 55–59.

16. SRO D/P/gla. j. 4/1/1.

17. John Moorman, *Church Life in England in the Thirteenth Century* (Cambridge: Cambridge University Press, 1955), 24; Christopher Harper-Bill, *The Pre-Reformation Church in England* (London: Longmans, 1989), 45.

18. Drew, *Early Parochial Organisation*, 12–15.

19. SRO D/B/reg. 2 (Register of Oliver King), fol. 2; *Register of Oliver King*, ed. H. C. Maxwell-Lyte, SRS 54 (1939), 341, no. 1295; David Gary Shaw, *The Creation of a Community: The City of Wells in the Middle Ages* (Oxford: Oxford University Press, 1993), 259; *Church-wardens Accounts of Croscombe, etc.*, 227, 262; "Churchwardens' Accounts for St. John's Glastonbury," ed. F. W. Weaver and C. H. Mayo, *Somerset and Dorset Notes and Queries* 4 (1895): 89. Yeovil's patron was the Middlesex convent of Syon, Glastonbury's was the abbey, and Tintinhull's the nearby priory of Montacute. *Calendar of Manuscripts of the Dean and Chapter of Wells*, Historical Manuscripts Commission 12a (London: H.M.S.O., 1907), 1: 78–79. Several parishes, such as Yatton, Wells, Pilton, and North Curry, were appropriated by the dean and chapter of Wells cathedral, or one of the other cathedral clergy. *Church-wardens' Accounts of Croscombe, etc.*, 49, 79; Michael Costan, *The Origins of Somerset* (Manchester: Manchester University Press, 1992), 45–47.

20. Drew, *Early Parochial Orginisation*, 25.

21. Blickle, *Communal Reformation*, 165; Forster, *The Counter-Reformation in the Villages*, 23–24; Drew, *Early Parochial Organisation*, 25–26; Paul Adam, *La vie paroissiale en France au XIVe siècle*, Histoire et Sociologie de l'Église 3 (Paris: Sirey, 1964), 80–85; Beat A. Kümin, "The English Parish in a European Context," in *The Parish in English Life: 1400–1600*, ed. Katherine L. French, Gary G. Gibbs, and Beat A. Kümin (Manchester: Manchester University Press, 1997), 15–32; Allyson Poska, *Regulating the People: The Catholic Reformation in Seventeenth-Century Spain* (Leiden: Brill, 1998), 55–56.

22. Dorothy Owen, *Church and Society in Medieval Lincolnshire*, History of Lincolnshire 5 (Lincoln: History of Lincolnshire Committee and Lincolnshire Local History Society, 1971), 120–21; Robert N. Swanson, *Church and Society in Late Medieval England* (Oxford: Basil Blackwell, 1989), 165–66; *Church-wardens' Accounts of Croscombe, etc.*, xii; Gasquet, *The Parish*, 106; Cox, *Churchwardens' Accounts*, 2.

23. PRO STAC 2/18/301.

24. PRO C1 1014/48–49.

25. PRO C1 1014/49.

26. PRO C1 1014/48.

27. SRO D/P/yat 4/1/1, fol. 86.

28. SRO D/P/yat 4/1/1, fol. 88. "Thomas Kew and John Harte (wardens in 1467) owying to the parasche 20s. that they delyvered to the peynter withowte leve of the parasche."

29. SRO D/P/yat 4/1/1, fols. 217 et passim.

30. PRO C1 9/428.

31. Kümin, *Shaping of a Community*, 95–96.

32. *Select Cases in the Court of Requests*, ed. Isaac Saunders Leadam, Selden Society 12 (1898), 17–29.

33. Ibid., 18.

34. Ibid., 20.

35. Ibid., 19.

36. For more discussion of this issue see Clive Burgess, "Shaping the Parish: St. Mary at Hill, London, in the Fifteenth Century," in *The Cloister and the World: Essays in Honour of Barbara Harvey*, ed. John Blair and Brian Golding (Oxford: Oxford University Press, 1996), 255–57.

37. SRO D/P/pilt 4/1/1, fol. 56; DD/CT 77.

38. Cox, *Churchwardens' Accounts*, 4; W.E. Tate, *The Parish Chest: A Study of the Records of Parochial Administration in England* (Cambridge: Cambridge University Press, 1946), 83–85. See also Burgess, "Shaping the Parish," 253–56.

39. D/P/ba. mi. 4/1/1, #14, 15, 17, 19, et passim.

40. SRO D/P/ban 4/1/1.

41. SRO D/P/ban 4/1/1, fols. 3 et passim. Glastonbury paid its wardens a much larger stipend of 6s. 8d. D/P/gla. j. 4/1/1.

42. *VHC-Somerset*, ed. R. W. Dunning (London: University of London, Institute for Historical Research, 1988), 5: 118.

43. Fenton and Doveridge in Devon both used a rotation system. In the late sixteenth century, when records from Aisholt in Somerset begin to survive, we find that the wardens were appointed by house row. Tate, *The Parish Chest*, 84.

44. Sons do not appear to take over from their deceased fathers.

45. SRO DD/WO 49/1, fols. 5, 35, 67.

46. SRO DD/WO 49/1, fols. 9, 41, 73.

47. SRO DD/WO 49/1, fols. 75, 78.

48. I use this term with hesitation. It seems, however, to be appropriate as a way of contrasting Yatton's local government with other parishes. Had the parish really been moving towards a democratic system, we might expect a higher number of repeating wardens as the community continued to reelect those who performed successfully.

49. Jennifer Kermode warns that the sign of a true oligarchy lies in its election or selection practices. This information can only be inferred from the surviving material. Jennifer Kermode, "Obvious Observations on the Formation of Oligarchies in Late Medieval English Towns," in *Towns and Townspeople in the Fifteenth Century*, ed. J. A. F. Thomson (Gloucester: Sutton, 1988), 89.

50. For the following discussion of Croscombe, see "The Church-wardens' Accounts of Croscombe," 1–48.

51. PRO STAC 2/18/301.

52. PRO STAC 2/12/180–84. See also *Proceedings of the Court of Star Chamber in the Reigns of Henry VII and Henry VIII*, ed. Gladys Bradford, SRS 27 (1911), 230–39.

53. "Church-wardens' Accounts of Croscombe," 46–47.

54. Ashburton, Chagford, Morebath, Stratton, Bodmin, all had parish guilds that contributed to the upkeep of the parish church. See *Churchwardens' Accounts of Ashburton, 1479– 1580*, ed. Alison Hanham, Devon and Cornwall Record Society, ns 15 (1970); *The Churchwardens' Accounts of St. Michael's Church, Chagford: 1480–1600*, ed. Francis Mardon Osborne (Chagford: Devon: Privately Printed, 1979); *Accounts of the Wardens of the Parish of Morebath, Devon: 1520–1573*, ed. Erskine Binney, *Devon Notes and Queries* 2, 3 (1904); Joanna Mattingly, "The Medieval Parish Guilds of Cornwall," *Journal of the Royal Institution of Cornwall* 10 (1989): 290–329; "Reports and Expenses in the Building of Bodmin Church: 1469–1472," ed. John James Wilkinson, in *Camden Miscellany VII*, Camden Society 14 (1874), iii–49.

55. SRO D/P/tin 4/1/1, fols. 1–32.

56. This is a ratio of 11:21 (between 1458 and 1500) compared to 11:24 (between 1433 and 1457).

57. John Stacey served from 1440–46 and again in 1453; Thomas Stacey served in 1465, 1479–81, 1487, 1496–97; Robert Stacey served from 1470–76, 1485, and 1497. SRO D/P/tin 4/1/1.

58. SRO D/P/tin 4/1/1, fols. 26.

59. SRO D/P/tin 4/1/1, fols. 15, 42; fols. 7, 8, 10–14. In 1455, the accounts refer to him as the bailiff (fol. 30).

60. SRO D/P/tin 4/1/1, fols. 81–104.

61. SRO D/P/tin 4/1/1, fols. 81, 87.

62. SRO D/P/tin 4/1/1, fol. 111.

63. Susan Reynolds, "Medieval Urban History and the History of Political Thought," *Urban History Yearbook* (1982): 20–21. She also notes that although Aristotle used the word, medieval people who ran towns did not.

64. Shaw, *Creation of a Community*, 177–215; Kermode, "Obvious Observations on the Formation of Oligarchies," 87–106.

65. *The Survey and Rental of the Chantries, Colleges and Free Chapels, Guilds, Fraternities, Lamps, Lights, and Obits in the County of Somerset: 1548*, ed. Emmanuel Green, SRS 2 (1888), 74, 89, 137.

66. H. S. Bennett, *Life on the English Manor* (Cambridge: Cambridge University Press, 1965), 154–92.

67. SRO D/P/ tin 4/1/1, fols. 39, 42, 120 for example.

68. Kümin, *Shaping of a Community*, 27–30.

69. Clive Burgess, "The Benefactions of Mortality: The Lay Response in the Medieval Urban Parish," in *Studies in Clergy and Ministry in Medieval England*, ed. D. M. Smith (York: Borthwick Institute of Historical Research, 1991), 80–82.

70. Shaw, *Creation of a Community*, 158–60.

71. WCR., *WCB* I, fol. 4. See also Shaw, *Creation of a Community*, 104–254 for more on borough government in Wells.

72. Serel, *Notes on the Church of Saint Cuthbert in Wells*, 38 (the original no longer survives).

73. Lépold Genicot, *Rural Communities in the Medieval West* (Baltimore: Johns Hopkins University Press, 1990), 104; Sylvia L. Thrupp, *The Merchant Class of Medieval London* (Chicago: University of Chicago Press, 1948), 186.

74. *Somerset Medieval Wills*, ed. F. W. Weaver, SRS 16 (1901), 1: 355–56, 359–60; *Somerset Medieval Wills*, ed. F. W. Weaver, SRS 19 (1903), 2: 80, 205; *Somerset Medieval Wills*, ed. F. W. Weaver, SRS 21 (1905), 3: 15; *Medieval Wills from Wells*, ed. Dorothy Shilton and Richard Holworthy, SRS 40 (1925), 35.

75. SRO D/P/yat 4/1/1, fols. 70 and 153.

76. SRO D/P/ba. mi. 4/1/1 #27.

77. PRO C1 679/61; C1 1014/48; STAC 2/8/190; STAC 2/18/301.

78. Shaw, *Creation of a Community*, 166.

79. Kümin, *Shaping of a Community*, 33–38.

80. Judy Ann Ford, "The Community of the Parish in Late Medieval Kent" (unpublished Ph. D. dissertation, Fordham University, 1994), 107–20.

81. PRO E179/239/153; E179/169/176; E179/170/194. Complete ones survive for Bath E179/169/142 and E179/169/178 (although taxpayers are not listed by parish), Ilminster E179/169/180 fol. 45–47 (which has very late and sparse churchwardens' accounts), Lydeard St. Lawrence E179/169/180 fol. 12, and Croscombe E179/169/173.

82. PRO E179/169/176, piece 6.

83. SRO D/P/bw #806–9; 811; 1648–49; 1763; 1773–74; 1776b. These are lists of names, by street, with the amount of money households gave during parish or town assessments.

84. I arrived at this conclusion by comparing the individual amounts donated by the churchwardens to the average amount given by their street or ward. Some gave above the average, some gave below. Because the collection sheets do not always explain the purpose of the collection, and never explain how the community decided how much each household should give, I treated each sheet independently of the others. The average donation for each ward or street is only a relative description of wealth, allowing me to compare them, but making the absolute amounts essentially meaningless since the criteria of contribution were never explicit. The street between the bridge and the church was consistently the largest contributor and hence would seem to be the wealthiest part of town.

85. WCR *WCB* II, fols. 209, 218, 257, 275, 279, 291, 296, 331, 345, 397, 419.

86. This may be related to the fact that the parish could not legally incorporate; so the office of churchwarden was only quasi-legal.

87. Cox, *Churchwardens' Accounts*, 7; Gasquet, *Parish Life*, 106. Outside of Somerset, other parishes had women churchwardens, although these are generally limited to the West Country. In 1426, in the parish of St. Patrick, Ingestre in Cornwall, Alice Cooke and Alice Pyppedon were wardens; in 1428 in the Exeter parish of St. Petrock Beatrice Braye served; in 1527, in the Bristol parish of St. Ewen's Margaret Mathew served; and in Morbath in Devon, Margaret Borson served in 1528, Joan Morse served in 1542, Joan Goodman served in 1543, and Lucy Scely served in 1548. One other possible female churchwarden was Maryan Gerens who was warden in 1508 in the London parish of St. Andrew Hubbard. The handwriting makes this identification unclear. See Kümin, *Shaping of a Community*, 40. See also David Palliser, "Introduction: The Parish in Perspective," in *Parish, Church, and People*, ed. Susan Wright (London: Hutchinson, 1988), 23.

88. Katherine L. French, "Maidens' Lights and Wives' Stores: Women's Parish Guilds in Late Medieval England," *Sixteenth Century Journal* 29 (1998): 421–42.

89. SRO D/P/yat 4/1/1, fols. 210–14.

90. See *Somerset Medieval Wills*, 1: 374–75 for her will and 272, for her husband's will. According to the pamphlet available in the parish church, she is "supposed to be the 'Grey Lady,' the benevolent ghost of Yatton Church." Gillian Keily, *A Guide to the Parish Church of St. Mary the Virgin in the Parish of Yatton Moor* (Yatton: Yatton Moor P.C.C., n.d.), 7.

91. Cox, *Churchwardens' Accounts*, 5. The parish of North Petherwin, in the diocese of Exeter, had difficulties getting individuals to serve as churchwarden in the late 1530s and 40s. See Robert Whiting, *The Blind Devotion of the People: Popular Religion and the English Reformation* (Cambridge: Cambridge University Press, 1989), 101.

92. SRO DD/WO 49/1, fol. 80.

93. SRO DD/CT 77, fol. 63.

94. SRO DD/CT 77, fol. 68.

95. SRO DD/CT 77, fol. 75.

96. SRO D/P/tin 4/1/1, fol. 147.

97. SRO D/P/hal 4/1/4.

98. PRO E179/169/176, piece 6.

99. Julian Cornwall, "English Country Towns in the 1520s," *Economic History Review* 15 (1962): 63.

100. PRO E179/170/194. Still, about a third of the population was too poor to pay the lay subsidy tax, so Sibyl Smith does not appear to have been destitute. Roger Schofield, "Parliamentary Lay Taxation: 1485–1547" (unpublished Ph. D. Dissertation, Cambridge University, 1963), 244–46.

101. Ford, "Community of the Parish," 117–20.

102. SRO D/P/bw #806, 617, 105, 17, 7.

103. SRO D/P/bw #105.

104. SRO D/P/bw #17.

105. WCR *WCB* II, fols. 21, 97, 155, 213, 218.

106. There is no consistent guild warden information.

107. This is also Burgess's point in his article "Shaping the Parish."

108. Virginia Bainbridge, *Gilds in the Medieval Countryside* (Woodbridge: Boydell, 1996), 131–35.

109. There is only one guild certificate for Somerset, and no communities with church-wardens' accounts have manorial accounts from the same period.

110. SRO D/P/tin 4/1/1 fols. 7, 8, 10–14; 30.

111. John Mirk, *Instructions for Parish Priests*, ed. Edward Peacock, EETS 31a (1902), 35.

112. John Mirk, *Festial: A Collection of Homilies*, ed. Theodor Erbe, EETS, es 96 (1905), 280.

113. SRO DD/WO 49/1, fols. 15, 47.

114. SRO DD/WO 49/1, fol. 79.

115. Jennifer Ward, *English Noble Women in the Later Middle Ages* (London: Longmans, 1992), 143–63; Jennifer Ward, "English Noble Women and the Local Community in the Later Middle Ages," in *Medieval Women in Their Communities*, ed. Diane Watt (Toronto: University of Toronto Press, 1997), 186–203.

116. Colin Richmond, "Religion and the Fifteenth-Century English Gentleman," in *The Church, Politics, and Patronage*, ed. R. B. Dobson (Gloucester: Sutton, 1984), 193–208; P. W. Fleming, "Charity, Faith and the Gentry of Kent 1422–1529," in *Property and Politics*, ed. A. J. Pollard (Gloucester: Sutton, 1984), 36–58; J. Catto, "Religion and the English Nobility in the Later Fourteenth Century," in *History and Imagination: Essays in Honor of H. R. Trevor-Roper* , ed. Hugh Lloyd-Jones, Valerie Pearl, and Blair Worden (New York: Holmes and Meier Pub. Inc., 1981), 43–55; for a dissenting opinion see Christine Carpenter, "Religion of the Gentry of Fifteenth-Century England," in *England in the Fifteenth Century: Proceedings of the 1986 Harlaxton Symposium*, ed. D. W. Williams (Woodbridge: Boydell, 1987), 53–74.

117. Carpenter, "Religion of the Gentry," 53–74.

118. Richmond, "Religion and the Fifteenth-Century Gentleman," 193–208, and "The English Gentry and Religion, c. 1500," in *Religious Beliefs and Ecclesiastical Careers*, ed. Christopher Harper-Bill (Woodbridge: Boydell and Brewer, 1991), 121–50, esp. 137. See also

Catto, "Religion and the English," 43–55; Peter Heath, "Between Reform and Reformation: The English Church in the Fourteenth and Fifteenth Century," *Journal of Ecclesiastical History* 41 (1990): 667–69.

119. SRO D/D/B reg. 4 (Register of Nicholas Bubwith), fol. 151d; *Register of Nicholas Bubwith, Bishop of Bath and Wells, 1407–1424*, ed. Thomas Scott Holmes, SRS 30 (1914), 341 no. 808.

120. PRO STAC 2/18/26.

121. PRO STAC 2/26/107.

122. *Somerset Medieval Wills*, 2: 197–98.

123. J. H. Betty, "From Norman Conquest to the Reformation," in *Aspects of the Mediaeval Landscape of Somerset*, ed. Michael Aston (Bridgwater: Somerset County Council, 1988), 59.

124. PRO C1 789/43.

125. SRO D/D/B reg. 6 (Bishop's Register of Thomas Bekynton), fols. 3–4. See also Michael Hicks, "Four Studies in Conventional Piety," *Southern History* 13 (1991): 12–13.

126. Betty, "From Norman Conquest to the Reformation," 59.

127. *Somerset Medieval Wills*, 1: 238.

128. *VHC-Somerset*, 3: 261.

129. Nikolaus Pevsner, *The Buildings of England: North Somerset and Bristol* (Middlesex: Penguin, 1958), 177–8.

130. *Church-wardens' Accounts of Croscombe etc.*, 3.

131. *Church-wardens' Accounts of Croscombe etc.*, xi; Pollock and Maitland also believe that the vestries carried out these responsibilities, but do not define their composition. Frederick Pollock and Frederic William Maitland, *The History of English Law Before the Time of Edward I*, 2nd ed. (Cambridge: Cambridge University Press, 1968), 1: 613.

132. Cox, *Churchwardens' Accounts*, 12–14.

133. Ian Archer, *The Pursuit of Stability: Social Relations in Elizabethan London* (Cambridge: Cambridge University Press, 1991), 69–74; Kümin, *Shaping of a Community*, 251.

134. Archer, *The Pursuit of Stability*, 85.

135. SRO D/P/l. st l. 4/1/1, fols. 1, 3, et passim.

136. SRO D/P/stogs 4/1/1 fol. 53.

137. Cox believes that twenty-four people was the standard number of vestry members, although he records many with less. Cox, *Churchwardens' Accounts*, 12–14.

138. Kümin, *Shaping of a Community*, 251.

Chapter 4. Parish Fundraising

1. A version of this chapter was published first as "Parochial Fundraising in Late Medieval Somerset," in *The Parish in English Life: 1400–1600*, ed. Katherine L. French, Gary G. Gibbs, and Beat A. Kümin (Manchester: Manchester University Press, 1997), 115–32.

2. Charles Drew, *Early Parochial Organisation in England; the Origin of the Office of Churchwarden*, St. Anthony Hall Publications 7 (York: Borthwick Institute of Historical Research 1954), 10–11.

3. *Church-wardens' Accounts of the Parishes of Pilton, Yatton, Tintinhull, Morebath and St. Michael's Bath*, ed. Edmund Hobhouse, SRS 4 (1890), xii–xiii.

4. Clive Burgess, "The Benefactions of Mortality: The Lay Response in the Late Medieval Urban Parish," in *Studies in Clergy and Ministry in Medieval England*, ed. D. M. Smith,

Borthwick Studies in History 1 (York: Borthwick Institute for Historical Research, 1991), 65–87.

5. Clive Burgess and Beat Kümin, "Penitential Bequests and Parish Regimes in Late Medieval England," *Journal of Ecclesiastical History* 44 (1993): 610–30; Andrew Brown, *Popular Piety in Late Medieval England: The Diocese of Salisbury, 1250–1550* (Oxford: Oxford University Press, 1995), 83–91.

6. Warren O. Ault, "Manor Court and Parish Church in Fifteenth-Century England: A Study of Village By-Laws," *Speculum* 42 (1967): 53–67. Ault discusses manorial regulations that turned over to the parish church part of the fines collected by the manorial court. There are a few examples in Somerset, but they are infrequent and do not appear to be a regular part of parish income. See SRO D/P/tin 4/1/1, fol. 2.

7. *Somerset Medieval Wills*, ed. F. W. Weaver, SRS 21 (1905), 3: 42–3.

8. *Somerset Medieval Wills*, ed. F. W. Weaver, SRS 19 (1903), 2: 172; see also p. 128 for another will which left another ship to the same parish.

9. Suffolk Record Office, FC 185/E1/1.

10. Brown, *Popular Piety*, 83–91.

11. Burgess and Kümin, "Penitential Bequests," 622–25.

12. Burgess, "Fond Thing Vainly Invented: An Essay on Purgatory and Pious Motive in Late Medieval England," in *Parish Church and People: Local Studies in Lay Religion, 1350–1750*, ed. S. J. Wright (London: Hutchinson, 1988), 56–84; J. J. Scarisbrick, *The Reformation and the English People* (Oxford: Basil Blackwell, 1984), 1–39.

13. J. Charles Cox, *Churchwardens' Accounts: From the Fourteenth to the Close of the Seventeenth Century* (London: Methuen, 1913), 158–59; F. A. Gasquet, *Parish Life in Mediaeval England* (London: Methuen, 1903), 222–25; Dorothy Owen, *Church and Society in Medieval Lincolnshire* (Lincoln: History of Lincolnshire Committee and the Lincolnshire Local History Society, 1971), 112–13; Eamon Duffy, *Stripping of the Altars: Traditional Religion in England, 1400–1580* (New Haven, Conn.: Yale University Press, 1992), 153–54.

14. SRO D/D/B reg. 10 (Register of Bishop Adrian de Castello), fols. 104b–105a.

15. SRO D/P/tin 4/1/1, fol. 56.

16. SRO D/P/bw #9, 17, 19, 18, 88, 4.

17. SRO T/Ph/bm 31 s/1800.

18. Peter Heath, "Urban Piety in the Later Middle Ages: The Evidence of Hull Wills," in *The Church, Politics and Patronage*, ed. R.B. Dobson (New York: St. Martin's Press, 1984), 209–34; Clive Burgess, "Late Medieval Wills and Pious Conventions: Testamentary Evidence Reconsidered," in *Profit, Piety, and the Professions*, ed. Michael Hicks (Gloucester: Sutton, 1990), 14–33.

19. *Somerset Medieval Wills*, 3: 35.

20. Christine Carpenter, "Religion of the Gentry of Fifteenth-Century England," in *England in the Fifteenth Century: Proceedings of the 1986 Harlaxton Symposium*, ed. D. W. Williams (Woodbridge: Boydell Press, 1987), 53–74; J. Catto, "Religion and the English Nobility in the Later Fourteenth Century," in *History and Imagination: Essays in Honor of H. R. Trevor-Roper*, ed. Hugh Lloyd-Jones, Valerie Pearl, and Blair Worden (New York: Holmes and Meier, 1981), 43–55.

21. *Somerset Medieval Wills*, 1: 244–45.

22. *Somerset Medieval Wills*, 2: 25–27.

23. Judith Bennett, "The Village Ale-Wife: Women and Brewing in Fourteenth-Century England," in *Women and Work in Preindustrial Europe*, ed. Barbara A. Hanawalt (Bloomington: Indiana University Press, 1986), 30.

24. SRO D/P/ban 4/1/1, fol. 9 is just one of many such examples. "Et de 4d. for the lyng of a chyld of John Byrd yn the chyrche."

25. Amy Louise Erickson, *Women and Property in Early Modern England* (London: Routledge, 1993), 156–222.

26. It is difficult to represent this numerically. In Croscombe, of the total number of times cash was given to the parish (170 times in 63 years) women gave 34 percent of the time or 57 times. For precious objects and jewelry, of the total number of times they were given to the parish—141 times—women contributed 72 percent of the time. Clothing appears in the accounts 25 times, and 68 percent of these gifts came from women. Parishioners gave liturgical items 23 times, and women's gifts make up 43 percent of the total. In Yatton, between 1445 and 1515, men and women gave clothing and liturgical items in equal or nearly equal numbers. Of the 77 items of jewelry given to Yatton during this period, 47 (or 61 percent) came from women and 30 (or 39 percent) from men.

27. Christopher Dyer, *Standards of Living in the Later Middle Ages: Social Change in England, c. 1200–1520* (Cambridge: Cambridge University Press, 1989), 78–87.

28. I have argued elsewhere that in this period women's contributions to the parish become more obvious and that the parish made more room for activities delineated by gender. Katherine L. French, " 'To Free Them from Binding': Women in the Late Medieval English Parish," *Journal of Interdisciplinary History* 27(1997): 387–412; "Maidens' Lights and Wives' Stores: Women's Parish Guilds in the Late Medieval English Parish," *Sixteenth Century Journal* 29 (1998): 399–425.

29. For more on women and the laws of inheritance see Kay E. Lacey, "Women and Work in Fourteenth and Fifteenth Century London," in *Women and Work in Pre-Industrial England*, ed. Lindsey Charles and Lorna Duffin (London: Croom Helm, 1985), 24–82; Erickson, *Women and Property*.

30. 44 percent of women's wills compared to 18 percent of men's wills left material goods to the church. Of these wills 31 percent of women's wills and 3 percent of men's wills left jewelry; 45 percent of women's wills and 17 percent of men's wills left clothing. For more on this see Katherine L. French, " 'I Leave My Best Gown as a Vestment': Women's Spiritual Interests in the Late Medieval English Parish," *Magistra* 4 (1998): 57–77.

31. SRO D/P/tin 4/1/1, fol. 57.

32. SRO D/P/yat 4/1/1, fol. 143.

33. SRO D/P/tin 4/1/1, fol. 96.

34. SRO D/P/yat 4/1/1, fols. 52, 61, 69, 80, 88.

35. SRO, DD/CT 77, fols. 20, 56; D/P/pilt 4/1/1, fols. 24, et passim; D/P/tin 4/1/1, fols. 6. 8, et passim.

36. SRO D/P/tin 4/1/1, fol. 6.

37. SRO D/P/ba. mi. 4/1/1 #50.

38. This is not the case for all parishes. The accounts for St. Edmund in Salisbury show that seats became an important way for the parish to raise money. In 1484/5, the wardens received 10s. 6d. Cox, *Churchwardens' Accounts*, 67.

39. SRO D/P/bw #15, 17, 8, 51, 51. In 1450, seats constituted 8 percent of the total income; in 1455, they made up 17 percent. This level drops to 3 percent for 1456 and 1457. In 1463 and 1464, the wardens sold more seats, and the sales constituted 10 percent and 11 percent respectively. For the last account from before the Reformation, 1471, seats sold made only 1 percent of the income.

40. The medieval seats still survive in Trull. Some were built in 1527 (SRO DD/CT 77, fol. 11). In Yatton, the wardens had seats installed in 1454 (SRO D/P/yat 4/4/1, fol. 38)

and in Tintinhull they were built between 1511 and 1513 (SRO D/P/tin 4/1/1, fols. 95–96). For further examples see Peter Poyntz Wright, *The Rural Benchends of Somerset* (Amersham: Avebury, 1983).

41. BL Add. Ms. 40, 729A; SRO T/PH/bm 31 s/1800.

42. Susan Reynolds, *An Introduction to the History of English Medieval Towns* (Oxford: Oxford University Press, 1977), 93.

43. W.O. Ault, "The Village Church and the Village Community in Medieval England," *Speculum* 45 (1970): 211–12.

44. SRO D/P/ba. mi. 4/1/1 #1, 4/1/2 #13, 4/1/4 #49.

45. SRO D/P/gla. j. 4/1/1–3. These accounts are very sporadic and often mutilated. It is difficult, therefore, to get as complete a picture from them as it is from other accounts.

46. SRO D/P/bw #22, 14.

47. PRO STAC 2/6/90–92.

48. BRO P/ST. T/ChW/1.

49. SRO D/P/yeo. j. 4/1/6, fols. 5, 28.

50. SRO D/P/stogs j. 4/1/1, fols. 4, 25.

51. *Somerset Wills*, 1: 368–70.

52. Burgess, "Late Medieval Wills and Pious Convention: Testamentary Evidence Reconsidered," in *Profit, Piety and the Professions*, ed. Michael Hicks (Gloucester: Sutton, 1990), 14–33.

53. Initially it was only 4s., but the sum increased continually throughout the rest of the period. In 1459, the parish could not collect £2 9d., and in 1547, it was short £2 5s. 6d. It may be that these properties were not leased, or the tenants were poor and the wardens did not vigorously demand payment. SRO D/P/ba. mi. 4/1/2#21, #28, 4/1/6 #68; "The Churchwardens' Accounts of the Church and Parish of St Michael Without the North Gate, Bath, 1349–1575," ed. C. B. Pearson, *Proceeding of the Somerset Archaeological and Natural History Society* 23 (1877): ii.

54. Reynolds, *English Medieval Towns*, 154–59; Charles Phythian-Adams, *Desolation of a City: Coventry and the Urban Crisis of the Late Middle Ages* (Cambridge: Cambridge University Press, 1979), 31–67.

55. Ault, "The Village Church," 211–12. Ault finds that rural churchwardens regularly appeared in the manorial courts and assumes that this means that the parish owned a great deal of property. However, just one acre of meadow could still bring the churchwardens into court on a regular basis and yet not provide much monetary support.

56. SRO DD/WO 49/1, fols. 1, 3, 17, 76

57. SRO D/P/ban 4/1/1, fols. 27, 69, et passim.

58. SRO D/P/tin 4/1/1, fols. 70, 116, 120, 127, 147.

59. David Farmer, "Prices and Wages, 1350–1500," in *The Agrarian History of England and Wales*, ed. Edward Miller (Cambridge: Cambridge University Press, 1991), 3: 436.

60. J. H. Betty, *Church and Community* (Bradford-on-Avon: Moonraker Press, 1979), 41, 51–53, 58–59; Patrick Cowley, *The Church House* (London: S.P.C.K., 1970) 15.

61. G.W. Copeland, "Devonshire Church-Houses," *Transactions of the Devonshire Association* 92 (1960): 118.

62. SRO DD/WO 49/1, fol. 82; D/P/yat 4/1/1, fol. 204.

63. *Survey and Rental of the Chantries . . . in the Country of Somerset, 1548*, ed. Emmanuel Green, SRS 2 (1888), 219–20.

64. We find similar arrangements in Shepton Bauchamp, Selworthy, Easton Gordano,

Long Ashton, Charleton Adam, and Weston. *Survey and Rental of the Chantries*, 85, 97, 112, 150, 186, 218.

65. The parishioners of Croscombe built their church house in 1480/1, spending £13 2s. 11½d. Pilton refurbished theirs extensively in 1512, Banwell built theirs in 1529, and both Nettlecombe and Trull had houses when their accounts start in 1515 and 1525 respectively. "Church-wardens' Accounts of Croscombe," 9; SRO D/P/ban 4/1/1, fols. 53–58; D/P/pilt 4/1/1, fols. 22–23; DD/CT 77, fol. 1; DD/WO 49/1, fol. 22.

66. SRO D/P/yat 4/1/1, fols. 1–4; 95–114; 121–28.

67. SRO D/P/tin 4/1/1, fol. 4.

68. SRO D/P/tin 4/1/1, fols. 3, 33, 41, 47, 74–75.

69. SRO D/P/tin 4/1/1 fol. 119.

70. Bennett, "The Village Ale-Wife," 20–36.

71. PRO 1090/34.

72. Cowley, *Church House*, 15–16.

73. J. H. Betty, *Church and Parish: An Introduction for Local Historians* (London: Batsford, 1987), 101–2.

74. Judith Bennett, "Conviviality and Charity in Medieval and Early Modern England," *Past and Present* 134 (1992): 19–41. Here Bennett makes the point that church houses also provided a place for ales that were held to help out neighbors or new couples in financial need. This can also be an example of the charity that the church sought to foster.

75. It was not a significant source of income, bringing in at the most 22d. It does not appear before 1521, and it is not a regular feature of the accounts. SRO D/P/stogs 4/1/1, fols. 25, 26, 28v, 36v et passim.

76. "Accounts of the proctors of the church of Yeovil, co. Somerset, 36 Henry VI, 1457–8," ed. John G. Nichols, *Collectanea Topographica et Genealogica* 3 (1834): 161–70 (original lost).

77. James E. Thorold Rogers, *A History of Agriculture and Prices in England*, 3 (rpt.; London: Kraus Reprint, 1963). Rogers's price index shows just how much of an investment these items could be. Brewing equipment could range from 1s. to 40s. a pan (555 iv; 559 iv; 561 ii). A set of weights sold for 9s. (549 i) and anvils ranged from 16s. 8d. to 33s. 4d. (558 ii; 577 ii).

78. SRO D/P/yeo. j 4/1/6; bishops had never approved of business being conducted in the church or churchyard. In 1334, the Bishop Ralph of Shrewsbury republished the diocesan statutes that forbade these kinds of activities. SRO D/D/B reg. 2, fol. 132.

79. Brown, *Popular Piety*, 104–10; Burgess and Kümin, "Penitential Bequests."

80. Gasquet, *Parish Life*, 125; Drew, *Early Parochial Organisation*, 13–14. There is some suggestion by Gasquet and Drew that the collections for wax were voluntary and those for the whole fabric were not. These distinctions are not clear in the accounts, but generally wax collections did not bring in enough money to make chasing defaulters into court financially worthwhile. Collections for the whole fabric were a different matter, as offenders, it could be argued, violated canon law, but again there is little evidence that churchwardens regularly pursued them into court.

81. SRO DD/CC 131908/5; DD/CC 131903/3.

82. SRO D/D/B reg. 1 (Bishop's Register of John Drokensford), fol. 240a.

83. SRO D/P/bw #3, 23.

84. SRO D/P/tin 4/1/1, fols. 3, 7, 119, 135.

85. Cox, *Churchwardens' Accounts*, 2. See Drew, *Early Parochial Organisation*, 12–13 for some earlier examples and Gasquet, *Parish Life*, 125–29 for later ones. Hobhouse com-

ments on how unusual Bridgwater's fundraising was (*Church-wardens' Accounts of Croscombe etc.*, 230–31).

86. SRO, D/P/bw #2 (1394) "Et de 108s. 6d receptis de quandam collectione assessa super parochianos ville pro reparatione fabrice ecclesie." D/P/bw #41 (1415) "Et de £20 receptis de quandam collectione assessata super parochianos tam infra villam quam extra pro diversis defectibus in ecclesia."

87. SRO D/P/bw #50.

88. SRO D/P/bw #22, #50.

89. SRO, D/P/bw #26. It is unclear how many years this list of debts might cover.

90. SRO D/D/B reg. 1 (Bishop's Register of John Drokensford), fol. 240a.

91. SRO, D/P/bw #41.

92. SRO D/P/ban 4/1/1; DD/WO 49/1; D/P/pilt 4/1/1.

93. Ronald Hutton, *The Rise and Fall of Merry England: The Ritual Year, 1400–1700* (Oxford: Oxford University Press, 1994), 50–51.

94. SRO D/D/Cd 17, fol. 42; see James Stokes, "The Hoglers: Evidences of an Entertainment Tradition in Eleven Somerset Parishes," *Notes and Queries for Somerset and Dorset* 32 (1990): 808.

95. SRO D/D/Cd 17, fol. 42v; see also Stokes, "The Hoglers," 808.

96. *Church-wardens' Accounts of Croscombe*, 251.

97. Stokes, "The Hoglers," 811–12.

98. Ibid, 807–17; *Church-wardens' Accounts of Croscombe*, 251; Hutton, *Merry England*, 50.

99. SRO D/P/ban 4/1/1, fols. 53–100.

100. SRO D/P/ban 4/1/1, fol. 164.

101. "Church-wardens' Accounts of Croscombe," 1–48; SRO D/P/tin 4/1/1, fols. 40, 74; D/P/gla. j 4/1/7, 8; D/P/pilt 4/1/1, fols. 27, 12, 17.

102. Gail McMurray Gibson discusses local drama as not only drawing upon local events and circumstances but further defining and identifying the community. Gail McMurray Gibson, *Theater of Devotion* (Chicago, Ill.: University of Chicago Press, 1989), 19–46.

103. For more on Hocktide see my article "To Free Them from Binding," 387–412.

104. "Church-wardens' Accounts of Croscombe," 20.

105. Barbara Hanawalt, *The Ties That Bound: Peasant Families in Medieval England* (New York: Oxford University Press, 1986), 193.

106. For more on women's guilds see my article "Maidens' Lights and Wives' Stores: Women's Parish Guilds in Late Medieval England."

107. SRO D/P/pilt 4/1/1, fols. 12, 27.

108. Hutton, *Merry England*, 28–29; 87–88.

109. Cox, *Churchwardens' Accounts*, 288; Alexandra F. Johnston, "Parish Entertainments in Berkshire", in *Pathways to Mediaeval Peasants*, ed. J. A. Raftis, Mediaeval Studies 2 (Toronto: Pontifical Institute of Mediaeval Studies, 1981), 335–38; Hutton, *Merry England*, 5–68.

110. For more on dramatic activities see *REED-Somerset, Including Bath*, 2 vols., ed. James Stokes with Robert J. Alexander (Toronto: University of Toronto Press, 1997).

111. *The Rymes of Robyn Hood: An Introduction to the English Outlaw*, ed. R. B. Dobson and J. Taylor (Gloucester: Sutton, 1989), 37.

112. For more on inversion see Natalie Zemon Davis, "The Reasons of Misrule," in *Society and Culture in Early Modern France* (Stanford, Calif.: Stanford University Press, 1965), 97–123.

113. Stephen Knight, *Robin Hood: A Complete Study of the English Outlaw* (Oxford: Basil Blackwell, 1994), 262–63.

114. James D. Stokes, "Robin Hood and the Churchwardens of Yeovil," *Medieval and Renaissance Drama in England* 3 (1986): 1–3.

115. Ibid., 7.

116. SRO, D/P/yeo. j. 4/1/6, fol. 5, T/PH/bm 31 s/1800; BL Add. Ms. 40,729A.

117. *Rymes of Robyn Hood*, 39.

118. "Church-wardens' Accounts of Croscombe," 9.

119. Ibid., 24.

120. Ibid., 28, 29 et passim.

121. WCR. *WCB* II fol. 203; See also "Wells Convocation Book," *First Report of the Royal Commission on Historical Manuscripts* (London: H.M.S.O, 1874), 107; E. K. Chambers, *The Mediaeval Stage* (Oxford: Oxford University Press, 1903), 1: 176; *Rymes of Robyn Hood*, 39.

122. SRO D/P/tin 4/1/1, fol. 96.

123. "Churchwardens' Accounts for St John's Glastonbury," ed. F. W. Weaver and C. H. Mayo, *Somerset and Dorset Notes and Queries* 4 (1895): 332–36.

124. *Rymes of Robyn Hood*, 38; Chambers, *Mediaeval Stage*, 1: 160–81, 205–27. In one of the Paston letters, John Paston complains that the servant he kept "this 3 year[s past] to play Saint George and Robin Hood and the Sheriff of Nottingham" has left him upon acquiring a good horse. *Paston Letters*, ed. J. Gairdner (rpt. Gloucester: Sutton, 1986), 5: 185.

125. Jonathan Bengtson, "Saint George and the Formation of English Nationalism," *Journal of Medieval and Early Modern Studies* 27 (1997): 317–40; John Wasson, "The Saint George and Robin Hood Plays in Devon," *Medieval English Theatre* 2 (1980): 66–69; Benjamin R. McRee, "Unity or Division: The Social Meaning of Guild Ceremony in Urban Communities," in *City and Spectacle in Medieval Europe*, ed. Barbara A. Hanawalt and Kathryn L. Reyerson (Minneapolis: University of Minnesota Press, 1994), 189–207.

126. "Statutes of Wells," 601–2, nos. 19–20.

127. *Dives and Pauper*, ed. Priscilla Heath Barnum, EETS 275 (1976), 1: 189.

128. Knight, *Robin Hood*, 105.

129. For more on Robin Hood's status see Knight, *Robin Hood*, 88–97.

130. "Church-wardens' Accounts of Croscombe," 36.

131. For a variation on this argument, but from a more literary standpoint, see P. R. Cross, "Aspects of Cultural Diffusion in Medieval England: The Early Romances, Local Society and Robin Hood," *Past and Present* 108 (1985): 35–79. See also Alexandra Johnston and Sally-Beth MacLean, "Reformation and Resistance in Thames/Severn Parishes: The Dramatic Witness," in *The Parish in English Life, 1400–1600*, 178–200.

132. John C. Coldewey, "Some Economic Aspects of the Late Medieval Drama" in *Contexts for Early English Drama*, ed. Marianne G. Briscoe and John C. Coldewey (Bloomington: Indiana University Press, 1989), 92; Mervyn James, "Ritual, Drama and Social Body in the Late Medieval English Town," *Past and Present* 98 (1983): 10–15; Charles Phythian-Adams, "Ceremony and the Citizen: The Communal Year at Coventry, 1450–1550," in *Crisis and Order in English Towns, 1500–1700*, ed. Paul Clark and Paul Slack (London: Routledge, 1972), 57–85.

133. Coldewey, "Some Economic Aspects of Late Medieval Drama," 92. Coldewey contends that financial reward and civic pride are mutually exclusive. I would suggest that this is not the case, and that fundraising could be another manifestation of local pride.

134. Ibid., 93.

135. SRO D/P/tin 4/1/1, fol. 21.

136. SRO D/P/gla. j. 4/1/7.

137. SRO D/P/gla. j. 4/1/7.

138. SRO D/P/yeo. j. 4/1/6, fol. 9.

139. There are a few exceptions, such as the 1428 ale held by the parishioners of St John's in Glastonbury or the occasional ones held at St Michael's in Bath. SRO D/P/gla. j 4/1/7; D/P/ba. mi. 4/1/5 #53, 54, 56. The ale at Glastonbury occurred the same year as the two plays and was part of the extra effort to pay for the new construction.

140. Lawrence Blair, *English Church Ales* (Ann Arbor, Mich.: Edwards Brothers, 1940), 1–2.

141. Cox, *Churchwardens' Accounts*, 289.

142. SRO D/P/yat 4/1/1, fols. 104, 108, 116 et passim.

143. SRO D/P/tin 4/1/1, fol. 99; DD/WO 49/1, fol. 10.

144. Stogursey, Nettlecombe, Yatton, and Ilminster all held ales on Whitsun.

145. SRO D/P/yat 4/1/1 fol. 43. In 1455, Banwell's ale was part of the group of ales patronized by the Yatton wardens.

146. SRO D/P/yat 4/1/1, fols. 229–331.

147. SRO D/P/tin 4/1/1, fols. 12–16, 25, 28, 61, et passim.

148. Income had dropped to only 16s. 8d. and £1 2s. 11d. in 1445 and 1447 respectively, whereas the previous five years had brought in an annual income ranging from £1 6s. 8d. to £3 8s. 8d.

149. SRO D/P/tin 4/1/1 fols. 121, 125, 147.

150. SRO DD/WO 49/1, f. 63.

151. Cox, *Churchwardens' Accounts*, 289.

152. SRO D/P/yat 4/1/1, fol. 378; 4/1/2 fols. 62, 79, 92, 99, 114, 124 et passim.

153. Colin Platt, *The Parish Churches of Medieval England* (London: Secker and Warburg, 1981), 97.

154. Robert Whiting, *The Blind Devotion of the People: Popular Religion and the English Reformation* (Cambridge: Cambridge University Press, 1989), 90–106.

155. Ales were one of the many abuses cited by Stubbes in his 1583 work *Anatomie of Abuses*, and Archbishop Laud did much to outlaw these gatherings completely. Cox, *Churchwardens' Accounts*, 288.

156. Bernard L. Manning, *The People's Faith in the Time of Wyclif* (Cambridge: Cambridge University Press, 1919), 123–44.

157. For the demise of church ales in the seventeenth century see David Underdown, *Revel, Riot and Rebellion: Popular Politics and Culture of England* (Oxford: Oxford University Press, 1985), 83–88; T. G. Barnes, "County Politics and a Puritan Cause Célèbre: Somerset Church Ales, 1633," *Transactions of the Royal Historical Society* 5th ser. (1959): 103–22.

158. By way of a contrast, in the Tyrol, on the border of what is modern day Italy and Austria, church ales were not as popular with the Reform-inspired peasants. During the peasant revolts of 1525, the peasants of Merano included in their list of demands the abolition of all church ales. They demanded that "All church ales should be abolished, for no good comes of them, only evil." Part of the objection was the extra financial support for maintaining the parish church above and beyond the tithes. "The Merano Articles, 30 May 1525," in *The German Peasants' War: A History in Documents*, ed. Tom Scott and Bob Scribner (Atlantic Highlands, N.J. and London: Humanities Press, 1991), 94 no. 59.

159. Ken Farnhill, "Religious Policy and Parish Conformity: Cratfield's Lands in the Sixteenth Century," and Caroline Litzenberger, "St. Michael's Gloucester 1540–80: The

Cost of Conformity in Sixteenth-Century England," in *The Parish in English Life: 1400–1600*, 217–29, 230–49; Kümin, *Shaping of a Community*, 202–21.

160. Manning, *People's Faith*, 123–44; Bennett, "Conviviality and Charity," 19–41.

161. "Statutes of Wells," 604–5, #28.

162. John Mirk, *Instructions for Parish Priests*, ed. Edward Peacock, EETS 31a (1902), 41.

Chapter 5. *The Architecture of Community*

1. *Dives and Pauper*, ed. Priscilla Heath Barnum, EETS 275 (1976), 1: 189–90.

2. Pauper refers specifically to the building of the Temple by the Jews and the Gospel story of the widow who gave everything she had to the temple. See Exodus 30: 11–16; Mark 12: 41–44.

3. Gervase Rosser, *Medieval Westminster* (Oxford: Oxford University Press, 1989), 263–71.

4. Charles Phythian-Adams, *Local History and Folklore: A New Framework* (London: Bedford Square Press for Standing Conference for Local History, 1975), 17.

5. Margaret Aston, "Segregation in Church," *Studies in Church History* 27 (1990): 237–94; Vanessa Harding, "Burial Choice and Burial Location in Later Medieval London," in *Death in Towns: Urban Responses to the Dying and the Dead, 100–1600*, ed. Steven Basset (Leicester: University of Leicester Press, 1992), 119–35; Robert Dinn, " 'Monuments Answerable to Men's Worth': Burial Patterns, Social Status, and Gender in Late Medieval Bury St. Edmund's," *Journal of Ecclesiastical History* 46 (1995): 237–55.

6. Rosser, *Medieval Westminster*, 271.

7. John Detjeman, ed., *Collins Guide to English Parish Churches Including the Isle of Man* (London: Collins, 1958), 322; Nikolaus Pevsner, *The Buildings of England: North Somerset and Bristol* (Middlesex: Penguin, 1958) 33–34; Nikolaus Pevsner, *The Buildings of England: South and West Somerset* (Middlesex: Penguin, 1958) 33–34; R. W. Dunning, "The Middle Ages," in *Christianity in Somerset*, ed. R. W. Dunning (Somerset: Somerset County Council, 1976), 6; A.K. Wickham, *The Churches of Somerset* (Dawlish: David and Charles, 1965).

8. See Pevsner, *North Somerset* or *South and West Somerset*, 34–44 for a detailed discussion of the styles and types of church towers. (The introductions are the same for both volumes.)

9. Wickham, *The Churches of Somerset*, 38–49. The eight schools are the cathedral group, west Mendip group, Quantock group, east Mendip group, north Somerset group, south Somerset group, Brislington group, and Devon group.

10. Ibid., 26–27.

11. SRO D/P/ban 4/1/1, fols. 11, 37, 51, 97, 98, 109, 118, 124; D/P/tin 4/1/1, fol. 32, 52; DD/WO 49/1, fols. 42, 65, 70, 71.

12. SRO D/P/yat 4/1/1, fols. 86, 89, 90; 4/1/2, fol. 151; 4/1/3, fols. 35 et passim.

13. "Churchwardens' Accounts for St. John's Glastonbury," ed. F. W. Weaver and C. H. Mayo, *Somerset and Dorset Notes and Queries* 4 (1895): 332–36.

14. J. H. Betty has mapped out the geographic range of services and goods for Yatton's rebuilding project. See J. H. Betty, "From Norman Conquest to Reformation," in *Aspects of the Medieval Landscape of Somerset*, ed. Michael Aston (Bridgwater: Somerset County Council, 1988), 54–58.

15. Edwin Smith, Graham Hutton, and Olive Cook, *English Parish Churches* (London: Thames and Hudson, 1976), 117–24; Colin Platt, *The Parish Churches of Medieval England*

(London: Secker and Warburg, 1981), 92–98; Richard Morris, *Churches in the Landscape* (London: J. M. Dent, 1989), 227–315; G. H. Cook, *The English Mediaeval Parish Church* (London: Phoenix House, 1954); J. Charles Cox and Charles Bradley Ford, *The Parish Churches of England* (London: Batsford, 1937), 59–63; Philip Ziegler, *The Black Death* (New York: Harper Torchbooks, 1969), 267–70; Colin Platt, *King Death* (Toronto: University of Toronto Press, 1996), 137–75.

16. Clive Burgess, "A Fond Thing Vainly Invented: An Essay on Purgatory and Pious Motive in Late Medieval England," in *Parish, Church and People*, ed. Susan Wright (London: Hutchinson, 1988), 66–68; Jacques Le Goff, *The Birth of Purgatory*, trans. Arthur Goldhammer (Chicago, Ill.: University of Chicago Press, 1981), 289–333.

17. J. G. Davies, *The Secular Use of Church Buildings* (London: S.C.M. Press, 1968), 36–95.

18. The description is Eamon Duffy's. *Stripping of the Altars: Traditional Religion in England, 1400–1580* (New Haven, Conn.: Yale University Press, 1992), 132.

19. John Leland, *The Itinerary*, ed. Lucy Toulmin Smith (Carbondale: Southern Illinois University Press, 1964), 1: 167.

20. Cook, *The English Mediaeval Parish Church*, 133.

21. As we have already seen, the earliest churchwardens' account in Bath and Wells covers Bridgwater's expenses for casting a new bell. At this point, bell-making was not a professionalized task, and the parishioners, perhaps with the supervision of a local smith, did much of the work themselves. By the fifteenth century, bell-founding was in the hands of professionals, and parishioners did not have to expend this kind of effort over the installation of a new bell. SRO D/P/bw #3; John C. Eisel, "Developments in Bell Hanging," in *Change Ringing: The History of an English Art*, ed. J. Sanderson (Cambridge: Central Council of Church Bell Ringers, 1987), 1: 17–21. Maintenance of the bells appears regularly in the churchwardens' accounts and consistently cost between 7 and 12 percent of total expenses. Bells required a lot of care. They needed to be greased and rotated to produce even wear. The leather thong that attached the clapper to the bell (the baldric) needed regular replacing, as did the ropes.

22. Eisel, "Developments in Bell Hanging," 18–20.

23. In 1447, the parishioners of Yeovil gave their bell-ringers ale in payment for having rung the bells while it thundered. "Account of the Proctors of the Church of Yeovil, Co. Somerset, 36 Henry VI, 1457–8," ed. John G. Nichols, *Collectanea Topographica et Genealogica* 3 (1834): 134–37.

24. PRO C1 520/33.

25. PRO C1 839/47.

26. PRO C1 520/33.

27. Of the 18 wills from this parish, 16 left money to support the bells; the 2 who did not were gentry buried at the Franciscan church in Bridgwater. *Somerset Medieval Wills*, ed. F. W. Weaver, SRS 16 (1901), 1: 1, 61–62, 66–67, 317, 324; 2: 18–19, 63, 157, 162–63, 204–5, 210, 211, 212, 261, 280–81, 283–84. *Medieval Wills from Wells*, ed. Dorothy Shilton and Richard Holworthy, SRS 40 (1925), 16, 18, 24–25, 35. Although there are sporadic bequests to bells in many wills, testamentary bequests to the bells appear to be a particular custom in this parish. Such an obvious local custom is not usually so visible in wills.

28. SRO D/D/B reg. 4 (Register of Nicholas Bubwith), fols. 212–13; *Register of Nicholas Bubwith, Bishop of Bath and Wells, 1407–1424*, ed. Thomas Scott Holmes, SRS 29 (1914), 460–64, no. 1266.

29. For a discussion of this dispute and its resolution see H. C. Maxwell-Lyte, *History of Dunster and the Families of Mohun and Luttrell* (London: St. Catherine's Press, Ltd., 1909), 2:

393–95. The original is apparently lost. A transcript of the contract between the parishioners and the mason can be found in L. S. Salzman, *Building in England Down to 1540* (Oxford: Oxford University Press, 1967), 514–15. See also Katherine L. French, "Competing for Space: The Monastic-Parochial Church at Dunster," *Journal of Medieval and Early Modern Studies* 27 (1997): 215–44.

30. Maxwell-Lyte, *History of Dunster*, 2: 394.

31. The prior of Bath, of which Dunster was a priory, initiated the suit, presumably at the request of the prior of Dunster.

32. PRO STAC 1/2/122.

33. PRO STAC 1/2/122.

34. Not all sets of churchwardens' accounts show building projects. The church at Tintinhull had been rebuilt prior to the start of its accounts in 1433. The parishioners in this tiny parish took on only one other major building project prior to the Reformation. In 1539, the parishioners renovated or expanded the bell tower. SRO D/P/tin 4/1/1, fol. 135.

35. SRO D/P/bw #23. Most of what survives today is Victorian.

36. Wickham, *Churches of Somerset*, 26.

37. Ibid.

38. SRO D/P/bw #1650.

39. SRO D/P/bw #22, 2; work on this building continued on and off for the next fifty years.

40. SRO D/P/bw #41.

41. SRO D/P/bw #41, 42.

42. SRO D/P/bw #17.

43. Jonathan Bengtson, "Saint George and the Formation of English Nationalism," *Journal of Medieval and Early Modern Studies* 27 (1997): 317–40; Kathleen Ashley and Pamela Sheingorn, "Introduction," in *Interpreting Cultural Symbols: St. Anne in Late Medieval Society*, ed. Kathleen Ashley and Pamela Sheingorn (Athens: University of Georgia Press, 1990), 1–68.

44. SRO D/P/gla. j. 4/1/3v.

45. SRO D/P/gla. j. 4/1/1 #7. This part of the project cost £10 16s. 4d. and was partially paid for by extra parish fundraising efforts. They held two plays and an ale that year to increase revenues.

46. This account only survives in a fragment, so the exact amount of repair is not clear. "Churchwardens' Accounts for St. John's Glastonbury," 235–37.

47. Pevsner, *North Somerset*, 35. The tower is 134½ feet tall. Only St. Mary Magdalene's church tower in Taunton is taller, with a 163½ foot tower. The tower in Taunton was built in the 1490s. The height of this tower was a likely consequence of competition between the parish and the priory located nearby. There are no building accounts, but many testators specifically provided money for work on the tower in their wills. *Somerset Medieval Wills*, 1: 279–80, 288–89, 298–300, 352–54, 378–80; 2: 25–27, 30–32, 37, 124–25, 211–12.

48. SRO D/P/ba. mi. 4/1/1 #12.

49. SRO D/P/ba. mi. 4/1/2 #20. Others then left money to the altar. *Somerset Medieval Wills*, 2: 326, 354–55.

50. It was first rebuilt in 1742 and then in 1835–37 when G.P. Manners erected the current church. See Pevsner, *North Somerset*, 107–8.

51. Barry Cunliffe, *The City of Bath* (Gloucester: Sutton, 1986), 66.

52. Wickham, *Churches of Somerset*, 22. A similar, but less dramatic, example of the difference between the chancel and the nave can also be found at Stoke St. Gregory.

53. SRO D/P/yat 4/1/1, fols. 16–17.

54. Platt, *Parish Churches*, 97; A. C. Edwards, "The Medieval Churchwardens' Accounts of St. Mary's Church, Yatton," *Somerset and Dorset Notes and Queries* 32 (1986): 536–47; SRO D/P/yat 4/1/1, fols. 46–48 the spire; fols. 48–58 the south porch; fols. 143–61 the nave.

55. *Somerset Medieval Wills*, 1: 272, 374–75.

56. Emmanuel Green, "On the Manor of Yeovil," *Proceedings of the Somerset Archaeological and Natural History Society* 32(1887): 5–8.

57. *Somerset Medieval Wills*, 2: 287–88.

58. "The claim is based on the likeness between the arcades of Yeovil and the arches of the antechapel at New College; between its tower, especially its parapet, and those of Wells; and on the fact that Robert de Samborne was a Canon of Wells, lived there, and would have known and wished to employ one of the leading architects of his time." Wickham, *Churches of Somerset*, 26.

59. John Mirk, *Instructions for Parish Priests*, ed. Edward Peacock, EETS 31a (1902), 9.

60. C. Pamela Graves, "Social Space in the English Medieval Parish Church," *Economy and Society* 18 (1989): 298–99 Gábor Klaniczay, "Religious Movements and Christian Culture: A Pattern of Centripetal and Centrifugal Orientations," in *The Uses of Supernatural Power: The Transformation of Popular Religion in Medieval and Early Modern Europe*, trans. Susan Singerman, ed. Karen Margolis (Princeton, N.J.: Princeton University Press, 1990), 28–50; Edmund M. Kern, "The 'Universal' and the 'Local' in Episcopal Visitations," in *Infinite Boundaries: Order, Dis-Order, and Re-Order in Early Modern German Culture*, ed. Max Reinhart, Sixteenth Century Essays and Studies 40 (Kirksville, Mo.: Sixteenth Century Journal Publishers, 1998), 35–54.

61. Graves, "Social Space," 306; Duffy, *Stripping of the Altars*, 124.

62. Graves, "Social Space," 306.

63. Ibid., 307.

64. Christopher Brooke, "Religious Sentiment and Church Design in the Later Middle Ages," in *Medieval Church and Society: Collected Essays* (New York: New York University Press, 1972), 162–82. Screens gradually became more important and more elaborate over the course of the middle ages. While in the twelfth century those in cathedrals were long and low, by the thirteenth century they were higher and obscured the altar. As parish churches sought to imitate cathedrals, we might assume that they had not always had such big screens.

65. Eamon Duffy, "The Parish, Piety, and Patronage in Late Medieval East Anglia: The Evidence of Rood-Screens," in *English Parish Life: 1400–1600*, ed. Katherine French, Gary Gibbs, and Beat Kümin (Manchester: Manchester University Press, 1997), 133–62.

66. J. J. Scarisbrick, *Reformation and the English People* (Oxford: Basil Blackwell, 1984), 43; Duffy, *Stripping of the Altars*, 113–14; Duffy, "Rood-Screens," 148–55; Virginia Reinberg, "Liturgy and the Laity in Late Medieval and Reformation France," *Sixteenth Century Journal* 23 (1992): 526–47.

67. Wickham, *Churches of Somerset*, 54.

68. Ibid., 54.

69. PRO C1 215/20.

70. *Somerset Medieval Wills*, 2: 228–29. The saints were John the Baptist, the Virgin Mary, Mary "de Bowe," Our Lady of Pity, St. Clement, St. Christopher, St. Lucy, St. Giles, St. Michael, and St. George.

71. Banwell, Bridgwater, Croscombe, Dunster, Glastonbury, Pilton, Tintinhull, Trull, Yatton. Three still survive: Trull, Banwell, and Dunster.

72. SRO DD/CT 77, fols. 41, 45, 51, 53.

73. SRO D/P/ban 4/1/1, fol. 25.

74. In 1521, the Banwell churchwardens paid "9d. for bred and ale for men to take downe the rode loft . . . 2d. for John Sayer dyner the same day . . . and 3d. for John Wyld the same day to helpe take downe the rode loft." SRO D/P/ban 4/1/1, fol. 30.

75. SRO D/P/ban 4/1/1, fol. 30.

76. SRO D/P/ban 4/1/1, fol. 31.

77. French, "Competing for Space."

78. SRO D/D/B reg. 9 (Register of Oliver King), fols. 137b–38b; for a calendared version, see *Registers of Oliver King, Bishop of Bath and Wells, 1496–1503, and Hadrian de Castello, Bishop of Bath and Wells, 1503–1518*, ed. H. C. Maxwell-Lyte, SRS 54 (1939), 34–35.

79. The rood screen still survives in the church and, at over fifty feet long, is one of the longest surviving wooden screens in Europe. R.G. Bryant, *Dunster Village: Church and Castle*, 3rd ed. (Dunster: privately printed, no date), 8. For discussion on the enlarged chancel, see Cook, *The English Mediaeval Parish Church*, 62; F. Hancock, *Dunster Church and Priory* (Taunton: Barnicott and Pearce Athenaeum, 1905), 126a–b.

80. We can read the tower that the parishioners built in the same way.

81. The feast days specified were Christmas, Epiphany, Palm Sunday, Easter, Ascension, Whitsun, Trinity, Corpus Christi, Purification of Our Lady, St. George's Day, the Assumption, All Saints, and the dedication of the church.

82. Maxwell-Lyte, *History of Dunster*, 2: 394.

83. Ibid.

84. Clifford Geertz, "Ritual and Social Change: A Javanese Example," in *The Interpretation of Cultures*, ed. Clifford Geertz (New York: Basic Books 1973), 142–69. Geertz's criticism of the social anthropological approach is its inability to deal with social change. Functionalism "emphasizes the manner in which belief and particularly ritual reinforce the traditional social ties between individuals" (142). In Dunster, the processional order was an attempt to enforce a relationship that clearly did not work. As the parish became increasingly important in England as a unit of local religion, the prescribed rituals could not contain the antagonism between the monks and parishioners of Dunster. To understand why these attempts continually failed, we need to recognize the changing nature of local religion in the late Middle Ages within the context of local practice. See also Catherine Bell, *Ritual Theory, Ritual Practice* (New York: Oxford University Press, 1992), 88–93. Specifically she writes: "Yet if ritual is interpreted in terms of practice, it becomes clear that formality, fixity, and repetition are not intrinsic qualities of ritual so much as they are a frequent but not universal strategy for producing ritualized acts." Later she adds: "Since practice is situational and strategic, people engage in ritualization as a practical way of dealing with some specific circumstances. Ritual is never simply or solely a matter of routine, habit, or 'the dead weight of tradition' " (92).

85. John Bossy argues that it does, in his article, "The Mass as a Social Institution, 1200–1700," *Past and Present* 100 (1983): 27–61.

86. When Mary became queen, the parish put up a new screen. In contrast, this one only cost 13s. 4d. and cost 12d. to install. Edwards, "The Medieval Churchwardens' Accounts of St. Mary's, Yatton," 54.

87. SRO D/P/yat 4/1/1, fol. 11. Three men went to Easton-in-Gordano "to se ye all'e" (an allure was an arch feature in the rood loft), Crosse and one of the wardens went to Selwood, and another man went to Bruton. Most stone rood screens imitate wooden ones, so the visit to these other parishes does not mean they had stone screens too. Francis Bond, *Screens and Galleries in the English Church* (London: Henry Froude, 1908), 34.

88. SRO D/P/yat 4/1/1, fol. 43.

89. There were four identifiable trips to Bristol for paint. (fols. 43, 44, 53.)

90. SRO D/P/yat 4/1/1, fol. 23 "yn costs yn sekyng of Crosse at Backwell—1d." and fol. 32 "costis atte laboryng to Wells for Crosse—3d."

91. SRO D/P/yat 4/1/1, fol. 43.

92. SRO D/P/yat 4/1/1, fol. 74.

93. SRO D/P/yat 4/1/1, fol. 136.

94. Duffy, "Rood Screens" 133, 151–53.

95. Scarisbrick, *Reformation and the English People*, 43; Duffy, *Stripping of the Altars*, 113–14; Reinburg, "Liturgy and the Laity," 526–47.

96. The earliest seats were probably reserved for the aged, infirm, and women. See Aston, "Segregation in Church," 237–94; J. Charles Cox, *Bench-ends in English Churches* (Oxford: Oxford University Press, 1916), 10.

97. SRO D/P/bw #8 43, 51.

98. SRO D/P/ba. mi. 4/1/2 #20.

99. SRO D/P/gla. j. 4/1/8; D/P/gla. j. 4/1/10; "Churchwardens' Accounts for St. John's Glastonbury, 1500," 332–36.

100. SRO D/P/yat 4/1/1, fol. 38.

101. SRO DD/CT 77, fol. 41; see also Mark McDermott, "Early Bench-Ends in All Saints' Church, Trull," *Somerset Archaeology and Natural History* 138 (1995): 118–20.

102. SRO D/P/tin 4/1/1, fols. 95–96.

103. SRO D/P/tin 4/1/1, fol. 96.

104. Cox, *Bench-ends in English Churches*; Peter Poyntz Wright, *Rural Benchends of Somerset* (Amersham: Avebury, 1983).

105. J. C. D. Smith, *Church Woodcarvings: A West Country Study* (New York: Augustus M. Kelley, 1969), 12–13.

106. Ibid., 88.

107. SRO DD/WO 49/1 fol. 80.

108. He dated his work in the church 1560. There are at least two styles of work in the remaining benches, as well as the clearly pre-Reformation images of the parish procession. See Poyntz Wright, 159–60.

109. Ibid., 159–60.

110. Poyntz Wright, in his book on rural bench-ends in Somerset, says that we can identify Simon's work by the edge moldings. "They are a uniform design of a continuous running stem pattern that is crossed obliquely by a leaf at regular intervals" (1). Based on this evidence, his work appears in Hatch Beauchamp, Combe Florey, Cheddon Fitzpaine, Fiddington, Bishop's Hull, Monksilver, Bicknoller, East Quontoxhead, and Cothelstone; see Poyntz Wright, 1, 43, 49, 75, 126, 159, 160.

111. McDermott, "Early Bench-Ends in All Saints' Church, Trull," 118–20.

112. Smith, *Church Wood Carvings*, 78–79.

113. PRO STAC 2/24/149; STAC 2/32/53; STAC 2/28/54; STAC 2/17/208; STAC 2/12/224–26; SRO D/D/Cd 17; D/D/Cd 35; D/D/Cd 37.

114. PRO STAC 2/12/224–26.

115. PRO STAC 2/2/224.

116. PRO STAC 2/32/53; 2/24/149; 2/17/208.

117. For more on male concerns over women's culture see Steve Hindle, "The Shaming of Margaret Knowsley: Gossip, Gender and the Experience of Authority in Early Modern England," *Continuity and Change* 9 (1994): 391–419.

118. Aston, "Segregation in Church," 269–81.

119. Ibid., 238–41.

120. See also Roberta Gilchrist, *Gender and Material Culture: The Archaeology of Religious Women* (London: Routledge, 1994), 128–49.

121. SRO D/P/yeo. j. 4/1/6, fol. 6.

122. SRO D/P/yeo. j. 4/1/6, fol. 6.

123. SRO, D/P bw #99.

124. *Bridgwater Borough Archives: 1200–1468*, vols. 1–4, ed. Thomas Bruce Dilks SRS 48, 53, 58, 60 (1933–48).

125. Based on the levels of individual contributions, the better-off members of the town appear to have lived on the street between the church and the bridge. *Bridgwater Borough Archives*, 4: 7–34.

126. There are collection reports surviving for three years, 1445, 1446, and an undated one from about the same time. In the first two lists, women comprise 5 percent of the listed individuals and gave 5 percent of the total income. In the undated list, the percentage of income is higher (11 percent) as is the percentage of women (22 percent). This last list also included servants, which helps account for the increase in women. SRO, D/P/bw #806, 807, 1649. See also *Bridgwater Borough Archives*, 4: 7–34.

127. *Somerset Medieval Wills*, 2: 275–78.

128. Pevsner, *South and West Somerset*, 151; the tomb was originally a table tomb, which in modern times was removed. The brass was reinstalled, and still survives. Arthur B. Connor, *Monumental Brasses in Somerset* (Bath: Kingsmead Reprints, 1970), 293.

129. *Somerset Medieval Wills*, 2: 275.

130. The Newtons built two family chapels in Yatton parish church, and Sir John Trevelyan left money in his will to build a new aisle and chapel in Nettlecombe parish church.

131. Graves, "Social Space," 311–17.

132. Ibid., 315.

133. Connor, *Monumental Brasses in Somerset*, 294–95.

134. Christopher Woodforde, *Stained Glass in Somerset: 1250–1830* (London: Oxford University Press, 1946), 99.

135. Gervase Rosser writes: "A common impetus to form fraternities was a desire (conscious or not) to transcend the limitations, geographical or institutional, of a parish. A concomitant of this proposition would be that guilds were most likely to be found in social contexts characterized by a relatively high degree of mobility, such as the parish could not accommodate." "Communities of Parish and Guild," 33.

136. Duffy, *Stripping of the Altars*, 150.

137. SRO D/P/pilt 4/1/1, fols. 34, 69, 71 et passim; D/P/stogs 4/1/1, fols. 49, 49v., 50, 52.

138. Taunton is one of the few parishes with enough surviving wills to allow for a comparison of bequests between men and women. Of the forty-four wills, seven (or 16 percent) are by women. Of the eleven wills leaving money or asking for admittance to the guild of St. Mary of the priory, only one is by a woman, and it is dated 1541, when Henry's reforms had already closed the priory and possibly changed the character of the endowment. *Somerset Medieval Wills*, 1: 356–57, 392–93; 2: 37, 42–43, 161–62, 228; 3: 31, 35–36, 66–67, 78–79, 82–83.

139. James Stokes, "The Hoglers: Evidence of an Entertainment Tradition in Eleven Somerset Parishes," *Notes and Queries for Somerset and Dorset* 32 (1990): 807–16; *Bridgwater Borough Archives*, 2 : nos. 427, 464; *Bridgwater Borough Archives*, 3: 56.

140. French, "Maiden's Lights and Wives' Stores."

141. SRO D/D/B reg. 6 (Register of Thomas Bekynton), fols. 110–11; *Register of Bishop Bekynton*, 147, no. 519.

142. *The Survey and Rental of the Chantries*, ed. Emmanuel Green, SRS 2 (1888), 259.

143. Graves, "Social Space," 301.

Chapter 6. Liturgical Celebrations and the Cult of the Saints

1. Christopher Wordsworth and Henry Littlehales, *The Old Service-Books of the English Church* (London: Methuen, 1904), 15.

2. F. A. Gasquet, *Parish Life in Mediaeval England* (London: Methuen, 1906), 140–63; Eamon Duffy, *The Stripping of the Altars: Traditional Religion in England: 1400–1580* (New Haven, Conn.: Yale University Press, 1992), 123–26; Wordsworth and Littlehales, *Old Service-Books*, 21–22.

3. *The Lay Folk's Mass Book*, ed. T. F. Simmons, EETS 71 (1879), 2.

4. SRO D/D/B reg. 6 (Register of Thomas Bekynton), fol. 303; *Register of Thomas Bekynton, Bishop of Bath and Wells, 1443–1465*, part 1, ed. M. C. B. Dawes, SRS 49 (1934), 414, #1582.

5. In the Gospel of John (9: 7), Jesus instructs a blind man to wash his eyes in a well, and when he does, he is healed.

6. H. Leith Spencer, *English Preaching in the Late Middle Ages* (Oxford: Oxford University Press, 1993), 202–7. In 1357, the archdiocese of York adopted this program. When the York version was translated into English it became known in the vernacular as *The Lay Folks' Catechism*. See *The Lay Folks' Catechism*, ed. Thomas Frederick Simmons and Henry Edward Nolloth, EETS 118 (1901).

7. Spencer, *English Preaching*, 202–7.

8. John Mirk, *Instructions for Parish Priests*, ed. Edward Peacock, EETS 31a (1902), 27–33.

9. Spencer, *English Preaching*, 58–60, 166–74.

10. G. R. Owst, *Preaching in Medieval England* (Cambridge: Cambridge University Press, 1922), 144–46.

11. Mirk was an Augustinian canon and prior of the Abbey of Lilleshall in Shropshire. He probably composed his *Festial* sometime between 1382 and 1390. It survives in numerous manuscripts, and based on the manuscript tradition, would seem to have been most influential in the late fifteenth and early sixteenth centuries. It was also one of the few medieval sermon collections to be printed. Caxton printed the *Liber Festivalis* in 1483, and the work continued to be printed until 1532. Mirk wrote this sermon collection for parish priests, possibly even a particular parish priest at the church of St. Alkmund's in Shrewsbury, whose tithes were a major portion of Lilleshall's income. Spencer, *English Preaching*, 62, 311–16. See also M. F. Wakelin, "The Manuscripts of John Mirk's *Festial*," *Leeds Studies in English* ns 1 (1997), 93–118.

12. *Speculum Sacerdotale*, ed. Edward Weatherly, EETS 200 (1936); *Middle English Sermons*, ed. Woodburn O. Ross, EETS 209 (1940). The introduction to the *Speculum Sacerdotale* says that it is not the original manuscript (p. xv), so the sermons might have been better known than this single manuscript suggests.

13. Spencer, *English Preaching*, 163–88.

14. Ibid., 65.

15. W. A. Pantin, *The English Church in the Fourteenth Century*, Medieval Academy Reprints (Toronto: University of Toronto Press, 1980), 193; Duffy, *The Stripping of the Altars*, 54.

16. SRO D/D/B reg. 5 (Register of John Stafford), fols. 107d–110; *Register of John Stafford, Bishop of Bath and Wells, 1425–1443*, ed. Thomas Scott Holmes, SRS 31 (1915), 173–80, no. 511.

17. SRO D/D/B reg. 4 (Register of Nicholas Bubwith), fol. 68d; *Register of Nicholas Bubwith, Bishop of Bath and Wells, 1407–1424*, ed. Thomas Scott Holmes, SRS 29 (1914), 139, no. 395.

18. W. A. Pantin, "The Fourteenth Century," in *The English Church and the Papacy*, ed. C. H. Lawrence (New York: Fordham University Press, 1965), 174.

19. SRO D/D/B reg. 5 (Register of John Stafford), fol. 15; *Register of John Stafford*, 32 no. 56. Similar licenses: D/D/B reg. 5, fols. 106, 121, 181; *Bishop Stafford's Register*, 169, no. 503; 190, no. 564; 270, no. 843.

20. *Register of Thomas Bekynton*, xxi; Judd, *Life of Thomas Bekynton*, 129–34.

21. SRO D/D/B reg. 6 (Register of Thomas Bekynton), fols. 75, 78, 155–6, 252, 257, 273–74, 98; *Register of Bishop Bekynton*, xxi, note 3, 4; 93–94, no. 338; 98–99, no. 355; 203, no. 742; 340, no. 1287; 347, no. 1318; 372–73, no. 147; 129, no. 469.

22. SRO D/D/B reg. 6 (Register of Thomas Bekynton), fol. 18; *Register of Bishop Bekynton*, 20–21, no. 73.

23. SRO D/D/B reg. 6 (Register of Thomas Bekynton), fols. 36, 53–54, 84; *Register of Bishop Bekynton*, 43, no. 138; 66, no. 223; 108, no. 395.

24. Miri Rubin, *Corpus Christi: The Eucharist in Late Medieval Culture* (Cambridge: Cambridge University Press, 1991), 222–28.

25. Thomas Mertok, a bachelor of theology and monk of Muchelney; John Lacok, monk of Bath; Thomas Daperfeld, John Crosse, William Frampton, and John Sant, bachelors of theology and monks of Glastonbury. SRO D/D/B reg. 6 (Register of Thomas Bekynton), fols. 15–16, 212, 225b, 234, 272; *Register of Thomas Bekynton*, 155, nos. 57–58; 282, no. 1041; 303, no. 1136; 314, no. 119; 369, no. 1417.

26. For example: Master William Silk, M.A., rector of Kyngesdon; John Huysshe, M.A., vicar of St. Mary de Stalles, Bath; Nicholas Pyttes, M.A., vicar of St. Mary Redcliffe; William Chyld, M.A., rector of Westlydford; Richard Swan, M. A., vicar of Burneham. SRO D/D/B reg. 6 (Register of Thomas Bekynton), fols. 145, 180, 194, 202, 705; *Register of Thomas Bekynton*, 190–91, no. 689; 195, no. 705; 231, no. 840; 248, no. 916; 265, no. 966.

27. Prior to this point the secular clergy were not receiving or asking for licenses to preach outside of their parishes. SRO D/D/B reg. 6 (Register of Thomas Bekynton), fols. 20, 111, 145, 149, 180, 193, 202, 225b, 252, 260, 261 303; 16, 37, 216, 234, 272; 38, 147, 211, 234, 283; *Register of Thomas Bekynton*, 23, no. 86; 148, no. 522; 190–91, no. 689; 195, no. 705; 231, no. 840; 248, no. 916; 265, no. 966; 303, no. 1136; 340, no. 1288; 352, no. 1343; 354, no. 1350; 414–45, no. 1584; 16, no. 58; 45, no. 145; 291, nos. 1064, 1068; 314, no. 1191; 369, no. 1417; 46, nos. 149,150; 186, no. 668; 192, no. 699; 282, no. 1041; 385, no. 1492.

28. Robert N. Swanson, *Church and Society in Late Medieval England* (Oxford: Basil Blackwell, 1989), 294, 298–99, 303–4; Duffy, *Stripping of the Altars*, 234–65.

29. The Franciscans came to England in 1224, and they probably settled in Bridgwater in the 1230s. Eccleston, the chronicler of the Franciscans' early years in England, comments that the new church built in the 1440s was the second Franciscan convent in the town. See *VHC-Somerset*, 2: 151, Thomas Eccleston, *On the Coming of the Friars Minor to England*, trans. Emma Gurney-Salter (London: E.P. Dutton, 1926), 62.

30. Peter Poyntz Wright, *The Rural Benchends of Somerset: A Study in Medieval Woodcarving* (Amersham: Avebury, 1983).

31. SRO D/P/ban 4/1/1 fol. 2; *Somerset Medieval Wills*, ed. F. W. Weaver, SRS 21 (1905), 3: 228–29.

32. *Somerset Medieval Wills*, ed. F. W. Weaver, SRS 19 (1903), 2: 54.

33. Arnold Williams, "Relations Between the Mendicant Friars and the Secular Clergy in England in the Late Fourteenth Century," *Annuale Mediaevale* 1 (1960): 22–95.

34. SRO D/D/B reg. 6 (Register of Thomas Bekynton), fol. 38; *Register of Thomas Bekynton*, 46–47, no. 151.

35. A. G. Dickens, *The English Reformation*, 2nd ed. (University Park: Pennsylvania State University Press, 1989), 68–74.

36. Peter Heath, *The English Parish Clergy on the Eve of the Reformation* (London: Routledge and Kegan Paul, 1969), xi.

37. Ibid., 70–92; Pantin, *The English Church*, 220–22.

38. Peter Marshall, *The Catholic Priesthood and the English Reformation* (Oxford: Oxford University Press, 1994), 51–59, 63. In one case, the parishioners' choice of cleric ran afoul of the bishop. In 1448, the parishioners of Pensford admitted one Thomas Northion to preach to them. As he did not have a license, the bishop placed them all under interdict. SRO D/D/B reg. 6 (Register of Thomas Bekynton), fols. 82–83; *Register of Thomas Bekynton*, 105–6, no. 381.

39. Swanson, *Church and Society*, 51–52.

40. Heath, *The English Parish Clergy*, 70–72; 91–92.

41. Christopher R. Cheney, "Rules for the Observance of Feast-Days in Medieval England," *Bulletin for the Institute of Historical Research* 34 (1961): 117.

42. Ibid., 119.

43. For a list of the feast days added to medieval English calendars see Richard Pfaff, *New Liturgical Feasts in Later Medieval England* (Oxford: Oxford University Press, 1970), 3–4.

44. The actual folio from the original register does not appear to have survived. The register has been repaginated since the Somerset Record Society published a calendar of the register in 1887. For the calendared entry, see *Calendar of the Register of John de Drokensford: Bishop of Bath and Wells 1309–1329*, ed. Edmund Hobhouse, SRS 1 (1887), 13. See also Rubin, *Corpus Christi*, 199–200.

45. SRO D/D/B reg. 2 (Register of Ralph of Shrewbury), fols. 273v.–274; see also Cheney, "Rules for the Observance of Feast-Days," 131, 143; Barbara Harvey, "Work and *Festa Ferianda* in Medieval England," *Journal of Ecclesiastical History* 23 (1972): 289–308.

46. Cheney, "Rules for the Observance of Feast-Days," 143.

47. Ibid.

48. J. Catto, "Religious Change Under Henry V," in *Henry V: The Practice of Kingship*, ed. G. L. Harriss (Oxford: Oxford University Press, 1985), 108–10; Sarah Beckwith, *Christ's Body: Identity, Culture, and Society in Late Medieval Writings* (London: Routledge, 1993), 74–76.

49. Catto, "Religious Changes," 107–8; see also W. R. Jones, "The English Church and Royal Propaganda During the Hundred Years War," *Journal of British Studies* 19 (1979): 18–30.

50. SRO D/D/B reg. 4 (Register of Nicholas Bubwith), fols. 107–8; *Register of Nicholas Bubwith*, 229, no. 601. See also Jonathan Bengtson, "Saint George and the Formation of English Nationalism," *Journal of Medieval and Early Modern Studies* 27 (1997): 317–40.

51. SRO D/D/B reg. 4 (Register of Nicholas Bubwith), fols. 128d–129; *Register of Nicholas Bubwith*, 273–76, no. 685.

52. SRO D/D/B reg. 6 (Register of Thomas Bekynton), fol. 86; *Register of Thomas Bekynton*, 112, no. 415.

53. SRO D/D/B reg. 4 (Register of Nicholas Bubwith), fols. 85–86; *Register of Nicholas*

Bubwith, 179–81, no. 498; SRO D/D/B reg. 5 (Register of John Stafford), fol. 177; *Register of John Stafford*, 262, no. 827; SRO D/D/B reg. 6 (Register of Thomas Bekynton), fol. 60; *Register of Thomas Bekynton*, 74, no. 265; SRO D/D/B reg. 9 (Register of Oliver King), fols. 97b–98a; *Registers of Oliver King, Bishop of Bath and Wells, 1496–1503, and Hadrian de Castello, Bishop of Bath and Wells, 1503–1518*, ed. H. C. Maxwell-Lyte, SRS 54 (1939), 80, no. 486; SRO D/D/B reg. 12 (Register of John Clerk), fols. 44–45v; *Registers of Thomas Wolsey, Bishop of Bath and Wells, 1518–1523, John Clerk, Bishop of Bath and Wells, 1523–1541, William Knyght, Bishop of Bath and Wells 1544–1547, Gilbert Bourne, Bishop of Bath and Wells, 1554–1559*, ed. H. C. Maxwell-Lyte, SRS 55 (1940), 65, no. 417; SRO D/D/B reg. 13 (Register of William Knyght), fols. 17b–18a, 22a; *Register of William Knyght*, 103–4, no. 561; 107, no. 583. See also A. K. McHardy, "Liturgy and Propaganda in the Diocese of Lincoln, During the Hundred Years' War," in *Studies in Church History* 18 (1982): 215–28.

54. SRO D/D/B reg. 5 (Register of John Stafford), fols. 159d, 172d; *Register of John Stafford*, 239, no. 753; 256, no. 800; SRO D/D/B reg. 6 (Register of Thomas Bekynton), fols. 39, 111–12, 196, 264, 308; *Register of Thomas Bekynton*, 47–48, no. 155; 149, no. 528; 251–52, no. 934; 359, no. 1378; 421–22, no. 1613; SRO D/D/B reg. 7 (Register of Robert Stillington), fol. 100b; *Register of Robert Stillington*, 109, no. 639; SRO D/D/B reg. 9 (Register of Oliver King), fol. 57a; *Register of Oliver King*, 54, no. 318; SRO D/D/B reg. 12 (Register of John Clerk), fol. 15v; *Register of John Clerk*, 38, no. 214.

55. SRO D/D/B reg. 5 (Register of John Stafford), fol. 172d; *Register of John Stafford*, 256, no. 800.

56. Pfaff, *New Liturgical Feasts*, 4–6.

57. Ibid., 4–5.

58. Ibid., 5; 11–12.

59. Ibid., 6.

60. Ibid., 8.

61. "Statutes of Wells, 1252 x 1258," in *Councils and Synods II*, ed. F. M. Powicke and C. R. Cheney (Oxford: Oxford University Press, 1964), 1: 599, no. 15; See also Duffy, *Stripping of the Altars*, 133.

62. For a more complete discussion of the various liturgical books see Wordsworth and Littlehales, *Old Service-Books*, 69–240.

63. Ibid., 78.

64. Ibid., 170–85.

65. Ibid., 39.

66. "Statutes of Wells," 599, no. 15.

67. *Somerset Medieval Wills*, 1: 104–5,108, 360; 2: 35–36, 43, 174–75.

68. *Somerset Medieval Wills*, 1: 360.

69. *Somerset Medieval Wills*, 1:67–68, 138–39, 301–2, 306–8, 330–32, 400; 3: 1–2.

70. *Somerset Medieval Wills*, 1: 162–63, 175–77, 213–15, 330–32; 2: 306–8, 316. Two of the rectors were also canons; I have counted them twice.

71. *Somerset Medieval Wills*, 2: 306–8.

72. Harvey, "Work and *Festa Ferianda*," 291. See also Dorothy Owen's discussion of Lincolnshire parishes in *Church and Society in Medieval Lincolnshire* (Lincoln: History of Lincolnshire Committee, Lincolnshire Local History Committee, 1971), 102–31. She relies on court records and didactic literature but organizes her discussion in the same way.

73. *Speculum Sacerdotale*, 4.

74. Ronald Hutton, *The Rise and Fall of Merry England: The Ritual Year, 1400–1700* (Oxford: Oxford University Press, 1994), 5–10.

75. *Speculum Sacerdotale*, 7.

76. SRO D/P/ba. mi. 4/1/1 #1.

77. SRO D/P/ba. mi. 4/1/1 #10; 4/1/2 #19.

78. These figures are for the years 1515–46, the extent of the pre-Reformation accounts. SRO D/P/ban 4/1/1.

79. For more on the symbolism of candles see David Postles, "Lamps, Lights, and Layfolk: 'Popular' Devotion Before the Black Death," *Journal of Medieval History* 25 (1999): 97–114.

80. SRO D/P/bw #14, 13, 17, 7, 1, 19.

81. SRO D/P/bw #13.

82. E. K. Chambers, *The Medieval Stage* (Oxford: Oxford University Press, 1903), 2: 44.

83. Expenditures to the clerk or member of the parish to cover the images and put up the Lenten veil appear very regularly in many accounts. For example, in Yeovil, in 1519, the account says: "payd ye fyrst Sonday in lent to ye clark & to ye Bedman for hangyng up the lent clothys—2d. SRO T/PH/bm 31 s/1800; BL Add. Ms 40,729A

84. SRO D/P/tin 4/1/1, fol. 2; D/P/bw #105.

85. *Dives and Pauper*, ed. Priscilla Heath Barnum, EETS 275 (1976), 1: 99.

86. SRO D/P/ban 4/1/1 fols. 3, 6, 12 et passim.

87. *Speculum Sacerdotale*, 122.

88. There are several examples of parishes using blessed bread during the mass as a substitute for the host; see Tintinhull, for example. See also J. Charles Cox, *Churchwardens' Accounts: From the Fourteenth to the Close of the Seventeenth Century* (London: Methuen, 1913), 96–98.

89. For a complete discussion see Pamela Sheingorn, *The Easter Sepulchre in England* (Kalamazoo, Mich.: Medieval Institute Publications, 1987).

90. Sheingorn, *Easter Sepulchre*, 34–5; J. Charles Cox, "Some Somerset Easter Sepulchres and Sacristies," *The Downside Review* 42 (1924): 84–88.

91. Alfred Heales, "Easter Sepulchres: Their Object, Nature, and History," *Archaeologia* 48 (1869): 301.

92. *Somerset Medieval Wills*, 2: 53. Agnes Burton alias Bascombe left "to the said spulchre service there my rede damaske mantell and my mantell lyned with silke . . . to thentente of Mary Magdalene play."

93. SRO D/P/yeo. j. 4/1/1, fols. 6 and 11.

94. The accounts mention it in 1420, 1429, and again in 1442. SRO D/P/bw #42, 15, 10.

95. SRO D/P/bw #11.

96. Sheingorn, *Easter Sepulchre*, 6.

97. Ibid., 26–32; Cox, *Churchwardens' Accounts*, 60.

98. Pamela Sheingorn in her study of English Easter sepulchers found them more frequently in the eastern and southern parts of the country. Sheingorn, *Easter Sepulchre*, 52–57.

99. SRO D/P/ba. mi. 4/1/1 #11; D/P/bw #42; "Accounts of the Proctors of the Church of Yeovil, Co. Somerset, 36 Henry VI, 1457–8," ed. John T. Nichols, *Collectanea Topographica et Genealogica* 3 (1834): 134–41.

100. "Churchwardens' Accounts, St. John's Glastonbury," ed. F. W. Weaver and C. H. Mayo, *Somerset and Dorset Notes and Queries* 4 (1895): 336. The account for 1500 apparently no longer survives.

101. SRO D/P/pilt 4/1/1, fol. 39.

102. SRO D/P/ban 4/1/1, fol. 115.

103. John Mirk, *Festial*, ed. Theodor Erbe, EETS, es 96 (1905),150.

104. Hutton, *Rise and Fall of Merry England*, 34.

105. SRO D/P/ba. mi. 4/1/16, 4/1/17, et passim.

106. Owen, *Church and Society in Medieval Lincolnshire*, 108–9; Duffy, *Stripping of the Altars*, 136.

107. Mirk, *Festial*, 173.

108. Ibid.

109. For more on the origins of this story, see Rubin, *Corpus Christi*, 116.

110. Ibid., 243–87.

111. Glynne Wickham, *The Medieval Theatre*, 3rd ed. (Cambridge: Cambridge University Press, 1987), 60–61.

112. The origin and celebration of this festival have been studied in some detail by many people. See: Rubin, *Corpus Christi*; Mervyn James, "Ritual, Drama and Social Body in the Late Medieval English Town," *Past and Present* 98 (1983): 3–29; Charles Phythian-Adams, "Ceremony and the Citizen: the Communal Year at Coventry 1450–1550," in *Crisis and Order in English Towns: 1500–1700: Essays in Urban History*, ed. Peter Clark and Paul Slack (London: Routledge and Kegan Paul, 1976), 57–85.

113. Rubin, *Corpus Christi*, 294–97.

114. The most recent and extensive coverage of the subject is Rubin's *Corpus Christi*.

115. Charles Phythian-Adams, *Desolation of a City: Coventry and the Urban Crisis of the Late Middle Ages* (Cambridge: Cambridge University Press, 1979), 178. See also "Ceremony and the Citizen," 58.

116. James, "Ritual, Drama, and the Social Body," 4.

117. Ibid., 11.

118. Rubin, *Corpus Christi*, 265–71. She continues this criticism of ideas of community in "Small Groups: Identity and Solidarity in the Late Middle Ages," in *Enterprise and Individuals in Fifteenth Century England*, ed. Jennifer Kermode (Gloucester: Sutton, 1991), 132–50.

119. Quoted in Phythian-Adams, "Ceremony and the Citizen," 58.

120. Beckwith, *Christ's Body*, 35.

121. The Bristol parishes in the diocese contributed to that city's procession. David Harris Sacks, *The Widening Gate* (Berekeley: University of California Press, 1991), 132–42; BRO P/ST.T/ChW/1 fol. 8. See also Margery Kempe's description in *The Book of Margery Kempe*, ed. S. B. Meech and Hope Emily Allen, EETS 212 (1940), 107.

122. SRO D/P/ba. mi. 4/1/1 #7.

123. SRO D/P/ba. mi. 4/1/3 #30, 31, 35, 36. The parish produced a play in 1482, although the occasion was not specified. Among the expenses for it were bread, ale, and cheese, and the scenery and props included stained skins and a chest. SRO D/P/ba. mi. 4/1/3 #39.

124. *The Municipal Records of Bath, 1184–1604*, ed. Austin J. King and B. H. Watts (London: Elliot Stock, no date), 46.

125. *Somerset Medieval Wills*, 2: 147.

126. SRO D/P/gla. j. 4/1/6b; 4/1/7.

127. "Churchwardens' Accounts for St. John's Glastonbury, 1500," 336.

128. "Churchwardens' Accounts for Yeovil, 1457–8."

129. SRO D/P/ yeo. j. 4/1/6, fol. 9.

130. Lawrence Clopper's work on Chester's medieval drama shows that the Reformation did not automatically lead to its end. "Lay and Clerical Impact on Civic and Religious

Drama and Ceremony," in *Contexts for Early English Drama*, ed. Marianne G. Briscoe and John C. Coldwey (Bloomington: Indiana University Press, 1989), 103–36.

131. SRO D/P/bw #42.

132. SRO D/P/bw #15, 16, 13 et passim.

133. SRO D/P/bw # 8.

134. SRO D/P/bw #1658, 1659, 1660, 35 et passim.

135. The records do not explain what is meant by a shepherds' pageant. *Bridgwater Borough Archives*, ed. Bruce Dilkes, SRS 60 (1948), 4: 55, no. 757.

136. SRO D/P/bw #33.

137. *Bridgwater Borough Archives*, 4: 92, no. 793.

138. Ibid., 98–99, nos. 797, 830.

139. T. Bruce Dilks, "Bridgwater and the Insurrection of 1381," *Proceedings of the Somersetshire Archaeological and Natural History Society* 73 (1927): 57–69.

140. Peter Brown, *Cult of the Saints: Its Rise and Function in Latin Christianity* (Chicago: University of Chicago Press, 1981); Benedicta Ward, *Miracles and the Medieval Mind: Theory, Record, and Event* (Philadelphia: University of Pennsylvania Press, 1982).

141. Duffy, *Stripping of the Altars*, 169–83.

142. Ibid., 185.

143. Mirk, *Festial*, 242–43.

144. *The Golden Legend: Readings of the Saints*, ed. William Granger Ryan (Princeton, N.J.: Princeton University Press, 1993), 1: 370.

145. Eamon Duffy, "Holy Maydens, Holy Wyfes: The Cult of Women Saints in Fifteenth- and Sixteenth-Century England," *Studies in Church History* 27 (1990): 194–96.

146. Letter 26 "Dr. Layton to Cromwell," in *Letters Relating to the Suppression of Monasteries*, ed. T. Wright, Camden Society 26 (1843), 58–59.

147. Duffy, *Stripping of the Altars*, 167; Judy Ann Ford, "Art and Identity in the Parish Communities of Late Medieval Kent," *Studies in Church History* 28 (1992): 225–37.

148. SRO D/P/bw # 105.

149. 26 percent of women who left material goods to their parish, compared with none of men, left something for an image of a saint. See Katherine L. French, " 'I Leave My Best Gown as a Vestment': Women's Spiritual Interests in the Late Medieval English Parish," *Magistra* 4 (1998): 57–77.

150. *Ancient Deeds Belonging to the Corporation of Bath*, ed. C.W. Shickle (Bath: Bath Record Society, 1921), 90.

151. *Somerset Medieval Wills*, 2: 2

152. SRO D/P/yat 4/1/1 fols. 77, 88, 91, et passim.

153. SRO D/P/yat 4/1/1 fol. 147.

154. Mirk, *Festial*, 201.

155. *Dives and Pauper*, 1: 81–91.

156. Ibid., 83–85; see also C. David Benson, "*Piers Plowman* and Parish Wall Paintings," *Yearbook of Langland Studies* 11 (1998): 10.

157. *Dives and Pauper*, 1: 91–93. The saints are Mary, Peter, Paul, John the Evangelist, John the Baptist, Katherine, and Margaret.

158. Karen Winstead, *The Virgin Martyrs: Legends of Sainthood in Late Medieval England* (Ithaca, N.Y.: Cornell University Press, 1997), 88.

159. Similarity in execution may not be only because of artistic convention, but also because of pattern books or outright imitation of another artist's work. M. D. Anderson, *History and Imagery in British Churches* (London: J. Murray, 1971),164–72. She talks about

misericords and windows specifically, but I think the process for choosing the depiction of images on walls might be similar.

160. Similarly, Christopher Woodforde, in his study of medieval stained glass, has found only a few examples of windows or fragments of window dedicated to local saints. The only examples in parish churches would appear to be windows of St. Dunstan in St. John's, Glastonbury and St. Joseph of Arimathea at Langport. Christopher Woodforde, *Stained Glass in Somerset, 1250–1830* (London: Oxford University Press, 1946), 180.

161. *Somerset Medieval Wills*, 2: 28–29.

162. Of the twenty parishes with churchwardens' accounts, six are dedicated to St. Mary, three to St. John, and two to St. Andrew.

163. SRO DD/WO 49/1, fol. 63.

164. E. Clive Rouse, *Medieval Wall Paintings* (Buckinghamshire: Shire Publications, 1991), 30.

165. Caxton printed the *Golden Legend* in 1483, and its organization follows the lines of a service book legenda rather than of de Voragine's original work. Wordsworth and Littlehales, *Old Service Books*, 137.

166. *Somerset Medieval Wills*, 1: 294. For another reference to the *Golden Legend* in Somerset wills see *Somerset Medieval Wills*, 3: 2.

167. Winstead, *Virgin Martyrs*, 71; see also Manfred Görlach, *The Textural Tradition of the "South English Legendary"* (Leeds: University of Leeds Press, 1974).

168. Winstead, *Virgin Martyrs*, 72–73.

169. Thomas Heffernan, *Sacred Biography: Saints and Their Biographers in the Middle Ages* (New York: Oxford University Press, 1988), 261–65; Winstead disagrees, see *Virgin Martyrs*, 98–111; for more on audience see p. 72, n. 21.

170. *Somerset Medieval Wills*, 1: 42.

171. Paul Strohm, "*Passioun, Lyf, Miracle, Legende*: Some Generic Terms in Middle English Hagiographical Narrative," *Chaucer Review* 10, 1 and 2 (1975–6): 62–75, 154–71.

172. SRO D/P/gla. j. 4/1/5.

173. Winstead, *Virgin Martyrs*.

174. Ibid., 110.

175. Ibid., 74–78; the author of *Dives and Pauper* makes the same point when describing St. Katherine. The author writes, "St. Katherine is painted with a wheel in one hand in token of the horrible wheels which the tyrant Maxentius ordained to tear her limb from limb. But the angel destroyed him and so many of the heathen people, and so they did her no harm. She has a sword in the other hand in token that her head was cut off with a sword for Christ's sake." *Dives and Pauper*, 1: 92–93, see also Winstead, 88.

176. Winstead, *Virgin Martyrs*, 100–1.

177. Ibid., 110.

178. Mirk, *Festial*, 6.

179. Winstead, *Virgin Martyrs*, 112; see also the *Festial*, 200–1.

180. Winstead, *Virgin Martyrs*, 112; see also the *Speculum Sacerdotale*, 243–44.

181. Winstead, *Virgin Martyrs*, 113, see also note 4. This new presentation coincided with other cultural initiatives to develop women's demeanor. Felicity Riddy, " 'Mother Knows Best': Reading Social Change in a Courtesy Text," *Speculum* 71 (1996): 66–86.

182. Winstead, *Virgin Martyrs*, 132.

183. Ibid., 121.

184. Ibid., 70; Rouse, *Medieval Wall Paintings*, 54.

185. These paintings were not frescos, painting done on wet plaster. English wall paint-

ings were typically another technique called secco, when the artist applied pigment to dry plaster. The paint did not become part of the plaster as in frescos. Rouse, *Medieval Wall Paintings*, 25.

186. E.W. Tristram, *English Wall Paintings in the Fourteenth Century* (London: Routledge and Kegan Paul, 1955), 4; Rouse, *Medieval Wall Paintings*, 30.

187. Benson, *"Piers Plowman* and Parish Wall Paintings," 5, note 11; see also Rouse, *Medieval Wall Paintings*, 35 for a slightly different list of categories. Scholars who work on glass have a similar scheme. See Woodforde, *Stained Glass in Somerset*, 165–66.

188. Woodforde, *Stained Glass in Somerset*, 166–94.

189. The doom fragment is in Axebridge. C. E. Keyser, *A List of the Buildings in Great Britain and Ireland Having Mural and Other Painted Decorations*, 3rd ed. (London: H.M.S.O., 1883), 11.

190. Woodforde, *Stained Glass in Somerset*, 178–79.

191. Compare, for example, the art discussed by Pamela Tudor-Craig in "Painting in Medieval England: the Wall-to-Wall Message" in *Age of Chivalry: Art and Society in Late Medieval England*, ed. Nigel Saul (London: Brockhampton Press, 1995), 106–19, with the rood screen paintings discussed by Eamon Duffy in "Holy Maydens, Holy Wyfes: the Cult of Women Saints in Fifteenth and Sixteenth Century England," 175–96.

192. SRO D/P/yat 4/1/1 fol. 80.

193. SRO D/P/yat 4/1/1, fols. 80–2, 86, 88.

194. WCR *WCB* I, fol. 89. This carving suffered much damage in the Reformation.

195. *Somerset Medieval Wills*, 1: 368–70.

196. Postles, "Lamps, Lights, and Layfolk," 97–114.

197. William A. Christian, *Local Religion in Sixteenth Century Spain* (Princeton, N.J.: Princeton University Press, 1981), 70–125; Keith P. Luria, *Territories of Grace: Cultural Changes in the Seventeenth-Century Diocese of Grenoble* (Berkeley: University of California, 1991), 106–36; Samuel Kline Cohn, *Death and Property in Siena, 1205–1800* (Baltimore: Johns Hopkins University Press, 1988), 171–75; Barbara A. Hanawalt, "Keepers of the Lights: Late Medieval English Parish Gilds," *Journal of Medieval and Renaissance Studies* 14 (1984): 21–37; Gervase Rosser, "Parochial Conformity and Voluntary Religion in Late-Medieval England," *Transactions of the Royal Historical Society* 6th ser. 1 (1991): 173–89.

198. SRO D/D/B reg. 9 (Register of Oliver King), fol. 97b; *Register of Oliver King*, 80, no. 485.

199. For more on this cult see Charles W. Jones, *St. Nicholas of Myra, Bari, and Manhattan* (Chicago: University of Chicago Press, 1978).

200. SRO D/P/gla. j. 4/1/1.

201. SRO D/P/ban 4/1/1, fol. 164; Woodforde, *Stained Glass in Somerset*, 38.

202. For more on this saint see Muriel C. McClendon, "A Moveable Feast: St. George's Day Celebrations and Religious Change in Early Modern England," *Journal of British Studies* 38 (1999): 1–27.

203. Bengston, "Saint George," 320.

204. Ibid., 320–28.

205. Chambers, *The Mediaeval Stage*, 1: 211–27.

206. SRO D/P/gla. j. 4/1/5. It is also interesting that St. Nicholas was an important saint in this parish as early as 1418 as well, long before 1503 and official recognition of his cult.

207. SRO D/P/gla. j. 4/1/7; "Churchwardens' Accounts for St. John's Glastonbury, 1500," 334.

208. SRO D/P/bw #105, 17.

209. *The Survey and Rental of the Chantries*, ed. Emmanuel Green, SRS 2 (1888), 70.

210. *Somerset Medieval Wills*, 1: 259–60.

211. *Somerset Medieval Wills*, 2: 197–98.

212. SRO DD/WO 49/1, fol. 61.

213. Duffy shows how the promotion of St. Sidwell's cult in Morebath, Devon, was the work of the vicar, Christopher Trychay. *Stripping of the Altars*, 168.

214. SRO D/P/stogs 4/1/1, fol. 26v.

215. "Church-wardens' Accounts of Croscombe," in *The Church-wardens Accounts for Croscombe etc.*, ed. Edmund Hobhouse, SRS 4 (1890), 30.

216. Ibid., 34, 36 et passim.

217. Bengston writes, "Edward IV aggressively used the image of the saint to aid in establishing the legitimacy of the Yorkist government. George represented a link between national identity and royal power and prestige, and it is said that Edward often prayed to the saint in order to reinforce his image of being devoted to the same ideals as his predecessors" (327).

Conclusion

1. Eamon Duffy, *The Stripping of the Altars: Traditional Religion in England, 1400–1580* (New Haven, Conn.: Yale University Press, 1992), 394–95.

2. Ibid., 407.

3. SRO D/P/ban 4/1/1, fol. 126.

4. SRO D/P/bw #1447, fol. 6.

BIBLIOGRAPHY

MANUSCRIPT SOURCES

BRISTOL, CITY RECORD OFFICE

Churchwardens' Accounts:
  St. Thomas': P/ST.T/ChW/1

DORCHESTER, DORSET RECORD OFFICE

Churchwardens' Accounts:
  Wimborne Minster: PE/WM/CW

IPSWITCH, SUFFOLK RECORD OFFICE

Churchwardens' Accounts:
  Walbersick: FC 185/E1/1

LONDON, BRITISH LIBRARY

Churchwardens' Accounts:
  Yeovil: Add. Ms. 40,729A

LONDON, GUILDHALL LIBRARY

Churchwardens' Accounts:
St. Mary at Hill: 1239/1 parts 1 and 2
St. Botolph Aldersgate: 1454/1–12

LONDON, PUBLIC RECORD OFFICE

Chantry Certificates: E117
Early Chancery Documents: C1
Early Proceedings for the Court of Star Chamber: STAC 1 and STAC 2
Lay Subsidies: E179

TAUNTON, SOMERSET RECORD OFFICE

Bishops' Registers:
Register of John Drokensford: D/D/B reg. 1
Register of Ralph of Shrewsbury: D/D/B reg. 2
Register of Henry Bowet: D/D/B reg. 3
Register of Nicholas Bubwith: D/D/B reg. 4
Register of John Stafford: D/D/B reg. 5
Register of Thomas Bekyngton: D/D/B reg. 6
Register of Robert Stillington:D/D/B reg. 7
Register of Richard Fox: D/D/B reg. 8
Register of Oliver King: D/D/B reg. 9
Register of Hadrian de Castello: D/D/B reg. 10
Register of Thomas Wolsey: D/D/B reg. 11
Register of John Clerk: D/D/B reg. 12
Register of William Knight: D/D/B reg. 13
Churchwardens' Accounts:
Bath: D/P/ba. mi. 4/1/1–6
Banwell: D/P/ban 4/1/1
Bridgwater: D/P/bw
Chedzoy: T/PH/vch 72/2 G/311
Glastonbury: D/P/gla.j. 4/1/1–11
Halse: D/P/hal 4/1/4
Ilminister: D/P/ilm 4/1/1
Lydeard St. Lawrence: D/P/l. st l. 4/1/1
Nettlecombe: DD/WO 49/1
North Curry: DD/CC 131908/5; 131903/3
Pilton: D/P/pilt 4/1/1–2
Stogursey: D/P/stogs 4/1/1
Tintinhull: D/P/tin 4/1/1–2
Trull: DD/CT 77
Yatton: D/P/yat 4/1/1–3
Yeovil: D/P/yeo. j. 4/1/6; T/PH/bm 31 s/1800

Witness Depositions:
    Keynsham and Wells: D/D/Cd 17
    Yeovil: D/D/Cd 35

WELLS, CITY RECORD OFFICE

Wells Convocations Book, 2 vols.

PRINTED PRIMARY SOURCES

"Accounts of the Proctors of the Church of Yeovil, Co. Somerset, 36 Henry VI, 1457–
    8." Edited by John G. Nichols. *Collectanea Topographica et Genealogica* 3 (1834): 134–41.
Accounts of the Wardens of the Parish of Morebath, Devon: 1520–1573. Edited by Erskine
    Binney. Devon Notes and Queries 2, 3. 1904.
Ancient Deeds Belonging to the Corporation of Bath. Edited by C. W. Shickle. Bath Record
    Society 1. 1921.
Bridgwater Borough Archives: 1200–1485. 5 vols. Vols. 1–4 edited by Thomas Bruce Dilks.
    SRS 48, 53, 58, 60. 1933–48. Vol. 5 edited by R. W. Dunning and T. D. Tremlett. SRS
    70. 1971.
Calendar of the Mannuscripts of the Dean and Chapter of Wells. 2 vols. Historical Manuscripts
    Commission, London: H.M.S.O., 1907, 1914.
Calendar of Inquisitions Post Mortem. 18 vols. London: H.M.S.O., 1904–87.
Calendar of Papal Letters. 18 vols. London: H.M.S.O., 1902–89.
Calendar of the Register of John de Drokensford: Bishop of Bath and Wells, 1309–1329. Edited by
    Edmund Hobhouse. SRS 1. 1887.
Churchwardens' Accounts of Ashburton, 1479–1580. Edited by Alison Hanham. Devon and
    Cornwall Record Society New Series 15. 1970.
"Churchwardens' Accounts of the Church and Parish of St. Michael Without the
    North Gate, Bath: 1349–1575." Edited by C. B. Pearson. *Proceedings of the Somerset
    Archaeological and Natural History Society* 23–26 (1877–80).
*Church-wardens' Accounts of Croscombe, Pilton, Yatton, Tintinhull, Morebath and St. Michael's
    Bath: Ranging from 1349–1560*. Edited by Edmund Hobhouse. SRS 4. 1890.
"Churchwardens' Account Book of Rotherfield." Edited by Canon Goodwyn. *Sussex
    Archaeological Collections* 41 (1898): 25–48.
Churchwardens' Accounts of St. Edmund and St. Thomas, Sarum. Edited by Henry J. F.
    Swayne. Wilts Record Society 1. 1896.
"Churchwardens' Accounts for St. John's Glastonbury." Edited by F. W. Weaver and
    C. H. Mayo. *Somerset and Dorset Notes and Queries* 4 (1895): 89–96, 137–44, 185–92,
    235–40, 281–88, 329–36, 379–84.
Churchwardens' Accounts of St. Mary the Great, Cambridge from 1504–1635. Edited by J. E.
    Foster. Cambridge Antiquarian Society 35. 1905.
The Churchwardens' Accounts of St. Michael's Church, Chagford: 1480–1600. Edited by Francis
    Mardon Osborne. Chagford, Devon: Privately Printed, 1979.
Churchwardens' Accounts of St. Michael's Church, Oxford. Edited by H. E. Salter. Ox-
    fordshire Archaeological Society 78. 1933.
Collectanea III. Edited by T. F. Palmer. SRS 57. 1942.

The Courts of the Archdeaconry of Buckingham: 1483–1523. Edited by E. M. Elvey. Buckingham Record Society 19. 1975.

Dives and Pauper. 2 vols. Edited by Priscilla Heath Barnum. EETS 275, 280. 1976, 1980.

Eccleston, Thomas. *On the Coming of the Friars Minor to England*. Translated by Emma Gurney-Salter. London: E.P. Dutton, 1926.

"Episcopal Statutes of Bishop Robert Grosseteste for the Diocese of Lincoln." Translated by John Shiners. In *Pastors and the Care of Souls in Medieval England*, edited by John Shinners and William J. Dohar. Notre Dame, Ind.: University of Notre Dame, Press, 1998.

The German Peasants' War: A History in Documents. Edited by Tom Scott and Bob Scribner. Atlantic Highlands, N.J. and London: Humanities Press International, 1991.

The Golden Legend: Readings of the Saints. 2 vols. Edited by William Granger Ryan. Princeton, N.J.: Princeton University Press, 1993.

Kentish Visitations of Archbishop William Warham and His Deputies, 1511–1512. Edited by Kathleen L. Wood-Legh. Kent Records 24. 1984.

Kempe, Margery. *The Book of Margery Kempe*. Edited by S. B. Meech and Hope Emily Allen, EETS 212. 1940.

Lambeth Churchwardens' Accounts, 1504–1645, part 1. Edited by Charles Drew. Surrey Record Society 40. 1940.

Lay Folk's Catechism. Edited by T. F. Simmons and H. E. Nolloth. EETS 118. 1901.

The Lay Folk's Mass Book. Edited by T. F. Simmons. EETS 71. 1879.

Leland, John. *The Itinerary*. 5 vols. Edited by Lucy Toulmin Smith. Carbondale: Southern Illinois University Press, 1964.

Letters Relating to the Suppression of Monasteries. Edited by T. Wright. Camden Society Original Series 26. 1843.

"Lydeard St. Lawrence Churchwardens' Accounts, 1524–1559." Edited by E. H. Bates. *Somerset and Dorset Notes and Queries* 7 (1901): 212–19.

Medieval Wills from Wells. Edited by Dorothy O. Shilton and Richard Holworthy. SRS 40. 1925.

Middle English Sermons. Edited by Woodburn Ross. EETS 209. 1940.

Mirk, John. *Instructions for Parish Priests*. Edited by Edward Peacock. EETS 31a. 1902.

——. *Festial*. Edited by Theodor Erbe, EETS, es 96. 1905.

The Municipal Records of Bath: 1184–1604. Edited by Austin J. King and B. H. Watts. London: Elliot Stock, no date.

The Paston Letters. Edited by James Gairdner. Reprint. Gloucester: Sutton, 1986.

Proceedings in the Court of Star Chamber in the Reigns of Henry VII and Henry VIII. Edited by Gladys Bradford. SRS 27. 1911.

Records of Early English Drama: Cambridge. 2 vols. Edited by Alan H. Nelson. Toronto: University of Toronto Press, 1989.

Records of Early English Drama: Somerset, Including Bath. 2 vols. Edited by James Stokes with Robert J. Alexander. Toronto: University of Toronto Press, 1997.

Register of John Stafford, Bishop of Bath and Wells, 1425–1443. Edited by Thomas Scott Holmes. SRS 31, 32. 1915, 1916.

Register of Nicholas Bubwith, Bishop of Bath and Wells, 1407–1424. Edited by Thomas Scott Holmes. SRS 29, 30. 1914.

Registers of Oliver King, Bishop of Bath and Wells, 1496–1503, and Hadrian de Castello, Bishop of Bath and Wells, 1503–1518. Edited by H. C. Maxwell-Lyte. SRS 54. 1939.

Register of Ralph of Shrewsbury: Bishop of Bath and Wells, 1329–1363. 2 parts. Edited by Thomas Scott Holmes. SRS 9, 10. 1896.

Registers of Robert Stillington and Richard Fox: Bishops of Bath and Wells, 1466–1494. Edited by H. C. Maxwell-Lyte. SRS 52. 1937.

Register of Thomas Bekynton: Bishop of Bath and Wells, 1443–1465. 2 parts. Edited by M. C. B. Dawes. SRS 49, 50. 1934.

Registers of Thomas Wolsey, Bishop of Bath and Wells, 1518–1523, John Clerk, Bishop of Bath and Wells, 1523–1541, William Knyght, Bishop of Bath and Wells, 1541–1547, and Gilbert Bourne, Bishop of Bath and Wells, 1554–1559. Edited by H. C. Maxwell-Lyte. SRS 55. 1940.

Registers of Walter Giffard, Bishop of Bath and Wells, 1265, and Henry Bowett, Bishop of Bath and Wells, 1401–1407. Edited by Thomas Scott Holmes. SRS 13. 1899.

"Regulations of the Vestry of St. Stephen, 1524." Edited by F. F. Fox. *Proceedings of the Clifton Antiquarian Club* 1 (1884–88): 198–206.

"Reports and Expenses in the Building of Bodmin Church: 1469–1472." Edited by John James Wilkinson. In *Camden Miscellany VII*. Camden Society 14. 1874, iii–49.

The Rymes of Robyn Hood: An Introduction to the English Outlaw. Edited by R. B. Dobson and J. Taylor. 1976. Reprint Gloucester: Sutton, 1989.

Select Cases Before the King's Council in the Star Chamber. Edited by Isaac Saunders Leadam. Selden Society 16. 1903.

Select Cases in Chancery, 1364–1471. Edited by Willaim Paley Baildon. Selden Society 10. 1869.

Select Cases in the Council of Henry VII. Edited by C. G. Bayne and William H. Dunham. Selden Society 75. 1958.

Select Cases in the Court of Requests, A.D. 1497–1569. Edited by Isaac Saunders Leadam. Selden Society 12. 1898.

Somerset Medieval Wills: 1383–1500. 3 vols. Edited by F. W. Weaver. SRS 16, 19, 21. 1901–5.

Speculum Sacerdotale. Edited by Edward Weatherly, EETS 200. 1936.

"Statutes of Exeter II." *Councils and Synods*, vol. 2, part 2. Edited by F. M. Powicke and C. R. Cheney, 982–1059. Oxford: Oxford University Press, 1964.

"Statutes for Wells: 1252 x 1258." *Councils and Synods*, Vol. 2, part 1. Edited by F. M. Powicke and C. R. Cheney, 586–626. Oxford: Oxford University Press, 1964.

The Survey and Rental of the Chantries, Colleges and Free Chapels, Guilds, Fraternities, Lamps, Lights, and Obits in the County of Somerset, 1548. Edited by Emmanuel Green. SRS 2. 1888.

"Visitation Returns of Hereford in 1397." Edited by Arthur T. Bannister. *English Historical Review* 44 (1929): 92–101; 45 (1930): 444–63.

Visitations in the Diocese of Lincoln: 1517–1531. Edited by A. Hamilton Thompson. Lincoln Record Society 33, 35. 1940–1.

"Wells Convocation Book." *First Report of the Royal Commission on Historical Manuscripts*. London: H.M.S.O., 1874.

Secondary Sources

Adam, Paul. *La vie paroissiale en France au XIVe siècle*. Historie et Sociologie de l'Église 3. Paris: Sirey, 1964.

Addleshaw, G. W. O. *The Development of the Parochial System: From Charlegmagne to Urban II*. St. Anthony's Hall Publications 6. York: Borthwick Institute, 1954.

Aers, David. "Altars of Power: Reflections on Eamon Duffy's *The Stripping of the Altars*." *Literature and History* 3rd ser. 3 (1994): 90–105.

Anderson, M. D. *History and Imagery in British Churches*. London: J. Murray, 1971.

Archer, Ian. *The Pursuit of Stability: Social Relations in Elizabethan London*. Cambridge: Cambridge University Press, 1991.

Ashley, Kathleen and Pamela Sheingorn. "Introduction." In *Interpreting Cultural Symbols: St. Anne in Late Medieval Society*, edited by Kathleen Ashley and Pamela Sheingorn, 1–68. Athens: University of Georgia Press, 1990.

Aston, Margaret. *Lollards and Reformers: Images and Literacy in Late Medieval Religion*. London: Hambledon Press, 1984.

——. "Iconoclasm at Rickmansworth, 1522: Troubles of Churchwardens." *Journal of Ecclesiastical History* 40 (1989): 524–52.

——. "Segregation in Church." *Studies in Church History* 27 (1990): 237–94.

——. "Bishops and Heresy: The Defense of the Faith." In *Faith and Fire: Popular and Unpopular Religion, 1350–1600*, edited by Margaret Aston, 73–93. London: Hambledon Press, 1993.

Aston, Michael. "Land Use and Field Systems." In *Aspects of Mediaeval Landscape of Somerset and Contributions to the Landscape History of the Country*, edited by Michael Aston, 83–99. Taunton: Somerset County Council, 1988.

Aston, Michael and Roger Leech. *Historic Towns in Somerset*. Taunton: Somerset County Council, 1977.

Ault, Warren O. "Manor Court and Parish Church in Fifteenth-Century England: A Study of Village By-Laws." *Speculum* 42 (1967): 53–67.

——. "The Village Church and the Village Community in Medieval England." *Speculum* 45 (1970): 197–215.

Avery, Margaret. "A History of Equitable Jurisdiction of Chancery Before 1460." *Bulletin of the Institute of Historical Research* 42 (1969): 129–44.

——. "An Evaluation of the Effectiveness of the Court of Chancery Under the Lancastrian Kings." *Law Quarterly Review* 86 (1970): 84–95.

Bainbridge, Virginia. *Gilds in the Medieval Countryside: Social and Religious Change in Cambridgeshire, c. 1350–1558*. Woodbridge: Boydell Press, 1996.

Baker, James N. "The Presence of the Name: Reading Scripture in an Indonesian Village." In *The Ethnography of Reading*, edited by James Boyarin, 98–138. Berkeley: University of California Press, 1993.

Baker, J. H. *An Introduction to English Legal History*. 3rd ed. London: Butterworths, 1990.

Bäuml, Franz H. "Varieties and Consequences of Medieval Literacy." *Speculum* 55 (1980): 237–65.

Barnes, T. G. "County Politics and a Puritan Cause Célèbre: Somerset Church Ales, 1633." *Transactions of the Royal Historical Society* 5th ser. (1959): 103–22.

Beckwith, Sarah. *Christ's Body: Identity, Culture, and Society in Late Medieval Writings*. London: Routledge, 1993.

Bedell, John. "Memory and Proof of Age in England." *Past and Present* 162 (1999): 3–27.

Bell, Catherine M. *Ritual Theory, Ritual Practice*. New York: Oxford University Press, 1992.

Bengtson, Jonathan. "Saint George and the Formation of English Nationalism." *Journal of Medieval and Early Modern Studies* 27 (1997): 317–40.

Bennett, H. S. *Life on the English Manor: A Study of Peasant Conditions, 1150–1400*. Cambridge: Cambridge University Press, 1965.

Bennett, Judith. "The Village Ale-Wife: Women and Brewing in Fourteenth-Century England." In *Women and Work in Preindustrial Europe*, edited by Barbara A. Hanawalt, 20–36. Bloomington: Indiana University Press, 1986.

———. "Conviviality and Charity in Medieval and Early Modern England." *Past and Present* 134 (1992): 19–41.

Benson, David. "*Piers Plowman* and Parish Wall Paintings." *Yearbook of Langland Studies* 11 (1998): 1–38.

Bettey, J. H. *Church and Community*. Bradford-on-Avon: Moonraker Press, 1979.

———. *Church and Parish: An Introduction for Local Historians*. London: Batsford, 1987.

———. *Suppression of the Monasteries in the West Country*. Gloucester: Sutton, 1989.

———. "From Norman Conquest to Reformation." In *Aspects of the Mediaeval Landscape of Somerset*, edited by Michael Aston, 54–58. Bridgwater: Somerset County Council, 1988.

Bindoff, S. T. *Tudor England*. Harmondsworth: Penguin, 1950.

Blair, John, ed. *Minsters and Parish Churches: The Local Church in Transition, 950–1200*. Oxford University Committee on Archaeology 17. Oxford: Alden Press, 1988.

Blair, John and Richard Sharp, eds. *Pastoral Care Before the Parish*. Leicester: Leicester University Press, 1992.

Blair, Lawrence. *A List of Churchwardens' Accounts*. Ann Arbor, Mich.: Edwards Brothers. 1939.

———. *English Church Ales*. Ann Arbor, Mich.: Edwards Brothers. 1940.

Blickle, Peter. *The Communal Reformation: The Quest for Salvation in Sixteenth-Century Germany*. Translated by Thomas Dunlap. Atlantic Highlands, N.J. and London: Humanities Press International, 1992.

Bolton, James L. *The Medieval English Economy, 1150–1500*. London: J. M. Dent, 1980.

Bond, Francis. *Screens and Galleries in the English Church*. London: Henry Froude, 1908.

Bossy, John. "The Counter-Reformation and the People of Catholic Europe." *Past and Present* 47 (1970): 51–70.

———. "Blood and Baptism: Kinship, Community and Christianity in Western Europe from the Fourteenth to the Seventeenth Centuries." *Studies in Church History* 10 (1973): 129–43.

———. "The Mass as a Social Institution, 1200–1700." *Past and Present* 100 (1983): 27–61.

———. *Christianity in the West, 1400–1700*. Oxford: Oxford University Press, 1985.

Bowker, Margaret. *The Secular Clergy in the Diocese of Lincoln, 1495–1520*. Cambridge: Cambridge University Press, 1968.

Brentano, Robert. *Two Churches: England and Italy in the Thirteenth Century*. Los Angeles: University of California Press, 1988.

Brigden, Susan. "Religion and Social Obligation in Sixteenth-Century London." *Past and Present* 103 (1984): 67–112.

———. *London and the Reformation*. Oxford: Oxford University Press, 1989.

Brooke, Christopher N. "Religious Sentiment and Church Design in the Later Middle Ages." In *Medieval Church and Society: Collected Essays*, edited by Christopher N. Brooke, 162–82. New York: New York University Press, 1972.

Brown, Andrew. *Popular Piety in Late Medieval England: The Diocese of Salisbury, 1250–1550*. Oxford: Oxford University Press, 1995.

Brown, Peter. *Cult of the Saints: Its Rise and Function in Latin Christianity*. Chicago: University of Chicago Press, 1981.

Bryant, R.G. *Dunster Village: Church and Castle*, 3rd ed. Dunster, Somerset: privately printed, no date.

Burgess, Clive. "'A Fond Thing Vainly Invented': An Essay on Purgatory and Pious Motive in Late Medieval England." In *Parish, Church, and People: Local Studies in Lay Religion, 1350–1750*, edited by S. J. Wright, 56–84. London: Hutchinson, 1988.

———. "Late Medieval Wills and Pious Conventions: Testamentary Evidence Reconsidered." In *Profit, Piety and the Professions*, edited by Michael Hicks, 14–33. Gloucester: Sutton, 1990.

———. "The Benefactions of Mortality: The Lay Response in the Medieval Urban Parish." In *Studies in Clergy and Ministry in Medieval England*, edited by D. Smith, 65–87. Borthwick Studies in History. York: Borthwick Institute of Historical Research, 1991.

———. "Shaping the Parish: St. Mary at Hill, London, in the Fifteenth Century." In *The Cloister and the World: Essays in Medieval History in Honour of Barbara Harvey*, edited by John Blair and Brian Golding, 246–86. Oxford: Oxford University Press, 1996.

Burgess, Clive and Beat Kümin. "Penitential Bequests and Parish Regimes in Late Medieval England." *Journal of Ecclesiastical History* 44 (1993): 610–30.

Burke, Peter. *The Historical Anthropology of Early Modern Italy: Essays on Perception and Communication*. Cambridge: Cambridge University Press, 1987.

Campbell, Bruce M. S. "Ecology Versus Economics in Late Thirteenth- and Early Fourteenth-Century English Agriculture." In *Agriculture in the Middle Ages: Technology, Practice, and Representation*, edited by Del Sweeney, 76–108. Philadelphia: University of Pennsylvania Press, 1995.

Carlson, Eric J. "The Origins, Function, and Status of the Office of Churchwarden, with Particular Reference to the Diocese of Ely." In *The World of Rural Dissenters, 1520–1725*, edited by Margaret Spufford, 164–207. Cambridge: Cambridge University Press, 1995.

Carnwath, Julia. "The Churchwardens' Accounts of Thame, Oxfordshire, c. 1443–1524." In *Trade, Devotion and Governance: Papers in Later Medieval History*, edited by Dorothy J. Clayton, Richard G. Davies, and Peter McNiven, 177–97. Gloucester: Sutton, 1994.

Carpenter, Christine. "Religion of the Gentry of Fifteenth-Century England." In *England in the Fifteenth Century: Proceedings of the 1986 Harlaxton Symposium*, edited by D. W. Williams, 53–74. Woodbridge: Boydell Press, 1987.

Carruthers, Mary. *The Book of Memory: A Study of Memory in Medieval Culture*. Cambridge: Cambridge University Press, 1990.

Catto. J. "Religion and the English Nobility in the Later Fourteenth Century." *History and Imagination*, edited by H. Lloyd-Jones, V. Pearl, and B. Worden, 43–55. New York: Holmes and Meier, 1981.

———. "Religious Changes Under Henry V." In *Henry V: The Practice of Kingship*, edited by G. L. Harriss, 97–115. Oxford: Oxford University Press, 1985.

Chambers, E. K. *The Medieval Stage*. 2 vols. Oxford: Oxford University Press, 1903.

Cheney, C. R. *English Synodalia of the Thirteenth Century*. Oxford: Oxford University Press, 1941.

———. *From Becket to Langton: English Church Government, 1170–1213*. Manchester: Manchester University Press, 1956.

———. "Rules for the Observance of Feast-Days in Medieval England." *Bulletin of the Institute of Historical Research* 34 (1961): 117–47.

———. "William Lyndwood's *Provinciale.*" In *Medieval Texts and Studies*, edited by Christopher Cheney 158–84. Oxford: Oxford University Press, 1973.

Chibnall, Marjorie. "Monks and Pastorial Work: A Problem in Anglo-Norman History." *Journal of Ecclesiastical History* 18 (1967): 165–72.

Christian, William A. *Local Religion in Sixteenth-Century Spain.* Princeton, N.J.: Princeton University Press, 1981.

Clanchy, Michael. *From Memory to Written Record: England 1066–1307.* Cambridge: Mass.: Harvard University Press, 1979.

Clopper, Lawrence. "Lay and Clerical Impact on Civic Religious Drama and Ceremony." In *Contexts for Early English Drama*, edited by Marianne G. Briscoe and John C. Coldewey, 103–37. Bloomington: Indiana University Press, 1989.

Cohn, Samuel. *Death and Property in Siena, 1205–1880: Strategies for the Afterlife.* Baltimore: Johns Hopkins University Press, 1988.

Coldewey, John C. "Some Economic Aspects of the Late Medieval Drama." In *Contexts for Early English Drama*, edited by Marianne G. Briscoe and John C. Coldewey, 77–101. Bloomington: Indiana University Press, 1989.

Coleman, Janet. *Medieval Readers and Writers, 1350–1400.* New York: Columbia University Press, 1981.

Collinson, John. *A History and Antiquities of the County of Somerset.* 2 vols. Bath: Cruttwell, 1791.

Connor, Arthur B. *Monumental Brasses in Somerset.* Bath: Kingsmead Preprints, 1970.

Constable, Giles. "Resistance to Tithes in the Middle Ages," *Journal of Ecclesiastical History* 13 (1962): 172–85.

———. *Monastic Tithes from Their Origins to the Twelfth Century.* Cambridge, Mass.: Harvard University Press, 1964.

Cook, George H. *The English Mediaeval Parish Church.* London: Phoenix House, 1954.

Copeland, G. W. "Devonshire Church-Houses." *Transactions of the Devonshire Association* 92 (1960): 116–41.

Cornwall, Julian. "English Country Towns in the 1520s." *Economic History Review* 15 (1962): 54–69.

Coss, P. R. "Aspects of Cultural Diffusion in Medieval England: The Early Romances, Local Society and Robin Hood." *Past and Present* 108 (1985): 35–79.

Costan, Michael. *The Origins of Somerset.* Manchester: Manchester University Press, 1992.

———. "The Church in the Landscape: The Anglo-Saxon Period." In *Aspects of the Medieval Landscape of Somerset*, edited by Michael Aston, 49–53. Bridgwater: Somerset County Council, 1988.

Cowley, Patrick. *The Church House.* London: S.P.C.K., 1970.

Cox, J. Charles. *Churchwardens' Accounts: From the Fourteenth to the Close of the Seventeenth Century.* London: Methuen, 1913.

———. "Some Somerset Easter Sepulchers and Sacristies." *Downside Review* 42 (1924): 84–88.

———. *Bench-Ends in English Churches.* Oxford: Oxford University Press, 1916.

Cox, J. Charles and Charles Bradley Ford. *The Parish Churches of England.* London: Batsford, 1937.

Crane, Susan. "The Writing Lesson of 1381." In *Chaucer's England: Literature in Histor-*

ical Context, edited by Barbara Hanawalt, 201–21. Minneapolis: University of Minnesota Press, 1992.

Cressy, David. *Literacy and the Social Orders: Reading and Writing in Tudor and Stuart England*. Cambridge: Cambridge University Press, 1980.

Crosby, Ruth. "Oral Delivery in the Middle Ages." *Speculum* 11 (1936): 88–110.

Cross, P. R. "Aspects of Cultural Diffusion in Medieval English Literature: The Early Romances, Local Society, and Robin Hood." *Past and Present* 108 (1985): 35–79.

Cunliffe, Barry. *The City of Bath*. Gloucester: Sutton, 1986.

Davies, J. G. *The Secular Use of Church Buildings*. London: S.C.M. Press, 1968.

Davis, Natalie Zemon. *Society and Culture in Early Modern France*. Stanford, Calif.: Stanford University Press, 1965.

———. "From 'Popular Religion' to Religious Cultures." In *Reformation Europe: A Guide to Research*, edited by Steven Ozment, 321–41. St. Louis, Mo.: Center for Reformation Research, 1982.

DeLeeuw, Patricia Allwin. "The Changing Face of the Village Parish I: The Parish in the Early Middle Ages." In *Pathways to Mediaeval Peasants*, edited by J. A. Raftis, 311–22. Papers in Mediaeval Studies 2. Toronto: Pontifical Institute of Mediaeval Studies, 1981.

Denholm-Young, N. *Seignorial Administration in England*. Oxford: Oxford University Press, 1937.

Denton, Sydney. *The Records of Banwell Church*. Bristol: St. Stephen's Press, no date.

Detjeman, John. *Collins Guide to English Parish Churches Including the Isle of Man*. London: Collins, 1958.

Dickens, A. G. *The Lollards and Protestants in the Diocese of York*. Oxford: Oxford University Press, 1959.

———. *The English Reformation*, 2nd ed. University Park: Pennsylvania State University Press, 1989.

Dilks, T. Bruce. "The Burgesses of Bridgwater in the Thirteenth Century." *Proceedings of the Somersetshire Archaeological and Natural History Society* 63 (1917): 30–59.

———. "Bridgwater Wills, 1310–1497." *Proceedings of the Somersetshire Archaeological and Natural History Society* 66 (1920): 78–97.

———. "Bridgwater and the Insurrection of 1381." *Proceedings of the Somersetshire Archaeological and Natural History Society* 73 (1927): 57–69.

Dinn, Robert. "'Monuments Answerable to Men's Worth': Burial Patterns, Social Status, and Gender in Late Medieval Bury St. Edmunds." *Journal of Ecclesiastical History* 46 (1995): 237–55.

Dohar, William J. *The Black Death and Pastoral Leadership: The Diocese of Hereford in the Fourteenth Century*. Philadelphia: University of Pennsylvania Press, 1995.

Drew, Charles. *Early Parochial Organisation in England: The Origin of the Office of Churchwarden*. St. Anthony's Hall Publications 7. York: Borthwick Institute of Historical Research, 1954.

Du Boulay, F. R. H. "The Fifteenth Century." In *The English Church and the Papacy in the Middle Ages*, edited by C. H. Lawrence, 175–95. New York: Fordham University Press, 1965.

———. *Age of Ambition: English Society in the Late Middle Ages*. London: Thomas Nelson, 1970.

Duffy, Eamon. *Stripping of the Altars: Traditional Religion in England, 1400–1580*. New Haven, Conn.: Yale University Press, 1992.

———. "Holy Maydens, Holy Wyfes: The Cult of Women Saints in Fifteenth- and Sixteenth-Century England." *Studies in Church History* 27 (1990): 175–96.

———. "The Parish, Piety, and Patronage in Late Medieval East Anglia: The Evidence of Rood-Screens." In *The Parish in English Life, 1400–1600*, edited by Katherine L. French, Gary G. Gibbs, and Beat A. Kümin, 133–62. Manchester: Manchester University Press, 1997.

Duggan, Charles. "From the Conquest to the Death of John." In *The English Church and the Papacy in the Middle Ages*, edited by C. H. Lawrence, 63–116. New York: Fordham University Press, 1965.

Dunning, R. W. "The Wells Consistory Court in the Fifteenth Century." *Proceedings of the Somerset Archaeological Society* 2 (1961–62): 46–61.

———. "The Middle Ages." *Christianity in Somerset*, edited by R. W. Dunning, 1–25. Somerset: Somerset County Council, 1976.

———. "The Reformation." *Christianity in Somerset*, edited by R. W. Dunning, 26–49. Somerset: Somerset County Council, 1976.

Dyer, Christopher. *Standards of Living in the Later Middle Ages: Social Change in England, c. 1200–1520*. Cambridge: Cambridge University Press, 1989.

———. "The English Medieval Village Community and Its Decline." *Journal of British Studies* 33 (1994): 419–24.

Edwards, A. C. "The Medieval Churchwardens' Accounts of St. Mary's, Yatton." *Somerset and Dorset Notes and Queries* 32 (1986): 537–47.

Edwards, Kathleen. *The Secular English Cathedrals in the Middle Ages: A Constitutional Study with Special Reference to the Fourteenth Century*. Manchester: Manchester University Press, 1949.

Eisel, John C. "Developments in Bell Hanging." In *Change Ringing: The History of an English Art*, vol. 1, edited by J. Sanderson, 17–21. Cambridge: Central Council of Church Bell Ringers, 1987.

Elton, Geoffrey. *Star Chamber Stories*. London: Methuen, 1958.

Erickson, Amy Louise. *Women and Property in Early Modern England*. London: Routledge, 1993.

Farmer, David. "Prices and Wages, 1350–1500." In *The Agrarian History of England and Wales*, vol. 3, edited by Edward Miller, 431–525. Cambridge: Cambridge University Press, 1991.

Farnhill, Ken. "Religious Policy and Parish Conformity: Cratfield's Lands in the Sixteenth Century." In *The Parish in English Life: 1400–1600*, edited by Katherine L. French, Gary G. Gibbs, and Beat A. Kümin, 217–29. Manchester: Manchester University Press, 1997.

Fleming. P. W. "Charity, Faith, and the Gentry of Kent, 1422–1529." In *Property and Politics*, edited by A. J. Pollard, 36–58. Gloucester: Sutton Publishers, 1984.

Fisher, John H. "Chancery and the Emergence of Standard Written English in the Fifteenth Century." *Speculum* 52 (1975): 870–99.

Foley, John Miles. "Orality, Textuality and Interpretation." In *Vox Intexta*, edited by A. N. Doane and Carol Braun Pasternack, 34–45. Madison: University of Wisconsin Press, 1992.

Ford, Judy Ann. "The Community of the Parish in Late Medieval Kent." Unpublished Ph.D. dissertation, Fordham University, 1994.

———. "Art and Identity in the Parish Communities of Late Medieval Kent." *Studies in Church History* 28 (1992): 225–37.

Forster, Marc. R. *The Counter-Reformation in the Villages: Religion and Reform in the Bishopric of Speyer, 1560–1720.* Ithaca, N.Y.: Cornell University Press, 1992.

Fox, Adam. "Custom, Memory, and the Authority of Writing." In *The Experience of Authority in Early Modern England*, edited by Adam Fox, Paul Griffiths, and Steve Hindle, 89–116. Basingstoke and London: MacMillan Press, 1996.

French, Katherine L. "Local Identity and the Late-Medieval Parish: The Communities of Bath and Wells." Unpublished Ph. D. dissertation. University of Minnesota, 1993.

——. "Competing for Space: The Monastic-Parochial Church at Dunster." *Journal of Medieval and Early Modern History* 27 (1997): 215–44.

——. "Parochial Fund-Raising in Late Medieval Somerset." In *The Parish in English Life, 1400–1600*, edited by Katherine L. French, Gary G. Gibbs, and Beat A. Kümin, 115–32. Manchester: Manchester University Press, 1997.

——. " 'To Free Them from Binding': Women in the Late Medieval English Parish." *Journal of Interdisciplinary History* 27 (1997): 387–412.

——. " 'I Leave My Best Gown as a Vestment': Women's Spiritual Interests in the Late Medieval English Parish." *Magistra* 4 (1998): 57–77.

——. "Maidens' Lights and Wives' Stores: Women's Parish Guilds in Late Medieval England." *Sixteenth Century Journal* 29 (1998): 399–425.

Gasquet, F. A. *Parish Life in Mediaeval England.* London: Methuen, 1906.

Geertz, Clifford. *The Interpretation of Cultures.* New York: Basic Books, 1973.

Genicot, Lépold. *Rural Communities in the Medieval West.* Baltimore: Johns Hopkins University Press, 1990.

Gibbs, Gary G. "Parish Finance and the Urban Community in London: 1450–1620." Unpublished Ph.D. dissertation, University of Virginia, 1990.

——. "New Duties for the Parish Community in Tudor London." In *The Parish in English Life, 1400–1600*, edited by Katherine L. French, Gary G. Gibbs, and Beat A. Kümin, 125–47. Manchester: Manchester University Press, 1997.

Gibbs, Marion and Jane Lang. *Bishops and Reform 1215–1272, with Special References to the Lateran Council of 1215.* Oxford: Oxford University Press, 1932.

Gibson, Gail McMurray. *Theater of Devotion: East Anglian Drama and Society in the Late Middle Ages.* Chicago: University of Chicago Press, 1989.

Gilchrist, Roberta. *Gender and Material Culture: The Archaeology of Religious Women.* London: Routledge, 1994.

Goering, Joseph W. "Changing Face of the Village Parish II: The Thirteenth Century." In *Pathways to Mediaeval Peasants*, edited by J. A. Raftis, 335–38. Papers in Mediaeval Studies 2. Toronto: Pontifical Institute of Mediaeval Studies, 1981.

Goldberg, P. J. P. *Women, Work, and Life Cycle in a Medieval Economy: Women in York and Yorkshire, c. 1300–1520.* Oxford: Oxford University Press, 1992.

Goody, Jack. *Domestication of the Savage Mind.* Cambridge: Cambridge University Press, 1977.

——. *The Logic of Writing and the Organization of Society.* Cambridge: Cambridge University Press, 1986.

Görlach, Manfred. *The Textual Tradition of the South English Legendary.* Leeds: University of Leeds Press, 1974.

Graves, Pamela. "Social Space in the English Medieval Parish Church." *Economy and Society* 18 (1989): 297–322.

Green, D. H. "Orality and Reading: The State of Research in Medieval Studies." *Speculum* 65 (1990): 267–80.

Green, Emmanuel. "On the Manor of Yeovil." *Proceedings of the Somerset Archaeological and Natural History Society* 32 (1887): 1–15.

Haigh, Christopher. *Reformation and Resistance in Tudor Lancashire*. Cambridge: Cambridge University Press, 1975.

——. "Recent Historiography of the English Reformation." In *The English Reformation Revised*, edited by Christopher Haigh, 19–33. Cambridge: Cambridge University Press, 1987.

Haines, Roy Martin. *The Administration of the Diocese of Worcester in the First Half of the Fourteenth Century*. London: S.P.C.K., 1965.

Hanawalt, Barbara A. "Keepers of the Lights: Late Medieval English Parish Gilds." *Journal of Medieval and Renaissance Studies* 14 (1984): 21–37.

——."Peasant Women's Contributions to the Home Economy in Late Medieval England." In *Women and Work in Preindustrial Europe*, edited by Barbara Hanawalt, 3–19. Bloomington: Indiana University Press, 1986.

——. *The Ties That Bound: Peasant Families in Medieval England*. New York: Oxford University Press, 1986.

Hanawalt, Barbara and Ben R. McRee, "The Guilds of *Homo Prudens* in Late Medieval England." *Continuity and Change* 7 (1992): 163–79.

Hancock, F. *Dunster Church and Priory*. Taunton: Barnicott and Pearce Atheneaum Press, 1905.

Harding, Vanessa. "Burial Choice and Burial Location in Later Medieval London." In *Death and Towns: Urban Responses to the Dying and the Dead, 100–1600*, edited by Steven Bassett, 119–35. Leicester, London and New York: Leicester University Press, 1992.

Hardy, W. J. "Remarks on the History of Seat-Reservation in Churches." *Archaeologia* 53 (1892): 94–98.

Harper-Bill, Christopher. *The Pre-Reformation Church in England*. London: Longmans, 1989.

Harrod, Henry. "Some Particulars Relating to the History of the Abbey Church of Wymondham in Norfolk." *Archaeologia* 43 (1890): 263–72.

Hartridge, R. A. R. *A History of Vicarages in the Middle Ages*. Cambridge: Cambridge University Press, 1930.

Harvey, Barbara. "Work and *Festa Ferianda* in Medieval England." *Journal of Ecclesiastical History* 23 (1972): 289–308.

Heales, Alfred. "Easter Sepulchers: Their Object, Nature, and History." *Archaeologia* 48 (1869): 263–308.

Heath, Peter. *The English Parish Clergy on the Eve of the Reformation*. London: Routledge and Kegan Paul, 1969.

——. "Urban Piety in the Later Middle Ages: The Evidence of Hull Wills." In *The Church, Politics and Patronage in the Fifteenth Century*, edited by Barrie Dobson, 209–34. New York: St. Martin's Press, 1984.

——. *Church and Realm, 1272–1461: Conflict and Collaboration in an Age of Crisis*. London: Fontana Press, 1988.

——. "Between Reform and Reformation: The English Church in the Fourteenth and Fifteenth Centuries." *Journal of Ecclesiastical History* 41(1990): 647–78.

Heffernan, Thomas. *Saints and Their Biographers in the Middle Ages*. New York: Oxford University Press, 1988.

Hicks, Michael. "Four Studies in Conventional Piety." *Southern History* 13 (1991): 1–22.

Hindle, Steve. "The Shaming of Margaret Knowsley: Gossip, Gender and the Experience of Authority in Early Modern England." *Continuity and Change* 9 (1994): 391–419.

Holdsworth, W. S. *A History of English Law*, vol. 1. London: Methuen, 1903.

Houlbrooke, R. A. "Women's Social Life and Common Action in England from the Fifteenth Century to the Eve of the Civil War." *Continuity and Change* 1 (1986): 171–89.

Huizinga, J. *The Waning of the Middle Ages*. New York: St. Martin's Press, 1924.

Hulbert, N. F. "A Survey of the Somerset Fairs." *Somerset Antiquarian and Natural History Society* 83 (1937): 83–86.

Humphreys, Arthur L. *Somersetshire Parishes: A Handbook of Historical Reference to All Places in the County*. London: 187 Picadilly W. 1905.

Hutton, Ronald. "The Local Impact of the Tudor Reformations." In *The English Reformation Revised*, edited by Christopher Haigh, 114–38. Cambridge: Cambridge University Press, 1987.

———. *The Rise and Fall of Merry England: The Ritual Year, 1400–1700*. Oxford: Oxford University Press, 1994.

James, Mervyn. "Ritual, Drama and the Social Body in the Late Medieval English Town." *Past and Present* 98 (1983): 3–29.

Jansen, Sharon L. *Dangerous Talk and Strange Behavior: Women and Popular Resistance to the Reforms of Henry VIII*. New York: St. Martin's Press, 1996.

Jewell, Helen M. *English Local Administration in the Middle Ages*. Newton Abbot, Devon: David and Charles; New York: Barnes and Noble Books, 1972.

———. "English Bishops as Educational Benefactors in the Later Fifteenth Century." In *The Church, Politics and Patronage in the Fifteenth Century*, edited by Barrie Dobson, 146–67. Gloucester: Sutton, 1984.

Johnston, Alexandra. "Parish Entertainments in Berkshire." In *Pathways to Mediaeval Peasants*, edited by J. A. Raftis, 335–38. Papers in Mediaeval Studies 2. Toronto: Pontifical Institute of Mediaeval Studies, 1981.

Johnston, Alexandra and Sally-Beth MacLean. "Reformation and Resistance in Thames/Severn Parishes: The Dramatic Witness." In *The Parish in English Life, 1400–1600*, edited by Katherine L. French, Gary G. Gibbs, and Beat A. Kümin, 178–200. Manchester: Manchester University Press, 1997.

Jones, Charles W. *St. Nicholas of Myra, Bari, and Manhattan*. Chicago: University of Chicago Press, 1978.

Jones, W. R. "The English Church and Royal Propaganda During the Hundred Years War." *Journal of British Studies* 19 (1979): 18–30.

Jordan, W. K. *Philanthropy in England, 1480–1660*. London: George Allen and Unwin, 1959.

Judd, Arnold. *The Life of Thomas Bekynton, Secretary to King Henry VI and Bishop of Bath and Wells, 1443–1465*. Chichester: Regnum Press, 1961.

Justice, Steven. *Writing and Rebellion: England in 1381*. Berkeley: University of California Press, 1994.

Keily, Gillian. *A Guide to the Parish Church of St. Mary the Virgin in the Parish of Yatton Moor*. Yatton: Yatton Moor P.C.C., no date.

Kemp, B. R. "Monastic Possession of Parish Churches in the Twelfth Century." *Journal of Ecclesiastical History* 31 (1980): 133–60.

Kermode, Jennifer. "Obvious Observations on the Formation of Oligarchies in Late Medieval English Towns." In *Towns and Townspeople in the Fifteenth Century*, edited by J. A. F. Thomson, 87–106. Gloucester: Sutton, 1988.

Kern, Edmund M. "The 'Universal' and the 'Local' in Episcopal Visitations." In *Infinite Boundaries: Order, Disorder, and Reorder in Early Modern German Culture*, edited by Max Reinhart, 35–54. Sixteenth Century Essays and Studies 40. Kirksville, Mo.: Sixteenth Century Journal Publishers, 1998.

Keyser, C. E. *A List of the Buildings in Great Britain and Ireland Having Mural and Other Painted Decorations*. 3rd ed. London: H.M.S.O., 1883.

Klaniczay, Gábor. "Religious Movements and Christian Culture: A Pattern of Centripetal and Centrifugal Orientations." In *The Uses of Supernatural Power: The Transformation of Popular Religion in Medieval and Early Modern Europe*, translated by Susan Singerman, edited by Karen Margolis, 28–50. Princeton, N.J.: Princeton University Press, 1990.

Knight, Stephen. *Robin Hood: A Complete Study of the English Outlaw*. Oxford: Basil Blackwell, 1994.

Kowaleski, Maryanne. "Introduction to 'Vill, Gild, and Gentry: Forces of Community in Later Medieval England' " *Journal of British Studies* 33 (1994): 337–39.

Kreider, Alan. *English Chantries: The Road to Dissolution*. Cambridge, Mass.: Harvard University Press, 1979.

Kümin, Beat A. *The Shaping of a Community: The Rise and Reformation of the English Parish, c. 1400–1560*. Aldershot: Scolar Press, 1996.

——. "The English Parish in a European Context." In *The Parish in English Life, 1400–1600*, edited by Katherine L. French, Gary G. Gibbs, and Beat A. Kümin, 15–32. Manchester: Manchester University Press, 1997.

——. "Parishioners in Court: Litigation and the Local Community, 1350–1650." In *Belief and Practice in Reformation England: A Tribute to Patrick Collinson From His Students*, edited by Susan Wabuda and Caroline Litzenberger, 20–39. Aldershot: Ashgate, 1998.

Lacey, Kay E. "Women and Work in Fourteenth and Fifteenth Century London." In *Women and Work in Pre-Industrial England*, edited by Lindsey Charles and Lorna Duffin, 24–82. London: Croom Helm, 1985.

Le Goff, Jacques. *The Birth of Purgatory*, translated by Arthur Goldhammer. Chicago: The University of Chicago Press, 1981.

——. "Merchants' Time and Church Time in the Middle Ages." In *Time, Work, and Culture in the Middle Ages*, translated by Arthur Goldhammer, 29–42. Chicago: University of Chicago Press, 1980.

Lehmberg, Stanford E. "Star Chamber: 1485–1509." *Huntington Library Quarterly* 24 (1961): 189–214.

Little, A. G. "Personal Tithes." *English Historical Review* 60 (1945): 67–89.

Litzenberger, Caroline. *The English Reformation and the Laity*. Cambridge: Cambridge University Press, 1997.

——. "St. Michael's Gloucester, 1540–80: The Cost of Conformity in Sixteenth-Century England." In *The Parish in English Life, 1400–1600*, edited by Katherine L. French, Gary G. Gibbs, and Beat A. Kümin, 230–49. Manchester: Manchester University Press, 1997.

Luria, Keith P. *Territories of Grace: Cultural Changes in the Seventeenth-Century Diocese of Grenoble*. Berkeley: University of California, 1991.

Machan, Tim William. "Editing, Orality and Late Middle English Texts." In *Vox Intexta*, edited by A. N. Doane and Carol Braun Pasternack, 229–45. Madison: University of Wisconsin Press, 1991.

McClendon, Muriel C. "A Moveable Feast: St. George's Day Celebrations and Religious Change in Early Modern England." *Journal of British Studies* 38 (1999): 1–27.

McDermott, Mark. "Early Bench-Ends in All Saints' Church, Trull." *Somerset Archaeology and Natural History* 138 (1995): 117–30.

McHardy, A. K. "Liturgy and Propaganda in the Diocese of Lincoln During the Hundred Years War." *Studies in Church History* 18 (1982): 215–28.

McRee, Benjamin R. "Unity or Division: The Social Meaning of Guild Ceremony in Urban Communities." In *City and Spectacle in Medieval Europe*, edited by Barbara A. Hanawalt and Kathryn L. Reyerson, 189–207. Minneapolis: University of Minnesota Press, 1994.

McSheffrey, Shannon. *Gender and Heresy: Women and Men in Lollard Communities, 1420–1530*. Philadelphia: University of Pennsylvania Press, 1995.

——. "Literacy and the Gender Gap in the Late Middle Ages: Women and Reading in Lollard Communities." In *Women, the Book and the Word*, edited by Lesley Smith and Jane Taylor, 157–70. Woodbridge: Boydell and Brewer, 1995.

Manning, Bernard L. *The People's Faith in the Time of Wyclif*. Cambridge: Cambridge University Press, 1919.

Manning, Roger. *Religion and Society in Elizabethan Sussex*. Leicester: Leicester University Press, 1976.

Marshall, Peter. *The Catholic Priesthood and the English Reformation*. Oxford: Oxford University Press, 1994.

Mason, Emma. "The Role of the English Parishioner: 1100–1500." *Journal of Ecclesiastical History* 27 (1976): 17–29.

Matthew, D. J. A. *Norman Monasteries and Their English Possessions*. Oxford: Oxford University Press, 1962.

Mattingly, Joanna, "The Medieval Parish Guilds of Cornwall." *Journal of the Royal Institution of Cornwall* 10 (1989): 290–329.

Maxwell-Lyte, H. C. *History of Dunster and the Families of Mohun and Luttrell*, 2 vols. London: St. Catherine's Press, 1909.

Moran, Jo Ann Hoeppner. *The Growth of English Schooling, 1350–1548: Learning, Literacy and Laicization in Pre-Reformation York Diocese*. Princeton, N.J.: Princeton University Press, 1985.

Moorman, John. *Church Life in England in the Thirteenth Century*. Cambridge: Cambridge University Press, 1955.

Morris, Colin. "A Consistory Court in the Middle Ages." *Journal of Ecclesiastical History* 14 (1963): 150–59.

Morris, Richard. *Churches in the Landscape*. London: J. M. Dent, 1989.

Nichols, Stephen G. "Voice and Writing in Augustine and the Troubadour Lyric." In *Vox Intexta*, edited by A. N. Doane and Carol Braun Pasternack, 137–61. Madison: University of Wisconsin Press, 1992.

O'Day, Rosemary. *The Debate on the English Reformation*. London: Methuen, 1986.

Ong, Walter. *Orality and Literacy: The Technologizing of the Word*. London: Methuen, 1982.

Orme, Nicholas. *Exeter Cathedral as It Was: 1050–1550*. Exeter: Devon Books, 1986.

——. "Indulgences in the Diocese of Exeter: 1100–1536." *Report of the Transactions of the Devon Association for the Advancement of Science* 120 (1988): 15–32.

——. "Church and Chapel in Medieval England." *Transactions of the Royal Historical Society* 6 (1996): 75–102.

Owen, Dorothy. *Church and Society in Medieval Lincolnshire*, edited by Joan Thirsk. History of Lincolnshire 5. Lincoln: History of Lincolnshire Committee and Lincolnshire Local History Society, 1971.

Owst, G. R. *Preaching in Medieval England*. Cambridge: Cambridge University Press, 1922.

Oxley, J. *The Reformation in Essex to the Death of Mary*. Manchester: Manchester University Press, 1965.

Palliser, David. "Introduction: The Parish in Perspective." *Parish, Church, and People*, edited by Susan J. Wright, 5–28. London: Hutchinson, 1988.

Palmer, Robert C. *English Law in the Age of the Black Death, 1348–1381*. Chapel Hill: University of North Carolina, 1993.

——. "Selling the Church: Law, Religion, Commerce, and the English Parish, 1348–1540." (Unpublished manuscript.)

Pantin, W. A. *The English Church in the Fourteenth Century*. Medieval Academy Reprints for Teaching. Toronto: University of Toronto Press, 1980.

——. "The Fourteenth Century." In *The English Church and the Papacy*, edited by C. H. Lawrence, 154–74. New York: Fordham University Press, 1965.

Parks, Malcolm B. "Literacy and the Laity." In *The Medieval World*, edited by David Daiches and Anthony Tholby, 555–77. London: Alaus Books, 1973.

Parkes, Ward. "The Textualization of Orality in Literary Criticism." In *Vox Intexta*, edited by A. N. Doane and Carol Braun Pasternack, 46–61. Madison: University of Wisconsin Press, 1991.

Pevsner, Nikolaus. *The Buildings of England: North Somerset and Bristol*. Harmondsworth: Penguin, 1958.

——. *The Buildings of England: South and West Somerset*. Harmondsworth: Penguin, 1958.

Pfaff, R. W. *New Liturgical Feasts in Late Medieval England*. Oxford: Oxford University Press, 1970.

Philipps, Elsbeth. "A List of Printed Churchwardens' Accounts." *English Historical Review* 15 (1900): 335–41.

Phythian-Adams, Charles. "Ceremony and the Citizen: The Communal Year at Coventry, 1450–1550." In *Crisis and Order in English Towns: Essays in Urban History, 1500–1700*, edited by Peter Clark and Paul Slack, 57–85. London: Routledge and Kegan Paul, 1972.

——. *Local History and Folklore: A New Framework*. London: Bedford Square Press for Standing Conference for Local History, 1975.

——. *Desolation of a City: Coventry and the Urban Crisis of the Late Middle Ages*. Cambridge: Cambridge University Press, 1979.

Platt, Colin. *The Parish Churches of Medieval England*. London: Secker and Warburg, 1981.

——. *King Death: The Black Death and Its Aftermath in Late Medieval England*. Toronto: University of Toronto Press, 1996.

Pollard, A. F. *Thomas Cranmer and the English Reformation*. London: Putnam, 1905.

——. *Wolsey: Church and State in Sixteenth-Century England*. London: Longmans, 1929.

Pollock, Frederick and Frederic W. Maitland. *The History of English Law Before the Time of Edward I*. 2 vols. 2nd ed. Cambridge: Cambridge University Press, 1968.

Poska, Allyson. *Regulating the People: The Catholic Reformation in Seventeenth-Century Spain*. Leiden: Brill, 1998.

Postles, David. "Lamps, Lights, and Layfolk: 'Popular' Devotion Before the Black Death." *Journal of Medieval History* 25 (1999): 97–114.

Poos, L. R. *A Rural Society After the Black Death: Essex, 1350–1525*. Cambridge: Cambridge University Press, 1991.

Poyntz Wright, Peter. *The Rural Benchends of Somerset: A Study in Medieval Woodcarving*. Amersham: Avebury Publishing, 1983.

Ramsay, Nigel. "Scriveners and Notaries as Legal Intermediaries in Later Medieval England." In *Enterprise and Individuals in Fifteenth-Century England*, edited by Jennifer Kermode, 118–31. Gloucester: Sutton, 1991.

Reinburg, Virginia. "Liturgy and the Laity in Late Medieval and Reformation France." *Sixteenth Century Journal* 23 (1992): 526–47.

Reynolds, Herbert Edward. *Wells Cathedral: Its Foundation, Constitutional History and Statutes*. Wells: Privately printed, 1882.

Reynolds, Susan. *An Introduction to the History of English Medieval Towns*. Oxford: Oxford University Press, 1977.

——. "Medieval Urban History and the History of Political Thought." *Urban History Yearbook* (1982): 14–23.

——. *Kingdoms and Communities in Western Europe: 900–1300*. Oxford: Oxford University Press, 1984.

Rhodes, Robert E. *Ecclesiastical Administration in Medieval England: The Anglo-Saxons to the Reformation*. Notre Dame, Ind.: University of Notre Dame Press, 1977.

Richardson, H. G. "The Parish Clergy of the Thirteenth and Fourteenth Centuries." *Transactions of the Royal Historical Society* 3rd ser. 6 (1912): 89–128.

Richardson, Malcolm. "Henry V, the English Chancery, and Chancery English." *Speculum* 55 (1980): 726–50.

Richmond, Colin. "Religion and the Fifteenth-Century English Gentleman." In *The Church, Politics and Patronage*, edited by R. B. Dobson, 193–208. Gloucester: Sutton, 1984.

——. "The English Gentry and Religion, c. 1500." In *Religious Beliefs and Ecclesiastical Careers*, edited by Christopher Harper-Bill, 121–50. Woodbridge: Boydell and Brewer, 1991.

Riddy, Felicity. "'Mother Knows Best': Reading Social Change in a Courtesy Text." *Speculum* 71 (1996): 66–86.

Rogers, J. E. Thorold. *A History of Agriculture and Prices in England*, 7 vols. Reprint. London: Kraus Reprint, 1963.

Rosser, Gervase. *Medieval Westminster*. Oxford: Oxford University Press, 1989.

——. "Anglo-Saxon Gilds." In *Ministers and Parish Churches: The Local Church in Transition, 950–1200*, edited by John Blair, 31–34. Oxford University Committee on Archaeology 17. Oxford: Alden Press, 1988.

——. "Communities of Parish and Guild." In *Parish, Church and People: Local Studies in Lay Religion, 1350–1750*, edited by S. J. Wright, 29–55. London: Hutchinson, 1988.

——. "Parochial Conformity and Voluntary Religion in Late Medieval England." *Transactions of the Royal Historical Society* 6th ser. 1 (1991): 173–89.

——. "The Cure of Souls in English Towns Before 1000." In *Pastoral Care Before the Parish*, edited by John Blair and Richard Sharpe, 267–84. Leicester: Leicester University Press, 1992.

——. "Going to the Fraternity Feast: Commensality and Social Relations in Late Medieval England." *Journal of British Studies* 33 (1994): 430–46.

Rouse, E. Clive. *Medieval Wall Paintings*. Buckinghamshire: Shire Publications. 1991.

Rubin, Miri. *Corpus Christi: The Eucharist in Late Medieval Culture*. Cambridge: Cambridge University Press, 1991.

——. "Small Groups: Identity and Solidarity in the Late Middle Ages." In *Enterprise and Individuals in Fifteenth Century England*, edited by Jennifer Kermode, 134–49. Gloucester: Sutton Press, 1991.

Sabean, David. *The Power in the Blood: Popular Culture and Village Discourse in Early Modern Germany*. Cambridge: Cambridge University Press, 1987.

Sacks, David Harris. "The Demise of the Martyrs: The Feasts of St. Clement and St. Katherine in Bristol, 1400–1600." *Social History* 11 (1986): 141–69.

——. *The Widening Gate*. Berkeley: University of California Press, 1991.

Salzman L. F. *Building in England down to 1540: A Documentary History*. Rev. ed. Oxford: Oxford University Press, 1967.

Sauzet, Robert. *Les visites pastorales dans le diocèse de Chartres pendant la première moitié du XVIIe siècle*. Rome: Edizioni di Storia e Letteratura, 1975.

Sayers, Jane. "Monastic Archdeacons." In *Church and Government in the Middle Ages: Essays Presented to C. R. Cheney on His 70th Birthday*, edited by C. N. L. Brooke, D. E. Luscombe, G. H. Martin, and Dorothy Owen, 177–203. Cambridge: Cambridge University Press, 1976.

Scarisbrick, J. J. *The Reformation and the English People*. Oxford: Basil Blackwell, 1985.

Schofield, Roger. "Parliamentary Lay Taxation: 1485–1547." Unpublished Ph.D. dissertation, Cambridge University, 1963.

——. "The Geographic Distribution of Wealth, 1334–1649." *Economic History Review* 2nd ser. 18 (1965): 483–510.

Serel, Thomas. *Historical Notes on the Church of Saint Cuthbert in Wells: The Priory of St. John, College of La Mountery and Chapels Formerly at Southober, Southway, Polsham, and Chilcote*. Wells: Atkins and Beauchamp, 1875.

Shaw, David Gary. *The Creation of a Community: The City of Wells in the Middle Ages*. Oxford: Oxford University Press, 1993.

Sheingorn, Pamela. *The Easter Sepulcher in England*. Early Drama and Art and Music Reference Series 5. Kalamazoo: Medieval Institute Publications, Western Michigan University, 1987.

Skeeters, Martha C. *Community and Clergy: Bristol and the Reformation, c. 1530–1570*. Oxford: Oxford University Press, 1993.

Smith, Edwin, Graham Hutton, and Olive Cook. *English Parish Churches*. London: Thames and Hudson, 1976.

Smith, J. C. D. *Church Woodcarvings: A West Country Study*. New York: Augustus M. Kelley, 1969.

Smith, Toulmin. *The Parish*. London: H. Sweet, 1857.

Spencer, H. Leith. *English Preaching in the Late Middle Ages*. Oxford: Oxford University Press, 1993.

Stenton, Frank. *Anglo-Saxon England*. 3rd ed. Oxford: Oxford University Press, 1971.

Stock, Brian. "Medieval Literacy, Linguistic Theory and Social Organization." *New Literary History* 16 (1984): 13–29.

——. *Implications of Literacy: Written Language and Models of Interpretation in the Eleventh and Twelfth Centuries*. Princeton, N.J.: Princeton University Press, 1983.

Stokes, James. "The Hoglers: Evidence of an Entertainment Tradition in Eleven Somerset Parishes." *Notes and Queries for Somerset and Dorset* 32 (1990): 807–16.

———. "Robin Hood and the Churchwardens of Yeovil." *Medieval and Renaissance Drama in England: An Annual Gathering of Research, Criticism and Reviews* 3 (1986): 1–25.

———. "The Wells Cordwainers Show: New Evidence of Guild Drama in Somerset." *Comparative Drama* 19 (1985–86): 322–46.

Strohm, Paul. *England's Empty Throne: Usurpation and the Language of Legitimation, 1399–1422*. New Haven, Conn.: Yale University Press, 1998.

———. "*Passioun, Lyf, Miracle, Legende*: Some Generic Terms in Middle English Hagiographical Narrative." *Chaucer Review* 10, 1 and 2 (1975–76): 62–75; 154–71.

Swanson, Robert N. *Church and Society in Late Medieval England*. Oxford: Basil Blackwell, 1989.

———. *Religion and Devotion in Europe, c. 1215–c. 1515*. Cambridge: Cambridge University Press, 1995.

Tanner, Norman P. *The Church in Late Medieval Norwich: 1370–1532*. Toronto: Pontifical Institute of Mediaeval Studies, 1984.

Tate, W. E. *The Parish Chest: A Study of the Records of Parochial Administration in England*. Cambridge: Cambridge University Press, 1946.

Thirsk, Joan. "The Farming Regions of England." In *The Agrarian History of England and Wales*, vol. 4, edited by Joan Thirsk, 71–79. Cambridge: Cambridge University Press, 1947.

Thompson, A. Hamilton. *The English Clergy and Their Organization in the Later Middle Ages*. Oxford: Oxford University Press, 1947.

Thomson, J. A. F. *Laity and the Clergy in London: 1376–1531*. Unpublished Ph.D. dissertation, Oxford University, 1960.

———. "Tithe Disputes in Later Medieval London." *English Historical Review* 306 (1963): 1–17.

Thrupp, Slyvia L. *The Merchant Class of Medieval London*. Chicago: University of Chicago Press, 1948.

Tristram, E. W. *English Wall Paintings in the Fourteenth Century*. London: Routledge and Kegan Paul, 1955.

Tudor-Craig, Pamela. "Painting in Medieval England: The Wall-to-Wall Message." In *Age of Chivalry: Art and Society in Late Medieval England*, edited by Nigel Saul, 106–19. London: Brockhampton Press, 1995.

Underdown, David. *Revel, Riot, and Rebellion: Popular Politics and Culture in England, 1603–1660*. Oxford: Oxford University Press, 1985.

Vauchez, André. "The Pastoral Transformation of the Thirteenth Century." In *The Laity in the Middle Ages: Religious Beliefs and Devotional Practice*, edited by Daniel E. Bornstein, translated by Margery J. Schneider, 95–106. Notre Dame, Ind.: University of Notre Dame Press, 1993.

The Victoria History of the County of Somerset. 6 vols., vol. 2 edited by William Page, vols. 3–6 edited by R. W. Dunning. London: Constable, 1911; London: Oxford University Press for the Institute for Historical Research, 1974, 1978, 1985, 1988, 1992.

Wakelin, M. F. "The Manuscripts of John Mirk's *Festial*." *Leeds Studies in English* n.s. 1 (1997): 93–118.

Ward, Benedicta. *Miracles and the Medieval Mind: Theory, Record, and Event*. Philadelphia: University of Pennsylvania Press, 1982.

Ward, Jennifer. "English Noble Women and the Local Community in the Later Middle Ages." In *Medieval Women in Their Communities*, edited by Diane Watt, 186–203. Toronto: University of Toronto Press, 1997.

———. *English Noble Women in the Later Middle Ages*. London: Longmans, 1992.

Wasson, John. "The Saint George and Robin Hood Plays in Devon." *Medieval English Theatre* 2 (1980): 66–69.

Weiss, Robert. *Humanism in England During the Fifteenth Century*. Oxford: Basil Blackwell, 1957.

Westlake, H. F. *The Parish Gilds of Mediaeval England*. London: S.P.C.K., 1919.

Whiting, Robert. *The Blind Devotion of the People: Popular Religion and the English Reformation*. Cambridge: Cambridge University Press, 1989.

———. *Local Responses to the English Reformation*. New York: St. Martin's Press, 1998.

Wickham, A. K. *The Churches of Somerset*. Dawlish: David and Charles, 1965.

Wickham, Glynne. *The Medieval Theatre*, 3rd ed. Cambridge: Cambridge University Press, 1987.

Wiles, David. *The Early Plays of Robin Hood*. Cambridge: D. S. Brewer, 1981.

Williams, Arnold. "Relations Between the Mendicant Friars and the Secular Clergy in England in the Late Fourteenth Century." *Annuale Mediaevale* 1 (1960): 22–95.

Winstead, Karen A. *The Virgin Martyrs: Legends of Sainthood in Late Medieval England*. Ithaca, N.Y.: Cornell University Press, 1997.

Wood-Legh, K. L. *Perpetual Chantries in Britain*. Cambridge: Cambridge University Press, 1965.

Woodcock, Brian. *Medieval Ecclesiastical Courts*. London: Oxford University Press, 1952.

Woodforde, Christopher. *Stained Glass in Somerset: 1250–1830*. London: Oxford University Press, 1946.

Wordsworth, Christopher and Henry Littlehales. *The Old Service-Books of the English Church*. London: Methuen, 1904.

Wunderli, Richard M. *London Church Courts on the Eve of the Reformation*. Cambridge, Mass.: Medieval Academy of America, 1981.

Yorke, Barbara. *Wessex in the Early Middle Ages*. London: Leicester University Press, 1995.

Ziegler, Philip. *The Black Death*. New York: Harper Torchbooks, 1969.

Zumthor, Paul. "The Text and the Voice." *New Literary History* 16 (1984): 67–92.

———. *Oral Poetry: An Introduction*. Translated by Kathryn Murphy-Judy. Minneapolis: University of Minnesota Press, 1990.

INDEX

All place-names unless otherwise specified
are in Bath and Wells

Bury St. Edmunds, Suffolk, 7
bylaws, 62, 76, 83, 92

Cambridge, 7; King's Hall, 60; St. Mary the
    Great, 60
Candlemas, 209
candles, 29, 34, 36, 99, 100, 114, 159, 161,
    187, 189, 190, 196, 203
candlesticks, 20, 144, 146, 188
canon law, 28
canonical sanctions, 116
canopy, 192
Canterbury, 36
cardinal virtues, 178
Carpenter, Christine, 92
carpenters, carpentry, 54, 85, 107, 145
carver, 145, 156, 158, 160, 162, 201, 205
carvings, 145, 156, 160, 179
cash, 104
cash economy, 44, 46, 105
cathedrals, 2, 28, 84, 155; canons, 183; town,
    192
cattle. *See* livestock
Caxton, William, 197
cemetery, 2, 144
chalice, 20, 29, 30, 34, 37, 38, 95, 115, 144,
    152, 187, 188
Chambers, E. K., 187
chancel, 60, 152, 154–58, 167, 170, 205
chancellor, 6, 8, 41, 42, 53, 55, 74
Chancery petitions, 41, 42, 46, 50, 53, 54, 56,
    67, 73, 74, 85. *See also* Court of Chancery
chantries, 155, 171, 180, 211–27; certificates,
    211–27; priests, 184
chapels, 18, 37, 87, 89, 93, 94, 95, 87, 148,
    152, 153, 155, 156, 160, 170–73, 181, 188,
    201–3, 205, 206, 211–27. *See also* depen-
    dent chapels; family chapels; private
    chapels
chaplains, 34, 193
charity, 11, 22, 23, 102, 11, 22, 23, 102, 113,
    134, 152
charnel house, 148
Chedder, 172
Chedzoy, 12, 48
childbirth, 195
children, 98, 104, 109
chivalry, 204

Chocke, Lady Margaret, 104
Chocke, Sir Richard, 94
choir, 38, 158, 160, 182, 184, 188
chrism, 30
Christ, 175, 186–95
Christmas, 35, 51, 71, 80, 91, 114, 116, 186,
    187, 189; candles, 71, 186; vigil, 187
church ales, 31, 51, 61, 82, 88, 91, 96, 100,
    109, 113, 114, 122–26, 130–39, 141, 162,
    170, 176, 190, 197, 205, 209; charitable
    113; hocktide, 134–36; Pentecost, 134,
    135; Robin Hood, 131, 162; St. George,
    132; St. Margaret, 123, 124, 135, 209; SS
    Philip and James, 122, 123, 135; Whitsun,
    124, 130, 134, 136
churches: building 18, 22, 23, 63, 73, 81, 87,
    89, 90, 93, 94, 106, 114, 116, 127, 131, 173,
    133, 142–54, 197, 200; house, 50, 63, 103,
    109, 112–15, 117, 127, 154, 176; receiver,
    69
churching of women, 26, 183
churchwardens, 15, 18, 25, 30–33, 37, 40–
    47, 51, 54–57, 60–99, 104, 106–8, 112,
    114–17, 131, 132, 134, 137, 146, 152, 161,
    162, 167, 169, 182, 185–88, 192, 195, 198,
    201, 205, 206; appointment, 83–84;
    capabilities 88–92; election, 54, 63, 83, 84,
    89; first mention, 69; incompetence, 91–
    92; presentments, 190; rise of the office
    68–72; rotation, 77–79, 84, 86, 87, 91;
    tenure, 76–83; term limits, 76–83; wills,
    85, 89
churchwardens' accounts, 11, 13, 15, 17, 18,
    30, 32, 33, 44–68, 73, 77, 84, 89, 91, 95,
    96, 100–105, 107, 112, 117, 148, 168, 170,
    183, 186, 187, 189, 190, 192, 195, 196, 198,
    201, 209, 211–27; audit accounts, 47; fif-
    teenth century, 13; fourteenth century, 13,
    68; missing, 67, , 2, 5, 15, 20, 26, 29, 31,
    32, 35, 38, 80, 90, 106, 113, 132, 141, 143,
    147, 159, 160, 173, 176, 192
civic culture, 152, 106
civic ordinance, 84
Clanchy, Michael, 44, 52, 55
class, 21, 44, 68, 86, 198
Claverham, 79, 135, 136
cleaning, 101, 145, 188, 195
Cleeve, 79, 135, 136

clergy, 11, 17, 20, 23, 28, 29, 31–33, 35, 50, 69, 71, 84, 90, 94, 99, 100, 107, 113, 141, 142, 144, 152, 155, 156, 162, 163, 176, 177, 179, 181, 183, 185, 188, 193, 203; benefice, 2, 6, 23, 26, 37; income, 26; neglect, 24, 25, 30, 34, 35; poverty, 6, 34; wrongdoing, 34. *See also* priests

clocks, 69, 80, 143, 148

cloth industry, 13, 85

clothing, 102, 105, 106

coastal plain, 101

coat of arms, 93, 104, 163, 171, 172

cockfights, 1

code of honor, 56

coercion, 16, 22–24, 27, 34, 36

Colchester, Essex, 94

collections, 29, 69, 80, 86, 89–91, 100, 112, 114–30, 148, 204, 205, 209; Christmas, 91; Easter, 209

collector, 88, 89

college of priests, 94

Combe St. Nicholas, 182

commissary-general, 34, 37, 176

common law, 39, 40, 41, 55, 199

community identity, 2, 3, 16–27, 31, 36, 38, 45, 49, 51, 52, 62, 66, 68, 98, 100, 107, 114, 134, 143, 144, 147, 155, 176, 193, 199, 200, 201, 207, 208

community trust, 88, 91

competition, 147, 172

confession, 2, 24, 26, 28, 134, 141, 145, 177, 179, 180, 187, 188; private confessors, 179, 199

conflicts, 159, 160, 193. *See also* Dunster conflict

Congresbury, 5, 134, 156

consecration, 29, 144

consolidation of parishes, 2

contracts, 39, 40, 42, 54, 55, 57, 77, 201

conversion to Christianity, 3, 5

Cornwall, 10, 81, 86, 205. *See also* diocese of Exeter

Cornwall, Julian, 88

corporas case, 188

corporations, 39, 199

corpse, 26, 90

Corpus Christi 181, 191–92, 196; processions, 133, 192–94, 206

costumes, 131, 187

Council of Constance, 6

countryside, 53, 131, 190

Court of Chancery, 41, 42, 46, 52, 53, 55, 67, 73, 74, 93, 94, 146. *See also* Chancery petitions; equity courts

Court of Requests, 41. *See also* equity courts

Court of the Star Chamber, 41, 93, 147, 167. *See also* equity courts; Star Chamber petitions

Coventry, Warwickshire, 133, 191

Cox, J. Charles 96

Creed, 177, 178

Crewkerne, 5

criminals. *See* outlaws

crisis, 151

Cromwell, Thomas, 208

crops, 1, 10, 101. *See also* agriculture

Croscombe, 12, 13, 48, 54, 63, 79, 80, 83–85, 90, 95, 105, 106, 112, 116, 117, 127–33, 154, 172, 184, 203, 205

cross, 74, 115

crowds, 186

crown, 69, 112

crucifer, 159, 164

crucifix, 155, 167, 188

cult of the saints, 19, 155, 176, 194–206

Cum ex eo, 178

curate, 178

cure of souls, 3, 34, 37, 176, 178

Curry Rivel, 6

custom, 29, 51

dado, 155, 201

dancing, 131, 34

dead, 35, 114, 145, 161

dean and chapter, 39

death, 11, 54, 55, 71, 80, 81, 90, 91, 93, 95, 102, 104, 180

debts, 54, 62, 64, 116, 133

deceased husband, 77, 78, 87

decision making, 75, 82

decorations, 81, 101, 115, 141, 145, 156, 166, 195

dedication day, 90, 182, 208

deeds, 11, 65

defamation, 37, 80

defaulters, 109, 114

democracy, 15, 68, 69, 79, 83, 97

demographic crisis of the fourteenth century, 5

dependent chapels, 2, 5, 13, 24, 25–27, 42, 115, 116

devil, 146, 167, 189

Devon, 3, 10, 81, 86, 156. *See also* diocese of Exeter

dialogue, 61

Dickens, A. G., 15

dictation, 62

didactic literature, 19, 154. *See also* education; moral instruction

diocesan statutes, 28–33, 42, 75, 69, 71, 132, 141, 144, 182, 183

diocese of Canterbury, 7, 8

diocese of Chichester, 40

diocese of Durham, 7

diocese of Exeter, 16, 45, 47, 58, 69, 74, 136, 137; statutes, 69

diocese of Lincoln, 40

diocese of Oxford, statutes, 29

diocese of Salisbury, statutes, 29

diocese of Worcester, statutes, 29

diocese of York, 6, 7, 133

diplomatic correspondence, 7

dirge, 180

disaster, 101, 149

disbelief, 190

disobedience, 80

dissolution of pilgrimage shrines, 209

Ditcheat, 197

Dives and Pauper, 87, 122, 132, 142, 195

divine office, 93, 155, 174, 175, 178, 183, 203

divorce, 208

Domesday Book, 5

Donyatt, 163

Dorchester, Dorset, 180

Dorset, 3

Doulting, 151

Dowlish Wake, 171

dowries, 104

drama. *See* plays

dressing saints, 195

Drew, Charles, 15, 30, 69, 71, 72

droughts, 182

drunkenness, 31, 136, 193

Duffy, Eamon, 16, 172

Dundry, 146

Dunster, 12, 37, 38, 103, 112 156–60, 199; conflict 37, 38, 147, 158–60, 199; rood screen, 156–58

dye stuffs, 13

earl of Arundel, 193

Earnshill, 6

East Anglia, 60, 60, 156, 163, 201

East Bergholt, Suffolk, 94

Easter, 24, 26, 51, 71, 114, 127, 134, 187, 188, 190; breakfast, 189; candle, 61, 71, 115, 188; sepulcher, 180–90, 196, 205, 206; vigil, 189

Eastham, 5

Easton-in-Gordano, 160

ecclesiastical court, 11, 14, 28, 31, 37–39, 40, 50, 57, 59, 158, 159; archdeacons' court, 114, 116, 190; bishop's court, 31, 37, 38, 40, 158; commissary court, 40; consistory court, 40; records, 11, 14; vicar-general's court, 37, 38

ecclesiastical law, 15

economy, 50; changes, 145; prosperity, 191; rationality, 135

education, 8, 176–86, 197, 209. *See also* didactic literature; moral instruction

Edward I, 39

Edward III, 41, 204

Edward IV, 204, 206

Edward VI, 80, 108, 113, 137

egalitarianism, 68, 115

elite, 85, 97, 98, 191, 197, 205

Elizabeth I, 15, 16

Elizabeth Lady Botreaux, 94

embezzlement, 76

endowments, 65, 114

English, 45, 48, 57–60, 178

entertainment, 100, 116–41. *See also* church ales; plays; revels

Epiphany vigil, 187

episcopal: expectation, 20; neglect, 30; regulation, 27–39, 45, 66, 67; statutes (*see* diocesan statutes)

equity courts, 38–43, 52, 53. *See also* specific courts

Essex, 41

Henry VIII, 6, 7, 11, 17, 63, 66, 80, 82, 135, 168, 193, 208

Henstridge, 178

heresy, 8, 32, 49, 80, 176, 179. *See also* Lollards

high altar, 36, 38, 156, 159, 184, 187

high mass, 159, 175, 203

Hobhouse, Edmund, 95, 96, 116

hocktide, 127, 134–36

hogling, 116, 117, 126, 127, 173; 134, 203; bread, 117; collection, 124, 125; light 117

holy bread, 25, 26, 65, 84, 188, 190. *See also* blesssed bread; mass bread; pax bread

Holy Cross, 69, 80, 89, 209

holy days, 24, 175, 176, 178, 181, 186, 187, 194, 208

Holy Ghost. *See* Holy Spirit

holy oil, 30

Holy Spirit, 189, 196

holy spring, 176

Holy Trinity, 84, 89, 148, 173, 196

holy water, 147, 155, 159, 173

honor, 67, 79, 87, 91, 143

Horsey, 116

host, 23, 30, 31, 84, 100, 143, 154, 156, 167, 175, 179, 23, 30, 31, 84, 100, 189, 190–93

household, householders, 51, 86, 92, 99, 104, 113, 115, 170

housekeepers, 105

houses, 102, 108, 109, 112, 137

humiliation, 36, 147,

Humphrey, duke of Gloucester, 7

Hundred Years' War, 181

husbandman, 73, 85

Hutton, Ronald, 16, 47

iconoclasts, 163

iconography, 195

Ignoranita Sacerdotum, 177, 197

Ilchester, 6, 32, 180

Ilminster, 12, 48

image, 67, 72, 99, 132, 135, 141, 160, 187, 195, 197, 200, 204–6

immoral behavior, 6, 11, 31, 34, 83

impersonation, 131

income, 45, 51, 64, 96, 99–41

incorporation, 63

incumbent, 2

inflation, 114

Innocent III, 28

Instructions for Parish Priests, 90, 154, 177

intercessory prayers. *See* masses for the dead

interdict, 35–37

inventories, 89, 112, 115, 183, 195, 198, 204

inversion, 127, 130

Ireland, 1, 10

Italian Humanism, 7, 178

Italian notary, 52

Italy, 197

Jacobus de Voragine, 197

James, Mervyn, 191

jewelry, 105

John (king), 13, 28

John Leland's *Itinerary*, 146

John Mirk's *Festial*, 177, 190, 198, 199

junior warden 76, 77, 79, 82, 83

keepers of the peace, 64

Ken, 134

Kent, 86, 89

Keynsham, 116

Kilmersdon, 42, 73

king's mother, 193

king's revel, 80

Kingston, 134

kitchen, 112

knights, 87, 189

Kümin, Beat, 16, 17, 47, 86

labor, 109, 145

lamps, 71

land, 39, 55, 93, 102, 108; disputes, 93

landholders 5, 92, 169

landlords, 28, 29, 85, 107

last rites, 183

Last Supper, 175

Latin, 7, 44, 45, 48, 53, 57–60, 178–80

laundry, 71, 145, 188; laundresses, 52

lawyers, 39

The Lay Folk's Mass Book, 175

lay subsidy, 86, 88

leases, 50, 77, 81, 91, 102, 107–14, 152

legacies, 92, 103

Leigh-on-Mendip, 25, 26

Lent, 134, 177, 187, 188; Lenten veil, 187

Reynolds, Susan, 83
Richmond, Colin, 92
rings, 61. *See also* wedding rings
riot 35, 36, 41, 147
ritual, 102, 160, 191, 182
rivalry, 159
River Axe, 10, 130
River Brue, 10
River Cary, 10
River, Parrett, 8, 10, 13, 130, 148
River, Tone, 8
River, Yeo, 10
rivers, 10
roads, 10, 26, 69
Robin Hood, 60, 126–34, 141, 162, 204, 205;
    Robin Hood revel, 205
Rogation, 190
Roman Curia, 7
rood, 186, 187; loft 54, 155, 156, 160; 18, 51,
    133, 136, 143, 155–62, 174, 187, 197, 201,
    209
Roodmas, 134
roof, 42, 99, 101, 143, 147, 148
rosary, 179
Ross Collection, 177, 198
Rosser, Gervase, 21, 23
Rotherfeld, Sussex, 65
Royal Order of the Garter, 204
royal patronage, 132
Rubin, Miri, 21, 24, 191
rummage sales, 107
rural dean, 6, 32, 37
rural parishes 13, 77–79, 83, 90, 100, 101,
    105, 107, 109, 113, 114, 130, 134, 137, 152,
    158, 162, 167, 170, 173, 190 203, 206
rushes, 188

sacerdotal efficacy, 179
sacramental rights, 2, 26
sacraments, 3, 25–36, 42, 100, 143, 177–79,
    183. *See also* specific sacraments
sacrilege, 141
sacring bell, 144, 146
saints, 81, 100, 127, 132, 135, 156, 161, 172,
    173, 181, 187, 190, 195, 211–27; patron,
    22, 133, 135, 186, 194, 196; torture, 192,
    198; veneration (*see* cult of the saints). *See
    also* vergin martyrs

saints' days, 22, 51, 66, 186, 195, 197, 198,
    200, 203, 206
Saints Peter and Paul, 134
Saints Philip and James, 122, 123, 135
salaries, 54, 57, 94, 99
sale of goods, 91, 100, 106–7, 114
Salisbury, Wiltshire, St. Edmund's, 59
salvation, 30, 36, 145, 174, 207
sandstone, 145
Sarum Use, 8, 182, 186
scaffolding, 59
scandal, 141
Scarisbrick, J. J., 16
scenery, 187
schools, 44, 178
scribes, 44, 58–61, 63, 64, 74, 91, 104, 183,
    209
scripture, 94, 177, 178. *See also* Bible
Seaborough, 5
seating, 18, 72, 84, 93, 106, 107, 132, 144, 155,
    162–71; plan, 168, 170. *See also* pews
secular courts, 28, 42, 57. *See also* common
    law courts; equity courts
secular priests, 5
self-aggrandizement, 144
Selwood, 160
Selworthy, 197
senior wardens, 62, 76, 77, 79, 82, 83
sermons, 22, 90, 145, 154, 177, 179, 184, 186,
    188, 190, 194, 195, 198
servants, 51, 86, 98
seven deadly sins, 141, 177. *See also* sin
seven principal virtues, 177
seven works of mercy, 177, 178. *See also* good
    works
sexual relations, 32, 186
Shaw, Gary, 21, 85
Shepton Mallet, 55
shipwreck, 1
shrines, 133, 179, 193
side altars, 18, 34, 39, 84, 89, 99, 148, 155,
    156, 171, 173, 180, 187, 203, 206
signatures, 57
sin, 141, 171, 180, 187. *See also* seven deadly
    sins
sixteenth-century depression, 109, 116, 136,
social change, 200
social commentary, 130

Stogursey, 10, 12, 14, 32, 63, 54, 67, 96, 103, 108, 109, 113, 136, 137, 172, 185, 205
Stoke, 134
Stokes, James, 116, 130
stone, 10, 106, 94, 143, 144, 148, 154, 160, 201
suffragan bishop, 8, 28
superstition, 16, 176, 180
synodial legislation, 15

talking in church, 154
tapers. *See* candles
Taunton, 6, 104, 109, 145, 163, 172, 179, 192; St. Mary Magdalene, 26, 34, 103, 189
taverns, 32
Tavistock, Devon, 74, 75, 81, 82,
ten commandments, 142, 177, 188
tenements, 108, 109
tension, 23, 80, 82, 87, 88, 132, 142, 156, 171, 175, 191, 193, 194, 198, 199, 201
testators, 37, 69, 106, 198. *See also* wills
textual communities, 49, 53, 56, 60–62, 67
theft, 67, 74, 135, 147, 158
theology, 24, 178
Thirsk, Joan, 10
three ages of the world, 186
tin mining, 10
Tintinhull 12, 13, 22, 32, 35, 48, 57, 59, 63, 79, 81–90, 95, 103, 106, 109, 112–15, 117, 122–23, 131, 133–37, 140, 154, 162, 183, 184, 187, 188, 203, 209; manor, 94
tithes, 2, 5, 8, 20, 22, 26, 32, 38, 60, 95, 99, 103, 158, 209
tombs, 93, 94, 171, 172, 188, 189
tools, 107, 114
torches, 71, 115, 192
towers, 32, 51, 69, 115, 131, 143, 144–48, 151, 152, 153, 158, 189, 206
town parishes, 13, 77, 79, 83, 90, 100, 101, 105, 107, 109, 114, 134, 137, 152, 162, 167, 186, 190, 206
towns, 13, 14, 63, 85, 101, 109, 131, 143, 146, 158, 174, 189, 192, 198, 204, 206; confraternities, 22, 172; governments, 13, 69, 83, 97, 109, 131, 191–93; hierarchies, 199; offices, 168, 170; walls, 71
trade, 10, 13, 105; guilds, 170; leather, 14; wool, 14, 148

transcription, 62
transubstantiation, 175, 191
travelers, 146
treason, 80
Tree of Jesse, 201, 202
trendal, 187
Trevelyan, Sir John, 93, 205
Trull, 12, 26, 48, 67, 76, 86, 87, 90, 106, 109, 112, 134, 154, 156, 158, 162–64, 173, 184, 185
trust, 56
trustees, 102
Tudor dynasty, 204
tutors, 45

unbeneficed clergy, 177, 179
urbanization, 44

Valor Ecclesiasticus, 3
vernacular, 44, 59, 180, 199; learning, 199; manuals, 180
vestments, 23, 30, 31, 34, 71, 89, 99, 100, 102, 104, 113, 114, 142, 186, 203
vestries, 46, 63, 95–97
vicar-general, 7, 8, 28, 32, 34, 37, 38,
vicars, 32, 34–38, 46, 58, 59, 75, 103, 158, 159, 161, 178, 178, 180, 182, 183, 188, 192; vicars' choral, 84
villages, 42, 83, 135, 143, 146,
violence, 35, 36, 38, 42, 136, 141, 167
virgin martyrs, 197–200
visitations, 11, 22, 31–35, 37, 42, 57, 72, 115, 116, 175, 190, 203; reports, 11, 32
vocalization, 49, 50, 65, 67
voluntary membership, 21

wage laborers, 98
Walberswick, Suffolk, 101
wall paintings 73, 189, 195, 197, 200, 201, 205; schemata, 200. *See also* paintings
walls, 99, 115, 143, 171, 172
Walter Lord Hungerford, 94
Walton, Lancashire, 1
war, 182
War of the Rose,s 7, 204
Warman, Simon, 163, 165
Warwickhire, 92
washing, 145, 187

water, 96

wax, 80, 114, 115, 186–88

Wayford, 5

wealth, 85, 98, 115, 186

weapons, 39, 189

weather, 143

wedding offerings, 147

wedding rings, 195

weights, 113

Wellington, 183

Wells, 6, 12, 13, 36, 84–86, 89, 133, 173, 199, 201, 205, 209; borough council, 69, 84, 89; cathedral, 3, 6, 14, 69, 70, 154; master of the city, 84, 86, 89, 109, 201; minster, 3, 5; St. Cuthbert's, 48, 63, 64, 69, 70, 72, 86, 89, 109, 131 201, 202

Wells Convocation Book, 64, 84

Wembdon, 115, 116, 148, 176

Westbury, 5

Westminster, 41, 209

Whiting, Robert, 16, 136, 137

Whitsun, 124, 130, 134–36, 187, 190

widows, 23, 77–79, 87, 88, 142, 105, 109, 167, 171, 147, 196, 198, 205, 211–27

William Lynwood's *Provinciale*, 8, 29, 183

wills, 6, 10, 11, 14, 15, 23, 37, 57, 85, 92, 102–5, 183. *See also* legacies; testators

Wimborne Minster, Dorset 59

Winchester cathedral, 154

Winchester, Hampshire, 7

windmills, 163, 166

windows, 18, 33, 93, 99, 142, 172, 179, 195, 197, 203. *See also* stained glass windows

wine, 13, 65, 193

Winstead, Karen, 198, 199

witness depositions, 54, 59, 116

wives, 105, 109, 167, 171, 147, 196, 198, 205, 211–27

Wolsey, Thomas, 41

women, 23, 26, 36, 51, 77–79, 82, 87, 88, 98, 104, 105, 109, 142, 145, 147, 155, 167, 169, 170, 172, 183, 188, 190, 195, 196, 198, 199, 201, 205

women churchwardens, 77, 78, 87, 88

women's guilds, 87, 127

Woodwik, 6

Wookey, 5

wool, 106

workshops, 108

Wrington, 134

writing, 44–46, 49, 50–67, 77

written records, 50, 54, 56, 57, 60, 61

Wunderli, Richard, 40

Wyke, 5

Yatton, 12, 13, 48, 58, 61, 64, 73, 74, 78, 79, 83–87, 90, 94, 105, 106, 109, 112, 134–40, 145, 152, 153, 160–62, 172, 184, 201, 206

yeomen, 85, 200

Yeovil, 12, 14, 35, 36, 48, 54, 58, 76, 79, 103, 105, 106–8, 113, 130, 133, 148, 151, 153, 154, 167, 173, 180, 184, 185, 188, 189, 190, 192, 173

Yeovilton, 34

young men, 128, 129

younglings' guilds, 127–29, 172, 173

Zumthor, Paul 49, 50, 52